Francis O'Reilly

ABOUT THE AUTHOR

Peter Harbison, who was archaeologist with the Irish Tourist Board from 1966 to 1984, is now editor of its magazine, Ireland of the Welcomes. *In 1986 he was elected chairman of the National Monuments Advisory Council. His books include* The Archaeology of Ireland, Pre-Christian Ireland *and* Irish High Crosses, *and he is the co-author of* Irish Art and Architecture. *He has also revised and up-dated* The Shell Guide to Ireland.

GUIDE

to the NATIONAL MONUMENTS
in the Republic of IRELAND

including a selection of other monuments not in state care

Peter Harbison

126 illustrations, reconstructions, plans and reference maps

GILL & MACMILLAN

Frontispiece. Conjectural reconstruction of the monastery at Kells, Co Meath as it might have been c. 1100.

Published in Ireland by
Gill and Macmillan Ltd
Goldenbridge
Dublin 8
with associated companies in
Auckland, Delhi, Gaborone, Hamburg, Harare,
Hong Kong, Johannesburg, Kuala Lumpur, Lagos, London,
Manzini, Melbourne, Mexico City, Nairobi,
New York, Singapore, Tokyo
© Peter Harbison, 1970
Typography and design by Jan de Fouw, Dublin
Maps by Michael Gleeson
0 7171 0758 2
Print origination in Ireland by
Richview Browne & Nolan Ltd, Dublin
Printed in Hong Kong

For my wife

Contents

Acknowledgments

My thanks are due to Bord Fáilte, and particularly to J C Coleman, E P Kearney and T J M Sheehy, for financial assistance towards the artwork and layout of this book, and to May Boyd, Clive Brooks and John McNulty for help with the illustrations. I should like to thank the staff of the National Parks and Monuments Branch of the Office of Public Works, and particularly John McCarthy, Director, Pascal Scanlan, D Newman Johnson, Jim Bambury, Robert Corrigan and Mary Purcell for help and encouragement in the collection of material for this volume. To the Regional Tourist Companies, Garda Sergeants and certain private individuals I am grateful for information about access to and the opening times of certain monuments. My thanks are due also to Jim Robson for Figs. 26-27 and for having checked and read through the typescript: to D Newman Johnson for his excellent sketches of Trim and Roodstown Castles and the reconstruction of a motte-and-bailey (Figs. 14-17), as well as for having checked the sections on castles; to Brian O'Halloran for his reconstructions of Kells (Frontispiece) and Jerpoint (Fig. 12); to Ruth Brandt for her drawings of Crosses and the Turoe Stone (Figs. 5, 8 and 53) and also to George Campbell for his delightfully witty sketches which adorn these pages. John Hunt has given me the benefit of his knowledge on the medieval tombs and Barry Raftery has kindly supplied details of the results of his excavations at Rathgall. I should particularly like to record my thanks to my wife, Edelgard, who has brought her pen to bear on enriching many of the illustrations in the book. My thanks are also due to Michael Gleeson for the fine maps, to Jan de Fouw for the layout, and to Michael Gill and Eamonn O'Rourke for all their trouble and patience in the production of this work.

I am also grateful to the following for permission to reproduce illustrations: Jim Bambury (Figs. 6, 13, 18, 22, 25, 34, 37-38, 43, 49, 50, 52, 61, 64 and 81); Bord Fáilte Eireann (Figs. 19-20, 28, 35, 47 and 55-56); J C Coleman (Fig. 39); The Commissioners of Public Works (Figs. 6, 10, 13, 18, 21-22, 25, 31, 33-34, 37-38, 40-41, 43, 48-52, 60-61, 64, 69-70, 74, 76-77 and 81); The Cork Historical and Archaeological Society (Figs. 2 and 23); R P Corrigan (Figs. 40 and 58a); Kevin Danaher (Fig. 4); Professor R de Valera (Fig. 1); The Dundealgan Press (Figs. 30, 44 and 68); Edward Fahy (Figs. 2, 3 and 7); Government Publications (Fig. 83); The Kerryman (Fig. 39); Mrs Ada K Leask (Figs. 23, 24, 30, 44 and 68); The National Library of Ireland (Fig. 4); P O hÉailidhe (Fig. 82); Professor M J O'Kelly (Figs. 2, 3 and 7); Dara O Lochlainn (Fig. 41); Sean Ó Nuallain (Figs. 65-66); Mrs G Ó Riordáin (Figs. 1 and 57); The Public Record Office (Fig. 24); Rex Roberts Studios (Frontispiece); The Royal Archaeological Institute (Figs. 42 and 58-59); The Royal Irish Academy (Figs. 1 and 7); The Council of the Royal Society of Antiquaries of Ireland (Figs. 3, 32, 46a, 67 and 82); The Stationery Office (Figs. 4 and 83) and the Ulster Society of Archaeology (Fig. 24).

Figures 35, 42, 47, 55, 57, 58, 65, and 66 and the map sections at the end of the book are based on the Ordnance Survey by kind permission of the Government (permit no. 1666).

List of Illustrations

List of Illustrations

List of Illustrations

Sketches on pages 1, 4, 7, 14, 15, 21, 29, 35, 36, 65, 70, 81, 94, 110, 120, 140, 144, 157, 165, 201, 211, 240, 242, 244, 250, 259, 260, 261 and 264 are by George Campbell.

Preface

Those who are interested solely in the Prehistoric and Early Christian periods in Ireland will be well served for descriptions of the monuments of these periods in Estyn Evans' book *Prehistoric and Early Christian Ireland—A Guide* (Batsford, London 1966), while the public who are interested in knowing a great deal about almost all the monuments, both great and small, throughout the country would be well advised to equip themselves with that excellent compendium of knowledge, *The Shell Guide to Ireland,* (Ebury Press, London, 2nd edition revised 1969). But since that most useful guidebook *The National Monuments of Ireland* (produced by Bord Fáilte—The Irish Tourist Board—with text supplied by the Commissioners of Public Works) went out of print about three years ago, nothing has appeared to replace it which gives details of the National Monuments of the country in a handy pocket size and at a reasonable price, despite the constant demand for such a book.

The present Guidebook can be seen as a second, but very much altered and expanded edition of the Bord Fáilte guidebook. Because its main purpose is to give a considerable amount of information about the major monuments in the Republic of Ireland, it has gone beyond the scope of the Bord Fáilte Guide in giving details not only of those monuments which are in State Care, but also of those monuments which are not in State Care but which are, nevertheless, worth visiting. It is thus a handbook giving details of National Monuments in State Care (though not all of these are necessarily important) and my own personal selection of about a hundred or so non-National monuments which are considered important. The guidebook has been designed to give an adequate description and history of these monuments, as well as to give more practical details about access to and location of monuments, to state whether or not they are signposted, and to quote the more important works where further details of the monuments can be obtained.

With very few exceptions, the monuments given here were erected before the year 1700. Many of the buildings built since that year are still in use, and not necessarily accessible to the visitor, and for this reason most of the great 18th century buildings, of which the country can be proud, are omitted. Those 'Stately Homes' which the public may visit are listed in Bord Fáilte's brochure entitled *Houses and Gardens*. The book limits itself to buildings in the Republic of Ireland; details of historic buildings in Northern Ireland may be obtained in the Northern Ireland publications *Ancient Monuments in Northern Ireland in State Charge* and *Ancient Monuments in Northern Ireland not in State Charge*.

The entries under each monument in the Guide are designed to give information not only about the monument itself and its history, but also to tell the reader how to find out more about it, as well as to give details as to how to locate and to get to it.

In the first line of the entry in the left-hand margin, you will find after the word *Map* a number, a letter and another number. These are indications as to where a monument may be located on one or other map at the end of the book. The first number refers to the map number, the letter and the other number to the co-ordinates of the square on the map where the monument can be located. Thus, if you see 'Map 8 E 5', it means that the monument will be found on map 8 in the square whose co-ordinates on the top and side of the map are denoted by the letter E and the number 5. The entry below this in the margin, beginning with the letters 'OS', gives details as to where the monument can be located to within a mile or less on the Ordnance Survey Half Inch map. While many monuments are marked on the Ordnance Survey Quarter Inch maps (of which there are five covering the whole country), it is best to use the Half Inch maps which have the advantage that the road network is marked in greater detail coupled with the fact that a great many monuments are also marked on them. There are 25 such Half Inch maps covering the whole country, and it is advisable to obtain at a booksellers the Half Inch maps covering the area in which you are touring. The monument can be located on the Half Inch map as follows. Take the entry for Ballintubber Abbey, Co Mayo, for instance. It reads

OS ½″ 11 M. 15.79

First get the Half Inch map number 11. Look at the bottom of the map and you will see that the country is divided into quadrants on the National Grid, each quadrant being marked with a letter. Then find on the map the corresponding quadrant with the letter you are looking for, in this case 'M'. Having located this large area on the map, look along the top or bottom edge of the map and find the number 15 and follow it upwards or downwards as the case may be to the point where it meets the number 79 on either side of the map, and the point where these two lines meet is roughly where the monument is located.

In the main body of the text, the first line of each entry gives the name of the place or the name by which the monument is known, and this may be followed by a number in brackets. This refers to the official number of the National Monument. Where the monument has no number, it means that the monument is not in State Care. After this comes the general description of the type of monument, such as 'Abbey', 'Castle' or 'Megalithic Tomb'. If the monument is illustrated or if a plan of it is given, the reference to the illustration or plan will be given in italics at the end of the first line of the entry.

How to Use the Guide

Below this comes an entry beginning with the word *Access* giving details as to how to get to the monument from the nearest tarred road. It may be either 'direct' i.e. just beside or near the road, or it may be that you will have to go over two fields to reach it. This is followed by details as to whether the monument is signposted or not. In general it should be noted that not all monuments are signposted; only those monuments are signposted which are either worth visiting or where access to them is easy.

Then comes the history and description of the monument itself. If a slightly technical word occurs, the meaning of which you are not sure of, you should find it explained in the Glossary on pages 261-264.

At the bottom of each entry, references are given to publications where further information can be found about each monument. These references are not exhaustive, but merely refer to the main sources in the archaeological literature where the more important details about the monuments can be found. Certain books and journals are referred to in abbreviated forms; the key to these abbreviations will be found in the list of abbreviations near the end of the book. A short general bibliography, giving a list of the more important general works, is also given on page 269.

If you are touring in an area and you want to know what monuments are worth visiting in that area, you should first consult the maps at the end of the book. Then try to find out what county you are in, and locate it on the map. You will find the more important monuments given by name, and the lesser ones given by number. Those given by name you will find in the text given in their alphabetical order under the county you are in. If in doubt, consult the Index. If only a number is given on the map, then look up in the text under the particular county, and you will find the number given immediately after the name of the monument on the first line of each entry. As few counties contain a great number of monuments, it is hoped that this task will not prove too difficult. The number on the map and in the first line of the entry corresponds to the official number of the National Monument, and also to the number given under the letters 'SN' (Séadchomharta Náisiúnta—Irish for 'National Monument') on the green and white road signposts which are usually reserved for ancient monuments, and if the monument is signposted, this should help you to find the monument on the ground.

If you are looking for information on and the location of a particular monument, then first look up the Index where you will find a reference to the page on which the monument is described. To locate this monument on the map, consult the references given in the margin and then you should be able to find it on the maps at the end.

For those wishing to visit museums, a selected list of museums will be found on page 270.

Seen on a map, Ireland always reminds me of a plump puppy dog standing on its hind legs begging for attention, or of a small child jumping up and down in the lap of mother Europe, with Britain serving as a comfortable cushion. Geographically, it rounds off the north-western corner of the Continent. Although its climate is softened by the mild winds of the Atlantic Gulf Stream, Ireland must have appeared so wild and remote in the eyes of the ancient Romans that they did not even go to the bother of conquering it. Had they done so they would undoubtedly have given Slea Head in Co Kerry the name of 'Finis Terra'—'The End of the Earth'; for up till the time of Columbus it was practically the most westerly point in Europe and the place where the endless western ocean began.

That 'Ireland is an island in the Atlantic' is true in as much as it is isolated from its neighbours by the sea surrounding it. This insulation has given rise in the past to the impression that Ireland is a sleepy and dreamy island living a delightful Rip van Winkle kind of existence, out of touch with the reality of the rest of the world. But while it may be a country with an old world charm, a country of talkers and dreamers, it has rarely been out of contact culturally with the rest of Europe. For that same sea which appears to isolate it physically from its neighbours has always acted as a connecting link between Ireland, England and the Continent. From the earliest times Ireland has always formed a part of Europe, and conversely Europe has always been very much a part of Ireland. If Ireland had been placed away out in the middle of the Atlantic Ocean, without any contact with the rest of Europe, it would have been very much the poorer for it, and its culture would have choked and died like the wayside seed in the gospel. The best of Irish culture has always had its roots on foreign shores. Ireland has invariably relied upon the sea to have new ideas fed to it from other lands; the sea is the lifeline which has always kept the country culturally alive. Indeed it has always been when that lifeline has been most active that the best of Irish culture has resulted. The builders of the megalithic tombs filtered in across the sea from Brittany and England and erected great tombs in Ireland; the introduction of Christianity and writing from the Roman world led to the foundation of the Irish monasteries which acted as lighthouses in the darkness of Europe after the barbarian invasions, while the coming of the English language heralded a great renaissance in Irish literature.

For a country seeming to be so far out in the Atlantic, Ireland has surprisingly far-flung links. The Gulf Stream has sometimes served to float innovations northwards to it from Spain, Portugal and Brittany, and it was from there that the builders of the great Passage-Graves on the Boyne ultimately came. Being Ireland's closest neighbour, Britain has naturally always played a great role in the formation of Ireland, and this is so from the earliest times up to the present day. It is to England, Scotland and Wales that Ireland owes its knowledge of Christianity, writing, church building and military fortification, and indeed England has acted as intermediary in introducing many continental ideas to Ireland. Despite the destruction wrought by the Scandinavian Vikings in Ireland, the country owes a debt to them because they introduced community settlement to Ireland in the form of towns and also gave it a number of artistic motifs during the 9th-12th centuries.

These far-flung connections certainly help to make Irish culture eclectic. No nation exists in complete isolation, and, as is the case with every country, Ireland is the result of the interplay of a great number of ideas and factors derived from various directions. But this is not to say that everything in Ireland is just a mirror of foreign influence trickling in from various areas of Europe. It has never been content simply to receive whatever impulses it has been given from outside; it has always had the capacity to make its own selection of these impulses and put them into a common melting pot. But while the ingredients of that pot could trace their origin to foreign shores, the mixture which emerged as a result was characteristically Irish. Irish Romanesque architecture, for instance, was introduced in its basic form from outside, but no one could say that Clonfert Cathedral—one of the finest achievements of Irish Romanesque—is anything but Irish.

Ireland's geographical position at the extremity of Europe is also of importance in understanding its culture, for it has helped to preserve old traditions which have been obliterated in other parts of Europe. Europe, indeed, can be compared to a whirlpool where things move faster at the centre than they do at the rim. In Central Europe, civilizations come and go at a much faster rate. Only some of these have sufficient force before they die to send out roots elsewhere, to spread like waves in a pond when a stone is dropped into it, or like sounds which continue re-echoing long after what caused the sound has ceased. The stronger the wave, the wider it spreads, but in the past only the strongest had the resilience to break through the barrier of geographical isolation and cross the sea to Ireland. The Celts, the Normans, megalithic tombs, and Christianity as well as Romanesque and Gothic architecture broke through that barrier; but the Romans, the Saxons and Baroque architecture did not. But each new wave which did arrive came to stay—it could go no further westwards, and the long interval between every new arrival ensured that each one had time to settle down and take tenacious roots. New peoples and ideas added to, but were also swallowed up and assimilated by, already existing groups and institutions, thus creating a great continuity in tradition, but a tradition which—if not shaken out of its complacency by new peoples and ideas—could, and often did, lead to stagnation. But this stagnation also served to preserve old institutions which, although they became almost archaic museum pieces in Ireland, were extinguished and exchanged for newer, though not always better ones, in other parts of Europe. Thus, on the edge of this European whirlpool, Ireland was enabled to retain some old traditions and characteristics which were irretrievably lost through the faster pace of change at the centre of the vortex. The culture of the Celts is a case in point. The Celts at one stage dominated much of Europe from Ireland almost as far as Turkey, and although the so-called La Tène Celts radiated out from and were strongest in Central Europe and north-eastern France, little remains of their culture there because it was overlain by Roman and later civilizations. It is only on the western periphery of these areas, in Brittany, Scotland, Wales and Ireland, that the Celtic culture remains. Ireland indeed is remarkable in preserving some of the best of these traditions in the language, music, dancing, folklore and literature of the Celts, whereas these have entirely disappeared in Central Europe. If for no other reason, Ireland repays study because it is a vastly rich treasure house and museum of Celtic tradition.

The fusion of a number of foreign elements in creating something new and specifically Irish, as well as the preservation of old traditions long lost elsewhere, are characteristics of Irish culture which can well be studied and exemplified in the great number of ancient monuments which the traveller can see covering the face of Ireland like daisies. These monuments, however, should not be simply regarded as gaunt and silent scarecrows standing in the middle of a field. Their stones can speak—or should be made to speak. They are skeletons which come to life when clothed with the flesh of history. History books can tell us of 'old forgotten far-off things and battles long ago', but the events they tell of, instead of being imagined in a visual vacuum, are best understood on the sites where they took place. Ancient monuments form the essential stage backdrop for the pageant that is history. When we visit these monuments, our mind's eye must visualize that it was in these very churches that the monks we read about prayed, that it was here in this castle that an Irish chieftain defended himself, or that it was really on that spot that such and such a saint was laid to rest. Being inside one of these monuments, we should almost feel that we can touch history. We could of course—with Byron and Scott—see the monuments as romantic and ivy-clad ruins where the owls 'to-whit-too-whoo', but we will gain immeasurably more from them if we use our historical imagination and study the monuments as an integral part of the history of the country. We must bring these ruins to life in our imagination, and by reconstructing them in our mind, see how they must have looked when first built and how they fitted into the original landscape; and we can also see how our ancestors lived—and died—in them. They give us as much insight as history books into the development of mankind, and can serve as illustrations of the successive waves of peoples who came to our shore.

But monuments can also help us understand our own world as we grew up to find it. The past is father of the present, and it is only by understanding all the facets of history and its products that we can comprehend why the world has turned out to be as it is and not otherwise. Through the monuments, too, we can follow the history and development of art in Ireland, for stone, being the lasting material it is, has preserved for us some of the most important aspects of the cultural and artistic heritage of the country, from the spirals at Newgrange through the Celtic patterns on the Turoe stone, to the figures on the High Crosses and the beasts and masks on Romanesque doorways up to the effigy of the mail-clad warrior atop his medieval tomb.

In short, Ireland's monuments repay study for a great number of reasons. The visitor who goes to the trouble of visiting them will not only find them exuding a peace and a calm which will make the effort worthwhile, but from the cultural, historical and artistic point of view he will also find them an enriching experience, for through them he can re-create an old and delightful world, and play a game with himself of tracing the history of the country from its earliest beginnings up to the present.

THE STONE AGE

When the glaciers retreated at the end of the Ice Age, Ireland was left with a landscape sufficiently enticing and attractive for both humans and animals to come and settle in it. Except for some dubious and unproven relics of the Old Stone Age, the first definite traces of man which we find in Ireland date from about 6,000 B.C. At this period the first settlers came across the straits from Scotland to Northern Ireland and then spread westwards and southwards, reaching Derry and Dublin. They used flint implements to carry out their domestic chores, but it was probably not for hundreds of years that they learned the use of pottery. Except for shells piled on heaps and also some stone implements, few of the material remains of these earliest settlers have been preserved. Throughout the course of the following four thousand years they were probably joined by other small groups of people from Britain and further afield who brought with them improved tools, such as polished stone axes, and with the help of these the first inroads were made into clearing the forests which must have covered considerable parts of the country. Space was thus provided for the planting of wheat and barley, and animal husbandry was practised with cattle, sheep and goats. The people lived in small round or rectangular huts with a stone base, and the upper parts were possibly made of dried mud, wattle and daub, or some such similar material, while the roof may have already been made with straw. The foundations of some of these houses were excavated at Lough Gur in Co Limerick, but little remains to be seen of them now. The most important remnants of this period are the tombs constructed over the graves of the dead which are so much more imposing and long-lasting than the homes of the living. These tombs are described as megalithic, which means 'of great stones', as they are usually constructed with stones of massive size and weight. The variety of Stone Age tombs mirror a number of different waves of inhabitants who filtered into the country during the period 3,000-2,000 B.C.

Court Cairns

On present evidence, court cairns are the earliest megalithic tombs in Ireland, possibly dating from the period 3,000-2,500 B.C. The basic unit is the tomb itself consisting of a long chamber divided into a number of compartments where the burials were placed. In front of the tomb itself lay a semi-circular open space or court flanked by standing stones, where funeral rites possibly took place before the actual burial of the dead. The tomb itself was covered by a stone mound broader at the front than at the back, and held in place by upright stones at the edges. Moytirra East, Co Sligo is not the best court cairn, but it serves to show the

COURT CAIRN

Fig. 1. Groundplans of the four main types of megalithic tombs.

MOYTIRRA EAST

PASSAGE GRAVE

CARROWKEEL - Cairn K

WEDGE-SHAPED
GALLERY GRAVE

BALLYEDMONDUFF

DOLMEN

CARROWMORE

shape of this type of tomb (Fig. 1). But this basic shape can be varied considerably (compare Fig. 2). Cohaw, Co. Cavan represents one of the variations where two tombs have been placed back to back thus forming one long burial chamber with a semi-circular forecourt at each end. Another and more impressive variation is where two courts were placed together face to face so that the tomb consisted of a large open oval court with one or two burial chambers at either end. Good examples of this can be seen at Magheraghanrush, Co Sligo and Glencolumbkille (Cloghanmore), Co Donegal, while Creevykeel, Co Sligo (Fig. 67) represents a variant with an entrance at one end of an oval open court and a burial chamber at the other end. Although much pottery and stone implements have been found in these tombs, we are not yet in a position to say where the builders of the tombs came from.

Passage-Graves

More interesting and more exciting to the general visitor are tombs known as Passage-Graves. These are set in round earthen or stone mounds, with a passage leading from the edge of the mound to a grave near or at the centre of the mound. The grave can be large or small, usually round but occasionally somewhat square in shape and often having burial chambers leading off it, one at each side and one at the back of the tomb. The burial chamber itself can be roofed by a flat stone or by the corbel technique, and large stone basins are occasionally found in the side chambers. The most interesting aspect of these tombs is the number of geometrical motifs on the stones which despite

many efforts made by mystics and those studying the history of religions have yet to be deciphered satisfactorily; they probably have something to do with the religion of the people who built the tombs. Spirals, concentric U's, zigzags and triangles are the most common motifs used; the sun with its rays can be seen, and at Fourknocks and Knowth stylized representations of the human face occur. These tombs are generally grouped together into cemeteries where they occupy neighbouring hill-tops. The best examples are Loughcrew (Fig. 55), Carrowkeel (Fig. 65) and those in the Boyne Valley (Newgrange [Fig. 56], Knowth, Dowth). There are also a number of individual examples dotted around the countryside, such as Baltinglass Hill, Co Wicklow, and Duntryleague, Co Limerick, while large mounds in the West, such as Heapstown and Knocknarea in Co Sligo, and Eochy's Cairn and Ballymacgibbon in Co Mayo probably conceal Passage-Graves beneath them also. The decoration so characteristic of the Boyne Valley tombs and of Loughcrew is absent in the western tombs. Newgrange has recently been dated by modern scientific methods to around 2,500 B.C. but it is likely that Passage-Graves continued in use for some centuries after that date. A tomb like Fourknocks is so similar to others in Portugal that one could believe that its builders came directly from Portugal, but recent discoveries at Knowth suggest that it is more likely that the people who built the Passage-Graves may have come to the east coast of Ireland directly from Brittany.

Portal Dolmens

Dolmen is a word which is taken from the Breton meaning a stone table, and in the past dolmens have been thought to be Druids Altars or the beds of the romantic couple Diarmuid and Gráinne while fleeing from the wrath of an elderly king. They are—more prosaically—just another type of megalithic tomb consisting of three or more standing stones covered by one large capstone which can weigh up to 100 tons (Browneshill, Co Carlow), though occasionally there are two capstones. Two of the standing stones are usually placed symmetrically near each other and appear to form a portal or door to the tomb. Some of these dolmens are so attractive that they could be termed works of sculpture, and we must certainly admire the technical skill with which the builders raised the often enormous stones to their positions. The large capstone on top was placed in position by being hauled up the side of an earthen mound which was built around the standing stones, but which has long since disappeared. The dolmens are largely found along the east coast from Proleek in Co Louth to the examples in Carlow (Browneshill [Fig. 19] and Haroldstown), Kilkenny (Kilmogue) and Waterford (Knockeen etc. [Fig. 79]). They were probably built around 2,000 B.C. by the descendants of those who built the court cairns.

Fig. 2. Conjectural reconstruction of a Court-cairn at Shanballyedmond, Co Tipperary. 3rd millennium B.C.

Wedge-shaped Gallery-Graves

These graves get their name because they are wider at one end than at the other. The long narrow burial chamber was often surrounded by a special setting of stones and was originally covered by a mound of earth and stones. A conjectural reconstruction of one of these tombs is shown in Fig. 3. These graves were built—possibly by a new wave of immigrants coming from France —shortly after 2,000 B.C. Good examples are Labbacallee and Island, Co Cork (Fig. 3), Moylisha, Co Wicklow and Ballyedmonduff, Co Dublin (Fig. 1), while simplified versions can be found in Co Clare.

THE BRONZE AGE

The Bronze Age began probably around 1,750 B.C. and lasted until about 500 B.C.; it gets its name from the main material used during the period. The widespread use of copper and bronze, together with the well-known Irish gold, must have made Ireland one of the best known metal-producers in western Europe during the Bronze Age. The bronze and gold products of this period can best be studied in the National Museum of Ireland, in Dublin. In comparison to the Stone Age, the Bronze Age has surprisingly few striking monuments. Ireland has no Stonehenge, but it has a number of stone circles such as Grange, Lough Gur, Co Limerick, Beltany, Co Donegal and the Piper's Stones, Co Wicklow which could date to the Bronze Age. But other stone circles, such as that at Drombeg, Co Cork—with one stone lying down—date to the ensuing Iron Age. Their use is unknown, but Drombeg (Fig. 22) certainly seems to have been used as an observatory to find out the shortest day in the year. Also possibly Bronze Age in date are a number of standing stones, one of which —Punchestown, Co Kildare—marked the site of a Bronze Age burial. Others may have been boundary stones, road-markers— or even scratching posts for cattle!

At the dawn of its history in the 5th century A.D. Ireland was
a completely Celtic country, but no one knows for certain when
the first Celts arrived in Ireland. Many think that they arrived
there in the last five centuries B.C., but the opinion is fast gaining
ground that the Celts must have arrived long before that, though
of course no definite confirmation of this theory has been found.
But if this latter theory is true, it could mean that the Celts were
already arriving in Ireland by about 1,500 B.C., and possibly
even slightly earlier.

THE IRON AGE

Iron came into use in Ireland probably somewhere around 500
B.C. While the Stone and Bronze Age monuments are largely
tombs, and very few dwelling places are known, the situation is
reversed with the arrival of the Iron Age: our knowledge of the
Iron Age stems from places of habitation while we know extraordinarily little about burial customs during this period.

Hill-forts

Some of the most imposing Iron Age monuments are the Hill-
forts, where a large stone wall with a ditch inside or outside
surrounds an area covering many acres of a hill-top, such as at
Rathgall, Co Wicklow, Dun Aillinne, Co Kildare and Moghane,
Co Clare. The strongest occupation of these sites would seem to
begin around the time of Christ, and continue into the Early
Christian period. The enormous size of the Hill-forts and the
fact that the ditch is sometimes inside and not outside the bank
make them less practical as fortifications. At Tara, Co Meath
and Baltinglass Hill, Co Wicklow, the walls enclosed much older
Bronze Age burial mounds which crowned the hill-top, suggesting
that their use may have been linked with older burial cults.
Possibly it was the priest-kings who were gaining the political
upper hand before the time of St Patrick who established themselves here in a conscious effort to forge a link between older
established religious burial customs and their own new cult
centres. None of the Hill-forts was inhabited for lengthy periods,
and they may have acted as meeting places as did also Teltown
and the Hill of Ward in Co Meath, and Ushnagh in Co Westmeath.

*Fig. 3. Conjectural reconstruction of a Wedge-
shaped Gallery-grave at Island, Co Cork. 2nd
millennium B.C.*

Earthen and Stone Ring-forts

Smaller than the Hill-forts are the Ring-forts—small circular areas protected by an earthen or stone wall with a ditch outside —which are usually situated on level ground. There must have been one or more round or rectangular houses of stone or wood inside these Ring-forts, and their isolated position in the landscape corresponds closely to that of the country cottages of today. Many of these Ring-forts are not to be imagined as strong military fortifications but as normal homesteads sheltered by a wall to keep the cattle and sheep in at night and the preying animals out, though they could also be defended if necessary in times of danger. Some forts have underground stone-built passages called souterrains which could have been used for storage, though some acted as living quarters. A good example of a simple ring-fort (though lacking a souterrain) is Danestown, Co Meath. The stone forts, which are particularly common in western Ireland where stone was more plentiful and where every inch of earth was needed for tillage, are much more like military fortifications in appearance. The Grianán of Aileach in Co Donegal and Staigue, Co Kerry (Fig. 37) are among the most imposing, while Cahermacnaghten, Co Clare and Knockdrum, Co Cork show us examples on a smaller scale. The Aran Islands also have a number of stone forts, and the semi-circular walls of Dun Aenghus with its back to a cliff dropping 200 feet to the sea below are among the most primitively massive and magnificent fortifications in western Europe. The ramparts connected by flights of steps and the long stone-lined entrance passage are features which it shares with some of the larger stone forts in the rest of the country. Ring-forts, be they of earth or stone, came into fashion during the Iron Age, but continued in use up till the 17th century, as the illustration of a fort at Tullaghoge, Co Tyrone shows (Fig. 4).

Promontory-forts and Crannógs

These are other types of fortifications used during the Iron Age and continuing in use into the medieval period. Promontory-forts get their name because they are sited on small promontories jutting out into the sea, or as in the case of Caherconree, Co Kerry, into lower surrounding land. They are defended by nature on three sides with steeply falling cliffs, while on the fourth side they were cut off from the neighbouring high ground by one or more banks and ditches. A good but dangerous example of a promontory fort is Dunbeg, on the Dingle Peninsula in Co Kerry. Slightly more inaccessible are crannógs—small artificial islands in the middle or at the edge of lakes which were defended by wooden palisades and were inhabited also well into the medieval period. The only example listed here—and a poor one at that—is at Lough Gur, Co Limerick.

Fig. 4. The fort at Tullaghoge, Co Tyrone as seen
in Barthelet's map ca. 1600. At bottom right is the
inauguration chair of the O'Neills.

Fig. 5. Stone from Turoe, Co Galway, decorated
with Celtic curvilinear designs. 3rd–2nd century
B.C. (?).

La Tène Decorated Stones

Two stones—those at Turoe, Co Galway (Fig. 5) and Castlestrange, Co Roscommon—are practically unique in Europe in
that they are decorated with curvilinear motifs in the style used
by the Celts on the Continent (called by archaeologists the La
Tène Celts) in the last five centuries B.C. The Turoe and Castlestrange stones belong presumably to this period also, and are
evidence that the La Tène Celts must have reached Ireland by
that time.

Ogham Stones

The earliest writing in Ireland began probably around 300 A.D.
and we know it from stones inscribed in the alphabet known as
Ogham—called after Ogmios, the Celtic god of writing. The
alphabet is made up of sets of up to five strokes on, diagonally
across or on either side of a central line—the central line being the
edge of a stone. The alphabet is as follows:

A O U E I   H D T C Q   B L F S N M G NG Z R

The HDTCQ group of strokes corresponds to the first letters of
the numerals one to five in the Old Irish language. The inscriptions using the alphabet are carved on standing stones; they begin
at the bottom and climb towards the top of the stone as at Dunloe
Co Kerry (Fig. 6) and, if necessary, continue downwards on the
opposite side. The inscriptions commemorate a person and give
details of his father or ancestors. While the inscriptions themselves
are simple, they are difficult to translate because they are written
in such an archaic and obscure form of the language that it is
often difficult to give even the exact name of the person commemorated. The precise relationship (son or descendant) of the
person to his ancestor is so difficult to interpret also that in most
cases a translation is not given here for the inscription. The use
of the script continued till the 7th or 8th century and possibly
later.

Fig. 6. An Ogham stone from Coolmagort and now
at Dunloe, Co Kerry. The Ogham inscription
reads 'CUNACENA'. Early Christian period.

THE EARLY CHRISTIAN PERIOD

The introduction of Christianity by St Patrick in the 5th century (though there were some Christians there before his arrival) brought about considerable change. The power of the pagan priest-kings, such as those at Tara, must have declined, and their place was taken by kings whose power was purely political. The organization of St Patrick's church was largely episcopal, and he founded a great number of bishoprics during his lifetime. But by the end of the 5th century the importance of these bishops was overshadowed by the foundation of an extraordinarily large number of monasteries which mushroomed particularly in the 6th and 7th centuries, and which were to become important cultural centres, destined to bring great glory to Ireland. From accounts which have been preserved, we can gather that the monks led an extremely severe and ascetical life, practising the most rigorous penances. One of the greatest of these was self-exile, and from the second half of the 6th century onwards a great number of monks voluntarily exiled themselves from their beloved native heath to preach Christianity in foreign lands. They started in Scotland, spread then to England and finally they reached the Continent where they founded great monasteries in France, Germany, Switzerland, Austria and even as far away as Italy. The Irish monasteries had been able to glean and preserve much of the ancient learning of the later Roman Empire before it was swept away by the onslaught of the barbarian invasions in the 5th century. When the invaders had settled down peacefully in Central Europe, the missionary monks began to re-introduce there the learning which they and their predecessors had preserved and cherished, and their efforts culminated in the foundation of the schools of learning centred around the court of Charlemagne in the early 9th century, when the Middle Ages may be said to have begun. Cardinal Newman summed up this rôle of the Irish monasteries when he described them as 'the storehouse of the past and the birthplace of the future'.

Although their fruit was great, their seed was indeed small. To the visitor of today, these Early Christian monasteries must appear small in extent. Little or nothing remains of the monasteries of this early period as all the buildings were of wood or wattle and daub and have long since succumbed to the effects of time and the weather. But small monasteries in the stony areas of the west of the country have preserved the layout and appearance of these original monasteries, such as the small hermits cells on the island of Skellig Michael off the coast of Co Kerry, Church Island in Valentia Harbour also in Co Kerry (Fig. 7) or Inishmurray, Co. Sligo (Fig. 68) The Dingle Peninsula and the Aran Islands have preserved primitive-looking examples in stone though they do not necessarily belong to the earliest period of the monastic foundations. The buildings consist of one or more small churches,

Fig. 7. Conjectural reconstruction of the Early Christian monastery on Church Island, Valentia, Co Kerry.

and a number of bee-hive huts where the monks lived. This cluster of buildings was enclosed by a wall which cut off the monastery from the outside world. The buildings were not laid out according to a plan; they just 'growed and growed' in any space which was available to them.

While these monasteries were peacefully continuing their existence during the 6th, 7th and 8th centuries, becoming centres of manuscript illumination producing such masterpieces as the Book of Durrow (c. 650) and the Book of Kells (c. 800)— both now in the Library of Trinity College, Dublin—the political life of the country went on uninterrupted. The local kings were invariably struggling for greater power and eventually for sovereignty over all the other kings, but basically the power lay with one great royal family—the O'Neills of the North— who held nominal sway though not complete control over the whole country. This comparative peace was shattered, however, by the arrival of the Vikings from Scandinavia in 795. In the following fifty years small swift bands of Vikings made lightning raids on Irish monasteries and settlements, and carried off their treasures back to Scandinavia where some are still coming to light in Viking graves today. By 840 the Vikings founded permanent settlements and trading colonies along the coast, and many of Ireland's larger coastal towns such as Dublin, Wicklow, Arklow, Wexford, Waterford and possibly Cork and Limerick as well owe their foundation to them. Though they caused a great deal of destruction, the Vikings put Ireland in their debt by the foundation of these towns, and by the introduction of more organized trade with the outside world; they taught the Irish much about the use of seaworthy vessels and introduced the first coinage to the country. Despite the influence of the Battle of Clontarf in 1014, when Viking power in Ireland was effectively broken, relations between Irish and Norse must have been more cordial than the historical sources would reveal. There was considerable inter-marriage between the two races, particularly in the towns, and the interchange of artistic motifs up till the 12th century shows that there must have been close contact between the two at a cultural level also. This has been strikingly borne out recently by the excavations at High Street in the centre of the old Norse town of Dublin where a number of native and Norse elements have been found intermingled in the period prior to the 13th century.

But the raids of the first 50 years of the 9th century must have had a considerable impact on the Irish population who, however, were incapable of uniting and fighting against the common foe. Up till that time all the monastic buildings had been made of wood or of some other perishable material which was all too easily set on fire. It was possibly the influence of the Viking raids which first encouraged the Irish masons to construct the first real stone churches in Ireland. In the 9th and 10th centuries there would appear to have been a sudden re-awakening to the monumental power of stone, manifesting itself in the building of churches and Round Towers as well as the sculpting of High Crosses and grave-slabs. The monasteries as we see them today are thus not the same as those from which the early missionary monks went out to their exiled labours; they are more the monasteries of the 9th-12th centuries when the standard of asceticism had declined in favour of a more lax rule, possibly even under the abbacy of laymen. The monks of these monasteries continued to live in small huts, all of which have disappeared, and we have been left with what they made of stone—the High Crosses, the Round Towers and the churches themselves. (Compare the conjectural reconstruction of the monastery at Kells, Co Meath given in the frontispiece.) If anything can be said to be typical of Ireland, and can also be said to have been the greatest contribution which Ireland has made to the art and architecture of Europe, it is the products of these monasteries, both in the field of manuscript illumination, and in their buildings and crosses in stone which are fortunately still so delightfully ubiquitous in the Irish countryside. Groups of these stone monuments can best be seen together at Glendalough, Co Wicklow, Clonmacnoise, Co Offaly, Monasterboice, Co Louth, Kilmacduagh, Co Galway and on the two Co Clare islands of Inishcaltra and Scattery.

High Crosses

The best known High Crosses are those where a ring surrounds
the meeting place of stem and arms of the cross, and where panels
show figured scenes from the Old and New Testaments. They
tell simple stories from the Bible and are the precursors of modern
epic films about the same subjects. Yet the first crosses had
neither rings around the centre nor scenes from the Bible. The
experts tell us that the development of these crosses began with
simple standing stones like those at Carndonagh (Fig. 8) and
at Fahan (Fig. 25) which are dated to the 7th century, and which
may be either in the form of a cross or they may have crosses on
them formed of interlaced bands with simple figures carved in
relief. By the 8th century the crosses such as those at Ahenny,
Co Tipperary (Fig. 8) are divided up into a number of panels
containing a variety of geometrical motifs so similar to the Book
of Kells that they seem to be contemporary with it. It is, however,
possible that the crosses were originally of wood and had these
motifs applied to them on sheets of bronze, and that at some later
stage these crosses were 'translated' into stone though retaining
closely the decoration and style of the wooden crosses.

The artistic development continued from there in the 9th
century to the stage when scenes from the Old Testament began
to creep in hesitatingly, such as on the Cross of St Patrick and
Columba in Kells, Co Meath (Fig. 8), or on the South Cross at
Clonmacnoise, Co Offaly. By the middle of the 10th century,
the High Crosses as we know them had fully developed and such
masterpieces as the Cross of Muiredach at Monasterboice, Co
Louth (Fig. 8), the Cross of the Scriptures at Clonmacnoise
(Fig. 62) and others at Durrow, Co Offaly (Fig. 63) and Kells,
Co Meath were created. These crosses were almost entirely
filled out with scenes carved in relief depicting Old and New

7th century   8th century   9th centu

Fig. 8. Crosses from Carndonagh, Co Donegal, Ahenny, Co Tipperary, Kells, Co Meath, Monasterboice, Co Louth, Drumcliffe, Co Sligo and Dysert O'Dea, Co Clare showing the development of High Crosses from the 7th to the 12th century.

Testament stories, with the Crucifixion often taking the central position on one face of the cross, and the representation of Christ in Glory on the Day of Judgment in the same position on the other face. The depiction of the Fall of Man showing Adam and Eve on either side of a tree with its apple-laden branches curving over their heads and down behind their backs is an almost constant scene on the crosses, usually accompanied by a picture of one of their off-spring Cain battering their other son Abel with a club. Other scenes from the Old Testament include Daniel in the Lion's Den, the Children in the Fiery Furnace, the Sacrifice of Isaac, Noah's Ark, David and Goliath, and David with his harp. The Passion and Resurrection also formed favourite subjects for the sculptors, and the Crucifixion, the Crowning with Thorns, the Arrest of Christ, the Soldiers guarding the Tomb, the Transfiguration and Doubting Thomas often occur on one or other cross. The early life of Christ is represented neither by the Annunciation nor the Birth of Christ but by the Adoration of the Magi, and by the Baptism in the Jordan, while the miraculous power of Christ (and by implication, of his church) is shown by the Multiplication of Loaves and Fishes and the Marriage Feast of Cana. The monastic ideal is also hinted at by the scenes representing Paul and Anthony in the desert. These crosses may be thought to mark the grave of some exalted person, but it is much more likely that they were erected as

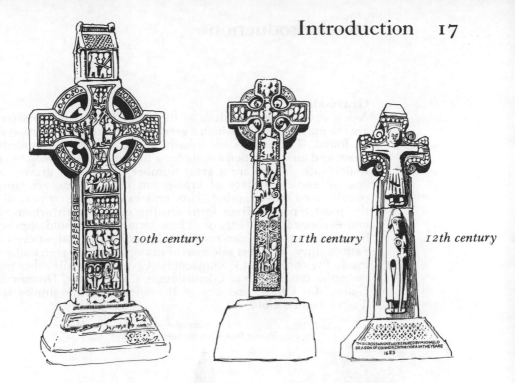

10th century   11th century   12th century

Picture Bibles for the edification of Christians just as statues or
stained glass are used in churches today. Intermingled with the
figures on these crosses are a number of geometrical ornaments,
including animal interlacing, animals prancing among vine
branches etc. which served to fill up all available gaps, for the
Celts had a horror of empty spaces.

Beside the larger and better known crosses, there are others
which represent local schools of sculpture. The most obvious of
these are the granite crosses found in Kildare (Old Kilcullen,
Castledermot) and Kilkenny (Ullard and St Mullins). Although
situated in the same area, the Moone, Co Kildare cross is unique
in shape and style, and is one of the most disarmingly and naively
beautiful of all the crosses.

By the 11th century, the figures began to stand out in high
relief on the crosses, as at Drumcliffe, Co Sligo (Fig. 8) and by
the 12th century, the Biblical scenes were largely discarded in
favour of animal interlacing in panels and the representations
of Christ and a local bishop or abbot standing out in very high
relief on one or both faces of the cross. The best examples of
these 12th century crosses come from Co Clare (Kilfenora,
Dysert O'Dea [Fig. 8] and Killaloe) and Co Galway (Tuam and
Aran Islands), and there is also a small example at Glendalough
and another at Cashel. The custom of erecting crosses continued,
though in a different form, well into the medieval period.

Grave-slabs

A less eye-catching product of the Early Christian monasteries
are the grave-slabs, on which a great deal of artistic expression can
be found. These slabs are usually flat stones with an inscribed
cross, and an inscription asking for a prayer for the person buried
underneath. There are a great number of types of grave-stone
and an endless variety of crosses on them. Some are simple
equal-armed crosses, others have crosses in square frames, while
the most typically Irish form are the crosses with ornamental
and expanded ends (Fig. 9). These latter types would appear to
have been common from the 9th till possibly the 11th or even the
12th century. The best selection of examples can be seen mounted
inside the entrance at Clonmacnoise, Co Offaly, while other good
examples can be seen at Glendalough, Co Wicklow, Durrow and
Gallen, Co Offaly, and one of the finest single examples is at
Tullylease, Co Cork.

*Fig. 9. A lost grave-slab of Suibine Mac Mailae
Humai from Clonmacnoise, Co Offaly. 887* A.D.

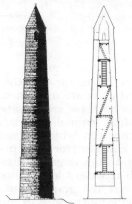

*Fig. 10. The Round Tower at Ardmore, Co Waterford
together with a cross-section. Probably 12th century*

Round Towers

It is through the Round Towers that Irish architects best showed
their paces. These towers are tall and slender like pared pencils,
with a doorway about ten or more feet above the ground; they
are five or more storeys high with a window for each storey and
four or more windows at the top immediately below the conical
roof. Today, they are bare within, but originally there were a
number of wooden landings joined by flights of stairs (compare
Fig. 10). With the aid of modern reconstructions, you can still
climb to the top of the towers at Kilkenny, Kildare, Monasterboice, Co Louth, Clondalkin, Co Dublin and at Kinneigh and
Cloyne, both in Co Cork. The Old Irish word for these towers
was Cloigtheach, or Bell Tower, and their main function was to

act as a bell tower or campanile to call the monks in from the fields to prayer, just as the Muslim muezzin does from the top of his minaret today. But the fact that the door was placed well above ground level suggests that the towers were also used as places of refuge both for the monks and for their treasures; the monks doubtless climbed up a wooden or rope ladder which they pulled up after them when all were safely installed inside, and then they closed the door in the face of Viking or indeed also Irish raiders (sometimes mercenaries of other monasteries!) who had a habit of descending upon them like the wolf on the fold. The latest of these Round Towers were built in the 12th century, such as those at Timahoe, Co Laois and at Kildare with their Romanesque doorways, but some must be as early as about 900; there is a report that the tower at Castledermot was built by a man who died in 919.

Early Christian and Romanesque Churches
The earliest stone churches in Ireland are scarcely likely to be older than the 9th century. Primitive-looking structures like the unusual boat-shaped oratory at Gallarus in the Dingle Peninsula, Co Kerry have often been taken to represent the first efforts at stone church building in Ireland, but they could even be 11th or 12th century instead of 8th century as supposed. Early Irish stone churches were probably modelled on the already existing wooden churches which they must have replaced one by one. Features of the wooden churches such as the end-rafters projecting out over the gable have been preserved in a church like that on St Macdara's Island, Co Galway (Fig. 34). The antae, or stone projections of the north and south walls beyond the east and west gables, which are such a common feature in early Irish church building, must also stem from a type of construction used in these wooden churches. The stones in the lowest parts of the walls in these early churches were often massive, and they decreased in size towards the top. Also typical are the rectangular and flat-headed doorways with sides narrowing towards the top. Good examples of these early church can be seen at St Mel's, Ardagh, Co Longford, Fore, Co Westmeath, Clonamery, Co Kilkenny, Labbamolaga, Co Cork, and also at Tuamgraney, Co Clare where the church is still in use. One of Ireland's most peculiar and interesting contributions to architecture are the stone roofs of some of these churches. St Kevin's Church at Glendalough, Co Wicklow, St Flannan's Oratory at Killaloe, St Doulagh's Church, Malahide, Co Dublin and Cormac's Chapel at Cashel, Co Tipperary all have well-preserved stone roofs with a steep pitch. The danger with a roof of stone is that it will tend to sag in the middle of the long side, and in order to counteract this, the Irish architects devised a system whereby the roof was supported by an arch underneath it which formed the walls of an attic room

above the main arch of the church below. The system is demon-strated from Cormac's Chapel in Cashel in Fig. 11.

At some stage, possibly around 1000 A.D. churches were built consisting of a nave and chancel, with a chancel arch where the two joined. Under the influence of this innovation, chancels were added to many of the older churches which up till then consisted of a simple rectangular nave. It was probably not until the 12th century that Romanesque architecture and decoration became such a common feature in Irish churches. The 12th century ushered in an unparalleled spate of church building activity in Ireland, encouraged by a number of ecclesiastical reforms which were taking place as a result of the Synod of Rathbreasail in 1110 and that of Kells in 1152. Through these synods a new church organization was being set up partially to replace the older monastic system, and the country was organized into a number of bishoprics, and—within that framework—into parishes. While not every parish church was necessarily Romanesque, Romanesque churches are found all over the country. Their typical features are round-headed doorways, chancel arches and windows which are decorated with a number of motifs such as fantastic animals, human masks (often with strands of beard intertwined) as well as various geometrical designs such as zig-zags, 'dog-teeth', bosses etc. A typically Irish feature is the pointed hood-moulding over the door which can be seen at Cormac's Chapel, Cashel, Co Tipperary (Fig. 72), Killeshin, Co Laois (Fig. 43), Freshford, Co Kilkenny, Donagh-more and Roscrea (Fig. 78), Co Tipperary as well as at Clonfert, Co Galway. While the Irish stone masons of the period did not have the opportunity of elaborating their designs on fully free-standing capitals as was the case on the Continent, they did develop a style of ornamentation which was entirely their own, and which conformed to the weird and almost rabelaisian fantasy common in the Europe of the 11th and 12th centuries. The best examples of Irish Romanesque architecture are to be seen at Cormac's Chapel in Cashel (Fig. 72) and Monaincha, both in Co Tipperary, Clonfert Cathedral and Tuam, Co Galway, Killeshin, Co Laois (Fig. 43), Ardfert and Kilmalkedar, Co Kerry, Ardmore, Co Waterford, Dysert O'Dea, Co Clare and Rahan, Co Offaly as well as at Glendalough, Co Wicklow. It will come as a surprise to those accustomed to visiting Romanesque churches in other countries to find that the Irish Romanesque churches are so small. They rarely exceed a length of about 40 feet or so. This smallness possibly stems from the fact that the churches were imitations of earlier wooden buildings which were small in size anyway, and it led to a much greater intimacy in the church too. As the population was not very large, and there was a great number of churches, it would also follow that there was no necessity for very large churches.

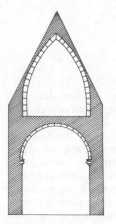

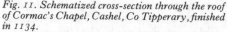

Fig. 11. Schematized cross-section through the roof of Cormac's Chapel, Cashel, Co Tipperary, finished in 1134.

THE MEDIEVAL PERIOD
Gothic Abbeys, Friaries and Churches

The 12th century saw the greatest changes which had taken place in Ireland since the advent of Christianity seven centuries before. Church leaders were reforming the structure of the church, assimilating a new spirit of religion which was spreading like lightning through Europe as Ecumenism is today. This spirit was finding expression in the Crusades and also in the foundation of new religious orders, starting with the Cistercians, and continuing with the Augustinians, Dominicans and Franciscans, as well as a host of lesser orders. The rapid spread of the Cistercian order did not escape the notice of St Malachy of Armagh, Ireland's most famous churchman in the first half of the 12th century. On his way to Rome in 1142 he visited the great St Bernard of Clairvaux, and induced him to send a handful of his monks to Ireland to found a new monastery of the order at Mellifont on the peaceful banks of the Mattock in Co Louth. This act sounded the death knell of the old Irish monasteries whose organization was as loose and disorganized as the buildings of the monasteries themselves. The arrival of the Cistercians brought with it an order, both within the religious community itself where every monk was assigned his specific post and with his day's programme carefully arranged for him, but also in the layout of the monastic buildings. The new system (Fig. 12) centred around an open square or quadrangle, with the church usually on the northern side of the square, the sacristy and Chapter or meeting room on the east, refectories and kitchen on the south, with store rooms etc on the west. On two sides of this quadrangle there was frequently an upper floor housing the monks' dormitories. The simple but stern life of the Cistercians must have obviously appealed to the Irish for the monks seem to have quickly abandoned the centuries old monasteries like Clonmacnoise and flocked to the new Cistercian foundations. By 1272 there were 38 Cistercian monasteries in the country. Some of the best-known medieval monasteries were Cistercian, and among their houses they can count such famous names as Jerpoint and Graiguenamanagh, Co Kilkenny, Dunbrody, Co Wexford, Boyle, Co Roscommon, Holycross and Kilcooly, Co Tipperary, Knockmoy, Co Galway and Corcomroe, Co Clare. The churches remaining at these places were undoubtedly begun in the 12th century, but a great many were not completed until the beginning of the 13th century. The period 1150-1250 comprised one of the most remarkable centuries in Irish architecture, and the obliquely chiselled stonework with its geometrical ornament and occasionally figured sculpture is one of the delights of the Irish countryside. Besides the monasteries listed above, good stonework can also be seen at the Cistercian foundations of Monasteranenagh, Co Limerick and Baltinglass, Co Wicklow.

Already by the end of the 12th century other orders were introduced to Ireland, such as the Augustinians, who were encouraged among others by that great church builder, Donal Mor O'Brien, King of Thomond. Athassel, Co Tipperary, Cong and Ballintubber in Co Mayo can be numbered among the most important Augustinian houses, while Killone and Inchicronan in Co Clare represent smaller examples. The Franciscans and Dominicans arrived in the first half of the 13th century. While the heyday of the Franciscans was only beginning, the Dominicans were already building their more important houses at Athenry, Co Galway, Kilmallock, Co Limerick and at Sligo, while the Benedictines were busy at the construction of Fore Abbey. The first half of the thirteenth century also brought forth great building activity in the Cathedrals which had been founded in the previous century. These include some of the few ancient Irish buildings still roofed and in use, and contain some of the best of Irish Gothic architecture. The two Dublin Cathedrals, Christchurch and St Patrick's, contain portions dating from this period, though they were heavily rebuilt later, and the same holds true for Kilkenny, Kildare, Cashel, Killaloe, Co Clare, Limerick and Clonfert, Co Galway. Tall slender lancet windows are characteristic features of this period. At the same time a number of larger parish churches were also being built, and prime among these is St Mary's, New Ross. By 1250 enough churches had been built to fit the needs of the community, and the earlier monastic zeal was beginning to wear thinner—we know of a number of instances of laxness in the Cistercian monasteries in the 13th century. The fight between Irish and English for control of the country persisted during the 13th and 14th centuries, and as less money was available for building, church construction declined after the mid-thirteenth century. The coming of the great European plague known as the Black Death which hit Ireland in 1348-49, and which killed eight Dominicans of the Black Friars monastery in Kilkenny in one day alone, denuded the population

JERPOINT ABBEY

Fig. 12. A conjectural reconstruction of Jerpoint Abbey, Co Kilkenny as it might have been in the 13th century.

of much of its life-blood, as well as its energy for building. It was not until the beginning of the 15th century that Ireland had regained sufficient strength to re-start its building activity again, and politically the 15th century was a felicitous one for Ireland.

The penal Statutes of Kilkenny of 1366 demanding that no monasteries should accept purely Irish monks, and that English and Irish should not intermarry, were connivingly disregarded, while the submission of the majority of Irish kings to Richard II on his visit to Ireland in 1394-95 meant nothing else than that the great landed magnates in Ireland who though Norman were becoming 'more Irish than the Irish themselves' were able to continue their careers and carve out their territories as before without any great hindrance from England. The period from 1400 up till 1535 was one of great freedom in Ireland, when the Lords of Ormond, Thomond and Kildare in turn held virtual sway over large parts of the country, and became great patrons of the arts by encouraging poetry and church building. It was thus that the 15th century saw a tremendous revival in ecclesiastical architecture. The Cistercians contented themselves with re-furbishing their own old foundations in a magnificent style, such as at Holy Cross (Fig. 75) and Kilcooly in Co Tipperary, which have excellent examples of 15th century stonework. But the 15th century was the age of the Franciscans, for it was in this century that they built some of their greatest monasteries in Ireland, and the good preservation of the remains of these friaries is an indication of the quality of their work. Muckross, Co Kerry, Timoleague, Co Cork, Ennis and Quin (Fig. 21) in Co Clare, Askeaton, Co Limerick, Claregalway, Kilconnell and Ross Errilly (Fig. 33), Co Galway, Rosserk, Co Mayo and Creevelea, Co Leitrim attest to the fine architecture produced by the Franciscans in the 15th and early 16th century. There is scarcely a church in Ireland which was founded after the coming of the Cistercians in 1142 which was not in some way or another either altered, transformed or added to in the period 1400-1535. New doors were inserted, old narrow and graceful lancet windows were blocked up or taken out and replaced by new broader traceried windows which let in much more light and which gave a great opportunity to the stonemason and the designer to express their virtuosity and delicacy in design. Large parts of the monastic buildings were rebuilt or repaired. At the same time a great number of parish churches were also either being built or re-built, such as at Carran, Co Clare, Howth and a number of churches in south Co Dublin, St Multose in Kinsale, Co Cork, Mungret and Killeen Cowpark, Co Limerick and Fenagh, Co Leitrim. But this movement was at its height when it was suddenly cut off in its prime because of the pride and greed of Henry VIII who closed down the monasteries in the years after 1535 in order to appropriate their lands. Many of the monasteries continued in clandestine use after this time, but their final downfall came when Cromwell hit the country like a tornado in 1649 and devastated all before him; he burned and looted any remaining churches, and put to the sword the few monks who had survived.

Medieval Tombs, Crosses and Fonts

For the beauties and joys it has to offer, medieval art has been singularly neglected and underestimated in Ireland. Beside the art which forms part of the actual stonework of churches, there is also a considerable amount of art preserved in stone which is well worth studying. Prime examples are the tombs which are scattered in churches throughout the country. Many of the 13th and 14th century tombs have effigies of knights and bishops on them; one of the finest is that at Kilfane, Co Kilkenny. By the 15th century and continuing on into the 17th a type of box tomb became common whereby the effigy of the Knight and sometimes of his Lady were placed on top of the tomb, while around the sides were placed figures of the Apostles and other saints, as well as the Crucifixion. Examples at Howth, Co Dublin (Fig. 27), Kilcooly, Co Tipperary (Fig. 13), Lismore, Co Waterford, Ennis, Co Clare (Fig. 20), Strade, Co Mayo (Fig. 52) and those at Jerpoint, Cashel and in Kilkenny Cathedral have carving which stands comparison with the best in Europe, and deserve much greater appreciation than they have got heretofore. Some of the best tombs were carved by members of the O'Tunney family, and particularly Rory. The region around Kilkenny also has a number of 17th century tombs specializing in the Instruments of the Passion, and again Kilkenny Cathedral houses a number of these.

Fig. 13. The tomb of Piers Fitz Oge Butler at Kilcooley Abbey, Co Tipperary, carved by Rory O Tunney circa 1526.

Baptismal fonts also of a very high quality have recently been brought to our notice through Miss Roe's excellent book 'The Medieval Fonts of Meath', and this book contains some of the best pieces which this country can offer. Co Meath and Westmeath seem to have the best collection, but other less ornamental fonts can be found by the diligent searcher in other parts of Ireland.

By the medieval period, the High Crosses with their scenes from the Scriptures had gone out of fashion. The craze was revived however in the 16th and 17th centuries with a number of delightful crosses erected on roadsides and usually commemorating a person or an event. Such is the cross at Balrath, Co Meath which asks for a prayer for the man who erected it, or the group of crosses at Killucan, Co Westmeath—where one of the crosses was erected to commemorate a road accident over four hundred years ago. Some of the best of these crosses were erected by Dame Jennet Dowdall in Co Meath around 1600 to keep afresh the memory of her husband William Bathe who died in 1599, and the crosses at Duleek (Fig. 53) and Athcarne are monuments which reflect credit on the taste of Dame Jennet herself. As well as this, crosses were erected outside family chapels at Rathmore, Killeen and Dunsany, Co Meath, all testifying to a great school of stone sculpture in Co Meath in the 16th and early 17th centuries.

Castles

Returning once again to the 12th century, it was a period of importance not only in the religious but also in the political sphere. After the death of Brian Boru in 1014, Ireland lacked a central power, and a number of lesser kings attempted to unite the country under them—but without success. The situation became unruly in the 12th century when in-fighting reached its peak. One chieftain, Dermot MacMurrough Kavanagh, having been deprived of his kingdom by others, resorted to seeking the help of foreign mercenaries in the form of the Normans who, when they appeared, overran considerable parts of the country within thirty years of their arrival. And even when one after the other of these Norman adventurers had died without sons to succeed them, the English King John sent over further supplies of men who continued the work. The earliest Normans established themselves in hastily made fortifications called mottes, consisting of a mound of earth, flat on top, and crowned by a wooden tower (Fig. 14). Around the base of the mound was a half-moon-shaped enclosure called a bailey where cattle and supplies were kept. Although the wooden towers have long since vanished, the mounds can still be seen, for instance, at Ardscull, Co Kildare, Callan, Co Kilkenny, Granard, Co Longford and at Knockgraffon, Co Tipperary. But by 1200, when the Normans had already conquered almost half the country, these temporary structures proved insufficient to hold the newly won territories, and a great wave of castle building was embarked upon. Some of these castles had strong rectangular keeps or towers standing in an area surrounded by a stout wall, such as Trim, Co Meath (Fig. 15), Adare, Co Limerick (Fig. 44), Maynooth, Co Kildare and Athenry, Co Galway (Fig. 29). In other cases the keeps were round, as at Shanid, Co Limerick or Nenagh, Co Tipperary (Fig. 77). Some of the castles in towns such as Limerick (Fig. 46), Dublin and Kilkenny had strongly fortified walls without the keeps, and this also applies to Roscommon, Ballintober, Co Roscommon, Ballymote, Co Sligo, Liscarroll, Co Cork, and two castles in Co Carlow—Ballymoon and Ballyloughan. The Normans also used sites on rock-tops to build their castles, as at Carlingford, Co Louth (Fig. 48), Castleroche, Co Louth and Dunamase, Co Laois. The castles at Carlow, Ferns, Co Wexford, Lea, Co Laois and Terryglass, Co Tipperary represent Norman fortifications of a typically Irish type consisting of a strong tall keep fortified by a rounded tower at each corner. Almost all these castles, except the last-mentioned type, had houses of wood inside their walls, and while none of these has survived, we have a description of Swords Castle in 1326 which gives some idea of the buildings which once stood inside the walls:

'There is in this place a hall, and a chamber adjoining the said hall, the walls of which are of stone, crenelated after the manner of a castle, and covered with shingles. Further there is a kitchen, together with a larder, the walls of which are of stone, roofed with shingles, and there is in the same place a chapel, the walls of which are of stone roofed with shingles. Also there was in the same place a chamber for friars, with a cloister. Also there are in the same place a chamber or apartment for the constable by the gate, and four chambers for soldiers and wardens, roofed with shingles, under which are a stable and bake-house. Also there were here a house for a dairy, and a workshop which are now prostrate; also there is on the premises in the haggard a shed made of planks and thatched with straw; also a granary, built with timber and roofed with boards; also a byre, for the housing of farm horses and bullocks.'

Alan, Liber Niger

Castles in the Norman style, particularly the rectangular type with rounded towers at the corners, continued to be built up till the 15th century at least, as evidenced by the castles of Ballinafad, Co Sligo, Dunmoe, Co Meath (Fig. 54) and Kilbolane, Co Cork. While many of the Irish were too slow off the mark to realize the military danger and significance of these castles, the O'Conors of Connacht seem to have been one of the few who did, for by

Fig. 14. Conjectural reconstruction of a Norman motte-and-bailey. Late 12th century.

1300 they had built a castle in the Norman style for themselves at Roscommon. By this period, the Irish chieftains were beginning to fight back the Norman invasion with partial success. O'Conor had been able to retain his kingdom practically intact, while the great O'Neill dynasties of the North held aloof. The 14th century marked a period of struggle both by the Irish native chieftains and also of the great Norman magnates for control one over the other, but while there was much repairing of castles at the time, few new ones appear to have been built.

As in church building, the 15th century also saw a revival in the building of castles and other fortifications. Some of the few remaining town walls we have date from this period, such as Youghal, Co Cork and Fethard, Co Tipperary, though the Athenry walls may be somewhat earlier. Clonmines, Co Wexford is an example of one of the walled settlements of medieval Ireland which have now practically disappeared. The 15th century was also the period *par excellence* of the great Norman princes who dominated the history of the country between 1400 and 1535. As they had showed their importance by fortifying themselves in castles, so too did the pure English of the Pale (the English part of the province of Leinster). In 1429 Edward VI promised

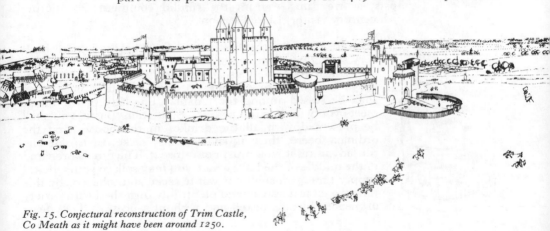

Fig. 15. Conjectural reconstruction of Trim Castle, Co Meath as it might have been around 1250.

a £10 grant to anybody who would build a castle to his specifications in order to strengthen the borders of the Pale, and Donore Castle, Co Meath, is probably one of these £10 castles. The castles were smaller and less impressive than the great Norman fortifications of the 13th century; they were square or rectangular in shape and had vaulted roofs. The lesser native chieftains in other parts of Ireland quickly adopted the idea of erecting these towers and built them for themselves both as defences and homes. It almost came to the stage where—like a good Victorian—nobody wishing to be respected could afford to do without his tower-house castle. Looking at Carrigafoyle Castle, Co Kerry, from the road, you can see a cross-section of one of these towers, and the same is shown in the illustration of a typical example from Roodstown, Co Louth (Figs. 16-17). The remaining floor timbers at Clara, Co Kilkenny show how low and dark the rooms in these towers must have been. This is confirmed by Boullaye le Gouz's description of these castles in 1644:

'The castles or houses of the nobility consist of four walls extremely high, thatched with straw; but to tell the truth, they are nothing but square towers without windows, or at least having such small apertures as to give no more light than a prison. They have little furniture, and cover their rooms with rushes, of which they make their beds in summer, and of straw in winter. They put rushes a foot deep on their floors and on their windows, and many ornament the ceilings with branches.'
— The Tour of the French Traveller M. de la Boullaye le Gouz, ed. T C Croker (1837) 40-41.

But while the furnishings were bare inside, the plates and glasses were not, for the owners of these castles were most generous hosts, as we can see from the candid comments of another 17th century visitor, Luke Gernon:

'We are come to the castle already. The castles are built very strong with narow stayres, for security. The hall is the uppermost room, lett us go up, you shall not come down agayne till tomorrow. Take no care of your horses, they shall be sessed among the tenants. The lady of the house meets you with her trayne . . . . Salutations paste, you shall be presented with all the drinkes in the house, first the ordinary beere, then aquavitae, then sacke, then olde-ale, the lady tastes it, you must not refuse it. The fyre is prepared in the middle of the hall, where you may sollace yourselfe till supper time, you shall not wante sacke and tobacco. By this time the table is spread and plentifully furnished with variety of meates, but ill cooked and without sauce . . . They feast

together with great jollyty and healths around; towards the middle of the supper, the harper begins to tune and singeth Irish rymes of auncient making . . . Supper being ended, it is at your liberty to sitt up, or to depart to your lodgeing, you shall have company in both kind. When you come to your chamber, do not expect canopy and curtaynes. It is very well if your bedd content you, and if the company be greate, you may happen to be bodkin in the middle. In the morning there will be brought unto you a cupp of aquavitae . . . it is a very wholesome drinke, and natural to digest the crudityes of the Irish feeding. You may drink a knaggin without offence . . . Breakfast is but the repetition of supper. When you are disposing of yourself to depart, they call for a Dogh a dores, that is, to drink at the doore, there you are presented agayne with all the drinkes in the house, as at your first entrance. Smacke them over, and lett us departe.'

—Luke Gernon, Discourse of Ireland (1620) printed in Faulkner, Illustrations of Irish History and Topography (1904) 360-1.

These castles became the staple house-fortification over many parts of Ireland in the period 1450-1650. Some of them are now simple towers like Roodstown (Figs. 16-17), but originally probably all of them had the extra protection of a walled bawn—a tall square or L-shaped wall with corner turrets—and the castle stood in one corner of the bawn. Examples abound, such as Derryhivenny (Fig. 30) and Aughnanure, Co Galway, Ballynacarriga, Co Cork, Carrigaholt, Co Clare, Pallas, Co Galway and Rathmacknee, Co Wexford. There are also a number of other good examples in East Galway. Large-size castles are also found as at Bunratty, Co Clare, Blarney, Co Cork and Dunsoghly, Co Dublin.

Figs. 16-17. Plan and section of Roodstown Castle, Co Louth.

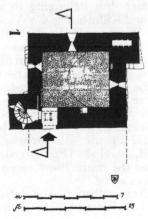

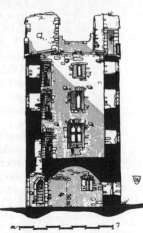

The suppression of the Rebellion of Silken Thomas in 1536 and the adoption by Henry VIII of the title of 'King of Ireland' in 1540 heralded a new era when the English under Henry and above all under Elizabeth I attempted by harsh means and also by planting a number of English settlers to subjugate Ireland completely. A new English Tudor style makes itself evident in the architecture of the second half of the 16th century, and becomes more common in the years 1600-50. The most important example is the Ormond castle at Carrick-on-Suir, Co Tipperary, where a 16th century mansion has been added to two already existing towers. It is one of the first Irish examples of a large house to be built which did not serve the primary purpose of defence. The remaining stucco work shows that it was richly decorated inside and was introducing a more spacious and gracious style of living into Ireland. The same can be seen in a well-preserved town house of 1594—Rothe House in Kilkenny. The defeat of Irish and Spanish forces in the Battle of Kinsale in 1601, the abolition of the old Gaelic Brehon Laws in 1606, and the Flight of the Gaelic nobility to Spain in 1607 left the English well and truly in the saddle in Ireland. They were now in a position to continue to build houses where fortification played a subsidiary role. The houses were two or three storeys high, had a great number of mullioned windows and tall gables, as well as some turrets over the door and at the corners just in case of attack. These fortified houses can be seen to good advantage at Kanturk, Mallow (Fig. 23) and Coppinger's Court, Co Cork, Burncourt and Loughmoe, Co Tipperary, Leamaneh, Co Clare, Glinsk and Portumna, Co Galway and Athlumney, Co Meath. Some new 'planters' who had been settled by James I in the lands which had been taken after the departure of the O'Neills were also building some of these fortified houses such as Sir Basil Brooke's castle at Donegal and Park's Castle, Co Leitrim. Other castles, different in character, but belonging to this period, are Castlebaldwin, Co Sligo and Killincarrig, Co Wicklow. The English Lord Deputy, Thomas Wentworth, Earl of Strafford, was in the process of building a grandiose new house for himself at Jigginstown, Co Kildare, using the latest fashion of red-brick, when he was recalled to London and hanged in 1641—and thus what would have been one of the finest of 17th century houses in Ireland remained incomplete. But while these houses were being built in imitation of the latest style over in England, the Irish in their characteristically traditional way continued to build the old fashioned tower-castles, and it comes as a surprise to find that a castle like Derry-hivenny, Co Galway (Fig. 30), dating from 1643, was built some years after the much more recent-looking Portumna castle only a few miles away.

The Cromwellian period (1649-50) interrupted most things in Ireland, including building, and it took the country a considerable time to recover from it. But in the second half of the 17th century the English were building strong star-shaped forts around the coast and elsewhere; they adapted Athlone castle, and built Charles Fort, Kinsale, Co Cork, around 1677. The architect of Charles Fort, Sir William Robinson, acts as a link between the old tradition of erecting fortifications, and the new idea of creating large and beautiful public buildings, for he is also the architect of the Royal Hospital, Kilmainham (not open to the public)—which is Dublin's oldest public building, dating to about 1680. The comparative calm in which the Royal Hospital was being built was shattered at the end of the decade when the final scenes of an almost European war were being fought out on Ireland's fields at Derry, the Boyne, Aughrim and Limerick in 1690-91. When James II lost the battle to William of Orange, one of Ireland's most tragic hours began; for what followed was a century of religious oppression of the native population. Yet, this picture is brightened by the beautifully designed houses with classical stucco work which the landed gentry were building in Ireland up till 1800, and by the great public buildings centred on Dublin, such as the Bank of Ireland, Trinity College, the Custom House and the General Post Office. Although our survey ends at 1700 and does not cover this period, there are one or two exceptions. The only 18th century building to be included here is the Casino at Marino near Dublin City, which is undoubtedly one of the greatest gems of the period in Britain or Ireland.

The other type of monument which is outside the historical scope of this guide, but of which a few examples are included, is the country cottage, and it is fitting that some of these should be preserved by the State. One, the Dwyer-MacAllister cottage in the Glen of Imaal in Co Wicklow (Fig. 18), is preserved because of its associations with the historic stand made by its inmate Samuel MacAllister in 1799 to save the life of Michael Dwyer; and two others—Pearse's Cottage at Rosmuck, Co Galway and Seán MacDiarmada's birthplace at Laghty Barr, Co Leitrim—are preserved because of their associations with two of the leaders who were shot in the Rebellion of 1916. These cottages at once represent the best and most typical in Ireland, and they are the embodiment itself of the timelessness and changelessness of the Irish tradition. The more things change, the more they remain the same!

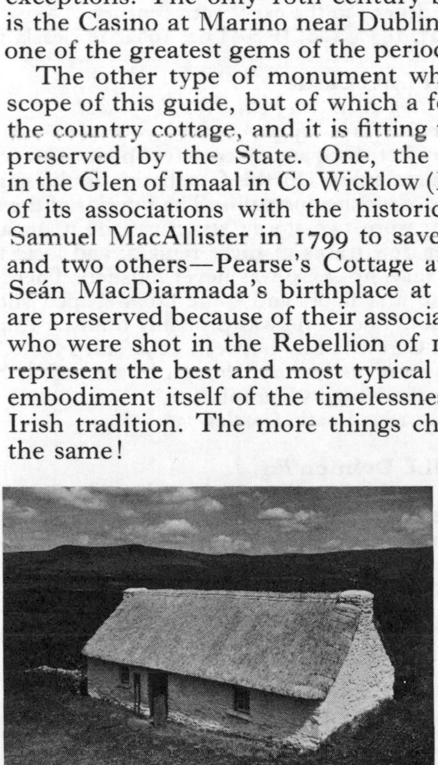

Fig. 18. The Dwyer-MacAllister Cottage, Derrynamuck, Co Wicklow.

AGHADE (347) Holed Stone ('Clochaphoill')

MAP 8 P 15
OS½″ 19S.85.70

Access: 30 yards up a lane, then up over a ditch on the left into field. Signposted
A large flat stone, now leaning though originally upright, with a hole 6
inches wide at one end. It may have been a so-called 'port-hole' stone
which closed the chamber of a megalithic tomb. However, the traditional
explanation—as usual, much more romantic and appealing—is that it was
a stone used at the dawn of history by Niall of the Nine Hostages to tie
up Eochaidh, son of Enna Cinnselach, by means of a chain which was
passed through the hole. But Eochaidh broke the chain and took his
revenge by killing the nine men whom Niall had sent to kill him. Up till
the 18th century, sick infants were passed through the hole to restore
them to health!
JCKAS 11, 1930–3, 248

BALLYLOUGHAN (351) Castle

MAP 8 N 16
OS½″ 19S.74.58

Access: Through gate into field. Signposted
The castle, which was probably built in the 13th century, originally consisted of a large open courtyard fortified by a high curtain wall with a
moat outside it. Only a small square tower at one corner survives, as well
as the entrance gate, flanked by two large rounded towers. The tower in
the north-eastern corner was abandoned in the 14th century, and the
whole castle may even have been abandoned at this time. Note the variety
of fireplaces. The castle formerly belonged to the Kavanaghs, and was
occupied by Donogh Kavanagh at the end of the 16th century. After the
Restoration it came into the possession of the Bagenal family, but was
bought by the Bruens in the early 19th century.
Arch Journal 93, 1937, 190; JRSAI 92, 1962, 1; Leask, Castles 72

BALLYMOON (486) Castle

MAP 8 N 15
OS½″ 19S.74.61

Access: Across deep ditch and field. Not signposted
The castle consists of a square central courtyard surrounded by walls
which are eight feet thick and twenty feet high, with square towers projecting from three sides. On the fourth side is the gate with a pointed
arch and a groove for the portcullis. The interior of the castle is bare, but
originally there were two-storey structures built up against the inside
walls. However, few traces of these remain, and local tradition explains
this by saying that the castle was never finished. There is a good double
fireplace on the first floor, and some cross-shaped slits through which
arrows were shot. The castle was probably built by Roger Bigod or by a
member of the Carew family between 1290 and 1310. Otherwise little or
nothing is known of its history, though in the past it has been wrongly
associated with the Knights Templars.
JRSAI 74, 1944, 183; Leask, Castles 73

BROWNESHILL Dolmen *Fig. 19*

MAP 8 N 15
OS½″ 19S.75.77

Access: Across two fences and one and a half fields. Signposted
The dolmen consists of a massive capstone embedded in the earth at one
end and supported at the other end by three stones, with a fourth standing
free nearby. The capstone is reputed to weigh about 100 tons, and is
claimed to be the heaviest in Europe.

CARLOW (306) Castle

MAP 8 N 15
OS½" 19S.72.77

Access : Only through Corcoran's Mineral Water factory (ask for permission and key in the factory's office). Closed Saturday and Sunday. The castle should be visited preferably in the morning. Not signposted

The original keep was 3 storeys high and was square in shape with stout three-quarters round towers at the corners, but only the eastern half still stands, with its two corner towers and the connecting wall. The entrance was through a door in the first floor of the north side. Around the year 1300 there was also a hall roofed with shingles, a prison and a palisade, but nothing remains of these. The topmost storey of the north-western tower is of 15th-16th century date.

Although the castle is only first mentioned in 1231, it was probably built by William the Marshall or by his son not long after he gave a charter to the town in 1208. William's grand-nephew handed it over to the Crown on his death in 1306. In 1312 it was granted to Thomas Plantagenet, surnamed 'de Brotherton' who became Earl of Norfolk, and it remained in possession of the same family until it was confiscated by the Crown in 1537 because the owners were absentee landlords. It was already in bad repair by 1307. Taken briefly by James Fitzgerald in 1494 and soon re-captured, it was again captured in 1535, this time by Silken Thomas but was once more re-taken after a short siege. Granted to Edward Randolf in 1552 and to Robert Hartpole in 1577, it was bought by Donough, Earl of Thomond, in 1616. During the 1640's it changed hands many times before being taken by Cromwell in 1650, but it was later returned to the Earl of Thomond. Having later passed into the hands of the Hamilton family, it was granted to a Dr Middleton who in order to create more room for the building of a lunatic asylum in 1814, blew up parts of the castle! As a result, most of the castle had to be demolished as a safety precaution, leaving only the two towers and adjoining wall of what was once one of the finest Norman castles in Leinster.

JRSAI 7, 1862-3, 140 and 10, 1869, 560; JCKAS 6, 1910, 311 and 365; Arch Journal 93, 1937, 168; Leask, Castles 47

Fig. 19. The Dolmen at Browneshill, Co Carlow.
Circa 2000 B.C. Its capstone is reputed to weigh about 100 tons.

CLONMORE Castle and High Crosses

MAP 8 P 15
OS½″ 19S.96.76

Access : Through gate and 30 yards across field. Not signposted
Typical of the late 13th century, the castle is nearly square in plan, with
rectangular towers at the two southern corners, and smaller turrets at the
other two corners. Remains of the main interior buildings can be seen on the
eastern side of the courtyard. While the castle is not mentioned in existing
records until the 14th century, the shape of the trefoil window in the south
wall shows that it was built probably towards the end of the 13th century.
Clonmore was captured by the Earl of Kildare in 1516 and by the Earl of
Ormond in 1598. It changed hands several times in the Confederate War,
and was finally taken by Cromwell's forces under Colonel Hewson in 1650.
    In the village graveyard, 300 yards to the east, there is one plain High
Cross in the churchyard on the north side of the road, and considerable
fragments of another in the graveyard on the south side of the road. The
road, in fact, cuts through the site of an old monastery founded by St
Mogue probably in the 6th century.
Arch Journal 93, 1937, 195

HAROLDSTOWN Dolmen

MAP 8 P 15
OS½″ 19S.90.78

Access : Through gate into field. Signposted
A good and well-preserved example of a portal dolmen, consisting of two
slightly tilted capstones supported by ten stones, two of which acted as
the 'door' to the tomb.

KILLOUGHTERNANE (393) Early Christian Church

MAP 8 N 16
OS½″ 19S.77.54

Access : Up over stile to church which is beside and above the road. Signposted
A small Early Christian church with antae and a round-headed east window.
Note the square baptismal font in the north-eastern corner. In this church
the Leinstermen venerated the founder, St Fortchern, who was the
teacher of St Finian of Clonard.
JRSAI 73, 1943, 98

LEIGHLINBRIDGE (438) 'The Black Castle'

MAP 8 N 15
OS½″ 19S.69.65

Access : Through nearby house. Signposted
Guarding an important bridge crossing the Barrow, this is a 16th century
tower, of which only the western half remains. It had a vault over the second
storey and a passage-way around the top. In an adjoining garden there
are remains of a bawn wall with slits for arrows or guns at the corner. The
original 'Black Castle' was built here by Hugh de Lacy in 1180. This was
superseded by a Carmelite Friary founded in 1260-70. The present castle
is said to have been built by Sir Edward Bellingham in 1547. The site
was long held by the Kavanaghs and the Butlers, and was also occupied
by Sir Peter Carew and the Bagenals. Leighlinbridge was captured by
Cromwellian forces under Colonel Hewson in 1650. The nearby bridge
incorporates much work of 1320.
JRSAI 18, 1887-8, 479

LORUM (350) Early Christian Cross-fragment

MAP 8 N 16
OS½″ 19S.72.57

*Access : Down lane beside Church of Ireland church; continue, leaving
farmyard to right, then into field through gate on right. The cross is beside the
gate. Not signposted*
A small and insignificant fragment of a narrow High Cross with two
panels on each side. The traces of carving are rather indistinct, but the
top panel on the east face would appear to have two figures on it.

NURNEY (352) Early Christian Cross

MAP 8 N 15
OS½" 19S.73.67

Access : Across wall into field. Signposted
Resting in a rectangular base, this is a squat granite cross with its ring unpierced. There is a large protruding boss at the intersection of the arms. The cross was divided into panels which possibly bore interlacing. It is the last remaining of three crosses which stood on the site.
JRSAI 23, 1893, 235

ST MULLIN'S (3) Early Christian and Medieval Monastic Site

MAP 8 N 17
OS½" 19S.73.38

Access : Direct to graveyard in which buildings stand. Signposted
The monastery was founded by St Moling who died in 696. Active in politics, he succeeded in convincing the Leinstermen to let the Munstermen off the Borama, a traditional tribute of cattle which they were forced to pay. St Moling is said to have been Bishop of Ferns and also of Glendalough. The Kings of South Leinster, including the McMurrough Kavanaghs, were buried here. St Mullin's Abbey is a medieval nave-and-chancel church with spiral staircase. Near it are the stump of a Round Tower, a tiny oratory ('St James's Chapel') and a small granite High Cross with a Crucifixion on the east face and interlacing and wave-like motifs on the other faces. Further down the slope is a medieval domestic building with an unusual diamond-shaped east window. Between the 'Abbey' and the graveyard gate is a small building with antae known as 'The Bath', while outside the gate is a Norman motte. The monastery was plundered by the Vikings in 951 and was burned in 1138. In a 7th century manuscript, known as 'The Book of Mulling', there is a plan of the monastery—the earliest known plan of an Irish monastery—which shows four crosses inside the round monastic wall and eight crosses outside it.
JRSAI 22, 1892, 377

STRABOE (452) Medieval Grave-slab

MAP 8 P 15
OS½" 19S.82.79

Access : Along laneway, through farmyard to field behind farm-house. Not signposted
A medieval grave-slab of little interest, with a double cross carved in relief. It probably marked the grave of a Knight Templar originally, but was possibly removed to its present site from Killerrig nearby.

COHAW (456) Double Court-cairn

MAP 5 N 8
OS½" 8H.64.13

Access : Through gate into field, 100 yards west of a National School. Signposted

A fine example of a double court-cairn, looking as if two single court-cairns were placed back to back. There is a semi-circular forecourt at each end, with five burial chambers between them. The tomb, which was excavated in 1949, stands in a rectangular stone mound delineated by kerb-stones. A Stone Age pottery vessel was found during the excavations.
PRIA 54, C, 1951, 75

DRUMLANE (4) Church and Round Tower

MAP 4 L 8
OS½" 8H.34.12

Access : Direct to graveyard in which buildings stand. Signposted

The oldest building on the site is a Round Tower with round-headed doorway and windows. On the north face, about six feet above the ground, are much weathered carvings of birds (cock and hen ?). Beside the tower stands a medieval church, possibly late 13th century in date, though much altered in the 15th century. The west doorway preserves some fine stonework. Unusual features are the heads (probably 15th century) of bishops or abbots, a king and others on the outer side of the door and windows. The first monastery here was founded in the Early Christian period, but in medieval times it was taken over by the Augustinian Canons from Kells. In 1431 an appeal was made for alms to build a cloister and refectory, and some of the church probably dates from this period of building. The western half of the church, however, may at least in part date from the 17th century.
UJA 5, 1857, 114; Breifny Antiquarian and Historical Society Journal II, ii, 1924, 132; JRSAI 78, 1948, 83

KILMORE Romanesque Doorway

MAP 4 L 8
OS½" 8H.38.04

Access : Direct to churchyard. Not signposted

Built into the modern Church of Ireland Cathedral of St Feidhlimidh is a fine 12th century Romanesque doorway which was removed from an early monastery on Trinity Island in Lough Oughter, three miles away. In the rebuilding of the doorway in its present position, some of the stones have been incorrectly replaced.
Leask, Churches I, 146

BALLYHICKEY (484) Dolmen

MAP 7 G 15
OS½" 17R.42.76

Access : Up private avenue, then over wall into field in front of ruined house.
Not signposted
A box-like megalithic tomb with six upright stones supporting two small capstones. Although somewhat similar in type to many dolmens found in Co. Clare, it is unusual in being almost square in shape.
Megalithic Survey Vol. I, Co. Clare (1961) 67, No. 87

BUNRATTY (478) Castle

MAP 7 G 15
OS½" 17R.45.61

Access : Direct. Advance approach notices on road. Open daily 9.30 a.m.–
5.30 p.m. There is an entrance fee to Castle and Folk-Park. Medieval banquet
should be booked well in advance.
Originally on an island, the site may have first been fortified by the Vikings. About 1250 Robert de Muscegros built a castle here, probably somewhere near the ruined church not far away on the other side of the road. Thomas de Clare, to whom Edward I granted the land after the death of de Muscegros, built a stone castle and imported English colonists to defend it. By the end of the 13th century, a town had sprung up around the castle. But the native Irish mistrusted the castle and by 1306 had already burned it twice. When the de Clares were defeated at the Battle of Dysart in 1318, they abandoned the castle and set fire to it. It was afterwards restored by Robert de Welle for Edward II, but the combined forces of the O'Briens and Macnamaras plundered it in 1332. Twenty one years later it was restored by Sir Thomas Rokeby, but the Irish again destroyed it a short time later. It was only about 1450 that the present castle was begun by Maccon MacSioda Macconmara and it was completed by his son Seán Finn in 1467. Around 1500 it was taken over by the O'Briens, and although Morrogh O'Brien submitted to Henry VIII, the castle remained in O'Brien hands. During the Civil War, it was defended by Admiral Sir William Penn, father of William Penn the founder of Pennsylvania, but he had to surrender it and sail away. It was later owned by the Studdert family before being bought by Lord Gort in 1954. It has since been excellently restored to its original splendour. Besides a basement now containing a shop, the castle consists of a large banqueting hall on the first floor approached by modern steps, and a magnificent hall on the floor above with high ceiling restored in 16th century style; a small chapel opens off the upper hall and above it to the south are the Great Earl's living quarters. The castle at present houses one of the best collections of 14th-17th century furniture and furnishings in Britain and Ireland, and twice nightly it is the scene of re-enacted medieval banquets. Beside the castle is a Folk-park where a number of house types found in Clare and its neighbouring counties can be seen together with their typical furnishings.
JNMAS 3, 1915, 220; NMAJ 8, 1960, 103.

CAHERAPHUCA (466) Wedge-shaped Gallery-grave

MAP 7 F 14
OS½" 14R.39.88

Access : Climb over wall into field beside road. Signposted.
A wedge-shaped gallery-grave consisting of a long wedge-shaped chamber of five standing stones supporting two capstones. As is usual with tombs of this type, one end is higher than the other.
Megalithic Survey Vol I, Co. Clare (1961) 63, No. 80

CAHERCOMMAUN (270b) Stone Fort

MAP 6 F 14
OS½" 14R.28.97

Access : A dangerous and hazardous walk, at least half a mile long, over field and crag to the fort which is situated on a cliff-edge. Not signposted

A stone fort dramatically situated on the edge of a steep valley. There are three concentric walls, all abutting on to the edge of the cliff, as at Dun Aenghus on the Aran Islands. The innermost wall, which is also the thickest, forms an almost complete circle, but the two outer walls (connected with each other by subsidiary walls, like a fan) only form a semi-circle. The innermost wall contains three chambers within the wall, and excavation by the Harvard Archaeological Expedition to Ireland in 1934 showed that the roughly circular area it enclosed had a dozen stone buildings in it at different times, two of which had souterrains. In the 35 years since the excavation, growth has covered many of the foundations of these buildings. Nothing is known of the history of the fort—not even the name of the family who built it, but a beautiful silver brooch found in one of the souterrains, and now in the National Museum of Ireland in Dublin, shows that it was already in existence by the 9th century A.D. It is one of the most elaborate of the hundreds of stone forts known from the Burren area in North Clare.

Hencken, Cahercommaun, Extra Volume Royal Society of Antiquaries of Ireland (1938).

Cashlaun Gar

Not far away, but difficult to find through the maze of hazel bushes, brambles and crags, is a smaller and irregularly-shaped stone fort, called Cashlaun Gar. Vertical joints, showing the different stages in which the wall-builders worked, can be seen on the outside of the wall, while inside the bare foundations of three or four beehive huts can be seen. It is unusual in being situated cleverly on a round and flat-topped piece of rock with a sheer drop all round.

JRSAI 26, 1896, 152

CAHERMACNAGHTEN (354) Stone Fort

MAP 3 E 13
OS½" 14M.19.00

Access : Through gate into field. Signposted

Caher is an Irish word meaning 'stone fort', and so this fort means the stone fort of the son of Neachtan. It is almost round in shape, with a diameter of about 100 feet. It was entered through a late medieval two-storeyed gateway. Foundations of rectangular buildings can be seen under the surface inside the fort, where the ground level—high in comparison with that outside the fort—suggests a long period of habitation. The fort was the home of one of Ireland's most famous medieval law schools, that run by the O'Davoren family. Early in the 17th century Duald Mac Firbis, the famous genealogist, lawyer and historian studied the old Irish Brehon laws here at the feet of Donald O'Davoren, himself author of a glossary. The fort was described as 'O'Davoren's town' in 1675, when it had a large house and a kitchen inside the walls, as well as a 'house of the churchyard' to the west, and various gardens.

JRSAI 27, 1897, 120; JNMAS 2, 1912, 63

CANON ISLAND (195) Augustinian Abbey

MAP 6 F 16
OS½" 17R.30.59

Access : Only by boat. Contact the Post-man, Mr Kelly, Telephone Ennis 26121, who is available on Monday, Tuesday, Thursday and Saturday. No fixed charge for crossing

Donal Mor O Brien founded a church on this island in the Shannon estuary for the Augustinian Canons some time towards the end of the 12th century. The present church is long and rectangular, and was built early in the 13th century. In the 15th century a tower was built to the south of the nave, and two chapels—one at the south-east corner, the other to the west of the tower—were added. Most of the domestic buildings are of the same period; they comprise a sacristy next to the church, a chapter room in the east side, and a kitchen, pantry and refectory on the ground floor of the south wing. There were no buildings in the western portion. The whole monastery was surrounded by a (or built inside an older) circular wall. We know little of the island's history while the monks inhabited it except that Mahon O'Griffy, Bishop of Killaloe, was buried there in 1483. In 1543, after the Dissolution of the monasteries, it was granted to Donatus O'Brien, and afterwards it belonged to various Earls of Thomond. Henry, 7th Earl of Thomond, granted it to Richard Henn in 1712.

JRSAI 27, 1897, 286 and 45, 1915, 271; Leask, Churches III, 96

CARRAN Medieval Church

MAP 6 F 14
OS½" 14R.24.97

Access : Through gate and field to churchyard. Not signposted
A good example of a medieval parish church which has a fine 15th century south doorway, and a contemporary east window. One of the corbels at the east end of the north wall is decorated with a carved head. An upper storey at the west end may have been used as a fortified residence.
PRIA 22, 1900-2, 133, No. 17

CARRIGAHOLT (427) Tower House

MAP 6 D 16
OS½" 17Q.85.51

Access : Through field into the castle bawn. Signposted
Finely situated overlooking the Shannon estuary and Carrigaholt pier, this is a tall and slender 5-storey tower standing in one corner of a bawn and built originally by the MacMahons, Lords of Corcabascin, around the end of the 15th century. The tower is complete with musket holes, 'murder holes' to drop things on intruders' heads when they come in the door, and it also has a vault on the 4th floor. Teige Caech, 'The Short-sighted' Macmahon was unsuccessfully besieged in the tower by Sir Conyers Clifford in 1598, but a few months later the Earl of Thomond succeeded in wresting the castle from him. It was then taken over by Daniel O'Brien who built the fireplace on the fifth floor which bears the date '1603', and it was probably he who built many of the present windows into the tower. In 1646 Admiral Sir William Penn called at the castle on his way to Kinsale, having just abandoned Bunratty to the Confederate troops. In 1651 it was taken by Cromwell's general, Ludlow, who kept a garrison there until 1652. Charles II, however, restored the castle to the O'Briens in 1666. But in 1691 William of Orange gave it to Keppel, Earl of Albemarle, who sold it almost immediately afterwards to the Burtons, who retained it up till the present century. The bawn protecting the tower is fairly well preserved, though the turret overlooking the pier is modern.
JNMAS 2, 1911, 29

CLAREABBEY (197) Augustinian Abbey

MAP 6 F 15
OS½" 17R.35.76

Access : Half a mile up a laneway (close gates behind you if you find them open), then across railway line (DANGER!) and into field. Signposted
The Abbey was founded by Donal Mor O Brien for the Augustinian Canons in 1189, and their charter was confirmed again in 1461. It was dedicated to

Saints Peter and Paul. In 1278 the Abbey was the scene of a great slaughter in the internecine strife between the various factions of the O Brien family. Some parts of the single-aisled church date back to the late 12th century, but the majority of the existing buildings date to the 15th century. It was probably in the reign of Teige Acomhad O Brien, around 1461, that the church was repaired, the well-preserved east window inserted, the tower built, and the domestic buildings with their unusual floral window at the south-eastern corner added. After the Dissolution of the monasteries in 1541, it passed to various members of the O Brien family, but the Canons seemed to have lived on in the Abbey until about 1650. JRSAI 30, 1900, 118

CORCOMROE (11) Cistercian Abbey

MAP 3 F 13
OS½" 14M.29.09

Access : Three quarters of a mile up a laneway to cemetery in which the Abbey stands. Signposted
The Abbey was given the name 'Sancta Maria de Petra Fertili'—'Saint Mary of the fertile rock'—a very well-chosen name for this remarkable Abbey which stands near the head of a limestone valley which brings forth lush green grass. The Abbey is supposed to have been founded by Donal Mor O Brien in 1182, but it is more likely to have been built by his son Donat, who brought monks from Inishlounaght (see under Marlfield, Co Tipperary) around 1195. As the domestic buildings have largely vanished, the church is the main item of interest. It is cross-shaped, with each transept having one chapel. The choir is constructed in stonework of a very high quality; the capitals are decorated with a lotus plant, leaves and acorns (a reference to the name of the monastery, and to its alternative name 'of the green rock') as well as human heads. The roof of the choir is delicately vaulted, showing still a strong influence from Irish Romanesque architecture; in the east wall there are three narrow lancet windows topped by another broader one. In a low tomb-niche in the north wall is the effigy of one of the Abbey's great benefactors, Conor na Siudaine O Brien (died 1267), which has often been wrongly supposed to depict Conor smoking a pipe! There is some fine carving in the transept chapels, the capitals in the south chapel bearing human masks. The nave has a south aisle running almost its whole length; it is uncertain if a north aisle was ever built. The wall screen across the middle of the nave is a 15th century insertion. In 1295 jurisdiction over the monastery was transferred from Inishlounaght to Furness in Lancashire. Dermot O Brien made the Abbey his headquarters after the battle of Drom Lurgan in 1317. After the Dissolution of the Monasteries it passed first to Murrogh, Earl of Thomond, in 1554, then to Donal O Brien, self-styled Chief of Clare in 1564, and afterwards to Donogh O Brien in 1584 and to Richard Harding in 1611. The monks may still have inhabited the buildings into the 17th century, for in 1628 Friar John O Dea, an Irish monk in Salamanca, was appointed its Abbot. A gate arch which existed outside the monastery fell in 1840. JRSAI 25, 1895, 280; JCHAS 33, 1928, 78; Leask, Churches II, 58

DRUMCLIFF (204) Church and Round Tower

MAP 6 F 15
OS½" 17R.33.80

Access : Direct to cemetery in which the monuments stand. Signposted
Nothing is known about the history of this old monastery, though the site is associated with a St Ciaran. Besides the remains of a Round Tower, still standing to a height of about 25 feet, there is a ruined 15th century church. The round-headed window in the west gable was probably taken from an older church and inserted when this church was built. JRSAI 24, 1894, 332

MAP 6 F 14
OS½" 14R.28.85

DYSERT O DEA (16) Church, Round Tower and High Cross *Fig. 8*
Access : Over stile and up path. Signposted
The church and Round Tower stand on the site of an Early Christian monastery founded by St Tola who died between 733 and 737. Where the church stands there was a 12th century Romanesque nave and chancel church with a plain chancel arch and a wonderfully decorated west doorway above which was an ornamental lancet window. Three narrow lancet windows were inserted in the east gable early in the 13th century. Some considerable time later the church must have fallen into decay. Possibly as late as 1683, when some of the corner stones of the church were used as a base for the re-erection of the High Cross in the adjoining field to the east, the church was reconstructed in its present form. The lancet window in the west gable was incorrectly replaced roughly in its original position; the Romanesque doorway, with its beautifully carved geometric motifs, foliage and almost mongoloid human masks, was inserted into the south wall, and the chancel (parts of which may still be original) reconstructed to its 13th century state. Near the outside of the door is placed a medieval grave slab. Near the north-western corner of the church stand the considerable remains of a Round Tower, most of which is probably contemporary with the Romanesque church. In the 16th century it was converted into a fortification as the narrow slits, and the window high up in the west wall, show. In a field to the east of the Church is a very fine 12th century High Cross which was re-erected on its present site by Conor O Dea in 1683, and again by the Synges in 1871. There is a representation of the Crucifixion and a Bishop (St Tola?) on the east face of the Cross, while the other sides and the base have panels of geometrical designs, animal interlacing and human figures.
JRSAI 24, 1894, 150 and 30, 1900, 415; JGAHS 26, 1956, 60

MAP 6 F 15
OS½" 17R.34.78

ENNIS (170) Franciscan Friary *Fig. 20*
Access: Direct. Key normally obtainable at police barracks, 100 yards to the north of the entrance to the friary. Signposted
The Friary was founded for the Franciscan Friars by Donchad Cairbreach O Brien, King of Thomond, sometime shortly before his death in 1242. In the following decades, the church must have suffered much damage, for the only considerable part remaining from the earliest foundation is the choir with its beautiful 5-light east window. Donchad's opponent and successor, Turlough O Brien, repaired the church and enlarged on his predecessor's work in 1287 and again in 1306, and put in blue stained glass—which has, of course, unfortunately vanished. By 1314 Maccon Macnamara had rebuilt the sacristy and refectory (which may be the vaulted room at present existing north of the chancel). Pope Clement granted indulgences to the Friary in 1350 and 1375, at which time there were about 350 Friars, as well as a flourishing and renowned school of 600 pupils. The cloister, to the north of the church, was added around 1400. It was probably in the second half of the 15th century that the fine west doorway abutting on to the street, the west window, and the windows in the south transept were inserted and the tower built. The nave of the church was dedicated to St Francis, and on the south-west face of the tower can be seen the figure of St Francis with the stigmata. Note also in the interior of the south arch of the tower a beautifully ornamented screen, as well as small representations of the Virgin and Child, and a Bishop. One of the glories of the Friary is the MacMahon tomb near the

*Fig. 20. 'Christ is laid in the Tomb' from the
MacMahon tomb at Ennis Friary, Co Clare.
Circa 1475.*

east end of the south wall which was built about 1475 and reconstructed
in 1843. In a slab on the west side may be seen a Bishop giving his Bene-
diction, and the Arrest of Christ with St Peter holding the ear of Malchus
who lies prostrate at the feet of Christ. The south face has three panels:
the Scourging at the pillar; the Crucifixion and Christ laid in the tomb.
On the east side are two panels: the Resurrection, and a woman, possibly
More Ni Brien, the foundress of the tomb. On the panel below are figures,
including those of the Apostles: Thomas (with the shaft of a long spear);
Paul (with sword); John (with lily); Simon (with saw); Peter (with the
keys of the Kingdom of Heaven); Christ enthroned; Matthew (with tax
bag); Bartholomew (with knife); James the Lesser (with club); Philip
(with small cross) and some other figures. Under the protection of Murrogh
O Brien, 1st Earl of Thomond, the Friary survived the Dissolution, and
was reformed in 1550. It was the last school of Catholic theology in
Ireland to survive the Reformation. It was granted to the Earl of Thomond
in 1578, and was the scene of the formal abolition of the old Irish Brehon
Law in 1606. In 1615, the Friary became a parish church. The last of the
old friars, Bruodin, died in 1617. A few friars returned in 1628, but were
decimated and turned out by the Cromwellians in 1651. Again under
Charles II the friars crept back, and in 1681 the transept was still roofed.
By the end of the 17th century the friary was finally deserted, but in 1969
it was formally handed back to the guardianship of the Franciscans.
JRSAI 19, 1889, 44 and 25, 1895, 135; Leask, Churches II, 118

GLENINAGH (509) Castle

MAP 3 E 13
OS½" 14M.19.10

Access : Quarter of a mile down a lane and then into a field. Signposted
An L-shaped tower of the 16th century, with one leg of the L being taken up by a spiral staircase. The tower has 4 storeys, the third being vaulted, and there is another underground vault supporting the ground floor. There is a good fireplace on the first floor, and the rounded corner turrets are well preserved. It is possible that the main doorway was taken from elsewhere and inserted here. The O'Loughlins occupied the castle up till 1840. Nearby is a Holy Well enclosed in the 16th century.
JRSAI 30, 1900, 425

INCHICRONAN (14) Augustinian Abbey

MAP 6 F 14
OS½" 14R.39.86

Access : Along avenue to farmhouse, then a one mile walk to near the end of the narrow peninsula. Inaccessible in winter due to flooding. Signposted
Standing on an earlier monastic site founded by St Cronán (of Tuam-graney?), the Church was granted to the Augustinian Canons of Clareabbey by Donal Mor O Brien in 1189. The church, with its unusual east window with foliage decoration on the outside, probably dates to this period. By 1302 it had become a parish church. In the 15th century conventual buildings (of which parts remain), a sacristy and a south transept were added. It was granted to Donogh, Earl of Thomond, in 1620. It is idyllically sited on a quiet peninsula jutting into a lake.
PRIA 22, 1900, 146, No. 71; JRSAI 30, 1900, 133

INISHCALTRA (5) Churches and Round Tower

MAP 7 H 14
OS½" 15R.69.85

Access : Only by boat. Contact John Carney in Scariff from whom rowing boats may be hired, and a return trip in a motor boat can be arranged. Please do not intrude upon or disturb any excavation in progress
St Caimin founded a monastery on this island in Lough Derg in the 7th century, but it is probable that there were also hermits on the island as well as monks. There is a somewhat doubtful report that the monastery was following the Benedictine rule in the 8th century. The Vikings burned the monastery in 836 and again in 922. Brian Boru is said to have built one of the churches on the island, while his brother, who died in 1009, was Abbot. Around 1043 a monk at Inishcaltra named Anmchad was ordered to leave the monastery because, as Guest-master, he had offered wine to the monastery's guests without the Abbot's permission. He left for Fulda in Germany where he shut himself up alone in his cell for 10 years. By the beginning of the 14th century, St Caimin's church was used as a parish church, but it may well have fallen into ruins in the course of the following two centuries. By the end of the 17th century the island had become a place of pilgrimage and penance. The buildings which remain are as follows:
St Michael's Church: Ruined oratory in ancient enclosure
St Brigid's Church: Rectangular church with Romanesque doorway, part of which has been incorrectly reconstructed
St Caimin's Church: Nave and chancel church with antae, and a 12th century Romanesque doorway which is possibly not in its original position. Chancel probably later than nave. There is also a Romanesque altar
St Mary's Church: Slightly later than the other churches, this is a long rectangular church, possibly of early 13th century date
'Anchorite's Cell': A minute building with two small apartments, possibly originally a tomb.

'Church of the Wounded Men': A small rectangular building of uncertain date; it has three doorways.

As well as these churches there is a Round Tower with round-headed window, a Holy Well, the remains of a cottage, a portion of the so-called 'Cross of Cathasach' with interlacing, fretwork and two sets of unidentified figures. Around the monastery are earthworks, delineating the old monastic enclosure.

PRIA 33 C 1916-7, 93

KILFENORA (8) Cathedral and Crosses

MAP 6 E 14
OS½″ 14R.18.94

Access : Direct to Cathedral ; over wall to one High Cross. Signposted
The Cathedral is on the site of a monastery founded by St Fachtna. It was first mentioned in 1055 when it was burned by Murtough O Brien. Little is known of its history, but the first bishop dates to 1189, the period in which the church was built. The western portion of the original church is still used for Divine worship, but the roofless chancel of the church has a fine three-light window with interesting figures carved on the capitals. The west gable has a stairs running up inside the wall. The chancel is decorated by some 13th and 14th century effigies of bishops, and a good triple sedilia in the north wall. The south doorway and some of the south windows were inserted in the 15th century. Opposite the door of the present church is the stem of a narrow High Cross with interlacing. To the west of the church is the Doorty cross showing three bishops with different types of croziers and a double headed bird (devouring skulls?) on the east face; the west face shows the Entry of Christ into Jerusalem (?) and a number of interlacings. There are strange heads on the south side. Near the north-western corner of the graveyard is another cross with interlacing. In a field, one hundred yards west of the church, is a tall and slender High Cross with a Crucifixion on the east face and a variety of geometrical and inter-lacing motifs. A fifth cross was removed to Killaloe in 1821. The Catholic Bishop of Kilfenora is—the Pope!

JRSAI 30, 1900, 393; JGAHS 21, 1956, 54

KILLALOE Cathedral and churches

MAP 7 H 15
OS½″ 18R.70.73

Access : Direct. Open daily 8.30–6 p.m. If locked the key is obtainable from Mr and Mrs Keane, 3 Abbey Street just around the corner on the right beyond the Cathedral. Signposted
The Cathedral.
The early monastery on this site at the southern end of Lough Derg was founded by St Molua, and he was followed as abbot by St Flannan who died around 639. The Cathedral was founded about 1185 by Donal Mor O Brien on the site of an earlier Romanesque church, the doorway of which is preserved in the south-west corner of the Cathedral. The Cathedral is in the form of a cross, and has three narrow lancet windows in the east gable. Beside the Romanesque door near the main entrance is one of the few stones in the country with a Viking Runic inscription; it is unique in that it also has the same inscription in Ogham asking for a prayer for Thorgrim who made the stone. Beside it is the cross removed from Kilfenora by Bishop Mant in 1821, having a Crucifixion, interlacings and geometrical ornaments on it.

St Flannan's (6) Oratory
In the grounds of the Cathedral is St Flannan's oratory (locked; key available from Mr and Mrs Keane, 3 Abbey Street), otherwise known as

'Brian Boru's vault', which is a 12th century Romanesque church which has lost its chancel but has retained a good Romanesque doorway and a well-preserved stone roof supported by the walls of a small loft above the vault.

St Molua's (279) Church
In the grounds of the Catholic church, further up the hill, is St Molua's oratory. It originally stood on Friar's Island in the Shannon, but was removed and re-erected here when the island was flooded and submerged in the Shannon Hydro-Electric Scheme in 1929. It consists of a nave, to which a chancel with its stone roof was added later. Both the west and south walls have lintelled doorways. The church was built probably some time prior to the 12th century.
JRSAI 59, 1929, 16 and 60, 1930, 130; Leask, Churches I, 36 and II, 54

KILLINABOY Medieval Church and Round Tower
MAP 6 F 14
OS½″ 14R.27.91
Access : Through gate into graveyard. Not signposted
An interesting medieval church of 16th century (?) date repaired in 1715, with simple south doorway over which is a Sheela-na-gig. On the outside of the west gable is the design of a two-barred cross in the masonry. Nearby is the stump of a Round Tower standing on the site of a monastery founded by the daughter of Baoithe.
JRSAI 24, 1894, 26

KILLONE (176) Augustinian Convent
MAP 6 F 15
OS½″ 17R.32.73
Access : One mile along laneway and then through fields. Signposted
Beautifully situated overlooking a peaceful lake, this building is unusual in that it is one of the few known old Irish convents for nuns. It was probably founded by that great church builder, Donal Mor O Brien, about 1190. Certain parts of the building, notably the fine Romanesque east windows with a passage through them within the walls, and presumably the vaulted crypt under the chancel date from around 1225. In the 15th century the church was shortened when the present west wall was built; at the same time much of the north wall was renewed and the domestic buildings were added. The convent was first mentioned in 1260, when an Abbess died. Of its subsequent history almost nothing is known except that it was vested in the Crown in 1584.
JRSAI 30, 1900, 126; Leask, Churches II, 63

KNAPPOGUE Castle
MAP 7 G 15
OS½″ 17R.44.72
Access : Direct. Open daily from 10 a.m. till 5 p.m. Signposted
A 16th century tower which has now been reconditioned inside by the private owners, and contains a number of pieces of old furniture. The Earl of Dunboyne added the lower front part in the middle of the last century. This is now used to stage banquets twice nightly at 6 and 9 p.m.

LEAMANEH (448) Castle
MAP 6 F 14
OS½″ 14R.23.93
Access : 20 yards up a path. Signposted
The eastern portion of the castle is a 5 storey tower built about 1480, with stone vault on the top floor, and a number of holes for guns. A four-storey mansion was added to the west of the tower in the first half of the 17th century, and it has some mullioned windows (some of which are

modern). Beside the castle was a large bawn, remnants of which can be seen on both sides of the road. The original gate, with an inscription saying that it was erected by Conor O'Brien and his wife Máire Ní Mahon in 1643, was removed and re-erected at Dromoland Castle in the last century. The castle was first mentioned in 1550 when it was granted to Donough O Brien, who was hanged in 1582. Lord Inchiquin claimed it unsuccessfully in 1603 and again in 1622. It abounds in legends about the Máire, known as Máire Rua, whose name appears on the gate inscription. One story goes that when she saw the apparently lifeless body of her husband being brought back from a skirmish with the Cromwellian general, Ludlow, in 1651, she refused to allow it in saying 'We need no dead men here'. But when she found out that he was still alive, she nursed him till he died later the same night. On the following day, she marched to Limerick to marry one of Cromwell's soldiers, Cooper, so that she could prevent the lands being taken from her by Cromwellian hands and could keep them for her infant son, Donat. Legend says that she later kicked Cooper out of a top window while he was shaving because he made a disparaging remark about her first husband! JRSAI 30, 1900, 403; Leask, Irish Castles 133

MAGH ADHAIR (224) Ancient Inauguration Place

MAP 7 G 15
OS½" 17R.44.77

Access : Half a mile up a laneway, then through stile into field. Signposted
Though it may have started its life as a burial place, this was the inauguration place of the Kings of Thomond, including Brian Boru. The inauguration possibly took place on the flat-topped mound which is surrounded by a bank and ditch. Near it is a raised area with a square building of unknown date, while across the stream is a stone pillar which probably also played its role in the crowning ceremony. The inauguration took place beside an oak pillar, and it is interesting to note that when, in 982, Malachy, High King of Ireland, and in 1051, Aedh O'Conor, King of Connacht, wanted to insult the sanctity of the place, they cut down a tree there which was probably regarded as sacred. There was a fierce battle here between Flan, High King of Ireland, and Lorcan, King of Thomond, in 877, when the High King, to show his superiority, started to play chess on the spot. But he was suddenly routed, and retired to a nearby wood where he got lost and had to surrender three days later. He was, however, allowed go away unharmed. PRIA 20, 1896, 55; JRSAI 30, 1900, 440

MOGHANE Hill-fort

MAP 7 G 15
OS½" 17R.41.70

Access : Through gate at gate-lodge, then 100 yards along path to stile, then turn right up hill along path, passing a ring-fort on the way. There is much undergrowth. Not signposted
One of the largest prehistoric hill-forts, it has three concentric banks and ditches around the top of the hill. The fort dates to the Early Iron Age (roughly 500 B.C.–500 A.D.). Not far away the largest find of prehistoric gold ornaments in Europe dating from about 700 B.C. came to light in 1854. JRSAI 23, 1893, 281

NEWTOWN Castle

MAP 3 F 13
OS½" 14M.22.07

Access : A quarter of a mile down a laneway to farmyard. Not signposted
A 16th century tower, which is unusual in that it is round but has a square base. It is 5 storeys high, with the first and third storeys having domed

roofs with well-preserved impressions of the wicker-work which kept the mortar in place until it dried. There are mullioned windows, and turrets on the parapet.

Leask, Castles 111

OUGHTMAMA (12) Early Christian Churches

MAP 3 F 13
OS½" 14M.30.08

Access : Almost a mile and a half up a laneway, then across two fields
Of the early monastic settlement founded by 'The Three Colmáns', three churches remain. The westernmost is the largest, and is a nave-and-chancel church with flat-headed doorway and a plain Romanesque arch. Nave and chancel are possibly contemporary. In the south-west corner a font portraying two animals with intertwined necks was inserted in the wall in the 15th century. To the west is a second church with round-headed doorway and window. Further to the west are the fragments of a third church with a narrow window in the east gable, and with a doorway in the south wall.

JRSAI 25, 1895, 283; PRIA 22, 1900, 130, No. 3

POULNABRONE Dolmen

MAP 3 F 13
OS½" 14M.24.00

Access : Over wall and 100 yards across field. Not signposted
A dramatic dolmen with gracefully tilted capstone supported by two long flag-stones, and situated among the unusual limestone formations in the centre of the Burren.

Megalithic Survey Vol I, Co Clare (1961) 23, No. 28

QUIN (15) Franciscan Abbey *Fig. 21*

MAP 7 G 15
OS½" 17R.42.74

Access : Through gate, and 100 yards along path. If locked, key from John Parnell Clune at Quin Gardens about 100 yards north of the gate leading to the Abbey, near the corner of the Ard Sollus road. Signposted
A church which stood on the site was burned in 1278, but two years later De Clare built it up as a castle forming a square with massive rounded towers at the corners. Parts of these towers still survive. In 1236 the garrison killed an Irish chief called O'Liddy, whereupon the Irish under Cuvea Macnamara attacked and ransacked the castle. By 1350 another church was built on top of the castle ruins, but much of this church was renewed by Sioda Cam Macnamara around 1433 when the Franciscans were brought to Quin. The church has a tower and well-preserved east, west and south windows, and a south transept. The cloisters are some of the best-preserved Franciscan examples in the country, with a dormitory on the first floor. In the church there is an interesting collection of 15th-19th century tombstones.

JRSAI 30, 1900, 427; Leask, Churches III, 102 and 139

St Finghin's Church

On the other side of the stream is St Finghin's Church, built between 1278 and 1285. It is a long rectangular church with triple lancet east windows and the remains of a richly moulded south window. The ivy-covered belfry at the south-western end is a later addition.

RUAN (17) Medieval Church

MAP 6 F 14
OS½" 14R.33.87

Access : Past modern Catholic church to churchyard behind. Not signposted
A 15th century parish church which, besides a carved east window, contains little of interest. The chapel to the south was added by Donough O'Kerin, whose tomb, dated 1687, it contains.

PRIA 22, 1900, 142, No. 55

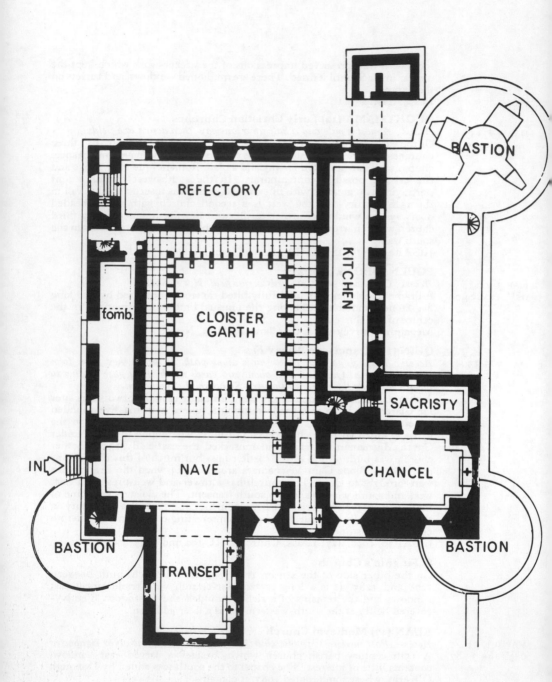

Fig. 21. Plan of the Franciscan Friary at Quin, Co Clare.

SCATTERY (10) Churches and Round Tower

MAP 6 D 16
OS½″ 17Q.97.52

Access : Only by boat. Boats leave from Cappa pier depending on weather and tides. To arrange crossing contact Mr Clancy, Telephone Kilrush 47. Cost £2 per person.

The island on which the monastery is sited was called Inis Cathaig, after a horrible monster who was defeated on it. St Senan, who died in 544, founded his monastery here in the first half of the 6th century. One of his pupils was St Ciaran of Clonmacnoise. The monastery was ravaged by the Vikings in 816 and again in 835, and was probably even occupied by them from 972 to 975, but was re-captured by Brian Boru. The most conspicuous part of the old monastery is the Round Tower, 120 feet high, which is unusual in that the door is at ground level. Just to the east of the tower is the Cathedral, a church with antae and with lintelled doorway; it was altered in the 13th or 14th century when the south and east windows were inserted. To the north is a Romanesque nave-and-chancel church of the 12th century. On a ridge north of the main group of buildings is Temple Senan, containing medieval work of no great interest. It houses an old grave slab, asking for a prayer for Moinach. South-west of the Round Tower is the Church of the Hill of the Angel where St Senan is alleged to have been placed by an angel before he defeated the horrible monster Cata; the church is early, but much ruined, and a medieval building was added to it. Near the east strand is the Church of the Dead, dating at earliest to the 14th century. In 1057 and in 1176 the island was plundered, and the churches were desecrated by William Hoel, an Englishman, in 1179. At about the same time, the monastery became part of the Diocese of Limerick. The Normans took over the church in the 13th century and appointed 'keepers'. In 1359, Pope Innocent VI at Avignon appointed a Bishop who was not recognized by the local clergy. The monastery regained importance in the 14th and 15th century as a Collegiate church, but it was destroyed in Elizabethan times. A castle was built on the island around 1577, but little remains of it. New boats sailed around the island 'sunwise' on their first cruise as a mark of respect, and sailors took pebbles from its shore to sea with them to avert danger.

JRSAI 27, 1897, 276; NMAJ 2, 1940-1, 14

SLIEVENAGLASHA (270a) Wedge-shaped Gallery-grave

MAP 6 F 14
OS½″ 14R.
28/9.97

Access: Across one and a half miles of stony crag. Difficult to find. Not signposted

A wedge-shaped megalithic tomb. The two long sides are each made of one slab of limestone about 10 feet in length; the capstone was damaged when a one-roomed hut was built up against it in the last century. It is known as 'Diarmuid and Gráinne's Bed'. There are other, more accessible, tombs in the same area.

Megalithic Survey Vol I, Co. Clare (1961) 47, No. 55

TEMPLE CRONAN (13) Early Christian Church

MAP 3 F 14
OS½″ 14M.29.00

Access : Half a mile along a lane, then down past a house to a hollow. Not signposted

A small church dedicated to St Cronán of Roscrea, or of Tuamgraney. The original lintelled doorway in the west wall was blocked up when an arched doorway was inserted into the north wall, probably some time in the 15th century. In the exterior walls there are some grotesque Romanesque heads, so the church probably dates from the 12th century. Near the church is a stone tomb-reliquary of uncertain date, which is locally said to mark the grave of St Cronán.

Dunraven, Irish Architecture I (1875) 105; Leask, Churches I, 74

TUAMGRANEY. Church

MAP 7 H 14
OS½" 18R.64.83

Access : Direct. If closed, key with Mrs Graham in second house on left up street. Not signposted

This is probably the oldest Irish church still in use. The western portion of the church, with its lintelled doorway, is said to have been rebuilt by the Abbot Cormac O Killeen in 969, and the church is reputed to have been repaired again by Brian Boru around 1000. The eastern portion of the church is 12th century in date; it has corner columns, but it is doubtful if the two south windows in the eastern part of the church are in their original position. The east window is modern. Note the carved head at the top of the east gable; it is locally said to represent St Cronán, who founded the original monastery on the site before 550. Loose Romanesque fragments in the church may have come from a church at Killaloe.

PRIA 22, 1900-2, 154, No. 110; Leask, Churches I, 69 and 152

If you are given a key—remember to return it

County Cork

ARDSKEAGH (314) Church

MAP 7 G 17
OS½" 21R.57.20

Access : Up private laneway and through two fields. Signposted

The insignificant remains of a 12th century church with round-headed doorway.

BALLYBEG (301) Augustinian Friary

MAP 7 G 18
OS½" 21R.54.08

Access : Across a stile into a field. Signposted

The friary was founded in 1229 or 1237 for the Augustinian Canons by Philip de Barry who dedicated it to St Thomas and erected a brass statue of himself on horseback in the church. David de Barry enlarged and enriched the monastery in 1235. The church was built shortly after the foundation and has two fine west windows. The central tower with interior staircase and the tower to the west were both added in the 15th century. The claustral buildings contain little of interest. The most unusual feature of the whole Friary is the dove-cot or pigeon-house to the east-south-east of the Church, which is probably the best preserved example in the whole country. In 1574 the friary was granted to George Bouchier. By 1605 it was in the hands of Sir David Norton and in 1610 it was taken over by Sir John Jephson.

JRSAI 2, 1852, 265; Leask, Churches II, 145

BALLYCROVANE (426) Ogham Stone

MAP 6 C 21
OS½" 24V.66.53

Access : 150 yards over private field. Not signposted

A standing stone, 17 feet high, looking almost like a modern piece of sculpture. An Ogham inscription, possibly added later, reads MAQI-DECCEDDAS AVI TURANIAS (Of the son of Deich descendant of Torainn).

Macalister, Corpus Inscriptionum I (1945), 70, No. 66

BALLYNACARRIGA (425) Castle

MAP 6 F 21
OS½" 24W.29.51

Access : Up steps. Signposted

A fine four-storey castle which is said to be older than the date of 1585 given in a window-recess on the top floor. It was built by Randal Hurley who married Catherine Cullinane. She may be the person whose initials are given as 'C.C.' in a window inscription on the top floor. The carvings and decorations in these windows are the most unusual feature of this castle; one shows a woman with three roses, thought to be Catherine Cullinane and her three children, and the other has a representation of the Crucifixion and the Instruments of the Passion. The windows are also decorated with a number of geometrical patterns. This top floor was used as a church until 1815. There are 'bartizans' or corner turrets at first floor level on diagonally opposite corners, and there are remnants of a round corner-tower of the bawn outside the entrance.
JCHAS 12, 1906, 26 and 76; 64, 1959, 53

BLARNEY Castle

MAP 7 H 20
OS½" 25W.61.75

Access : Quarter mile along a path. Entrance fee charged. Not signposted

A fine and excellently situated strong tower built by Cormac Laidir MacCarthy probably around 1446. The tower is L-shaped in plan; its first floor is vaulted and has a fireplace; above it are three other floors, the topmost of which had been a chapel. On the parapet is the famous stone of eloquence; if you lie on your back, put your head backwards and downwards and kiss the underside of the stone you will have the eternal gift of eloquence, so runs the local legend. Below the castle is a round bastion which may be older. The iron gate to the castle was rehung in its original position in the last century. The castle was taken by Lord Broghill in 1643. After the Restoration it was returned to the MacCarthy's but it was taken from them again in 1690. In 1703 it was sold to the Jefferyes, who still hold it.
JRSAI 23, 1893, 339 and 32, 1902, 372

BRIDGETOWN Augustinian Priory

MAP 7 H 19
OS½" 22W.69.00

Access : 200 yards down a laneway. Not signposted

The Priory was founded for the Canons Regular of St Augustine by Alexander Fitz Hugh Roche in the early 13th century. Its buildings are unfortunately much overgrown with ivy. They are placed around the usual quadrangle. The church is on the north side, and is divided into two parts, with the eastern section having 13th century lancet windows and a good 15th century tomb niche. The three lancet windows were reduced in size in the 15th or 16th century. Considerable portions of the domestic buildings remain, including a covered passage beside the cloister on the east side and a fine refectory with 13th century lancet windows on the first floor of the southern range of buildings. The Priory was suppressed at the time of the Reformation.
JCHAS 2nd Ser. 3, 1897, 261

BUTTEVANT (202) Franciscan Friary

Access : Direct to churchyard in which church stands. If locked, key available from the caretaker, Michael Sweeney, 6 Knockbarry, Buttevant, or from the Parish Priest. Signposted

MAP 7 G 18
OS½" 21R.54.09

This Friary was founded for the Franciscans by David Oge Barry in 1251 and was dedicated to St Thomas à Becket. Of the monastic complex only

the church remains; the domestic buildings have disappeared. The church consists of a long nave and choir, with a south transept. The door originally stood in the south part of the nave, but it was transferred (presumably in the 15th century) to the west gable; at the same time the original gable windows were blocked up and later Tudor windows inserted. The choir has 8 lancet windows in the south wall and two early windows in the west gable which were later reduced in size. In order to support the choir on the steep incline down to the river, a crypt was built underneath it. It is gruesomely filled with human bones which tradition says were put there after a battle at Knocknanuss nearby. Two out of the three original lancet windows of the transept were later built up and other windows inserted. The church shows well how the 13th century stone masons worked their decorative windows in sandstone, while the 15th century masons used limestone. There are two early de Barry tomb-recesses in the walls of the nave. After the Dissolution, the Abbey passed into the hands of the Barrys who had agreed not to let the Friars return. But the Friars did return, and in 1609 they adopted the Franciscan reform and remained on intermittently until 1783.
JRSAI 2, 1852, 83; JCHAS 18, 1912, 66

CAHERVAGLIAR (233) Ring-fort

MAP 6 F 20
OS½″ 24W.31.60

Access : Across stile into field. Signposted
An earthen ring-fort with concentric bank and ditch, with the remains of a monumental flat-headed stone doorway on the eastern side. Partially covered in undergrowth.

CARRIGAPHOOCA (255) Castle

MAP 6 F 20
OS½″ 21W.29.73

Access : Through gate and across a boggy field. Not signposted
Situated on an outcrop of rock ('The Fairy Rock'), this is a 16th century tower of 4 storeys below a vaulted roof. There are turrets on opposing corners at the top. It was built by the MacCarthys of Drishane, and Teig MacCarthy retired here after the battle of Kinsale in 1601, but O'Sullivan Bere attacked and sacked the castle shortly afterwards. There is also a stone circle two fields to the east of the castle.
JCHAS 16, 1910, 130; JRSAI 48, 1918, 139

CASTLELYONS (411) Dominican Friary

MAP 7 J 19
OS½″ 22W.84.93

Access : Direct from road. Not signposted
Founded in 1307 by John de Barry for the Carmelite Friars, and dedicated to the Blessed Virgin Mary. The present ruins are, however, probably of 15th century date, consisting of a nave and chancel church, and the eastern and western portions of the domestic buildings which are of little interest. There is a fine west doorway in the church with a twin-lighted window above it. The tower which divides the nave and chancel of the church is only partially preserved, though the spiral staircase within its walls is preserved up to the top level. After the Reformation the Friary came into the hands of the Earl of Cork who gave a life interest in the property to his daughter Alice 'to buy her pins'. During the Penal times, the Carmelites, Franciscans and Dominicans were associated titularly or otherwise with the Priory. The last titular Carmelite Prior was John O Neile who died in 1760. In the 18th century it served as a hedge-school. The south wall of the church fell in 1871.
JCHAS 4, 1898, 61; JCHAS 32, 1927, 50

CLEAR ISLAND (22) Medieval Church

MAP 6 D 22
OS½″ 24V.95.22

Access : June-September : One boat leaving Baltimore at 2.15–3 p.m., returning from Cape Clear at 6–6.45 p.m.

A church built about 1200 on the site of an earlier monastery founded by a pre-Patrician saint called Ciarán. Situated on the west side of the North Harbour of the island, it is a simple rectangular church. The south wall has a door with a rough arch. The east window has its upper portion in the shape of an inverted W, and there is another window in the south wall. 70 yards south of the church is a cross-inscribed pillar.

JCHAS 14, 1908, 118 and 18, 1912, 2

CLOYNE Cathedral and Round Tower

MAP 7 J 20
OS½″ 25W.92.68

Access : Direct from road. The key to the Round Tower may be obtained from the house in the corner of the Cathedral grounds. Not signposted

An Early Christian monastery was founded here by St Colman Mac Lenen who died around 600, but all its buildings were burned in 1137. The Cathedral of the present Church of Ireland Diocese was started around 1250, but because of much modernization, comparatively little of this early church can be seen. The chancel has been heavily modernized; the chancel arch was blocked up in 1705 and removed completely in 1775. The east window was inserted in 1856. The Cathedral's most famous Bishop was George Berkeley, a celebrated philosopher who died in 1753. In the north-east corner of the Churchyard stand the foundations of an earlier oratory called 'The Fire House'. Some Gothic fragments were found in it in the last century. On the opposite side of the road is a Round Tower; its original conical top was later replaced by battlements.

JRSAI 27, 1897, 334

CONNA (240) Castle

MAP 7 J 19
OS½″ 22W.93.94

Access : Through old tree-lined garden. Key at Garda Station at Ballynoe, some miles away. Signposted

Very dramatically situated, perched on a rock overlooking the river Bride, this tower was built around 1500 by one of the Earls of Desmond. Only one ceiling is retained, while there are also some scant remains of the bawn. It was the residence of Sir Thomas Fitzgerald, father of the betrayed Sugán Earl, until his death in 1595. It was the scene of fighting with the Earl of Essex in 1599. James I granted it to Richard Boyle, afterwards Earl of Cork. Captured in 1645 by Lord Castlehaven, it was assaulted but not taken by Cromwell in 1650. It was burned in 1653, killing three daughters of the occupant. Afterwards it passed to the Duke of Devonshire's family.

JCHAS 21, 1915, 129; JRSAI 45, 1915, 172

COOLE (395) Churches

MAP 7 J 19
OS½″ 22W.86.95

Access : Over stile into field. Not signposted

Little is known about the history of the place, but a monastery may have been founded here by St Alban, though it is also connected with other saints. Near the road is a 12th or 13th century church with antae, and with an unusual pointed east window which is off-centre. The west end would seem to have been added on later, as were possibly the other buildings to the north and south of the church, of which only the foundations remain. A few hundred yards to the north-north-east is a larger church.

JRSAI 49, 1919, 47; JCHAS 46, 1941, 80

COPPINGER'S COURT Fortified House

MAP 6 F 22
OS½" 24W.26.36

Access : Through gate and field. Not signposted
The ruins of a 4-storey house consisting of a central block flanked by two
fortified square blocks on the east side and with another in the centre of
the west side. There are some mullioned windows on the top floor on the
western side, while there are well preserved turrets on the southern side
and at the north-western corner just below the parapets. The chimney-
stacks are well preserved. The house was built by Sir Walter Coppinger
who surrendered his estates to James I in 1616 and had them re-granted
to him the following day.
JCHAS 65, 1960, 130

DRISHANE (296) Castle

MAP 6 F 19
OS½" 21W.28.92

Access : Through convent grounds. Key to be obtained at convent. Signposted
A tower-house with rounded corners built in 1450 by Dermot MacCarthy,
Lord of Munster. The top is modern. There is an ogee-headed window
in the third floor. In 1641 it was garrisoned in support of Charles I. About
1643 additions were made to the Castle, and several fireplaces were inserted
with the monogram 'W'—the Wallis family who owned it till the end of
the 19th century. It was again garrisoned in the Fenian rising of 1867,
and repaired in the last century by Lady Beaumont. It is now the property
of the Holy Child nuns.
JCHAS 20, 1914, 64

DROMANEEN (339) Castle

MAP 7 G 19
OS½" 21W.50.97

*Access : Three quarters of a mile up a private laneway, then through the
farmyard to castle in the field beyond. Not signposted*
Finely situated overlooking the river Blackwater, this is a fortified house
and castle erected by the O'Callaghans around 1600. It is an L-shaped
tower with a fine fireplace on the first floor and three- and four-mullioned
windows. At a later stage the eastern portion with its finely moulded gate
was added to form a bawn to the east of the tower. It suffered much in
the Rebellion of 1641, when it was taken from the O'Callaghans and
granted to Sir Richard Kyrle, and later it was sold to Richard Newman of
Cork. It was restored after 1694 by Dillon Newman, after whose death it
was used to garrison soldiers, but it was abandoned shortly afterwards.
JCHAS 2, 1893, 43 and 11, 1905, 34

DROMBEG (381) Stone Circle, Hut and Cooking-place *Fig. 22*

MAP 6 F 22
OS½" 24W.25.35

Access : Along path for 400 yards and then over a stile. Signposted
This is the best of a number of stone circles in Co Cork. There are 17
standing stones. The westernmost stone lies flat and has something
looking like a human foot carved in it. A cremated body was found in the
centre of the circle when it was excavated. The circle is dated to somewhere
between 153 B.C. and 127 A.D. Sixty yards to the west of the stone circle
are two round huts joined together. The eastern part of the east hut
contained a roasting oven. A stone causeway led from the huts to a cooking-
place containing a hearth, a well and a water-trough in which water was
heated. Experiments have shown that hot stones could boil water five
times their volume and keep it hot for two and three-quarter hours. The
site was probably a seasonal hunting place. The huts are dated to between
109 and 349 A.D. and the cooking-place to between 368 and 608 A.D.
JCHAS 64, 1959, 1 and 65, 1960, 1

Fig. 3. Conjectural reconstruction of a Wedge-shaped Gallery-grave at Island, Co Cork. 2nd millennium B.C.

MAP 6 F 20
OS½" 24W.22.61

FARRANAHINEENY (374) Standing Stones
Access : Across a boggy field. Not signposted
An alignment of four standing stones and one fallen one on the slopes of the Shehy mountains.

MAP 7 H 19
OS½" 21W.60.91

ISLAND (502) Wedge-shaped Gallery-grave *Fig. 3*
Access : Over two fences into the second field from the road. Not signposted
A neat example of a wedge-shaped gallery grave; it was excavated about 13 years ago. The long rectangular burial chamber has two tall stones marking the entrance and was surrounded by a double row of stones placed in the shape of a U. The tomb was covered by a mound of stones, the edges of which were marked by small standing stones. The entrance façade of the tomb was straight, and in front of it lay a semi-circular arrangement of stones. Some burned bones were found during the excavations.
JRSAI 88, 1958, 1

Fig. 22. Stone Circle at Drombeg, Co Cork built possibly around the time of Christ.

KANTURK (517) Castle

MAP 6 F 18
OS½″ 21W.38.02

Access : Over a stile into field. Not signposted
The castle is rectangular in shape with massive square towers at each corner. The main block has four storeys, the towers have five. There is a fine Renaissance door in the first floor on the north side and a more traditional pointed door on the ground floor on the south side. The flat 'Burgundian' arch is a feature of the ground-floor windows, while those on the upper storey are Tudor with two or three mullions. The castle has a remarkable number of well preserved fireplaces, that on the south wall of the third floor being particularly fine. This building is an interesting combination of the traditional Irish tower-house architecture with pointed arches and the new Tudor architecture with Renaissance doorways and mullioned windows. It was built by Dermod MacOwen MacDonagh around 1601 as a defence against the English. But news of its building reached England where the Privy Council, being uneasy about its purpose, ordered that building work should stop—and it did, possibly as a result of the disastrous Battle of Kinsale or possibly because MacDonagh could not borrow any more money from English moneylenders. So the castle was probably never completed. Dermot MacCarthy, into whose hands it later came, mortgaged it in 1641 to Sir Philip Perceval who afterwards took possession of it.
JCHAS 3, 1894, 158; Leask, Irish Castles 126

KEALKIL (450) Stone Circle

MAP 6 E 21
OS½″ 24W.05.55

Access : Over a fence and across two fields. Partially signposted
Five stones forming a miniature stone circle, two standing stones and the remains of another circle with small stones. From the hill-top where it is sited, there is a good view of Bantry Bay.

KILBOLANE (490) Castle

MAP 7 G 17
OS½″ 21R.42.21

Access : Through gate into field. Signposted
The remains of a square castle with rounded turrets at the corners and surrounded by a moat. Although in the style of the castles of the 13th century, it was built in the 15th or 16th century, probably by the Cogans from whom it was acquired by the Earls of Desmond. It was granted to H. Ughtrede in 1587 as part of the estate of David Gybbin, Lord of the Greatwood, and it was granted to Sir W. Power in 1613.
PRIA 26, 1906-7, 231

KILCREA (182) Franciscan Friary

MAP 7 G 20
OS½″ 21W.51.68

Access : 100 yards along grassy path. Signposted
A Franciscan Friary founded by Cormac Laidir MacCarthy, Lord of Muskerry, in 1465. The long church has a south aisle and transept, but the lack of decoration gives a rather austere impression. The tower is contemporary with the church. An unusual feature is the multi-windowed sacristy and scriptoria to the north of the chancel which is the most decorative part of the building. Although nothing remains of the cloister, the buildings which surrounded it are well preserved. The Friary may not have been suppressed until 1577, when it was granted on lease to Sir Cormock MacCarthy. Although he himself left the friars in peace, the friary was raided after his death by a company of English soldiers from Cork in a dispute as to who should be his successor. It was plundered again in 1599. The friars restored the building in 1604, but were expelled 10 years later. When Cromwell's troops occupied the place in 1650 they

altered the internal arrangements of the building, and later the church was robbed of many of its decorative stones. Charles II granted it to Donough, 1st Lord Clancarty, who kept it until the end of the 17th century. JCHAS 14, 1908, 167 and 18, 1912, 57; Leask, Churches III, 107

KILLEENEMER (316) Church

MAP 7 H 18
OS½" 22R.78.07

Access : Across field. Signposted
A 12th century church with antae. It originally had a round-headed door-way, now fallen, and also round-headed windows, one of which is still preserved. Parts of the original stone wall surrounding the monastery survive.
Leask, Churches I, 75

KILNARUANE (436) Carved Pillar Stone

MAP 6 D 21
OS½" 24V.98.48

Access : Through gate and field. Signposted
An Early Christian pillar stone which may have formed the shaft of a High Cross. On the south-western face are panels with interlacing, a praying figure, a cross and Saints Paul and Anthony in the Desert. On the north-east face are panels with interlacing, four animals and, facing upwards, a boat with four oarsmen. Its date is uncertain.
NMAJ 2, 1940-1, 153; Antiquity 38, 1964, 277

KINNEIGH Round Tower

MAP 6 F 21
OS½" 24W.33.57

Access : Direct to Churchyard. Signposted
On the site of a monastery founded by St Mo-Cholmog, this Round Tower is unique in that the lower 18 feet are hexagonal, and above that it is round. It has a square-headed doorway. An internal ladder leads to the top which was altered in the last century to make a belfry.
JRSAI 57, 1927, 67

KINSALE Church, Tower and Fortifications

MAP 7 H 21
OS½" 25W.64.51

Kinsale was a town which was insignificant until it became the scene of one of the great disasters in Irish history in 1601 when a combined Spanish and Irish force under de Aguila, O Neill and O Donnell was routed by the English under Mountjoy. In the 17th and 18th centuries Kinsale was an important English naval base. This is reflected in the architecture of the town which, with its 18th century flavour and a whiff of the distant southern shores reached by its mariners, makes Kinsale into the town with what, in my opinion, is the most individual character in the country. In the town and its surroundings are some interesting monuments.

St Multose Church

Access : Direct. Not signposted
The present Church of Ireland Parish church, founded probably by de Cogan at the end of the 12th century. It consists of an aisled nave and chancel, as well as a north transept. An unusual feature is the tower at the north-west corner which is contemporary with the church, and, thus, around 1200. The now ruined chancel was added about 1560. The original chancel was removed in 1730, and further repairs, including the provision of a new roof, were carried out in 1835. The door of the tower is Roman-esque in detail, while the west door of the church has a niche above it with a small statue (15th century?) supposed to be that of the founder of the original monastery on the site, St Multose. The interior of the church houses an interesting collection of 17th century grave-slabs while in the

porch are the town stocks. Not far away, up a hill, are the charming 'Almshouses' built by Sir Robert Southwell in 1682, with a unique doorway of moulded red-brick.
Darling, St Multose Church, Kinsale (1895)

The 'French Prison' (360) Tower
Access : Direct from Cork Street. Key with Edward Wright, 5 Cork Street, 60 yards up street. Not signposted
A small 15th or 16th century tower known also as 'Desmond Castle'. It has three storeys, with a finely decorated doorway (inserted later?) giving on to the street and a number of attractive ogee-headed windows particularly at the corner of the first floor. Behind the castle are garrison and prison rooms. The tower got its name because it was used as a prison for captured Spaniards, Portuguese, Dutch, French and even Americans from 1630 until 1800. The old Courthouse down the road is now used as a museum.
JCHAS 18, 1912, 133

Charles Fort
Access : Over grassy patch. The fort is dangerous—and nobody takes responsibility if you injure yourself! Not signposted
About two miles south of Kinsale, passing through the delightful village of Summercove, you come to Charles Fort which is the best preserved fort of its type in the country. Charles Fort is a massive star-shaped structure with the outer defences over 40 feet high. It has a fine classical doorway. It was built by Sir William Robinson in 1677 on the site of a medieval castle. The buildings inside the fort are ruined 19th century barracks. There is a lighthouse at the south-western corner. While the parapets are extremely dangerous, they afford a magnificent view of Kinsale harbour. On a tongue of land on the opposite side of the harbour (but about 10 miles away by road) are the ruined remains of an earlier star-shaped fort called James Fort)

KNOCKDRUM (284) Stone Fort
MAP 6 E 22
OS½" 24W.17.31
Access : 200 yards along path, then up steps. Signposted
This is a circular fort, repaired before 1860, with a stone wall 95 feet in diameter. It is entered at the north-east through a narrow entrance with a small sentry chamber on the right. Just to the left of the entrance is a stone with a cross inscribed on it. In the interior of the fort are the foundations of a square building, at one corner of which is the entrance to a souterrain. Outside the entrance of the fort is a large boulder with cup-marks.
JCHAS 2A, 1893, 154; JRSAI 61, 1931, 1

KNOCKNAKILLA (420) Stone Circle
MAP 6 F 19
OS½" 21W.29.84
Access : Across a patch of bog. Not signposted
Stone circle with 5 stones still standing. Nearby is a stone twelve feet high.
JRSAI 45, 1915, 316; JCHAS 36, 1931, 9

LABBACALLEE (318) Wedge-shaped Gallery-grave
MAP 7 H 18
OS½" 22R.78.02
Access : Over stile. Signposted
One of the biggest wedge-shaped gallery-graves in the country. There is a large rectangular chamber, with a smaller chamber behind it, carrying three large capstones sloping towards the back. It stands in a wedge-shaped

stone cairn (which possibly covered it originally) and is bounded by massive standing stones. Outside this again there was a further row of stones running off at an angle, but few of the original stones remain. Excavation in 1934 produced a number of inhumation burials, fragments of a late Stone Age decorated pot and a few fragments of bone and stone. PRIA 43, 1936, 77

LABBAMOLAGA (18) Early Christian Church and Grave-slabs

MAP 7 H 18
03½″ 22R.76.18

Access : Over stile. Signposted
On the site of a monastery founded by St Molaga who lived in the 7th century, there is a small primitive-looking church with antae and a flat-headed doorway made of 3 stones. Near the south wall of the church is a stone with a spiral volute which is said to mark the tomb of St Molaga. Nearby are the remains of a later church of little interest. The present graveyard is surrounded by a wall which is probably ancient.
JNMAS 1, 1909, 35; JCHAS 18, 1912, 4

LISCARROLL (333) Castle

MAP 7 G 18
OS½″ 21R.45.12

Access : Up path from village street. Not signposted
A 13th century castle built by the de Barrys, possibly by David Oge de Barry. It is a large square in shape, with rounded turrets at each corner. The entrance was through the south wall where there is a large oblong tower with a long passage which was closed by a heavy door and which possibly had a portcullis. This tower was heavily modified in the 15th or 16th century. Opposite it, in the north wall, there is another square tower. Buildings undoubtedly were built against the interior walls, but none of these survives. Around 1625 the castle fell into the hands of Sir Philip Perceval, but he lost it in a siege in 1642 when it was taken by Lord Castle-haven for the Irish. In Cromwellian times it was returned to the Percevals, and it remained in the possession of their descendants, the Earls of Egmont, for many years.
Journal of the Waterford Archaeological Society 7, 1901, 33; JCHAS 42, 1937, 92; Leask, Castles 71

Fig. 23. Conjectural reconstruction of Mallow Castle, Co Cork built shortly before 1600.

MALLOW (281) Castle *Fig. 23*

MAP 7 G 19
OS½" 21W.56.98

Access: Up private avenue and then to the right. Not signposted

A castle probably built by Sir Thomas Norreys who died in 1599. It is a long rectangular building with polygonal turrets (one incorporating a staircase) at the corners of the north wall. Wings project from the centre of the north and south walls, the northern one containing the entrance with a finely moulded doorway. The windows are mullioned and have holes for muskets below them. The castle was besieged by Mountgarrett in 1642, but Jephson (who had married Sir Thomas Norrey's only daughter, Elizabeth) resisted successfully. Three years later Lord Castlehaven took the castle, and it was abandoned some time after this. It still remains in the possession of the Jephson family who built their present mansion from the old stables, and who have now built a small museum beside the castle. Nearby are the fragments of a 13th century castle.

JCHAS 2, 1893, 42 and 49, 1944, 19; Leask, Castles 129

MONKSTOWN Castle

MAP 7 H 20
OS½" 25W.76.66

Access: Up golf-club avenue. Not signposted

Now the club-house of Monkstown Golf-club, this castle was built by Anastasia Archdeacon; née Gould, about 1636. She built it while her husband was away at sea, and having deducted the cost of the mason's board and lodgings from the total cost, she found that she had only paid 4d for the whole castle! It consists of a square central block flanked at the corners by four massive square towers, and it has gables at the top. It was used as a barracks in the 18th century.

JRSAI 27, 1897, 330

SHERKIN ISLAND (169) Franciscan Friary

MAP 6 E 22
OS½" 24W.03.26

Access: June-September: Boat service only from Baltimore every half hour.

Founded in 1460 or 1470 by Fineen or Dermot O'Driscoll for the Franciscan Friars of Strict Observance. The church consists of a nave and chancel, as well as a south transept with two chapels. The main doorway is unusual in that it is in the south and not in the west wall. Most of the original windows have disappeared. Although nothing remains of the cloister arcade, the eastern portion of the domestic wing is preserved; it contained the Chapter Room into which a fireplace was later inserted. The 3-storey sacristy (reached from outside) and the tower were probably built after the fire of 1537 when the men of Waterford sacked and burned the Friary as an act of vengeance against the O'Driscolls. After the Dissolution it was leased successively to James Heydon, Thomas Wye and John Bealinge, being bought in the 17th century by Sir Walter Coppinger (builder of Coppinger's Court) and coming later again into the hands of the Becher family. The Friars returned for some time around 1627 when a house was bought for them nearby.

JCHAS 11, 1905, 64; 18, 1912, 6; 29, 1923-4, 106 and 44, 1939, 40

TIMOLEAGUE (21) Franciscan Friary

MAP 7 G 21
OS½" 25W.47.44

Access: Direct. Signposted

Founded possibly by MacCarthy Reagh, Lord of Carbery, in 1240 or by William de Barry during the reign of Edward II for the Friars of the Strict Observance of St Francis. The buildings date from various periods. The original church was much shorter than the present one, extending only as far westwards as the third arch from the tower. The church was probably lengthened when the tower was added by Edmund Courcy, Bishop of Ross, who died in 1518. There is an aisle and a transept with a later chapel on the south side of the nave. An unusual feature is the stairs which begin at the passage leading from the choir to the sacristy, and go across the east windows to the south wall of the choir. There was a kitchen on the west side of the cloister; the north side consisted of store-rooms below and a library on the first floor, but the eastern side was adapted, possibly in 1604, to serve as a store-room. At the north-east corner is the attractively sited dining-hall, with 5 windows looking out over the water, and beyond it lies the infirmary. In 1577 the Friary was granted to Sir James Barry, Viscount Buttevant, and leased to Thomas Wye in 1582 and to John Champen in 1589. Probably some time after this, English soldiers ransacked the Friary and smashed the stained glass. The Friars remained on intermittently until at least 1629 when Brother Michael O'Cleary visited the Friary to copy manuscripts for the compilation of the 'Annals of the Four Masters'.

JCHAS IA, 1892, 173; 18, 1912, 14; 29, 1923-4, 104 and 44, 1939, 39; Coombes, A History of Timoleague and Barryroe (1969)

TULLYLEASE (299) Church and Grave-slabs

MAP 6 F 18
OS½″ 21R.36.18

Access : Direct. Signposted
An Early Christian monastery founded by St Berichter or Berchert who, with his father (a Saxon Prince) and two brothers, came to Ireland after the Synod of Whitby in 664. Another saint of the same name, who was possibly also Abbot of the monastery, died in 839. The existing church is of various dates. The south end of the east wall is probably the oldest part (12th century?) while the south door and window are early 13th century. The present chancel was built in the 15th century, and a number of fragments of Early Christian grave-slabs were incorporated in its walls. Fastened to the interior of the east gable is what is possibly the finest Early Christian decorated cross slab, with the inscription QUICUMQUE LEGERIT HUNC TITULUM ORAT PRO BERECHTUIRE (Whoever reads this inscription, let him pray for Berichter—probably referring to the founder). Because of its resemblance to the Book of Lindisfarne, the slab has been dated to the 8th century. The church formed part of an Augustinian Priory which was transferred to Kells in Co Kilkenny in 1415.

JCHAS 17, 1911, 66; 43, 1938, 101 and 109; 58, 1952, 12; PRIA 61C, 1961, 154

YOUGHAL Churches and Town Wall

MAP 7 K 20
OS½″ 25X.10.78

Youghal has been a flourishing town since the 13th century, if not before. It was sacked by the Rebel Earl of Desmond in 1579. In 1588-9 its mayor was Walter Raleigh, who, though he spent little time in it, is alleged by tradition to have planted the first Irish potato there. Owned by Richard Boyle (afterwards Earl of Cork) in the early 17th century, it was blockaded by Lord Castlehaven in 1645. Cromwell, to whom the town gave allegiance, used it as his base for his Irish expedition, and sailed from there in 1650. The town has a number of interesting items. The most important are:

St Mary's Church

Access : Direct. If locked, key with Mr Atkins at cottage at entrance to church grounds. Not signposted
Now the Church of Ireland Parish church, it was founded by Richard

Bennet and his wife, Ellis Barry, early in the 13th century, though it may replace an earlier church which was burned in 1192 and to which two small windows above the chancel arch may belong. The church consists of a nave and chancel and a north and south transept. The nave has two side-aisles, and outside the west wall were two external staircases, but these were removed in 1853. The floor-level was raised some feet during re-building around 1400. The chancel was heavily re-built around 1468 by Thomas Fitzgerald, 8th Earl of Desmond, but was desecrated by Gerald, the 16th Earl, in 1579. Its present ugly form is a result of 'rebuilding' by Drew in 1854, whereby some original features were plastered over. In the north wall is the 15th century tomb of Thomas Fleming. An interesting feature in the walls of the chancel are the holes behind which are pottery vessels inserted for acoustic purposes. The south transept was bought by Sir Richard Boyle as a mortuary chapel, and he erected a fine tomb for himself and his wife there in 1619. The church contains a 14th century eight-sided Baptismal font, and a number of grave-stones, one of which depicts Thomas Paris holding a falcon or dove in his hand. Near the north-west corner of the church is a square tower originally built in the early 13th century, but re-strengthened later (15th century ?).
JRSAI 23, 1893, 340 and 33, 1903, 333

The Town Walls
Access : Direct. Not signposted
An area behind St Mary's Church is bounded by the old town walls. These walls, dating probably to the 15th century but re-fortified in 1642, are possibly the best preserved medieval town walls in Ireland. They include two semi-circular turrets at the highest point. The Clock Gate, on Main Street, built in 1777 and now a tourist office and Museum, stands on the site of one of the town gates. In the same street are the 16th century Tynte's Castle (now a grain store), the deserted 16th century Almshouses and a 15th or 16th century doorway of a Benedictine Abbey, now dis-appeared.
Fleming, The Town-wall Fortifications of Ireland (1914) 61; Wain, The History of Youghal (1965)

North Abbey (286)
Access : Direct to graveyard. Signposted
Founded in 1268 by Thomas Fitzmaurice Fitzgerald (known as 'The Ape'!) for the Dominicans, and dedicated to the Invocation of the Holy Cross, and later to St Mary of Thanks. All that remains are portions of the west gable of the church with a three-light window, as well as a part of the centre aisle at the crossing, with architectural details similar to St Mary's; these date from shortly after the foundation. General Chapters of the Dominican Order were held here in 1289 and 1304. In 1586 it was granted to Sir Walter Raleigh, who pulled some of it down in 1587. In 1602 he sold it to Richard Boyle. A 15th century Italian 'Madonna and Child' owned by the monastery is now in the Dominican church at Pope's Quay in Cork.
JRSAI 3, 1854-5, 333 and 33, 1903, 331

If you open a gate—then close it too

Molana Abbey (Actually in Co Waterford)

MAP 7 K 19
OS½" 25X.08.83

Access : Up private avenue, then along raised wall to the right as far as the 'island'. Not signposted

This Abbey, standing on the site of an island monastery founded in the 6th century by St Maelanfaidh, was re-founded for the Canons Regular of St Augustine towards the close of the 12th century. The buildings now form a square around a cloister garth. The church is rectangular, and may contain elements from an older church; it is lighted by 10 fine lancet windows. On the east side of the cloister is the Chapter Room, where Raymond Le Gros is said to have been buried in 1186, while there is a refectory on the south and a kitchen on the west side of the cloister. A two-storey building to the north of the choir of the church was probably the Prior's lodging. In the middle of the cloister garth is an incongruous weathered modern statue of the founder. A half a mile to the south of this delightfully situated monastery is the Castle of Rhinecrew, built by the Knights Templars.

JRSAI 33, 1903, 313 and 62, 1932, 142

*Fig. 24. Burt Castle,
Co Donegal as it was in 1601.*

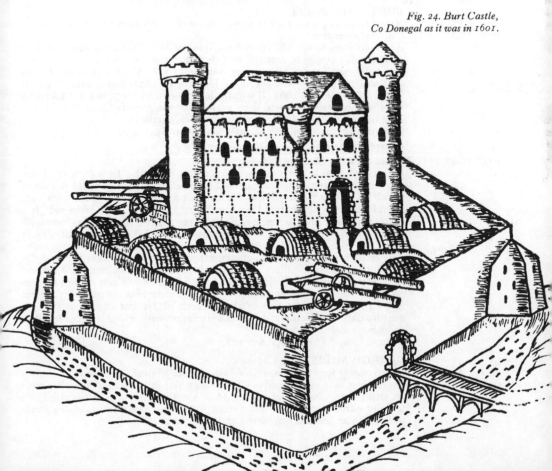

BELTANY (463) Stone Circle

MAP 2 L 3
OS½" 4C.25.00

Access : Through private farmyard, and 300 yards along path to top of hill.
Signposted
A fine stone circle on a hill-top with a commanding view. It is still composed
of 60 stones, though originally there were many more. There is one stone
standing outside the circle.
UJA 3rd Ser. 2, 1939, 293

BUNCRANA (435) O'Doherty's Keep

MAP 2 L 2
OS½" 1C.34.32

Access : Over bridge and down path. Not signposted
Having started off its life possibly as a Norman castle after 1333, this tower
was extensively repaired by Hugh Boy O'Dogherty in 1602 to act as a
bridgehead for the Spaniards who were supposed to land on the Inishowen
Peninsula. It was burned by the English shortly afterwards, but was
repaired either in 1641 or in 1689, and used as a manor. It is beautifully
situated beside the Crana stream, but its three storeys contain little of any
architectural or artistic interest.
UJA 3rd Ser. 2, 1939, 183

BURT Castle *Fig. 24*

MAP 2 L 3
OS½" 1C.32.19

Access : 200 yards up path to farmyard, then up through two fields to top of
hill. Not signposted
A small oblong tower, with two three-quarter round turrets (one a staircase)
at diagonally opposite corners, and dating to the late 16th century. It was
originally surrounded by a strong wall, and traces of the ditch outside this
wall still remain. It was taken by Docwra in 1601, but returned to Sir
Cahir O'Doherty in 1603. It was besieged again in 1607, but not taken by
the English until 1608 and later granted to Sir Arthur Chichester. For a
long time it remained an important English garrison.
UJA 3rd Ser. 2, 1939, 188; Leask, Castles 108

CARNDONAGH (271) Cross and Slabs *Fig. 8*

MAP 2 M 1
OS½" 1C.47.45

Access : Direct. Not signposted
Re-erected beside the entrance to the town on the Buncrana road are
three Early Christian monuments. The most important of these is a cross
which on one side has interlacing forming a cross, and a figure with out-
stretched hands surrounded by four figures, while on the other side is a
figure and more interlacing. Beside the cross are two small pillars, one with
a man with sword and shield, a bird, David and his harp, and a curvilinear
motif, while the other stone has on it a number of men, one with two bells.
The cross has been dated to the eighth century, but at least some of the
carving on the small pillars could be 9th century. In the graveyard behind
is an interesting early pillar on one side of which are carved two figures
on either side of a marigold supported by a stem; on the other side there
is a Crucifixion. The door of the Church of Ireland church is of 15th
century date, and beside the door is a stone (possibly a lintel) with a number
of bishops depicted on it.
Henry, Irish Art Vol. I (1965) 128

CARROWMORE High Crosses

MAP 2 M 1
OS½" 2C.52.45

Access : Over wire fence into field on both sides of road. Signposted
On the east side of the road is a tall cross pillar in the shape of a cross with
an angel cut in low relief on one face. On the west side of the road is a
tall and narrow cross with only stumps of arms, and there is also a stone
pillar with an incised ring-cross and a zigzag motif.

CLONCA (25) Church and Cross

MAP 2 M I
OS½" 2C.52.47

Access: Through gate and across field. Signposted

The church, on the site of a monastery founded by St Buodán, was built probably in the 17th century, but the lintel over the door, with worn carved figures on it, was taken from an earlier church. In the north-east angle of the church is a grave-slab erected by Magnus MacOrristin (possibly a Scotsman) with a sword and a hurley stick on it. In the adjoining field to the west is a very pleasing High Cross. On its east face is the Miracle of the Loaves and Fishes, and on the west face two men with folded arms (Saints Paul and Anthony in the Desert?), and on each side there is a number of geometric patterns.
JRSAI 32, 1902, 297 and 45, 1915, 197

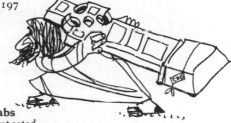

CONWAL Church and Grave-slabs

MAP 2 K 3
OS½" IC.14.10

Access: Direct to graveyard. Not signposted

Beside the medieval church, which is of little interest, are a pile of stones on which are mounted a number of Early Christian grave-slabs; one of these has a cross in relief with interlacing motifs and another has an inscribed human figure. In the graveyard is buried Godfrey O'Donnell who, though dying, ordered himself to be borne in his coffin into battle against Brian O'Neill in order not to disappoint his soldiers, and who died immediately after he had won the battle.
JRSAI 45, 1915, 230

COOLEY Churches and Cross

MAP 2 N I
OS½" 2C.60.38

Access: Direct. Signposted

Outside the graveyard is a slender Cross, ten feet high, in a rectangular stone base. As well as the normal perforations, the cross has a hole in the 'head' of the cross. In the graveyard are the remains of churches, and a small building called 'The Skull House', which is probably a tomb-shrine.
JRSAI 45, 1915, 190 and 200

DOE (319) Castle

MAP 2 K 2
OS½" IC.08.32

Access: 300 yards down untarred lane. Signposted

A four-storey house standing in a square turreted bawn built early in the 16th century on a beautiful site on Sheep Haven Bay by MacSweeney na dTuath, foster father of Red Hugh O'Donnell. Note that the moat on the landward side has been hewn out of the rock. The castle is first mentioned in 1544 in connection with internecine wars between the sons of MacSweeney Doe. Wrecked sailors from the Spanish Armada were granted refuge here in 1588. By 1600 it had been taken over by Eoghan Og MacSweeney, an ally of the English, who was unsuccessfully besieged there by his brother Rory in 1601. Red Hugh O'Donnell attacked the castle unsuccessfully in 1601, but shortly afterwards the castle was granted by the Crown to Rory O'Donnell. Taken again by the MacSweeneys in 1606, it was captured again by Rory O'Donnell in the following year. In the same year it was granted to Sir Basil Brooke, but was taken in 1608 by Sir Cahir O'Doherty's allies and shortly afterwards retaken by Crown forces. It was then granted to a number of Englishmen before it fell into Irish hands again in 1641. In the following year it greeted Owen Roe O'Neill back to Ireland. Captured by surprise by Coote for the Cromwellians in 1650, it later served as a Royal garrison under Charles II. In the Williamite wars it was captured by Donough Og MacSweeney but was taken by the English again shortly afterwards. It was extensively repaired by Harte at the end of the 18th century and inhabited by his family until 1843, after which it was deserted.

JRSAI 45, 1915, 223; The Donegal Annual, 2, 2, 1952, 381

DONEGAL (174-75) Castle and Franciscan Friary

Access : Direct. Friary signposted

MAP 2 J 5
OS½″ 3G.93 78

The Castle

The Castle is situated in the centre of Donegal town on a rock outcrop overlooking the river Eask. The massive tower at the north angle was erected by the O'Donnells either in 1474 or in 1563. It was the residence of Hugh Roe O'Donnell, last chief of Tir Connell, who died in Spain in 1602 and who possibly burned it in 1595 before he left it to prevent it falling into English hands. Note the floral decoration on the corner turret. In 1616 it was granted to Sir Basil Brooke for 21 years, and granted to him forever in 1623. He carried out extensive renovations in the tower, adding a bay-window above the old door and also other mullioned windows, and on the first floor he built a magnificent fireplace decorated with carved fruit, his own coat-of-arms and those of Leicester. It was probably shortly after 1623 that he erected the fine manor house beside the tower. This is a fine gabled three-storey house with two-, three- and four-mullioned windows. It incorporated earlier doorways, but there is also a fine Renaissance-style Jacobean door in the first floor, the stairs to which have disappeared. The gatehouse of the present entrance and the wall on either side of it were built by Brooke, but the turret at the western end of this wall is contemporary with O'Donnell's original tower.

100th Annual Report of the Commissioners of Public Works, 1932, 12; Leask, Castles 134

Franciscan Friary

On the seashore south of the town are the unfortunately scanty remains of a Franciscan Friary founded by the first Red Hugh O'Donnell and his wife Nuala O'Brien in 1474. Of the church only the chancel and a gable of the south transept remain. Better preserved are the remnants of the cloister arcade. The English seized and fortified the Friary in 1591 but were driven out the following year by Red Hugh O'Donnell. Ten years later, the English seized it again. During a battle between Niall Garbh O'Donnell, who held it for the English, and his cousin Red Hugh O'Donnell, the magazine blew up, and the resulting fire gutted the building. The Friary was granted to Sir Basil Brooke in 1607. The Franciscan community stayed on until 1600, under the protection of the O'Donnells. After that they wandered from place to place, and four of the Friars—three O'Clerys and a Duignan—made the community immortal by their compilation known as 'The Annals of the Four Masters' (1632-6), which is one of the most important sources for the early history of Ireland.

UJA 2nd Ser. 6, 1901, 224; Leask, Irish Churches III, 151

FAHAN Early Cross-Slabs *Fig. 25*

MAP 2 L 2
OS½″ 1C.34.26

Access : Direct to graveyard. Not signposted

St Mura founded a monastery here early in the 7th century; records testify to its existence up till 1098. The present church is modern, but to the east of the church there is a cross slab which has been dated to the 7th century. On one face it has two figures surrounding a cross composed of interlaced bands, and on the other face is a cross of similar design. Beside the gate of the cemetery, set into the outside wall, is a grave-slab with a ringed cross in a square. The crozier of St Mura and the shrine of St Mura's bell from the monastery are now in the National Museum of Ireland in Dublin.

JRSAI 45, 1915, 183 and 193; Henry, Irish Art I (1965), 127

Fig. 25. A Cross-slab at Fahan, Co Donegal dating possibly from the 7th or 8th century.

GLENCOLUMBKILLE (139) Megalithic Tombs and Early Cross-Slabs

MAP 2 G 4
OS½" 3G.
52-54. 82-85

Access : Partly direct, partly in over fields. Partly signposted
There was probably an Early Christian monastery in the valley where, according to tradition, St Columbkille banished demons who enveloped the valley in a fog. The most conspicuous remains of this monastery are the pillars decorated with cross-motifs and geometric designs which may originally have been grave-slabs, but are now the centres or 'stations' of the pilgrimage which takes place on the Saint's Feastday on 9th June. The pilgrims walk around each 'station', often three times, occasionally adding a stone to the pile already accumulated at the base of the pillar. The pillars are spread over an area in the valley 3½ miles long, and the pilgrimage has to be completed before sunrise. The most accessible pillars are near the Church of Ireland church (which also has a souterrain in the grounds) and another (broken) one near the police station. Within a radius of about three miles from the village there are two fine court-cairns, one at Farranmacbride ('Mannernamortee'), north of the village and another at Malin More ('Cloghanmore'), both of the central court variety. A Folk-Village, with cottages typical of the valley, has recently been opened to the west of the village.
JRSAI 71, 1941, 71; PRIA 60 C 1960, 107-8, Nos. 17 and 19

GREENCASTLE Castle

MAP 2 N 1
OS½" 2C.65.40

Access : Best through gate of 'Castle Inn' and then left into field. Not signposted
Called 'New Castle' by the Irish, and 'Northburgh' by the Normans, this castle was built by Richard de Burgo, the 'Red' Earl of Ulster, in 1305. It served as a port of supply for English armies in Scotland in the early part of the 14th century. The castle is roughly oblong in shape and is enclosed by strong walls. In the middle of the north wall is a projecting rectangular tower (probably earlier than the castle), which has very thick walls, a well and, in the centre of the lowest room, a peculiar hollow pillar. The castle entrance was at the western end, between two large polygonal towers which enclose a gatehouse. In 1332 Walter, son of Sir Walter Burke, was taken a prisoner by the Brown Earl of Ulster and starved to death in the castle. In revenge the Burkes murdered the Brown Earl in the following year. Subsequently, the castle passed to Lionel, Duke of Clarence. In 1555 the castle was demolished by Calbhach O'Donnell with the aid of a 'crooked gun'. Later the castle was granted to Sir Arthur Chichester.
UJA 2nd Ser. 16, 1911, 10; JRSAI 43, 1913, 44 and 45, 1915, 201; Arch Journal 93, 1937, 161; Leask, Irish Castles 39

GRIANAN OF AILEACH (140) Stone Fort

MAP 2 L 3
OS½" 1C.37.20

Access : Direct. Signposted
A very fine stone fort built on a hill-top with a superb commanding view over Lough Foyle and Lough Swilly. The tall stone circular wall encloses an area 77 feet in diameter, and the walls are 13 feet thick. In the walls are small chambers, while on the interior walls there are a series of steps to enable the defenders to reach the ramparts. The fort is entered by a long lintelled entrance. Legend says it was built by the ancient gods, but though its date is unknown, it was probably built some time in the early centuries of the Christian era. It served as the royal seat of the O Neill sept of Aileach possibly from the 5th to the 12th century. One of its most famous kings was Muircheartach of the Leather Cloaks who marched through Ireland in 941, and brought back many hostages with him to the Grianán.

In 1101, it was demolished by Murtogh O Brien, King of Munster, in revenge for the destruction of his own royal seat at Kincora near Killaloe in Co Clare. To make his destruction even worse, Murtogh made each of his soldiers take away a stone from the fort with him. We do not really know whether the fort originally looked as it does now, with its wall-walks etc., as it was greatly reconstructed by Dr Bernard of Derry in 1870. Surrounding the stone fort are three concentric walls which are not very high, but which formed part of the original fortification.

Ordnance Survey of the County of Londonderry, Vol I (1837) 217; JRSAI 45, 1915, 204; PRIA 15, 1879, 415

PLUCK (453) Standing Stone

MAP 2 L 3
OS$\frac{1}{2}$" 1C.23.10

Access : Through gate into field. Not signposted
A standing stone.

RAPHOE Carved Fragments

MAP 2 L 3
OS$\frac{1}{2}$" 4C.26.03

Access : Direct. Not signposted
In the Church of Ireland church of this town which is dominated by the comparatively uninteresting ruins of a 17th century castle, there are carved fragments possibly of 10th century date. In the hall of the church is a large stone bearing a representation of the Arrest of Christ. In the centre is Christ being arrested by two men; St Peter stands near, sword in hand, to cut off the ear of Malchus, and the group is surrounded by soldiers. A similar stone bearing unidentified figures is embedded in the outside of the north wall of the church. The carving is in the style of the High Crosses, though the figures are bigger. It has been suggested that they form part of a lintel of a church. Other fragments of 15th–17th century date are also built into the walls of the church.
Henry, Irish Art Vol 2 (1967) 189

RATHMULLAN Carmelite Friary

MAP 2 L 2
OS$\frac{1}{2}$" 1C.29.28

Access : Direct. If locked, key at house beside entrance. Not signposted
A Carmelite friary founded by MacSwiney, Lord of Fanad, in the 15th century. It consists of a nave and chancel church with south transept and some domestic buildings. The friars still seem to have been in occupation as late as 1595 for in that year George Óg Bingham raided it and took 24 Mass Vestments, church plate and other things. It was leased to Captain Ralph Bingley in 1602, when it consisted of 'one ruinous church, a steeple, a cloister, a hall, three chambers, an orchard and one and a half quarters of stony and infertile land'. King James granted it to James Fullerton in 1603, and about 1617 Bishop Knox took possession of it. He converted the south transept and the nave into a residence for himself, adding a western extension to the transept, inserting new windows, adding two fine corner turrets in the Scottish style at the east end of the nave, and building a fine new doorway in dark stone, putting his own initials and the date 1617 on it. Of the domestic buildings only the north-east corner survives, the upper part of which may have been the Abbot's room.
JRSAI 45, 1915, 222

RAY (23) Church and Cross

MAP 2 J 2
OS$\frac{1}{2}$" 1B.95.33

Access : Down a long grass-covered laneway. Not signposted
The 16th century church presumably stands on the site of an Early Christian monastery. It has four large round-headed windows in the south wall and an undecorated pointed doorway. Inside is a quernstone. Lying

flat on the ground in front of the door of the church is an unfinished High Cross, 21 feet long. It is said to have been carved in the hills to the south, and was intended for the monastery on Tory Island. However, when it was being transported, legend says that it began to rain, and St Colmcille realized that he had forgotten his prayer-book. He promised the cross to whichever of his disciples would go back and get his book for him. Fionán, founder of the church, went back and found the book being kept dry by a crow spreading its wings over it. When Fionán brought the book to St Colmcille, he claimed his prize, but not without some protestations from Colmcille. A pilgrimage used to be held here on the first Monday in May until it was stopped because it had become too rowdy!
Ordnance Survey Letters, Co. Donegal

TORY ISLAND (24) Round Tower, Cross and Churches

MAP 2 J 1
OS½" 1B.85.46

Access : Mail Boat from Magheraroarty pier ; sailing time depends upon the weather conditions. Intending passengers should contact the Post Office at Meenlaragh
On this island, which is still inhabited, St Colmcille is said to have founded a monastery in the 6th century. From the old monastery there remain a small undecorated T-shaped cross which is 7 feet high, a unique Round Tower, 57 feet high, built of rounded beach stones and with a round-headed doorway, as well as scanty remains of two churches.
JRSAI 25, 1895, 240

County Dublin

BALDONGAN (310) Church

MAP 5 R 11
OS½" 13 O.24.57

Access : Across field. Signposted
The remains of a church built possibly in the 15th century. The eastern portion is probably the earliest; the western part, with its massive tower and belfry, was added later. In the 13th century the site was attached to the church at Balrothery and was granted to the religious house at Kilbixy by the Archbishop of Dublin. It was subsequently made tributary to Lusk. Just to the north of the church are the insignificant remains of a castle which was owned successively by the Barnewalls, the Berminghams and the Lords of Howth, but which was largely destroyed by the Cromwellians.
JRSAI 44, 1914, 250

BALLYEDMONDUFF (437) Wedge-shaped Gallery-grave *Fig. 1*

MAP 5 Q 12
OS½" 16 O.18.21

Access : Up three fields. Signposted
A wedge-shaped megalithic tomb with a rectangular chamber divided into three unequal parts, and set into a wedge-shaped cairn bounded by standing stones, and the whole placed in a double-walled U-shaped setting of large stones. Cremated bone and pottery were found inside. The date of the tomb has been assigned to the Early Bronze Age (c. 1700 B.C.).
PRIA 55 C 1952, 61

BRENANSTOWN (291) Dolmen

MAP 5 R 12
OS½" 16 0.23.24

Access : Only down through a private garden. Please ask the permission of the landowner to visit it. Not signposted
Unfortunately difficult of access, this is an excellent example of a Portal Dolmen. Looking like a bird about to take off, it consists of seven stones forming a chamber and supporting a large capstone 15 feet long and wide.
JRSAI 44, 1944, 226

CLONDALKIN (32, 285) Round Tower, Church, Cross and Castle

MAP 5 Q 12
OS½" 16 0.07.31

Access : Direct. Key of Round Tower to be obtained from Christopher Mulryan, who lives in Rose Cottage, about 50 yards away on opposite side of the road going towards Clondalkin village. Round Tower signposted
The foundation of the first monastery is attributed to St Cronán, otherwise called Mo-Chua, who lived possibly in the 6th century. The monastery is first mentioned in 776. It was plundered by the Vikings in 832. In 1076 the southern half of Ireland demanded the expulsion of O'Ronáin from the Abbacy, as it was claimed that he held it against the rightful abbot. This probably means that the monastery had fallen into lay hands by that time. The most important remnant of the monastery is the Round Tower which is 84 feet high and has its original conical cap. The plinth and outside staircase are possibly original. In the Church of Ireland graveyard opposite there are two granite crosses (one a ringed cross, the other having traces of very worn figures), a granite baptismal font, and the remnants of a medieval church which was largely destroyed as a result of the explosion of 260 barrels of gun-powder at a neighbouring powder-mill in 1787! At the eastern end of the town are the uninteresting remains of a narrow 16th century tower called Tully's Castle which has crenellations and a later lean-to building.
JRSAI 44, 1914, 272 and 74, 1944, 212

DALKEY (444) Tower known as 'Archbold's Castle'

MAP 5 R 12
OS½" 16 0.27.27

Access : Direct. Key from Mr McDonald, 59 Castle Street, 1st house on left towards Dunlaoire. Not signposted
A 16th century granite tower of three storeys with a vault over the second. It has parapet machicolations. Together with the reconstructed Dalkey Town Hall, further along on the opposite side of the street, it is the last of the seven castellated buildings which once stood in the old walled town of Dalkey.
JRSAI 26, 1896, 415 and 39, 1909, 187

DALKEY ISLAND (33) Early Christian Church

MAP 5 R 12
OS½" 16 0.28.26

Access : By boat. Boat trips are operated by local fishermen from Coliemore Harbour, Dalkey.
A small, almost square church, dedicated to St Begnet. It has antae at each corner, a flat-headed west doorway and an unusual two-tiered south window. The belfry is a later addition. When the builders of the nearby martello tower lived in the church in the earlier part of the 19th century, they constructed a fireplace in the east gable. Excavations uncovered slates and glazed decorated tiles of medieval date from the roof of the church, showing that the church was also used in the medieval period. Opposite the west gable of the church is a rock with a Greek equal-armed cross inscribed on it.
PRIA 24, 1903, 195 and 66 C 1968, 126

DUBLIN CITY

The city started its life as a base founded by the Vikings in 841 for raids both inland and overseas. By 1000 it had become a trading centre of some importance ruled by a Viking dynasty which in time came to be recognized as an entity within Ireland, but which was occasionally subjugated by the Irish. It lost its power as a Viking city after the famous Battle of Clontarf in 1014 when Brian Boru defeated the Vikings, but despite this the Norsemen still controlled the city. But throughout the 11th and the first half of the 12th century, it came increasingly under the control and power of the Irish kings. On the arrival of the Normans in 1170, Strongbow seized the town by treachery, but in 1171-2 Henry II demanded that Strongbow hand over the town to him, which he did. From that time until 1922, the city remained the centre of English power in Ireland. By the late medieval period, Dublin had dwindled to a small town albeit walled and with a strong castle; in the 17th century it had a population of only about 9,000. Throughout the whole 18th century, however, the town boomed, became the 'second city of the Empire' and had a number of sumptuous town houses built in it which, although vanishing, make Dublin one of the finest Georgian cities anywhere in Britain or Ireland. Time has dealt harshly with Dublin's ancient buildings, and there are now little more than a handful of important buildings surviving which are earlier than 1700. Of these, Dublin Castle, the administrative centre of English power, gained its present form largely since 1700 and is thus not discussed further here. The fine Royal Hospital in Kilmainham, built about 1680 by Sir William Robinson, architect of Charles Fort in Kinsale, is not open to the public. The other most important pre-1700 buildings are given below.

Christchurch Cathedral *Fig. 26*

MAP 5 Q 12
OS½″ 16 O.15.34

Access: Direct. Open May-September 9.30 a.m.–5.30 p.m.; October-April 9.30 a.m.–4 p.m. Not signposted

Founded by Dunan, first Bishop of Dublin, about 1038 on land given by Sigtryggr Silkenbeard, King of Dublin. It remained under the See of Canterbury until 1152 when it became independent. Around 1163 it was transferred to the Canons Regular of St Augustine. The building of a new Cathedral was begun about 10 years later. The crypt of this church, which is still well preserved below the present structure, is the only one of this period in England or Ireland which stretches under the whole length of the church. The crypt contains many 12th and 13th century architectural fragments which formed part of the church, and also statues of Charles I and II made in 1684 for the Tholsel which no longer exists. Otherwise the only parts of the original 12th century church which survive are the north and south transepts which are constructed in the best Romanesque style with three sets of windows one above the other. Some of the capitals might be later, including one capital with figures at the corner of the nave and north transept; the use of such figures shows English influence in the building of the church. The present nave was probably built by Archbishop John Comyn around 1212, but the western bay was added after 1234, and in its lower portions it has been considerably restored in the last century. A new belfry was erected in 1330 to replace an earlier one which had been blown down. The choir was rebuilt soon after 1250, but its present form

Fig. 26. A carved double-capital from Christ Church Cathedral, Dublin, showing men, birds and plants. Circa 1200.

is due largely to Street's reconstruction of 1871-8 during which very considerable parts of the Cathedral as it now stands were rebuilt. To the north-east of the choir is the chapel of St Mary the Great (not normally accessible) which was rebuilt in the second half of the thirteenth century. The effigy of an armoured knight now under one of the south bays of the nave, is traditionally thought to represent Strongbow, but it really dates to around 1340. In the choir of the Cathedral are preserved some other tombstones, including one of a 12th or 13th century bishop. Remains of the 13th century Chapter House of the Augustinians can be seen to the south of the south transept; originally it fronted on to a cloister to the south of the nave which has long since disappeared. The Priory was suppressed in 1539 and given over to the Dean and Chapter. In 1562 the roof and the south wall of the nave fell, and the tower was replaced in 1608.
Arch Journal 88, 1931, 346

St Audoen's (34) Church

MAP 5 Q 12
OS½" 16 0.15.34

Access : Occasionally open 10 a.m.–12 in the morning, and 2.30–4 p.m. in the afternoon, and for service at 10 a.m. on Sunday mornings. Otherwise closed, and the key is not available locally. Not signposted
The church was founded by the Anglo-Normans and dedicated to the Norman saint, St Audoen of Rouen. It was once a group of Guild Chapels, and one of the leading churches in Dublin in its day. Public announcements, such as the Pronouncements of Papal Bulls, were made here, and public penances performed. The west doorway probably dates to around 1200, but the lower portion of the tower above it is largely 17th century in date. The present church consists only of the nave of the original church dating to the first half of the 13th century; new windows were inserted into it in the 15th century. The original chancel is now roofless. In 1431 a chapel was built and dedicated to St Ann. About twenty years later Sir Roland Fitzeustace, Baron of Portlester, built a chapel in the south side of the nave. The Portlester cenotaph, with effigies of himself and his wife, was later removed from this chapel to its present position in the porch beneath the tower. On the north side there was also a chapel dedicated to the Blessed Virgin. The Baptismal Font is Norman in date.
Wheeler and Craig, Dublin City Churches (1948) 12

St Mary's Abbey (401) Cistercian Abbey

MAP 5 Q 12
OS$\frac{1}{2}$" 16 0.15.35

Access: Entrance on right-hand side of Meeting House Lane off Mary's Abbey which is at a right angle to Capel Street. Key available from Mrs M. Brennan, 9 St. Mary's Abbey. Not signposted

A church possibly stood on the site, outside the city walls and on the opposite side of the river, as early as 998, but it must have fallen into decay. It is possible that around 1120, the Savignian order may have built a new church here, but the Cistercian foundation dates to 1139, and the monks probably came from Chester. Nothing survives of the church, although many of its old floor tiles were discovered during an excavation in 1886. To the south of the church lay a cloister surrounded by domestic buildings, but only the Chapter House and a passage to the south of it remain. These are, in fact, the only remnants of the old Abbey. The Chapter House is a fine vaulted room, with its floor well below present street level. It dates to about 1190, though it and the neighbouring passage have been partially rebuilt. It was in the Chapter House that Silken Thomas, Lord Deputy at the time, threw down the Sword of State in 1534 thereby starting his famous Insurrection and, on hearing the false report that his father had been executed in London, forthwith declared himself an enemy of the King.

JRSAI 56, 1926, 22 and 79, 1949, 110; Arch Journ 88, 1931, 348

St Michan's Church, Church Street

MAP 5 Q 12
OS$\frac{1}{2}$" 16 0.15.35

Access: Open week-days 10–1 and 2–5, except Saturday, when it is open from 10–1. Vaults normally closed on Sundays. Not signposted

Dedicated to St Michan, a Dublin saint, in 1095, it formed part of the parish of the same name which was the only city parish north of the river for 600 years. In its present form, it is a rectangular church with a gallery and with a tower at the west end, all dating probably to 1683-6. In the entrance hall are the remains of an organ said to have been played by Handel at the first performance of the 'Messiah'. An 18th century organ adorns the west wall; it is decorated with fine carvings of 14 musical instruments. Noteworthy are an 18th century Stool of Repentance, an early 19th century movable pulpit and the font where Edmund Burke, the orator, was baptised. Below the church are the late 17th century vaults containing mummified bodies (Crusaders according to tradition). The bodies have been preserved because of the peculiar atmospheric conditions in the vaults.

Wheeler and Craig, The Dublin City Churches (1948) 29

St Patrick's Cathedral

MAP 5 Q 12
OS$\frac{1}{2}$" 16 0.15.34

Access: Direct. Open 9 a.m.–6.15 p.m. daily except Saturdays when it closes at 5 p.m. Signposted

The site of the Cathedral was traditionally associated with St Patrick, and old stones preserved in the nave show evidence of an earlier church on the site. In 1213 the church was raised to Cathedral status, and was almost totally re-built in the years following. The Lady chapel at the east end of the choir was built at this time, though it may not have formed part of the original design. In 1316, the spire was blown down and the church was damaged by fire when the citizens burned the suburbs on the approach of Edward Bruce. After the fire, the north-western part of the nave and the four western bays of the north aisle were rebuilt by Archbishop Thomas Minot who also built the great tower at the western end of the north wall.

The stone vault of the nave collapsed in 1544. After the Reformation the Cathedral was reduced to the status of a parish church, but regained its Cathedral status in 1555. Large portions of the present church are, however, the result of rebuilding carried out by Sir Benjamin Guinness from 1864 onwards. There are a number of noteworthy tombs in the church, including those of the Earl of Cork (1631) in the south-west corner, the 17th century tomb of Thomas Jones near the west end of the north wall, Dean Swift, the church's most famous incumbent, in the south aisle of the nave, Archbishop Tregury (1471) in St Stephen's Chapel, Archbishop Fulk de Saundford (1271) in the north wall of the choir, and two fine brasses commemorating Dean Sutton (1528) and Dean Fyche (1537) in the south wall of the choir. In the south transept is a door with a hole in it, through which James, Earl of Ormond and Gerald, Earl of Kildare, shook hands in 1491 after years of distrust and treachery. Hanging in the church are the banners of the former Knights of St Patrick.
Arch. Journ. 88, 1931, 372

St Werburgh's Church, Werburgh Street

MAP 5 Q 12
OS½" 16 0.15.34

Access: Through the passage in 8 Castle Street, around the corner to the north. Open daily 10–4. Not signposted
Though the place was dedicated to St Martin of Tours in Early Christian times, the first English church on the site was dedicated to St Werburgh. The present church, with the remains of its facade, dates to 1715-9, and a later rebuilding to 1759-68. It was the parish church of Dublin Castle. Its main interest for us lies in the fact that its entrance hall houses the early 16th century tomb of one of the Purcell family with his effigy and that of his wife on top, and figures of various saints in the niches below. It originally stood either in the Monastery of All Hallows (where Trinity College now stands) or in the church of St Marie del Dam. It was transferred to St Werburgh's in 1663, and re-erected in its present position in 1914.
Wheeler and Craig, The Dublin City Churches (1948) 38

In the suburbs to the north-east of the city centre is the
Marino Casino (302)

MAP 5 Q 12
OS½" 16 0.18.37

Access: Up private avenue of O'Brien Institute (cars not allowed). Prior permission to visit must be obtained from the National Parks and Monuments branch of the Office of Public Works, Ely Place Upper, Dublin 2. Not signposted
This was a little pleasure house built by James Caulfield, 1st Earl of Charlemont, beside his country residence, Marino House, where he could go from his town house (now the Municipal Gallery in Parnell Square) to enjoy a little leisure in the countryside (as it was then). It was designed by Sir William Chambers and cost £60,000 which, in 1765-71, was a tidy sum. But it was worth it! It is possibly the greatest gem of eighteenth century architecture in the whole of England or Ireland. It is covered in the most delicately executed decorations in the Greek and Roman style. The Casino is a model of compactness, for although it gives the impression from outside of consisting of only one room, it has 8 rooms, a staircase and an extensive basement. The basement is square, but the ground and upper floors are in the shape of an equal armed cross. One enters through a hall with finely moulded mahogany doors; this leads into another room, off which, to the right, is the boudoir, and to the left the Zodiac room which

gets it name from the signs of the zodiac which are modelled around the base of the vaulted ceiling. Upstairs, reached by the stairs from the left-hand door on entering the entrance hall, is the Earl's bedroom, divided in half by two full and two half-columns, an adjoining room with the remains of a bed, and other rooms as well. Some of the statues in the basement were removed there from the balustrade of Aldeborough House in Dublin.

DUNSOGHLY (230) Castle

MAP 5 Q 11
OS½" 13 0.12.43

Access : Get the keys first at the house of Richard McNally, 12 Newtown, Dunsoghly. Signposted

The castle was built by Sir Thomas Plunkett probably some time around the middle of the 15th century. It consists of a central block, four storeys high, and square corner towers, which have corbelled roofing. The wooden roof on the top floor, which has only recently been partially replaced, is the last original 15th–16th century roof in the country to survive; it served as a model for the modern reconstructed roofs at Rothe House, Kilkenny and Bunratty Castle, Co Clare. Just to the south of the castle is a small chapel which has lost its chancel and which bears over its north doorway a representation of the Instruments of the Passion, the inscription 'I.P.M.D.D.S.' and the date 1573. Parts of the old bawn of the castle are incorporated in a neighbouring farm building.

JRSAI 27, 1897, 448 and 52, 1922, 85; Leask, Castles 118

FINGLAS High Cross

MAP 5 Q 12
OS½" 16 0.13.39

Access : Inside Wellmount Road entrance to old graveyard. Not signposted

The cross marks the site of a monastery founded by St Canice, a disciple of St Finian of Clonard. Possibly of 12th century date, it is a granite cross set in a square base. The cross bore figures which are no longer recognizable, and the ring of the cross is not pierced. The nearby church is of little interest.

JRSAI 27, 1897, 451

GLENCULLEN (276) Standing Stone

MAP 5 Q 12
OS¼" 16 0.19.20

Access : Across wall into field. Not signposted

A standing stone about 6 feet high.

HOWTH (36) St Mary's Church *Fig. 27*

MAP 5 R 12
OS½" 16 0.28.39

Access : Through gate and down steps to cemetery. Normally open during the day but if locked, apply for key to Mrs Florence McBride, 20 Church Street, Howth. Not signposted

The first church on the site was founded by Sigtrygg, King of Dublin around 1042. But when, around 1235, the old church was amalgamated with the church on Ireland's Eye, a new church was founded by Luke, Archbishop of Dublin, and it was granted land by Sir Almeric St Lawrence. Little remains of either of these two churches, and much of the present church is scarcely earlier than the late 14th or early 15th century. While the church of 1235 was probably a long single-aisled church, the present church has two aisles, the southern one being the longer, and each aisle had a gable roof. Some time later, probably during the course of the 15th century, the arches dividing the aisles were repaired and the twin-gable roof given up in favour of one single, but taller gable, and for this purpose the eastern and western gables were raised. It was possibly at this period that the porch and south doorway were added. The tall arch in the west gable was added and the bell-cot raised above it late in the 16th century when the east window in the north aisle was also inserted. Towards the eastern end of the south aisle is a well-preserved tomb of the St Lawrence family, probably carved around 1470. On top is a fine double effigy; at the western end is the Crucifixion, St Michael and two angels with censers, while on the eastern end are four figures including St Peter with the Keys, St Thomas of Canterbury and St Katherine of Alexandria (whose name has recently been deleted from the list of saints!) with her wheel. The church was a Collegiate church, served by a *Collegium* of three or more priests. A private house to the south-east of the church, which is reached by a flight of steps outside the cemetery, formed part of the old priests' house.

JRSAI 26, 1896, 1 and 37, 1907, 355

KILGOBBIN (226) Cross

Access : Beside road. Signposted

MAP 5 Q 12
OS½″ 16 0.19.24

A tall granite cross in a square base. The south part of the ring and arm are missing, but a simple representation of the Crucifixion may be seen on both faces (12th century?).

JRSAI 44, 1914, 228

Fig. 27. An unidentified saint, St Thomas of Canterbury, St Katherine of Alexandria and St Peter on the St Lawrence tomb at St Mary's Church, Howth, carved around 1470.

KILLINEY (35) Church

MAP 5 R 12
OS½" 16 O.26.25

Access : Direct to graveyard, but the gate is locked. Key from Mr Rafferty, Town Hall, Dun Laoire. Signposted

The church was dedicated to a saintly daughter of Lenin(!) who lived in the early 7th century. The southern portion of the church is the oldest. It consists of an apparently contemporary nave and chancel, with a rounded chancel arch and a flat-headed doorway with a Roman cross underneath it. It possibly dates to the 11th or 12th century. Probably in the 16th century, though perhaps considerably earlier, the northern aisle was built alongside the existing church and it contains a round-headed east window. Presumably at the same time the mullioned window was inserted in the south wall of the church. After the Dissolution it was given to the Dean of Christ Church, and in the 16th century was served by chaplains from Dalkey.

JRSAI 22, 1892, 101

KILL OF THE GRANGE (207) Church

MAP 5 R 12
OS½" 16 O.23.27

Access : Through housing-estate to graveyard. Not signposted

A small church with antae and a (partly reconstructed) flat-headed doorway to which a chancel was added. The original church is Early Christian in date, but the chancel was added possibly as late as the 16th century. The round-headed doorway in the south wall is later than the original church. Inside the church is a cross-base with small cross which was removed there recently from the housing-estate 100 yards south-west of the church. In the graveyard are one cross-inscribed slab, and the base and fragments of a cross recently broken by vandals.

JRSAI 21, 1891, 405 and 89, 1959, 207

KILMASHOGUE (493) Wedge-shaped Gallery-grave

MAP 5 Q 12
OS½" 16 O.15.25

Access : About 150 yards up hill-side from gate leading to forestry area. As this is occasionally a military shooting ground, do not enter if you see a red flag! Not signposted

A megalithic gallery-grave allied to the wedge-shaped gallery-graves; it consisted of a roughly rectangular chamber and a small ante-chamber set in an oval mound of stones, dating probably to the earlier part of the second millennium B.C. Later in the same millennium burials took place and a fireplace was constructed.

PRIA 56 C 1954, 461

KILTIERNAN (343) Dolmen

MAP 5 Q/R 12
OS½" 16 O.20.22

Access : Along cul-de-sac, up private avenue and then up through three fields. Not signposted

A late Stone Age dolmen (say about 2000 B.C.) with a most impressively large capstone 22 feet long, 13½ feet wide and 6 feet thick. Some of the ten or so stones supporting it have, in the course of time, been pushed side-ways by its great weight.

JRSAI 44, 1914, 226

LUSK (157) Round Tower

MAP 5 R 11
OS½" 13 O.21.55

Access : Direct to cemetery. Key obtainable from Miss Hunt at the shop about 50 yards from the back entrance to the churchyard. Not signposted

The original monastery was founded about 500 by St Macculin, but St Maurus is another saint also identified with Lusk. St Adamnán held a

synod here in 695. The monastery was plundered in 825 and burned in
1069. Many people were killed when a stone church (now no longer
existing) was burned by the Munstermen in 1089, and the church was
burned again together with its relics in 1133. Of the Early Christian
monastery only the Round Tower remains. It is five storeys high and still
retains its original conical roof. The level of the ground has grown considerably so that the flat-headed doorway is not very high off the ground.
In 1197 the monastery was granted to the See of Dublin and in 1219 to the
Precentor of St Patrick's Cathedral. King Edward I conferred it on John
of Spain in 1294, but it was restored to St Patrick's in 1467. The square
tower, which had three other round-towers at its corners to match the
original one, was built in the 15th or 16th century. The church was built
in 1847, but contains a number of fine medieval tombs, including that of
James Bermingham (1527) and the fine double-effigy tomb of Sir Christopher Barnewall and his wife, Marion Sharl (1589).
JRSAI 21, 1891, 502 and 44, 1914, 251

MONKSTOWN (494) Castle

MAP 5'R 12
OS½" 16 O.23.28

*Access : Direct. Key obtainable from John Galligan, Gate Lodge, Monkstown.
Not signposted*
The original castle was built in the 13th or 14th century by the Cistercian
monks of the Abbey of St Mary's in Dublin and was used for the protection
of the monks and the local inhabitants. The main tower, however, probably
dates to the 15th or 16th century, and is 2 storeys high with a little sentry
box half-way up the stairs. The western portion of the tower was added
later. The castle formed part of a bawn which in its present form is largely
19th century, but the gateway with its small south window and stairs
leading to the second storey, together with the once vaulted room beside
it, are largely 15th-16th century. In the 16th century the castle passed to
John Travers, and was later owned successively by the Eustaces, Sir
Henry Wallop and Henry Cheevers. In the Cromwellian period, Ludlow
took over and lived in the castle, but after the restoration of Charles II,
it was returned to the Cheevers who sold it to Archbishop Boyle. After
Boyle's death it was let to Anthony Upton. The castle was much mutilated
in the 19th century.
JRSAI 23, 1893, 349 and 30, 1900, 109

NEWCASTLE Church

MAP 5 P 12
OS½" 16N.00.29

*Access : Direct. If locked, key with Mrs Jobson at Old Rectory to the east
of graveyard. Not signposted*
St Finnian established a monastery here in the 6th century. The church,
consisting of a nave and chancel as well as a tower at the west end, was
built in the 15th century. The nave and chancel are of almost equal length.
The original east window was removed, and inserted in a new wall at the
east end of the nave which was constructed and re-roofed to serve as a
Church of Ireland church in 1724. A carved head, locally identified as
St Finnian, is inserted high up near the east end of the south wall, and
may have been part of a Romanesque church which previously stood on
the site. The tower, which has two upper storeys, has an almost military
look. The church was one of the prebends of St Patrick's Cathedral,
Dublin, from about 1200, but was annexed to Glendalough in 1467. In
the graveyard to the south of the church is a granite cross of Early Christian
date with a ringed cross on one side and a simple cross on the other.
JRSAI 44, 1914, 276

RATHMICHAEL (162) Church and Round Tower

MAP 5 R 12
OS½" 16 O.23.22

Access : 300 yards or so up untarred laneway to graveyard. Signposted
It was possibly St Comgall of Bangor who founded the first monastery here. The present nave-and-chancel church may have been built or re-built as late as the 16th century, but it incorporates part of an earlier church. Attached to the south wall of the church are a number of unusual Early Christian grave-slabs and a cross. Near the south-west end of the church is the stump of a Round Tower. Remains of the old monastic stone wall surround the graveyard. In a laneway leading down from the graveyard to the Old Connaught road is a base holding a small (12th century?) cross bearing a Crucifixion on each face, one in high and the other in low relief.
JRSAI 30, 1900, 186; 44, 1914, 228 and 87, 1957, 75

ST DOULAGH'S Church and Cross

MAP 5 R 11
OS½" 13 O.21.42

Access : Open in Summer on Saturdays 2.30–4.30 and Sundays 2.30–6.00 p.m. Signposted
Founded by St Doulagh, who lived around 600. The old church is entered through that part of the church now used for Divine Service which was built in 1864. The old church, built in the 13th century, is rectangular in shape and vaulted; it has a contemporary south window. Above the vault is an attic room whose walls also serve to prevent the steep-pitched stone roof from caving inwards. At the west end of the church is a small room called 'The Hermit's Cell' which is reputed to be the burial place of the founder, and it may contain parts of an earlier cell. Above this a square tower rises in stages; it is of the same date as the church. One of the floors connects with the croft or attic above the church, though the two may originally have been separate, and above this room, called 'The Bishop's Room', is the belfry. A considerable amount of alteration took place in the 15th and 16th centuries, as evidenced by the present shape of some of the windows and other details. In a field about 100 yards to the north-east of the church is a well, covered by an octagonal building (13th century?); according to tradition its interior walls were decorated with pictures.
JRSAI 27, 1897, 458 and 44, 1914, 264; Guidebook

SWORDS (340) Castle

MAP 5 Q 11
OS½" 13 O.18.47

Access : Direct. Key at Savage's shop, 5 doors up the Dublin road on the right-hand side. Not signposted
The castle was built around 1200 as an episcopal manor. It is 5-sided, enclosing a courtyard of considerable size. It is entered by a strong gateway with a porter's room on the left, and on the right a priest's room with remains of mid-13th century windows and a first floor reached by a spiral staircase. Beyond it is a chapel of fourteenth century date; its windows have been built up. The tower at the north end of the wall was the residence of the Constable of the Castle. For a description of the castle as it was in 1326, see the Introduction. The buildings mentioned in the 14th century description have largely disappeared, including the lean-to buildings built against the wall. The crenellations are 15th century. A weekly court was held in the castle, and Queen Elizabeth I gave the town municipal rights in 1578. There is a Round Tower in the grounds of the Church of Ireland church about 200 yards to the south-west of the castle.
JRSAI 44, 1914, 259; Arch. Journ. 93, 1937, 194; Leask, Castles 72

TIBRADDEN (464) Cairn

MAP 5 Q 12
OS½″ 16 0.15.22

Access : 500 feet up mountainside over boggy terrain. Not signposted
An Early Bronze Age burial was discovered here in 1849, but the mound of stone, with a passage leading to a circular chamber in the centre surrounded by a bench, was erected in the 19th century to allow people to gaze in wonderment at the site of such an ancient burial!
JRSAI 63, 1933, 252; O Ríordáin and Daniel, Newgrange (1964) 98

TULLY AND LAUGHANSTOWN (216 and 225) Church and Crosses

MAP 5 R 12
OS½″ 16 0.23.23

Access : Direct to church and one cross; over fence into field for another cross. Not signposted
The church, which was dedicated to St Bridget, is unusual in that the chancel is broader than the nave. The chancel has a rounded chancel-arch and two round-headed east windows. It is of 12th or 13th century date. It contains some Early Christian grave-slabs. After the Norman conquest it was granted to the Monastery of the Holy Trinity, and was attached to Kill of the Grange. In a field on the opposite side of the road is a tall, narrow cross with a bishop on one face and a head on the other, while a little down the road an undecorated granite cross has been re-erected on a modern base.
JRSAI 30, 1900, 183 and 87, 1957, 81

County Galway

ANNAGHDOWN (49) Church and Priory

MAP 3 F 12
OS½″ 14M.29.38

Access : Direct for churches, 100 yards down lane for Priory. Partially signposted
The first monastery was founded by St Brendan, who founded a convent for his sister here. Near the southern end of the graveyard is the Cathedral— a 15th century building incorporating a very fine window and a doorway dating to about 1200. Other fragments of the same date may be seen inside the church. They may all have been removed here either from the Priory (see below) or may come from an earlier church on the site of the Cathedral. To the north of the Cathedral are the foundations of an early church which is the oldest on the site, and may be of 11th or 12th century date; it was added to at a later period. Further north again are the remains of a medieval parish church of little interest. 100 yards west of the Cathedral, and reached by a lane to the south of it, is the Priory. This was originally built shortly after 1195 when the monastery was granted to the Arroasian nuns. There is still some good Romanesque carving in the church, including a north window in the chancel. To the south of the church was a cloister of which some of the surrounding buildings remain and which are almost military in character. It is a good example of an early fortified monastery. Fragments of a fine Romanesque chancel arch are built into the wall in the south-west corner. In 1321 the monastery was rather half-heartedly annexed to the Archbishopric of Tuam, but in fact it still kept its own bishops up till the end of the 15th century.
Wilde's Loch Coirib (1938) 63; JRSAI 31, 1901, 317

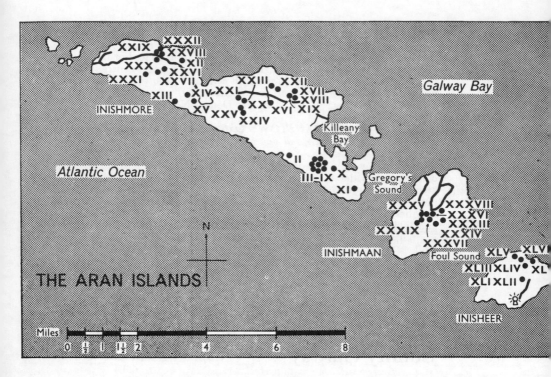

Fig. 28. Map of the National Monuments on the Aran Islands, Co Galway.

ARAN ISLANDS *Fig. 28*

MAP 3 c/d 13
os½″ 14L.
76-99.00-13
See map, Fig. 28

Access : Boats ply from Galway to each of the islands. For sailing time-table, apply to a CIE office. Access to each monument can be direct, via a path or over walls and through stony fields. Some monuments signposted

There are three Aran islands, Inishmore (the large island), Inishmaan (the middle island) and Inisheer (the eastern island), all three lying in Galway Bay, but closer to Co Clare, to which culturally they have been more closely linked until recently than to Co Galway to which they now belong. The earliest inhabitants are said to have been the Firbolgs, who, having escaped after the Battle of Moytura, fled first to Meath. But they were not prepared to pay the exorbitant rents imposed upon them there by Cairbre Nia-Fer, King of Tara in the first century A.D., and retired to Connacht where they were granted lands along the western seaboard, including the Aran Islands. They fortified themselves on the Islands, and called their fortresses after their chiefs Aengus, Eoghanacht and Eochla. The Firbolgs later lost the islands to the Eoghanacta of Munster. Some time around 490, St Enda founded a monastery at Killeany on Inishmore, and many of the founders of other great Irish monasteries, such as St Ciarán of Clonmacnoise, St Finnian of Moville and St Jarlath of Tuam, came and studied under him. St Enda's monastery was one of the first and one of the most important monasteries in the whole of Ireland. It was set on fire in 1020, raided by the Northmen in 1081 and its last recorded abbot died in 1400. Possibly some time in the 11th century, the O'Brien's took possession of the island, which was plundered and burned by Sir John Darcy, Lord Justice of Ireland, in 1334. As and from about 1400 the O'Flaherty's were laying claim to the islands, or at least to parts of them, and they succeeded in expelling the O'Briens in the 16th century. A Franciscan monastery was founded on Inishmore in the 15th century. Arkin's Castle was erected also on Inishmore in 1587 by John Rawson who had been granted the islands by Queen Elizabeth. The castle was probably occupied by the Cromwellian forces when they invaded the islands in 1651. Afterwards Aran passed to Erasmus Smyth and later to Richard Bentley, who was created Earl of Aran in 1662. The islands were garrisoned by the English after 1691. John Millington Synge drew some of his best literary inspiration for his plays from the people of the Aran Islands. Because of their comparative isolation, the islands have preserved a considerable amount of traditional Irish culture which has been lost elsewhere, and to this day it is one of Ireland's last and strongest Irish-speaking areas. The main monuments are listed below, and the numbers correspond to those of the accompanying map. Even tentative dates are omitted as the majority of the monuments are extraordinarily difficult to date, even approximately.

Inishmore (43)
Killeany Townland
   i Arkin's Castle. A long low castle beside the shore of the bay. Built probably by John Rawson around 1587, and garrisoned by Cromwellian troops in 1651.

  ii Doocaher (The Black Fort). A promontory fort with a 220 foot long stone wall with interior terraces which cuts off the promontory. Inside are two rows of stone houses, while stone stakes, known as *chevaux-de-frise,* are stuck into the ground outside.

 iii St Eany's Well (Dabhach Eanna).

 iv Temple Benen. A well preserved but small stone oratory with flat-headed doorway and a small east window. The side-walls are built with inordinately large stones.

  v Beehive huts and enclosures.

 vi Stone cells.

 vii An altar.

viii A cross.

 ix St Eany's Round Tower. Only fragments remain, as much of it fell in a storm in the last century. Nearby are the remains of the Franciscan Friary founded in 1485.

  x Tighlagh Eany and St Eany's Grave. This is a fine early church with antae and a round-headed east window. The north window and door are later insertions, and the west gable as it stands is the result of a later re-building. St Enda is reputed to be buried here.

 xi Turmartin. This is the stump of a Round Tower, reputed to be St Gregory's grave. As a mark of respect to the saint, sailors occasionally dip their sails when passing it.

Kilmurvy Townland

xii   Clochán na Carraige. A large stone hut, oval in shape with a south window, and doors facing east and west.

xiii   Dun Aenghus. One of the most magnificent and dramatic stone forts of western Europe, perilously perched on the edge of a cliff which drops about 200 feet sheer to the sea below. It has three rows of defences forming roughly concentric semi-circles. The innermost one has wall-walks and wall-chambers, and a massive flat-headed entrance passage. It has been extensively restored. The buttresses on the exterior of the north-western portion of the wall are modern. Outside this are a second and third wall, though parts of these were joined together at some stage. Beyond these stand thousands of stones, placed close together in the ground, serving to deny easy access to unwanted intruders; the technical name for these stone stakes is *chevaux-de-frise*. Outside these again is a further wall.

xiv   Temple MacDuagh. An early church built of massive masonry, with a flat-headed doorway leading to a nave and chancel. Certain additions were made to the chancel in the 16th century.

xv   Templenaneeve (Church of the Saints). An early church.

xvi   Oghil fort. A fine stone fort of two concentric walls, with steps leading up to the ramparts. There were traces of two bee-hive huts inside.

xvii   St Kieran's Church and well. An early church; its west doorway was later built up when a door was inserted in the north wall in medieval times.

xviii   Six crosses.

xix   A dolmen.

xx   Teampul an Cheathrair Aluinn (The Church of the Four Beautiful Saints). The four saints referred to are St Fursey, St Brendan of Birr, St Conall and St Berchan. The church is medieval, with a re-built trefoil-headed east window and a pointed north door.

xxi   Leaba an Cheathrair Aluinn (The grave of the four beautiful saints mentioned above).

xxii   Temple Soorney. (Teampall Assurnidhe). A rather ruined small church with the remains of an altar.

xxiii   St Soorney's Bed.

xxiv   Bee-hive huts.

xxv   A dolmen near Cowragh.

xxvi   Dun Onaght stone fort. The fort is almost circular.

xxvii   Kilcholan Church.

xxviii   Templebrecan (St Brecan's Church). An early church which was much altered in late medieval times. The western portion was probably a priest's house. In the graveyard is a stone with the inscription VII ROMANI—erected to 7 Roman saints. To the west of the church is St Brecan's grave, while in the rocks above the church are the remains of an ornate cross.

xxix   Other ecclesiastical ruins near Temple Brecan.

xxx   Cross and inscribed slabs.

xxxi   Two bee-hive huts.

xxxii   A 'Castle' and a square stone fort.

Inishmaan (42)
Carrownlisheen Townland

xxxiii Kilcanonagh (Church of the Canons). A small oratory with a flat-headed doorway and an angular east window.

xxxiv Doonfarvagh or Dun Moher. A stone fort, with interior steps.

xxxv Templesaghtmacree (Church of the Seven Sons of Kings). A ruined stone church.

xxxvi A cross.

xxxvii Labbanakinneriga or The Bed of St Kinerg.

xxxviii Dermot and Gráinne's Bed. A dolmen with two standing stones carrying a capstone.

Carrowntemple Townland

xxxix Dun Conor. An oval stone fort with two additions and with steps leading to an interior platform. Originally there were two bee-hive huts outside. It has been much restored.

xl Dunbeg. A ring-fort.

Inisheer (41)

xli Creggankeel fort. A large irregular stone fort.

xlii The Grave of the Seven Daughters. Ruins of a church in an enclosure surrounded by a stone wall.

xliii Great Fort.

xliv Stone cells.

xlv Kilgobnet (St Gobnet's Church). A small oratory with a round-headed east window and an altar. It has a flat-headed doorway which narrows towards the top.

xlvi Knockgrania burial ground.

xlvii O'Brien's Castle. A low castle of irregular plan.

xlviii St Cavan's Church. Now partially covered by sand, it is a church with nave and chancel. The west and north walls of the chancel are old, but the chancel arch and the south door are later insertions. The flat-headed west doorway only gives access to a sacristy behind it. The grave of the saint lies to the north-east of the church.

JRSAI 25, 1895, 250 and 68, 1938, 196; The Aran Islands and Galway City (1969)

ARDAMULLIVAN (252) Castle

MAP 7 G 14
OS½″ 14R.44.95

Access : Through gate and across field to an enclosure. Signposted

A fine 16th century tower, built in two sections, situated among trees on a hillock. The tower has five storeys, with vaults over the ground floor and third storey, that on the ground-floor preserving well-preserved traces of the wicker-work which kept the plaster in place. The north window on the top floor bears carvings of floral motifs. The two mullioned windows in the west wall on the first and second floors as well as the fire-place on the first floor are later insertions. The castle is first mentioned in 1567 when it was claimed by Dermot 'The Swarthy' O'Shaughnessy on the death of his brother, Sir Roger. But Dermot, a protegé of Queen Elizabeth's, betrayed Dr Creagh, Archbishop of Armagh, and as a result, the local people supported the claim of Dermot's nephew, John, as owner of the castle, though William O'Shaughnessy is given as the owner of the castle in 1574. In a fight between Dermot and his nephew John in 1579 to decide the ownership of the castle, both claimants were killed.

JGAHS 1, 1900-1, 114; JRSAI 34, 1904, 213

ATHENRY Castle, Friary and Town Walls

MAP 3 G 12
OS½″ 14M.50.28

Access : Direct to castle (though it may be locked), and across old graveyard to the friary. Castle only open Monday–Friday, 8 a.m.–5 p.m. Partially signposted

Richard de Burgo granted a charter to Meiler de Bermingham in 1235, and shortly afterwards de Bermingham started building his castle at Athenry. Shortly after 1312 walls were built around the town, and the de Berminghams fought the O'Connors outside the walls in 1316. The sons of the Earl of Clanrickarde sacked the town in 1577. It was restored in 1585, but in 1596 Red Hugh O'Donnell and Tibbot MacWilliam Burke burned the town once more.

Fleming, The Town-wall Fortifications of Ireland (1914) 75

The Castle (406) *Fig. 29*

Meiler de Bermingham built the castle some time after 1235, and he had probably completed it by 1250. It consists of a three storey tower surrounded by remains of a strong outer wall. The basement of the tower has a vault carried by three pillars. The door is on the first floor, though the steps leading to it are modern; the doorway is well preserved and has capitals which are reminiscent of Irish Romanesque decoration. Three trefoil-headed windows remain on the first floor, and the high pitch of the gable is unusual in such an early castle. One of the rounded corner turrets of the enclosing wall is original, but much of the wall has been restored.

JGAHS 11, 1920-1, 1; Arch. Journ. 93, 1937, 156; Leask, Castles 36

Fig. 29. Athenry Castle, Co Galway in 1791. The castle was built in the 13th century.

Dominican Friary (164)

The Friary was founded for the Dominicans by Meiler de Bermingham, 2nd Lord of Athenry, in 1241 and dedicated to Saints Peter and Paul. The building of the church can really be described as a community effort, as a number of people joined together to build it. The refectory (now destroyed) was built by Felim O'Connor in 1265; Eugene O Heyne built the Dormitory, Cornelius O'Kelly the Chapter House, Dermot O'Treasy the Guest Room and Art MacGallyly the Infirmary. The Chapel of the Blessed Virgin Mary was built by Mac-a-Wallyd de Bermingham and completed by William Wallys who died in 1344. But practically nothing remains of the domestic buildings. What is preserved is the nave-and-chancel church, together with a north aisle and transept. The tall lancet windows in the choir belong to the original church of the 13th century, but considerable portions of the church (including the aisle arches and pillars) are the result of rebuilding in the 14th century, probably by William de Burgo and his wife, Finola, (who added 20 feet to the choir) while Joanna de Ruffur (who died in 1408) inserted a new east window. In the church there is a fine collection of tomb niches of 13th–15th century date. Chapters of the Dominican Order in Ireland were held in the Friary in 1311, 1312, 1482, 1491 and 1524. A fire gutted the building in 1423, and in the same year Pope Martin V granted indulgences to people visiting the monastery on March 17th and August 1st—and who paid towards the building and repair of the monastery. It was possibly during this rebuilding that the north transept was added. Although the Abbey escaped the Dissolution because the 'custos', Adam Copynger, agreed to adopt a secular habit, it was confiscated by order of Queen Elizabeth in 1574 and burned in the same year by John and Ulick Burke. It remained in the possession of the town of Athenry until 1627, when it was granted to Galway merchants who allowed the friars to return. The newly established prior, Dominick de Burgo, restored all the buildings, and in 1644 it was raised to the status of a university. The Cromwellians expelled the friars in 1652, and 70 years later the friary was ruined. It was used as a barracks in the 18th century. The old belfry fell sometime after 1792.
JGAHS 2, 1902, 65; JRSAI 43, 1913, 197; Leask, Churches II, 126

AUGHNANURE (470) Castle

MAP 3 E 11
OS½" 11M.15.42

Access: Along path beside stream, then over natural stone bridge. Open in summer 11 a.m.—1 p.m. and 3 p.m.—7 p.m. Admission fee charged. Key available from Thomas Walsh nearby. Signposted
A fine castle built by the O'Flaherty's around 1500. It is a six-storey tower with a good fireplace on the 3rd storey and a vault over the 4th. The roof is a good modern reconstruction. There are two corner bartizans on the 3rd floor. The castle is unusual in having two bawns. The inner one is well preserved along the riverside and has a rounded turret with a fine corbelled roof at the south-western corner. The outer bawn also has a turret at the south-western corner, and encloses the 16th century banqueting hall, most of which collapsed onto the originally underground river below (now dry because its course has been changed recently). On the interior of the windows of the banqueting hall there are some slightly stiff vine-scrolls and other decorative motifs. The castle was destroyed by Sir Edward Fitton in 1572. James I granted it to Hugh O'Flaherty in 1618, and his family held it until they were expelled towards the end of the century.
JRSAI 39, 1909, 181; Wilde's Loch Coirib (1938) 287

88   Galway

AUGHRIM (371) Two Ring-forts

MAP 4 H 12
OS½″ 15M.79.27

Access : Across fence and into fields. Not signposted
Two ringforts in neighbouring fields, each with a diameter of about 100 feet and each surrounded by a bank, about 6 feet high, outside which is a ditch. It was in the one nearest the road that the Jacobean general, St Ruth, died in battle against the Williamite forces on 12 July, 1691. The defeat brought an end to the hopes of James II, and heralded one hundred of the blackest years in Irish history.
The Irish at War (ed. Hayes-McCoy) (1964) 59

CAHERAVOLEY (369) House Site

MAP 3 F 11
OS½″ 11M.40.42

Access : Up path for 250 yards, then straight across two fields (leaving a small hazel wood on the left), through a cleared path, and finally through another hazel wood into the next field. Signposted
A roughly square enclosure surrounded by a 6-ft. high wall having, at two opposing corners, rounded bastions with arrow-slits. Remains of the gateway to the enclosure are preserved. The wall resembles castle bawns, but inside, instead of a tower, there are just the remains of one central rectangular house and a number of subsidiary rectangular buildings. Nothing is known about the history of the place, but it was possibly built by a retainer of the de Burgos as a fortified homestead.
JGAHS 24, 1950-1, 118

CASTLEKIRKE (245) Castle

MAP 3 D 11
OS½″ 11L.00.50

Access : By boat. There is no regular boat service, but boats can be hired locally
This is a rectangular castle with square turrets at each corner and with an oblong tower in the south wall; the bases of its walls slope outwards. It covers almost the whole of a small island in Lough Corrib. It was built about 1235, probably replacing an earlier castle built about 1200 by the sons of Roderick O'Connor assisted by Fitzadelm de Burgo and which was burned in 1233. The existing castle was built by Fedlim, King of Connacht but later passed to the O'Flahertys. It was destroyed in Cromwellian times.
JRSAI 27, 1897, 381; Wilde's Loch Coirib (1938) 270; JGAHS 24, 1950-1, 118

CLAREGALWAY (165) Franciscan Friary

MAP 3 F 12
OS½″ 14M.37.33

Access : Through gate and field to graveyard. Signposted
This Franciscan Friary is said to have been founded by John de Cogan in 1290 and was richly endowed by the De Feoris or de Bermingham family. But the wide lancet windows in the church suggest a building date about 50 years earlier. The ruins consist of a nave-and-chancel church and portions of the cloister. The chancel has six side-windows and has a triple sedilia of about 1300. The north aisle was added to the nave at a later stage. In 1368 Lord Athenry granted the rich lands of Cloonmoylan to the Friary. In the 15th century the lancet windows in the east wall were replaced by the present well-preserved splayed window, the tower was added, and it was probably also at this period that the north transept was built. After the Suppression, it was granted to Richard de Burgh, but the Franciscans lingered on until 1765. A primitive plough is represented on one of the tomb-stones in the church.
JRSAI 25, 1895, 287 and 31, 1901, 324; Leask, Churches II 94 and 130

CLONFERT Cathedral

MAP 4 J 12
OS½" 15M.96.21

Access : Direct to churchyard. Signposted
The original monastery was founded here by St Brendan in 563. The earliest part of the present church dates to the 12th century. Its doorway is the crowning achievement of Irish Romanesque decoration. It is in six orders, and has an amazing variety of motifs, animal heads, foliage, human heads etc. Above the doorway is a pointed hood enclosing triangles alternating with bizarre human heads, and below this is an arcade enclosing more human heads. The east windows in the chancel can be numbered among the best late Romanesque windows. The chancel arch was inserted in the 15th century, and is decorated with angels, a rosette and a mermaid carrying a mirror. The supporting arches of the tower at the west end of the church are also decorated with 15th century heads, and the innermost order of the Romanesque doorway was also inserted at this time. The sacristy is also 15th century. The church had a Romanesque south transept which is now in ruins, and a Gothic north transept which has been removed. In the Roman Catholic church one mile to the south is a 14th century wooden statue of the Madonna and Child, and on the roadside near this church is a 16th century tower house.
JRSAI 42, 1912, 1; Leask, Churches I, 137

CLONTUSKERT (512) Augustinian Abbey

MAP 4 J 12
OS½" 15M.86.26

Access : Over wall and then a quarter of a mile across a field. Signposted
Nothing remains of an early monastery founded here by St Baedán who died around 809. Some time in the 12th century the Augustinians were introduced, and the earliest surviving parts of the present church, such as certain windows near the altar, show that the church was erected in the 13th century. By the end of that century it had become one of the richest monasteries in the diocese. In the second half of the 14th century it had become corrupt, and in 1413, when the monastery consisted of a Prior and only 12 canons, it was completely burned. Shortly afterwards, 10 years indulgences were granted to all those who contributed to its repair, and most of the present building is due to this 15th century reconstruction. Unfortunately little remains of the dressed stonework except for the very fine west door erected by Matthew MacCraith, an Augustinian Canon, and Patrick O'Neachtain in 1471. The top of the door has sculptures of St Michael with scales for judging the souls, St John, St Katherine and a Bishop or Abbot (the last two standing on a serpent); the sides include a pelican giving its blood for its young, a mermaid with mirror, 2 deer with intertwined heads and a dog biting its tail. Two years after the building of this door, the Prior was accused of keeping concubines and homicides! After the Dissolution the monastery passed to the de Burgos, but the monks returned in 1637 and built a new west wall for the choir and re-roofed it. The domestic buildings, originally built in the 13th century, were re-used too, as one of the rooms served as an oven. The south wall of the nave fell in 1968.
JGAHS 22, 1946, 1

DERRYHIVENNY (283) Castle *Fig. 30*

MAP 4 J 13
OS½" 15M.87.08

Access : Up laneway for 200 yards, then across three fields. Signposted
This is a well preserved four-storey tower with good fireplaces on the three upper floors. The two- and three-mullioned windows, and the oval hole at the bottom of the stairs were probably copied from Portumna

Fig. 30. Conjectural reconstruction of Derry-hivenny Castle, Co Galway. The castle was built in 1643.

Castle nearby, which had only recently been built. The tower forms part of an L-shaped bawn with rounded turrets at opposite corners. On the corbels of the turret at the north-eastern corner of the tower is the inscription 'D : OM ME : FIERI : FECIT : 1643' which states that a man with initials D O M (probably Daniel O'Madden) built the castle in 1643. It is thus one of the few dated castles in Ireland.
JGAHS 18, 1938-9, 72; Leask, Castles 89

DRUMACOO (254) Church

MAP 3 F 13
OS½″ 14M.40.17

Access : Direct to cemetery in which church stands. Signposted
A church and well dedicated to the nun, St Surney. The original small stone church, which had a flat-headed doorway and walls built of large stones, forms the south-western portion of the present church, but the whole was expanded to its present elongated form early in the 13th century when the two east windows and the excellently carved south door were created. The north wing of the church was added around 1830. A house of hospitality is known to have been kept here, and in 1232 the death is reported of the Abbot Fachtna O'Halgaith 'who kept a house of hospitality for the learned, and for the relief of the sick and the poor.'
JRSAI 31, 1901, 231; JGAHS 3, 1903-4, 117; Leask, Churches II, 73

DRUMHARSNA (365) Castle

Access : 300 yards along good untarred road, then over stile. Not signposted
Known to have been owned by Shane Ballagh in 1574, this is a 16th century tower of five storeys, with the ground and second floor vaulted. A spiral staircase, as usual, leads to the top. The castle was damaged when it was occupied in 1920.
JGAHS 1, 1900-1, 113 and 24, 1950-1, 119

DUNMORE Castle and Friary

MAP 3 G 10
OS½" 11M.
50/51.64

Access : To castle, up laneway then through gate into field ; to church, directly beside road, but key (temporarily kept at the Garda Station in the town) is necessary. Castle signposted

The Castle (248)

The first castle was built here by de Bermingham about 1225, but it was burned by the sons of the kings of Connacht in 1249, by Fiachra O'Flynn in 1284 and by Rory O'Connor in 1315. The present castle was probably built after the last burning. It is a massive rectangular tower of four storeys situated on a motte with the remains of a fortifying wall around it. The tower is bare inside, and the mullioned windows on the top floor suggest that it was partially rebuilt and used in the late 16th or early 17th century. Although taken by Sir Henry Sidney, it remained in de Bermingham hands until the Cromwellian plantations, and was inhabited until the last century.
JGAHS 1, 1900-1, 117 and 8, 1913-4, 98

The Friary (273)

The Friary, near the centre of the town, was founded for the Augustinian Eremites by Walter de Birmingham, Lord Baron of Athenry, in 1425. Of the whole monastery, only the church remains, consisting of a nave and chancel with a tower. There is a fine and decorative 15th century west doorway. Lord Athenry saved the monastery from suppression in 1541, but in 1574 John Burke-Fitzthomas seized it. However, he was later expelled, and as late as 1641 there were still a prior and 30 friars in the community.
JGAHS 8, 1913-4, 98; Leask, Churches III, 76

FEARTAGAR (428) Jenning's Castle

MAP 3 F 11
OS½" 11M.38.58

Access : Half a mile up a lane, then over fence into field. Signposted
A well-preserved tower built by the de Burgos in the 16th or 17th century. It has four storeys, the second of which is vaulted. There are two staircases in the walls. It got its name 'Jenning's Castle' because, as tradition states, several of its owners were called Eoin, anglicised John or Jenning. The last occupant, who was a lady, was dispossessed by the Cromwellians.
JGAHS 24, 1950-1, 119

FIDDAUN (206) Castle

MAP 7 G 14
OS½" 14R.41.96

Access : Half a mile up a lane, then half a mile along a path. The key can be got from Mr Forde, whose house is near the main road, but as access from where the key is kept to the castle is rough and through bog, only those with strong shoes should attempt to visit the castle. Not signposted
This is a fine early 16th century tower standing in a bawn. The ground and third floors are vaulted, and there are mullioned windows and a fine fireplace on the 3rd floor. The six-sided bawn is one of the best preserved in the country, and the projecting angle in the west wall, constructed so as to have a wider range of fire, is probably imitated from the star-shaped forts. Nearby are the ruins of a contemporary gate-house. The castle was one of three built and owned by the O'Shaughnessy family. They are known to have lived in it in 1574, and they continued to own it until the family estates were confiscated in 1697, forcing the then owner, Colonel William O'Shaughnessy, to fly to France for safety.
JGAHS 1, 1900-1, 114 and 4, 1905-6, 79; JRSAI 34, 1904, 215

GALWAY Castle and Church

MAP 3 F 12
OS½″ 14M.
29/30.25

Access : Direct. Not signposted

The town grew up around the castle built by Richard de Burgo in the early 13th century. In 1396 it became a royal borough, and a stronghold of the English Crown. It became a wealthy trading centre ruled by the fourteen 'tribes' of Galway including the Joyces and the Lynchs. The town was burned in 1473, surrendered to the Cromwellians in 1652 and suffered heavily in the Williamite wars.

St Nicholas Church

Access : Open weekdays 10 a.m.–1 p.m. and 2.30–6.30 p.m. Tuesdays, Wednesdays and Thursdays in June–August 7.30–9 p.m.

In Market Street is the Church of Ireland church of St Nicholas of Myra, standing on the site of an earlier church (remains of which can be seen in the south wall of the chancel), and preserving much of the medieval parish church. The vicarage was re-organized by Pope Urban VI in 1385 and changed into a collegiate church in 1484. It became Protestant in 1568, was mutilated by the Cromwellians and has been unfortunately altered in more recent times. The south aisle was enlarged to its present size between 1486 and 1535, and in 1561 the south transept was lengthened. The tower was added around 1500. The north aisle was enlarged to its present size between 1538 and 1583, while the Blessed Sacrament Chapel dates to about 1538. The 15th century west doorway and the 16th century south doorway are both insertions. There is a fine 16th century Joyce wall-tomb in the south transept and a fine 15th century reader's desk re-erected near the entrance to the Blessed Sacrament chapel, as well as a number of interesting grave-slabs on the floor. In a wall to the north of the church is a plaque alleging to mark the spot where Mayor Lynch hanged his son Walter in 1493.

JGAHS 17, 1936, 1

Lynch's Castle

At the junction of Shop Street and Upper Abbeygate Street is Lynch's Castle, a 16th century castle which was heavily altered in 1966 when it was converted into the Munster and Leinster Bank. The exterior preserves some of the few remaining Irish gargoyles as well as the arms of Henry VII, the Lynch family and the Fitzgeralds of Kildare. The stonework of the windows is of good quality. In the ground floor, historical material dealing with the castle is displayed. A doorway and first floor window of one of the many fine 16th and 17th century houses which adorned the city has been re-erected in isolation on the north side of Eyre Square. It belonged to a house of the Browne family which formerly stood in Lower Abbeygate Street. The so-called Spanish Arch, in the south-western portion of the old town, was one of the gates in the old city wall and a new museum is to be opened beside it shortly.

The Aran Islands and Galway City (1969)

GLINSK (439) Castle

MAP 4 H 10
OS½″ 12M.71.67

Access : Over stile into field. Key to be obtained from Mr Timothy Pettit in the two-storey house on the hill beside the castle. Signposted

A four-storey castle, roughly rectangular in plan, with two projecting

towers of the south side with turrets. The mullioned windows are well preserved, and the chimneys are some of the finest of their type in Ireland. The castle had a roof of two parallel gables, but the interior is gutted. It was built by the Burkes, possibly around 1630.
JGAHS 24, 1950-1, 120; Leask, Castles 131

HIGH ISLAND (52) Early Monastery

MAP 3 B 11
OS½" 10L.50.57

Access : By boat. There is no regular boat service. For transport apply to Miss Eileen O'Malley, O'Malley's Bar, Cleggan
The monastery was probably founded by St Feichín of Fore who died in 664. St Gormgall 'Chief Confessor of Ireland' died and was buried here in 1017. One of the important manuscripts of the Life of St Feichín was written on the island. The most important ruin is a rectangular church, with a flat-headed doorway. The doorway may not be original as the lintel of the door is an old grave-slab. The east end of the church is destroyed. Around the church are the remains of bee-hive huts, and a number of grave-slabs decorated with crosses. The wall which surrounded the old monastery is still preserved. The island is no longer inhabited.
JRSAI 26, 1896, 197

INCHAGOILL (412) Early Monastery

MAP 3 E 11
OS½" 11M.13.49

Access : By boat. There is no regular boat service to the island. To hire a private boat, apply to hotel owners in Oughterard
Little or nothing is known of the history of the monastery; its name signifies 'Island of the Foreigners'. Two churches remain. St Patrick's was originally a simple rectangular church, with a flat-headed doorway, but a chancel was later added to it. Linked to it by an old roadway is The Saint's Church, which is a Romanesque nave-and-chancel church restored in the last century by Sir Benjamin Guinness. Its main feature is the fine Romanesque west doorway with heads on the capitals and on the outer order of the arches. It has a simple rounded chancel arch and a small round-headed east window. There is an early cross-slab in the south-western corner of the nave. Not far from the church is a pillar with an inscription LIE LUGUAEDON MACCI MENUEH (The stone of Luguaedon son of Menueh), which may be a transliteration of an older Ogham inscription.
JRSAI 27, 1897, 381 and 31, 1901, 236

ISERT KELLY (272) Castle

MAP 4 G 13
OS½" 14M.52.12

Access : Down an untarred road and over a wall into field. Signposted
A fine mid-16th century tower house. The first floor is vaulted and has a fireplace. The second floor had a fine room with arcades, and a very good fireplace, inserted in 1604, with a Latin inscription asking that the builder (whose initials were W. H.) be preserved from all evil. The stairs leading to this floor is very twisty. The tower stands at the corner of a bawn, foundations of which remain. The castle was built by the MacHubert Burkes, and re-built by MacRedmond Burke about 1617.
JGAHS 4, 1905-6, 3 and 24, 1950-1, 120; Leask, Castles 94

KILBENNAN (48) Church and Round Tower

MAP 3 G 11
OS½" 11M.41.55

Access : Direct to graveyard. Signposted
The old monastery was founded by St Benen or Benignus, St Patrick's successor at Armagh, and the land for it was given by the local chieftain, Lugaid, who had been baptized by St Patrick. It was burned in 1114.

There are portions of a Round Tower with a round-headed doorway. The Franciscans founded a monastery here in 1428 and built the existing church which has a partly blocked-up trefoil-headed east window, but little else of interest. A fragment of a Romanesque doorway indicates the former existence of a Romanesque church on the site.
JRSAI 31, 1901, 379

KILCONNELL (47) Franciscan Friary

MAP 4 H 12
OS½″ 15M.73.32

Access : Along path from village, through stile and field. Get key beforehand from Miss Lyons in the middle of three cottages opposite the Catholic church in the village. Signposted

William O'Kelly, Lord of Hy Many, founded this new friary for the Franciscans in 1353 on the site of an older monastery founded by St Conall in the sixth century. The buildings consist of a church with nave, choir, south transept and aisle, and some domestic buildings. The nave is entered by a finely moulded west doorway with a 15th century window above it. The other windows also appear to be of 15th century date. The north wall of the church has two fine tomb-niches. That near the west door has well carved figures of Saints Johanes (John), Lodovic (Louis), Maria, another John, Jacoib (James) and Dinois (Denis); the names Louis and Denis suggest French influence. It is not known to whom this tomb belonged, as the inscription has worn away. The other fine tomb is that of the O'Daly's in the choir. Tradition says that the daughter of the founder built the tower and the main part of the church; certainly the tower was added later. The sacristy to the north of the choir was also added later. There are remains of a simple cloister with a wide variety of mason's marks, as well as conventual buildings with the refectory in the north-west corner. The friars adopted the Observantine rule of the order in 1460, and the friary was suppressed in 1541. In 1595 it was granted to Ludovick Briskett, but his grant lapsed because he did not pay his rent. The Catholics repaired the church in 1604. In 1614 James I granted it to a man named Callthorp, and two years later there were 6 friars left. It was besieged but not taken by the Cromwellians in 1650. Tradition says that the friars were finally expelled only a few weeks before the Battle of Aughrim in 1691.
JGAHS 1, 1900-1, 145; 2, 1902, 3; 3, 1903-4, 11; 21, 1945, 184; Leask, Churches III, 167

KILLURSA (231) Church

MAP 3 F 11
OS½″ 11M.24.47

Access : Direct to graveyard in which church stands. Key obtainable from John Coen who lives nearby

The church stands on the site of an old monastery founded by St Fursey in the 7th century. The south-western end of the church incorporates an early (10th century?) church with a flat-headed doorway. In the 15th century the church was expanded to its present size with the addition of an attractive east window.
JRSAI 10, 1868, 134

KILMACDUAGH (51) Churches and Round Tower *Fig. 31*

MAP 3 G 13
OS½″ 14M.40.00

Access: Over stile. Key of Cathedral obtainable from Coleman Finegan, Kilmacduagh. Signposted.

The monastery was founded early in the 7th century by St Colman son of Duagh, a member of one of the local royal families. It has one of the finest collections of churches in Ireland. The most conspicuous feature is the excellently preserved Round Tower which shares a lean with its more famous counterpart at Pisa. Beside it is the Cathedral, of which the west gable, with its blocked-up flat-headed doorway (11th–12th century?), is the earliest part. The rest of the nave dates largely to about 1200. In the 15th century a fine doorway with the head of a bishop above it was inserted in the south wall, and it was probably then that the west doorway was blocked up. Probably at the same period the two transepts were added, the west window inserted, and the chancel was possibly also rebuilt. Note the folk-art Crucifixions in the north transept, which were removed from the south transept after 1765. Not far away, in a field to the north, is St John's Church, a small (12th century?) church with rounded and pointed windows; a chancel was added to it later. Further north is 'Glebe House'— a two-storey house of military appearance (possibly the Abbot's house)— built in the 13th century, though altered later. In a field to the north-west is O'Heyne's Church, built in the first half of the 13th century with a beautiful chancel arch supported by pillars with animal and floral decoration, and also with two excellently carved east windows. When the north wall of the church collapsed, probably in the 14th or 15th century, a new wall was built inside it, incorporating the original north doorway, and much of the west wall was built at the same time. Beside this church are

Fig. 31. Plan of the monastery at Kilmacduagh, Co Galway.

the remains of another of uncertain date, but with a 15th century window above the door. East of the Cathedral, and on the other side of the road, is St Mary's church with a round-headed east window, built around 1200. The south doorway seems to have been inserted in its present position in the 15th century. The churches were much plundered early in the 13th century. After the Reformation, the monastery passed to Richard, 2nd Earl of Clanrickarde.
JRSAI 34, 1904, 220

KILTARTAN or BALLINAMANTAIN (259) Castle

MAP 3 G 13
OS½" 14M.46.05

Access : Across 2 fields and stone walls. Not signposted
The ruins of a 13th century castle built by the De Burgos. The tower, which is three storeys high and has very thick walls, stands at the corner of a roughly square enclosure surrounded by a wall. The entrance to this enclosure is flanked by two massive semi-circular turrets. The castle is now in a rather ruinous condition.
JGAHS 4, 1905-6, 4

KILTIERNAN (446) Church

MAP 3 G 13
OS½" 14M.44.16

Access : Across wall into field. Not signposted
An early stone church with flat-headed doorway, and a chancel which was added later. It is surrounded by the remains of a stone wall.
JRSAI 49, 1919, 178 and 81, 1951, 73; Leask, Churches I, 67

KNOCKMOY (166 and 278) Cistercian Abbey *Fig. 32*

MAP 3 G 11
OS½" 11M.51.44

Access : 200 yards up lane, then across two fields. Signposted
An Abbey dedicated to the Blessed Virgin Mary, and founded for the Cistercians from Boyle in 1189-90 by Cathal Crovdearg O'Connor, King of Connacht. The church has a nave, chancel and a transept with two chapels. The nave is simple and austere, with little ornament except at the top of the pillars. In contrast, the rib-vaulted chancel has beautifully carved stonework with fine capitals and east windows. It has a 13th century tomb-niche. On the north wall of the chancel is one of the few remaining medieval frescoes in Ireland. The bottom of the picture shows an angel with scales (now almost invisible), Christ with his hand raised in blessing, and the martyrdom of St Sebastian. Above is a scene from the medieval morality legend of the Three Dead Kings and the Three Live Kings. Under the Dead Kings was the inscription 'We have been as you are, you shall be as we are', while the Live Kings seem to be part of a hawking scene. It was commissioned probably around 1400 by Malachie O'Nollan and Conaire O'Eddichan. Except for the black outlines, none of the original colours remains. The central tower of the church, now partly fallen, was probably inserted in the 15th century. The east wing of the domestic building is well preserved, although the effect of the excellently carved windows of the Chapter House was ruined when the room was divided into three parts in the 14th or 15th century. Practically nothing remains of the cloister, but parts of the refectory on the south side of the domestic buildings can still be seen. The monastery was plundered in 1200 and again in 1228. In 1240 the Abbot was censured for having had his hair washed by a woman! After the Dissolution, the Abbey passed to Hugh O'Kelly and various others, and in 1662 was granted to Valentine Blake, and remained in the hands of his descendants until the last century.
JRSAI 34, 1904, 239 and 49, 1919, 25; Leask, Churches II, 37

LOUGHREA Carmelite Priory

MAP 4 H 13
OS½" 14M.62.17

Access : Direct. Key at nearby monastic house on the far side of the modern church. Not signposted

Founded probably in the 13th century for the Carmelites by Richard de Burgo. The church consists of a nave, chancel, tower, south transept and a small south chapel near the west end of the nave. The chancel (not accessible) has a number of 13th century lancet windows in the south wall, and a 15th century window in the east wall. Much of the nave, which has been over-heavily pointed on the outside, seems to be 15th century work. The tower was added in the 15th century; its base is now a tasteless grotto. In the Catholic Cathedral not far away, there is a beautiful collection of 20th century stained glass windows.

MEELICK Franciscan Friary

MAP 4 J 13
OS½" 15M.94.14

Access : Direct. Not signposted

This 15th century Franciscan friary, situated on a hill overlooking the River Shannon, is one of the few medieval churches in Ireland still used by the Catholic church. Of the original church there remain the walls, the west doorway and, in the south wall, two aisle arches (with a figure of St Francis inserted later between them) and another beside the altar which led to a now no longer existing south transept. The east window is a modern insertion, but the west window probably dates to a partial reconstruction in the 17th century, when a door to the sacristy was inserted. Parts of the east and west portions of the domestic buildings still stand.

Fig. 32. The Three Dead Kings and the Three Live Kings, and other scenes from a 15th century fresco at Knockmoy Abbey, Co Galway.

MOANMORE EAST (498) 'The Seven Monuments'

MAP 4 H 13
OS½" 15M.65.15

Access : Direct. Not signposted
A stone circle of seven stones, with a heap of stones in the middle. While the stone circle may possibly be old, the heap of stones is probably a 19th century folly, as is also a box-like structure nearby. Excavations produced only negative results.
JRSAI 44, 1914, 352 and 45, 1915, 310; PRIA 33, 1917, 505

PALLAS (462) Castle

MAP 4 H 13
OS½" 15M.76.08

Access : Half a mile up untarred laneway into backyard of house. Signposted
Possibly the best preserved tower-house in a county which has many well-preserved examples. The tower is 5 storeys high, with the third storey vaulted. Besides having a guard's room, and a 'dog's hole', the ground floor has an oven which was added later. There are a number of good fireplaces preserved on the various floors, with a head on that of the first floor. The fourth floor has attractive mullioned windows framed in arches. The tower is surrounded by an extremely well-preserved bawn, which was entered by a two-storey gate-house. The bawn has two towers with turrets at each corner, and has internal steps and parapets. On the west side of the bawn is a house which was built as part of the bawn, and which had its own entrance through the bawn wall. Some buildings in the south-west corner probably date from the 19th century. The castle was built by the Burkes, possibly around 1500. In 1574 it was in the hands of Jonyck FitzThomas Burke, but after the Restoration it passed to the Nugent family, Lords of Westmeath.
JGAHS 1, 1900-1, 21 and 111; 5, 1907-8, 213

PEARSE'S COTTAGE, Rosmuck (431)

MAP 3 D 12
OS½" 14L.92.34

Access : Across stile into garden. Normally open during the summer, but if closed, key is obtainable at house on main road, 100 yards west of the turn off to the cottage. Signposted
A three-roomed cottage which the patriot Padraig Pearse (1879-1916) used as his summer residence. There are bedrooms on either side of the living room which has a fireplace, cooking and eating utensils as well as a spinning wheel. The west bedroom also served as a study. The items on display are replicas of those used in Pearse's time.

PORTUMNA Friary and Castle

MAP 4 J 13
OS½" 15M.85.04

Access : Along lane in Forestry property to friary, and from there along a small path to castle. Signposted
Dominican Friary (461)
For a long time the Cistercians of Dunbrody had a chapel here dedicated to Saints Peter and Paul, but when it was abandoned by them, O'Madden, the local chieftain, gave it to the Dominicans who, with the consent of the Cistercians, erected a friary and a church which they dedicated to the Blessed Virgin. Pope Martin V granted a Bull to confirm their possessions in 1426. The remains consist of a church with nave, chancel and transepts, a cloister and domestic buildings. The two easternmost narrow and pointed windows in the north and south walls seem to be the oldest part of the building; they date to the thirteenth century and were presumably part of the original Cistercian church. The rest of the church was built by the Dominicans in the 15th century. The finest feature is the four-light east window, but the ornate window in the south transept is also of

good quality. In the sacristy to the north of the chancel is an unusual
quatrefoil window; note also the head upside down at the bottom of the
doorway. Little remains of the original cloister, which was partially
re-erected in 1954. Parts of the domestic buildings remain; there is a
refectory at the north-western end.
Leask, Churches III, 185

Castle (515)

This is the tragic shell of a Jacobean mansion built in 1618. It is a large
rectangular fortified house with square towers at the corners. There is a
fine Renaissance-style doorway in the first floor on the south side, with
gun-holes on one side. There are some good two- and three-mullioned
windows. To the north is the garden, and the ruined remains of the Adam
entrance gate. The castle has a fine view overlooking Lough Derg. It was
lived in until fairly recently, but is at present under repair.
JGAHS 6, 1909-10, 107; Waterman, in Studies in Building History, ed.
Jope (1961) 257

RATHSONNY and RAHANNAGROAGH (499) Ringforts

MAP 4 H 13
OS½" 15M.66.15

Access: Through gate into field. Not signposted
Rathsonny is a big ringfort, 288 feet in diameter, surrounded by a ditch
and two banks, and with a souterrain in the interior. Rahannagroagh is a
simple ringfort surrounded by a ditch and bank.
JGAHS 10, 1917-8, 82; JRSAI 49, 1919, 184

ROSCAM (46) Church and Round Tower

MAP 3 F 12
OS½" 14M.34.24

Access: Half a mile along laneway, then across 3 fields. Not signposted
An old monastic site associated with St Patrick. There are remains of a
Round Tower, which may never have been finished. It has a square-headed
doorway, and the holes used for scaffolding on it were never blocked up.
Nearby is a 15th century (?) parish church of little interest. The semi-
circular wall surrounding the buildings obviously incorporates the old
monastic cashel or surrounding wall. East of the church, and about 100
yards from the sea, there is a passage inside the wall which has an unusual
pointed roof.
JRSAI 25, 1895, 284

ROSS ERRILLY (50) Franciscan Friary *Fig. 33*

MAP 3 F 11
OS½" 11M.25.48

*Access: Direct. Get key beforehand from Mr Kyne who lives in the second
last house on the left before reaching the monastery. Signposted*
The Friary was founded around 1351 by Sir Raymond de Burgo for
the Franciscans. It is the most extensive and best preserved of the
Franciscan friaries in Ireland. Although founded in the 14th century,
most of the building dates from the late 15th century. The church consists
of a nave and chancel, and has a double south transept with a later chapel
added to it. The church windows, which are all well preserved, present
a good cross-section of the types of window used in the late 15th century.
The tower was added in 1498. There are two sets of cloisters to the north
of the church, one of which has a cloister arcade. In the north-west corner
of these domestic buildings is the kitchen, with a water-tank for holding
fish, and also an oven extending into the mill-room beyond. It is not
easy to know what the many other rooms were used for. In 1470 the
friars changed over to the Strict Observance. The community remained on

intermittently in the friary until as late as 1753, although they no longer legally owned the buildings. It was granted to the Clanricardes, who made two efforts to restore it to the monks. An important Chapter of the order took place in the friary in 1647. The Cromwellians took the buildings in 1656, but had to relinquish it to the friars again eight years later.
JRSAI 31, 1901, 334; Leask, Churches III, 108 and 149

ST CUAN'S WELL (467)

MAP 4 H 11
OS½″ 15M.79.41

Access : 100 yards down path and then right into field. The well is in the middle of the field. Partially signposted
A small insignificant well which is not worth a visit, and which is scarcely worthy to be a National Monument. Stones in the wall surrounding the well include a 17th century gravestone with the Instruments of the Passion. The whole is surrounded by a ditch.

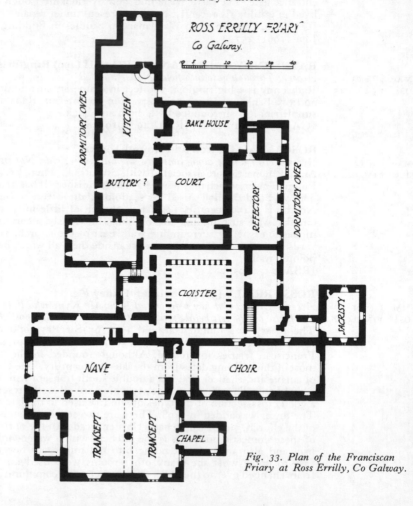

Fig. 33. Plan of the Franciscan Friary at Ross Errilly, Co Galway.

ST MACDARA'S ISLAND (242) Church etc *Fig. 34*

MAP 3 C 12
OS½″ 10L.72.30

Access: By boat. For transport to the island, apply 24 hours in advance to Mr Micheál Ó Moráin, Carna

The church on the eastern shore of this 60 acre island is on the site of a monastery founded by a sixth century saint named Mac Dara, or son of the fox. The saint's festival is on the 16th July and 28th September, and on these days pilgrims used come to the island from the mainland. The saint was venerated so much by sailors that they lowered their sails in his honour when they passed the island. The church is a small rectangular structure built of very large stones. It has a flat-headed doorway and a round-headed east window. The most unusual feature of this church is that the antae continue right up the gable and meet at the top, thus suggesting that this is a feature copied from wooden churches. Parts of the original stone roof still remain. To the east of the church is the Saint's Bed. Nearby was found a stone finial decorated with a head and geometric motifs; it probably originally adorned the top of one of the gables of the church. There are also remains of several pilgrimage 'stations' with Early Christian decorated slabs.

JRSAI 26, 1896, 101; Leask, Churches I, 29 and 46

THOOR BALLYLEE

MAP 3 G 13
OS½″ 14M.48.06

Access: Direct. Open daily May 1st to October 15th. Admission fee charged.

A four-storey tower of the 16th century, beautifully situated beside a stream. Its main interest lies in the fact that it and the adjoining cottage were repaired and lived in by the poet W.B. Yeats in the 1920's. A tablet in the wall commemorates this in the following lines:

'I, the poet William Yeats
With old mill boards and sea-green slates
and smithy work from the Gort forge
Restored this tower for my wife George;
and may these characters remain
when all is ruin once again.'

All was ruin once again shortly after Yeats left it in 1929, but in 1965 it was restored as a Yeats museum, and now contains an interesting collection of first editions of the poet's works. He wrote his volume *The Tower* here, and his poem 'Meditations in Time of Civil War' (1923) describes the tower and the life around it.

Thoor Ballylee (1965)

TUAM Cathedral and High Cross

MAP 3 G 11
OS½″ 11M.44.52

Access: Direct. Open daily 10 a.m.–5 p.m.

The Cathedral

A monastery was founded here by St Jarlath in the late 5th or early 6th century. In the 12th century a Romanesque nave and chancel church was built. Fire destroyed the nave in 1767, but the barrel-vaulted chancel is incorporated in the present Cathedral. It was added to in 1312, and for almost a century served as a porch. Its outstanding features are the chancel arch of six orders showing Scandinavian influence in its ornamentation, and a very fine east window. The Cathedral is a 19th century building. In the aisle of the south nave is the shaft of a 12th century High Cross with interlacing and other ornament; it bears an inscription in Irish which being translated reads 'A prayer for the King, Turloch O'Conor.

A prayer for the craftsman Giolla-Críost O'Toole' and another 'A prayer for the successor of Jarlath, Aedh O Hession, for whom this cross was made'. To the north-west of the Cathedral are the remains of Temple Jarlath with an east window of c. 1200.
Leask, Churches I, 153 and II, 131

'Market Cross' (505)

This 12th century cross stands in the centre of the town, surrounded by a railing. It is made up of a number of pieces which did not necessarily belong together originally. The base, which has figures (one of an abbot or bishop) on two sides bears the inscription (repeated on the modern base) 'A prayer for Turloch O'Connor and for . . . O Hession by whom it was made'. The shaft has interlacing panels with beasts in the Scandinavian style; there is a Crucifixion on one face of the head, and an abbot or bishop surrounded by figures on the other, while there are unidentified figures on the ends of the arms.
Henry, Irish High Crosses (1964) 34

TUROE (327) Stone with Celtic decoration *Fig. 5*

MAP 4 H 12
OS½" 14M.62.23

Access: 300 yards up untarred road, then right into field beside house
This stone, about three feet high, was removed here from its original position beside the Rath of Feerwore some miles away. The lowest portion has no decoration; in the middle is a Greek step-pattern. The top half of the stone is covered in a profusion of curvilinear ornament in relief which is typical of the Celtic art style known as La Tène. It is the finest example in Europe of a series of presumably ritual stones decorated with Celtic ornament, some other examples of which have also been found in Ireland (see Castlestrange, Co Roscommon). The fort beside which the stone originally stood was dated through excavation to the last pre-Christian centuries, and the stone probably belongs to the same period.
PRIA 24, 1903, 260; JRSAI 74, 1944, 23

Fig. 34. Temple Macdara, St Macdara's Island, Co Galway. Early Christian period.

Fig. 5. Stone from Turoe, Co Galway, decorated with Celtic curvilinear designs. 3rd-2nd century B.C. (?).

AGHADOE (53) Church and Round Tower

MAP 6 D 19
OS½″ 21V.93.93

Access : Over stile into graveyard. Signposted

An old monastery was founded here by St Finian the Leper in the 7th century. It is referred to as existing in 992, and a stone church here is mentioned in 1044. The site became part of the diocese of Ardfert and Aghadoe in the late 12th century. The western part of the church is the oldest. It was finished in 1158 by Auliff Mor na Cuimsionach, a member of the O'Donoghue family, who was buried here in 1166. It has a Romanesque west doorway, with the innermost order plain, and the two outer ones bearing Romanesque decoration. The east window, with a head and a flower at the intersection, was inserted in the 13th century. The eastern part of the church was added at about the same period; a part of the eastern portion may have served as living quarters at some stage. On top of the south wall is an Ogham stone bearing the inscription BRRUANANN. The nearby Round Tower has been much altered, but it still stands to a height of about 22 feet.

JRSAI 2, 1852, 242 and 22, 1892, 163; Dunraven, Irish Architecture II (1877) 35; Macalister, Corpus (1945) 237

Parkavoncar Castle (236)

In a field to the south-west of the church is a round castle dating from the 13th century. The two storeys which remain are joined by a staircase within the wall, and the first floor has the remains of a fireplace. It stands in the middle of a roughly square enclosure surrounded by a wall and moat. Nothing is known of its history, though it is traditionally known as 'The Bishop's Chair or Pulpit'.

JRSAI 22, 1892, 166; Kerry Arch. Mag. 1, 1908, 150

ANNAGH (56) Church

MAP 6 D 18
OS½″ 21Q.80.12

Access : 200 yards up lane and through stile into cemetery. Signposted

A medieval parish church (15th century?) with doorways in the north and south walls. A plaque with a damaged representation of a rather ghoulish horseman on it has been inserted into the inside wall beside the south doorway.

JRSAI 2, 1852, 247

ARDCANNAGHT (430) Ogham Stones

MAP 6 D 18
OS½″ 21Q.82.03

Access : Half a mile up laneway, then through gate into field ahead. Signposted

One large standing stone and two fragmentary Ogham stones bearing the slightly dubious inscriptions V MAQI and LMCDV.

Macalister, Corpus I, 251, No. 246

ARDFERT Cathedral, Churches and Friary

MAP 6 C 17
OS½″ 21Q.
78/79.21

Cathedral signposted

Cathedral and churches (54)

Access : Direct to graveyard

An extraordinarily interesting group of churches. The Cathedral goes back to the 12th century, and its oldest parts are the Romanesque doorway and blind arcade on the west wall as well as some masonry under the two windows in the north wall. The two small square niches in the north-eastern corner of the church may also be Romanesque. In the middle of the 13th

century the nave-and-chancel church took its present shape, with its characteristic triple lancet window in the east wall and the nine slender windows in the south wall. In a niche in the north-west corner is the effigy of a bishop, said to be that of Bishop Stack who died in 1488. The remains of a triple sedilia can be seen in the south wall. To the north-west of the cathedral is Temple na Hoe, a remarkable Romanesque nave-and-chancel church; its chancel has long since vanished. Unusual features include the columns at the external corners and the floral decoration on the interior of the south window. To the north-west of it lies Temple na Griffin, a 15th century church named after the griffins sculpted inside it. A Round Tower which stood opposite the west doorway of the Cathedral has now vanished.
Leask, Churches I, 124 and 155; II, 111

Franciscan Friary (358)
Access : 300 yards down a lane, then into a field.
Founded probably by Thomas FitzMaurice around 1253 for the Franciscans of the Conventual Rule, though the Observantine Rule was adopted in 1518. The 13th century church had a single aisle, with 9 lancet windows in the south wall of the aisle and another five in the east wall. The round pillars of the nave are also 13th century. The aisle was built possibly in the 14th century. In the 15th century a south transept was added, which has a fine south window, and tomb-niches and a tower at the western end were also inserted in the chancel at the same time. Also dating from the 15th century are the cloisters, two sides of which are preserved. The cloisters were roofed with stone 'tiles' which channelled the water ingeniously into the grassy area in the centre of the cloister. The tower was turned into a barracks in Elizabethan times, but was later taken over by the Protestant Bishop who probably once more used the chancel for religious service.
JRSAI 25, 1895, 30; Leask, Churches II, 113 and III, 148

BALLINSKELLIGS (168) Augustinian Monastery
MAP 6 B 20
OS½″ 20V.
43.65 (inset)
Access : Half a mile up an untarred road to cemetery in which ruins stand. Signposted
This monastery was founded for monks who came to the mainland here from the off-shore island of Skellig Michael and who probably adopted the Augustinian rule when they transferred here in the 12th or 13th century. As with their former monastery, the monastery was dedicated to St Michael. The buildings have been partially eroded by the sea. The two remaining churches seem to date however from the 15th century, and have windows and a door with dressed stones. Adjoining one of the churches is a 15th century cloister-garth with a large hall on the other side of it. After the Suppression of the monasteries, it came into the possession of the Hardings and later of the Sigersons.
JRSAI 32, 1902, 344

BALLYMALIS (364) Castle
MAP 6 D 19
OS½″ 20V.84.94
Access: Half a mile up untarred road and then 150 yards through field. Not signposted
A 16th century rectangular tower of 4 storeys and an attic in the gable. Tradition says that it was built by the O'Moriarty's, but it was probably really built by the Ferrises. The third floor has fine triple-mullioned

windows on the north and south sides; that on the north side having representations of doves on the outside. There are two bartizans on opposite corners of the tower which have holes for muskets; that on the south-western corner has rams heads or bunches of flowers (whichever you like!) on the corbel-stones supporting it. Note the geometrical design on the doorway between the spiral staircase and the fourth storey room. The tower was confiscated in 1677 and granted to Sir Francis Brewster, from whom it passed to Alexander Eager. It is beautifully situated on a peaceful stretch of the River Laune, with a good view of Carrantuohill—Ireland's highest mountain.

Kerry Arch. Mag. 1, 1908, 150; Leask, Castles 105

BEENBANE (380 and 492) Fort and Bee-hive Huts

MAP 6 B 20
OS½" 24V.51.66

Access : Half a mile down a lane almost down to the shore of Lough Currane. Not signposted

A stone fort shaped practically like a horse-shoe. It opens on to, and is delightfully situated beside Lough Currane. Inside is a shallow souterrain. In a field to the right of the path before reaching the fort are the ruins of a massive bee-hive hut with walls seven feet thick and with large stones on the bottom.

PRIA 58, 1956-7, 132

BEGINISH (500) Stone House

MAP 6 B 20
OS½" 20V.42.78

Access : Can be reached on foot at low tide from Church Island, otherwise by boat

A small circular house near the east end of the island. A shed was built on to it later. Originally roofed probably by thatch supported by beams resting in holes high up in the wall, the house had been sunk into the ground and was reached apparently by a ramp. The innermost stone over the door bore one of the few known Runic or Viking inscription in Ireland (now removed to the Museum, University College, Cork) which in translation reads 'Lir erected this stone; M . . . carved [the] Runes'. As the inscription is dated to the 11th century, the house must have been built some time after the original erection of the stone on another site. The inhabitants probably practised stock-breeding, while earlier inhabitants of the island, who used ground-level round huts and who built field-walls and small animal shelters, probably practised tillage.

PRIA 57, 1956, 159; Johsen, Stuttruner, Vikingtidens Innskrifter (1968) 220

CAHERGALL (227) Stone Fort

MAP 6 B 19
OS½" 20V.45.81

Access : Across two fields. Signposted

A large stone fort with stairs on the inside walls, as at Staigue fort (see below). Inside there are two buildings built in dry stone walling. One is a bee-hive hut and the other is a rectangular house built against the ramparts. A few hundred yards away is Leacanabuaile stone fort (see below).

Kerry Arch Mag 2, 1912-4, 155 and 3, 1914-16, 49; PRIA 58, 1956-7, 62

CALLANAFERSY (238) Fort

MAP 6 C 19
OS½" 20V.78.99

Access : A quarter of a mile up a lane, then through gate into field. Not signposted

A ringfort with a wall and ditch, and two souterrains inside. It is nicely situated overlooking the estuary of the River Laune.

Fig. 7. Conjectural reconstruction of the Early Christian monastery on Church Island, Valentia, Co Kerry.

CARRIGAFOYLE (349) Castle

MAP 6 D 16
OS½″ 17Q.99.48

Access: Along a path which is liable to be submerged at very high tides. Signposted

A 15th or 16th century castle built by O'Conor Kerry, and beautifully situated on an inlet of the sea. It is a five storey castle with the 2nd and 4th storeys vaulted. It is built of small stones beautifully layered. A spiral staircase leads up to the battlements. Originally the castle formed an island, and was fortified by a square bawn with rounded turrets, and outside that again on the land side was another bawn with square towers at the corners. The area between the bawns was used as a dock for boats. Parts of the inner bawn with the rounded turrets remain; one of these turrets seems to have been used as a dove-cot. The castle was besieged and taken in 1580 by Sir William Pelham who levelled the western portion of the castle with his cannon. It was later taken by O'Conor Kerry but it had to surrender again to Sir George Carew in 1600, when it was granted to Sir Charles Wilmot.
JRSAI 9, 1867, 202; Leask, Castles 121

CHURCH ISLAND Valentia (59) Church *Fig. 7*

MAP 6 B 20
OS½″ 20V.43.79

Access: No regular boat service. To arrange a trip leaving from Cahirciveen Pier contact Mr C O'Driscoll, c/o Court House and Library, Cahirciveen.
A small monastic settlement on a small island off Beginish Island in Valentia Harbour. Nothing is known of its history. Originally the monastery consisted of a small wooden oratory and a round hut of which nothing remains. These were later replaced by the existing long rectangular stone corbel-vaulted oratory, a rounded stone hut probably roofed with straw, as well as a square house near the edge of the island. The wall surrounding the monastery is a later addition. A stone with an inscribed cross, to which an Ogham inscription was later added, was found during the course of excavations. The excavator suggested that the church was built about 750 A.D., but it could have been built much later.
JCHAS 59, 1954, 101; PRIA 59 C, 1958, 57

CHUTE HALL (295) Ogham Stones

MAP 6 D 18
OS½″ 20Q.88.15

Access: Quarter of a mile up an untarred avenue to the stones which are in a field opposite a cottage on the left of the avenue. Signposted
Two Ogham stones which were removed from Ballinrannig near Smerwick Harbour in the last century and presented by Lord Ventry to his nephew Richard Chute of Chute Hall. The inscriptions read LUBBAIS MAQQI DUN....S (L. son of D.) and CCICAMINI MAQQI CATTINI (C. son of C.). It is possible that the stones will be moved to Ardfert shortly.
Macalister, Corpus I, 147, Nos 152-3

CLOGHANECARHAN (228) Fort and Ogham Stone

MAP 6 B 20
OS½″ 20V.49.72

Access : Through gate into field. Not signposted

A ringfort with a clay wall four feet high and lined with stones. Near the south side are the foundations of a bee-hive hut. The original entrance was probably on the west, and five stones still stand outside. Inside is an Ogham stone with the inscription D..... A..... AVI DALAGNI later superseded by EQQEGGNI MAQI MAQI-CARRATTINN.
JRSAI 39, 1909, 164; Macalister, Corpus I 224, No. 230

DERRYNANE (346) Ogham Stone

MAP 6 B 21
OS½″ 24V.54.59

Access : Beside road. Not signposted

An Ogham stone found below the waterline and re-erected in its present position. The inscription reads ANM LLATIGNI MAQ M..N..RC M...Q...CI. Nearby is Derrynane Abbey—home of 'The Liberator', Daniel O'Connell.
Macalister, Corpus I 214, No. 220

THE DINGLE PENINSULA *Fig. 35*

MAP 6 A-C 18-19
OS½″ 20.
See map, Fig. 35

The western end of the Dingle Peninsula, and its off-shore islands, preserve a great many ancient monuments, most of which are in state care. They include some fine Iron Age fortifications such as Dunmore and Dunbeg; bee-hive huts (of various dates) used probably for secular purposes and forming settlements such as those near Glenfahan; Early Christian monuments such as monastic sites, cross-inscribed pillars, and

Fig. 35. Map of the National Monuments in the Dingle Peninsula, Co Kerry.

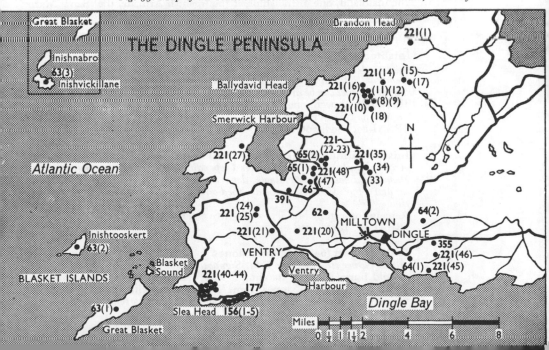

MAP 6 A-C 18-19
OS½″ 20.

small stone oratories; Ogham stones; a fine Romanesque church at Kilmalkedar, influenced by Cormac's Chapel at Cashel, and a promontory fort at Dunanoir which played a tragic role in the Elizabethan wars. It is almost impossible to date most of these monuments, and even approximate dates are avoided below. Some of these monuments display archaic characteristics and show features of a type of prehistoric architecture which have disappeared elsewhere, or are translations into stone of types of wooden buildings which have long since ceased to exist. They are listed below as they appear on the accompanying map, *Fig. 35.*

Teampull Geal (White Church), Ballymorereagh (62) Stone Oratory
Access : Up a laneway, left around farmyard, then right further along path, and then left up into a field. Not signposted
An incomplete Early Christian stone oratory of the same type as Gallarus, with a flat-headed doorway. On top of the gable over the doorway is a finial which originally stood on top of the gable. Opposite the entrance is a pillar with a simple cross inscribed on each side and an Ogham inscription QENILOCI MAQI MAQI AINIA MUC, and the inscription in Latin FECT QUENILOC (made by Qeniloc).
Macalister, Corpus I (1945) 163, No. 170

Great Blasket Island (63/1) Church Ruins
Access : Daily cruise in Summer (depending on weather) arranged by Mr Bennison, Cloughmore, Dingle, departing around 10 a.m., returning around 6 p.m. Visitors can be dropped at the island and collected again at an agreed time
Ruins of a church of uncertain date. In the Sound between the island and the mainland, one of the ships of the Spanish Armada, the 'Santa Maria de la Rosa' sank in 1588.
JRSAI 27, 1896, 306

Inishtooskert (63/2) Oratory, Crosses and Bee-hive Huts
Access : Daily cruise in summer (depending on weather) arranged by Mr Bennison, Cloughmore, Dingle, departing around 10 a.m., returning around 6 p.m. Visitors can be dropped on the island and collected at an agreed time
Ruins of a church, one nearly perfect and other imperfect bee-hive huts, as well as three crosses.
JRSAI 27, 1897, 306

Inishvickillane (63/3) Oratory, Cell and Cross
Access : Daily cruise in Summer (depending on weather) arranged by Mr Bennison, Cloughmore, Dingle, departing at around 10 a.m., and returning around 6 p.m. Visitors can be dropped on the island and collected at an agreed time
Remains of a stone oratory, a bee-hive cell and a cross.
JRSAI 27, 1897, 306

Ballintaggart (64/1) Ogham Stones
Access : Over stile and into field. Signposted
An old burial ground, its church long disappeared, but still containing a number of Ogham stones, some cigar-shaped with rounded ends and two with crosses inscribed. The Ogham inscriptions read

MAP 6 A-C 18-19
OS½" 20.
See map, Fig. 35

MAQQI-IARI KOI MAQQI MUCCOI DOVVINIAS
DOVETI MAQQI CATTINI
SUVALLOS MAQQI DUCOVAROS (Suall (grand)son of Dochar)
MAQI-DECCEDA MAQI GLASICONAS
TRIA MAQA MAILAGNI (3 sons of Mailagnos); on the other side
    CURCITTI INISSIONAS
CUNUMAQQI AVI CORBRI (Conmac grandson of Coirpre)
NETTA-LAMINACCA KOI MAQQI MUCOI DOVIN.S.
Very few of these, as usual, are translatable.
Macalister, Corpus I (1945), 151, Nos. 155-63

Garfinny (64/2) Cemetery
Access : Direct. Not signposted
A cemetery which originally contained a church and which now contains
nothing of interest!

Gallarus (65/1) Castle, Ogham Stones and Cells
Access : Down laneway into farmyard. Not signposted
One of the few surviving castles on the Dingle Peninsula, this is a four-
storey tower of the 15th or 16th century with a vaulted ceiling on the
4th floor. Its round-headed and pointed windows are of an archaic type.
It was built by the Knight of Kerry before 1600. Legend tells of a chief
on his deathbed who wanted to be carried to the window of the castle to
take one last look at the waves of Smerwick Harbour. His servants propped
him up at the window, making many attempts to get him back to bed.
But finally he made no reply and they saw that he had died looking out
over the waves of his beloved bay.
JRSAI 27, 1897, 297; Kerry Arch Mag. 1, 1908, 152

Kilmalkedar (65/2) Church, Cross, Ogham Stone, Alphabet Stone, Sundial and St Brendan's House
Access : A few yards up a lane, then along a path to cemetery. Signposted
This is one of the most important ecclesiastical sites in the whole of the
Dingle Peninsula. The monastery was founded by St Maolcethair who
died in 636. The church is 12th century Romanesque, consisting of a
nave and chancel. Animal heads can be seen at the top of the antae. Part
of the original stone roof is still preserved. The Romanesque doorway
has a tympanum with a head on one side and an imaginary beast on the
other. The chancel arch also bears Romanesque decoration. The chancel
was enlarged, probably some time around 1200. The blind colonnade on
the interior walls of the nave shows, together with the tympanum, that this
church has been strongly influenced by Cormac's Chapel in Cashel, and
historical evidence testifies to certain links between the two places. Two
finials are preserved—one on the gable, one on the ground near the chancel
arch. Inside the church is a stone inscribed with a cross; there is another
with the Alphabet inscribed. In the graveyard outside are a very attractive
early sun-dial, a large cross carved out of one stone, and an Ogham stone
with the inscription ANM MAILE-INBIR MACI BROCANN (The
name of Mael Inbir son of Brocán). About 150 yards north-east is St
Brendan's House, a two-storey medieval building which probably served
as the priest's residence. Its walls are thick, and are wider at the bottom.
JRSAI 10, 1869, 560 and 27, 1897, 295; Macalister, Corpus I (1945) 181;
Leask, Churches I, 121

MAP 6 A-C 18/19
OS½" 20
See map, Fig. 35

Gallarus (66) Oratory and Inscribed Stone
Access : Along path for 100 yards. Signposted
The most perfectly preserved of the boat-shaped oratories in Co. Kerry.
It has a flat-headed doorway, inside which are stones from which a door
or curtain hung, and a small round-headed east window. In shape it
resembles an upturned boat, and all its walls slope inwards towards the
top. Nearby is a cross-inscribed stone.
JRSAI 27, 1897, 297; Leask, Churches I, 21

**Illauntannig, Maharee Islands (67) Old Monastic Enclosure,
Church etc**
Access : For transport contact Mr Kennedy at (066)39146.
This wind-swept island is called after St Senan who founded a monastery
here. Inside the old stone wall which surrounded the monastery are two
stone oratories, one with a doorway with sloping sides, and with herring-
bone masonry in the south wall, the second with a white cross over the
door. There are three bee-hive huts and three burial-places. About 100
yards from the old stone wall is a cross-inscribed slab.
Dunraven Irish Architecture I, 37; JRSAI 27, 1897, 291

Glenfahan (156/1-5) Bee-hive Settlements
*Access : Up paths leading from road up hill, then into field. You are liable
to be charged something for trespassing! Not signposted officially*
A number of separate conglomerations of bee-hive dwellings surrounded
by walls. Caher Murphy is oval, and was full of buildings which must
have had a dark interior and which had souterrains inside. Passages inside
the walls without apparent access may have got their present shape
through reconstruction. Caher Martin is circular with a series of huts
varying in shape from round to rectangular. A souterrain inside has been
filled in. There is a 'sentry-box' at the entrance. Caher Conor is very
similar, though smaller. There are also a number of other groups of
huts beside these. At least some of these buildings, particularly those
on heights, are thought to be huts where herdsman spent the summer
with their flocks. Some at least must have been in use up till the last century;
others have even been built in this century.
JRSAI 81, 1951, 139 and 94, 1964, 39; TRIA 31, 1899, 209

Dunbeg (177) Promontory Fort
*Access : Down through private field to cliff-edge. Very dangerous! Not
signposted officially*
A fine promontory fort with four outer defensive banks of stone and earth
cutting off a tongue of land which falls precipitously to the Atlantic Ocean

MAP 6 A-C 18/19
OS½" 20
See map, Fig. 35

below. Inside these banks is a strong stone wall which was originally straight but became curved during a later reconstruction. The inner half of the wall is the older; the outer portion was added as a strengthener later. In the flat-headed entrance passage through this wall is a small 'dog-hole' at ground level. Inside the fort are the remains of a house which is round on the outside and square on the inside, and also remains of a bee-hive hut. There is also a souterrain leading from the interior to the front of the defences. Note also the water-drain around one of the buildings.
TRIA 31, 1899, 209; JRSAI 40, 1910, 267

Caherconree (184) Inland Promontory Fort

Access : Half a mile across bog, then a climb of 1500 feet up steep mountain. Partially signposted

A stone wall, 350 feet long, and 14 feet thick, which cuts off a tongue of land 2050 feet above sea level. There is a shallow ditch outside the wall, and there appear to have been terraces on the inside wall. The original entrance may have been about 90 feet from the northern end. The story says that the fort was built by Cú Roi. He defeated and degraded Cú-Chulainn by a gross insult, carrying off CúChulainn's girl-friend Blathnad. But Blathnad helped CúChulainn to get his revenge on Cú Roi who was now her husband. CúChulainn was waiting for a sign from Blathnad as to when he should attack the lofty fort where Cú Roi kept her. She poured milk into a stream which became white, and when CúChulainn and his men saw this, they attacked and killed Cú Roi.
UJA 8, 1860, 111; JRSAI 29, 1899, 5 and 40, 1910, 288 and 357

Arraglen (221/1) Ogham Stone with Inscribed Cross

Access : Miles up mountain path to a point north-east of old signal tower. Signposted at road where path begins

A pillar, now lying on the ground, with a Greek cross inscribed in a circle, and bearing the Ogham inscription QRIMITIR RONANN MAQ COMOGANN (Ronán the priest, son of Comgán).
JRSAI 67, 1937, 276; Macalister, Corpus I (1945) 140, No. 145

Ballynavenooragh (221/7-12) Stone Forts and Bee-hive Huts

Access : Three-quarters of a mile along good untarred road. The monuments are spread out at the foot of Brandon Mountain, between two and five fields from the road. Not signposted

A series of bee-hive huts. There are also two stone forts, one containing a double bee-hive hut, another containing four simple ones—one built into the wall of the fort. An isolated example, called 'The Baker's Hut', contains what is probably an oven. There are two double bee-hive huts.

Ballinknockane (221/14) Stone Fort and Bee-hive Huts

Access : Up five fields from the road. Not signposted

A stone fort with the remains of four bee-hive huts inside.

Ballinknockane (221/15) Bee-hive Hut and Cross-slab

Access : 2 fields in from road

This is an old and disused burial ground containing fragments of a cross-slab, and remains of a church.

Ballinknockane (221/16) Stone Fort with Bee-hive Huts

A stone fort with the remains of a bee-hive hut.

MAP 6 A-C 18/19
OS½" 20
See map, Fig. 35

St Brendan's Oratory and Cells (221/17)
Access : Up path to top of Brandon Mountain
St Brendan's rectangular oratory and remains of bee-hive huts.

Ballybrack (221/18) Bee-hive Hut
A bee-hive hut with a covered chamber.

Kilcolman, Maumanorig (221/20) Old Burial Ground
Access : Half a mile up lane, then down two fields
An old religious enclosure which originally contained an oratory. The main interest of the site is a boulder with a Maltese Cross in a circle, surrounded on two sides by an Ogham inscription which reads ANM COLMAN AILITHIR (the name of Colmán the pilgrim).
JRSAI 67, 1937, 277; Macalister, Corpus I (1945) 186, No. 193

Rahinnane (221/21) Castle, Fort and Souterrain
Access : Down a lane and across two fields. Signposted
The ruins of a 15th or 16th century castle built by the Knight of Kerry. The castle is two-storeyed, with unusual arcades on the ceiling of the second floor. The castle and the foundations of other buildings stand in the middle of a circular area, possibly an earlier fort, surrounded by a most impressive ditch 30 feet deep. The castle was taken by Sir Charles Wilmot in 1602 and destroyed in the Cromwellian wars.
JRSAI 3, 1854-5, 393

Kilmalkedar (221/22) 'The Keeler's' Stone
Called 'The Keeler's Stone', this is a flat stone in the middle of a field not far from the church. It has three large holes in it.

Kilmalkedar (221/23) Stone Oratory
A stone oratory similar to Gallarus. It is called St Brendan's Oratory.

Ballywiheen (221/24) Stone Fort and Ogham Stone
Access : Down two fields. Not signposted
A round stone fort, known as Cathair-na-gcat (The Cat's Fort), together with an Ogham stone which was placed here for safe keeping. But it has recently been broken in two. The inscription reads TOGITTACC MAQI SAGARETTOS.
Macalister, Corpus I (1945) 165, No. 172

Ballywiheen (221/25) Huts and Crosses
Access : Direct from road. Not signposted
An old monastic enclosure containing a ruined square oratory, a stone with an incised Maltese cross in a circle, and other undecorated slabs. The road cuts through the old enclosure, and the monumental cross on the other side of the road was thus part of the original enclosure.
JRSAI 67, 1937, 278

Dunanoir, Smerwick Harbour (221/27) Promontory Fort
Access : Over stile and along path. Signposted
A small promontory fort with an outer wall on the land-ward side, cutting off a tongue of land which drops to the sea below. Lord Grey and Admiral Winter besieged and entered the fort on November 17th, 1580, and mercilessly slaughtered James Fitzmaurice and 600 others, including Italians, Spaniards and Basques who had come by sea from Spain to help him.

MAP 6 A-C 18/19
OS½″ 20
See map, Fig. 35

JRSAI 40, 1910, 193; A O'Rahilly, The Massacre of Smerwick (1580), Historical and Archaeological Papers No. 1 (1938)

Glin North (221/33) Bee-hive Hut

Glin North (221/34) Stone Fort with Bee-hive Huts
Access : Along old path and then across four fields. Not signposted
A stone fort with two concentric walls enclosing the remnants of some bee-hive huts. One of these had a stone-paved path leading up to its entrance.

Reenconnell (221/35) Burial Ground with Cross
Access : Three fields in from the road, over field hedges. Not signposted
An old disused burial ground harbouring a stone roughly hewn in the shape of a cross, with a ringed cross incised on it.

Coumeenole South (221/40-4) Bee-hive Huts and an Inscribed Cross
Four bee-hive huts on the summit of a hill, two other bee-hive huts, three other huts and an inscribed cross.

Doonmore (221/45) Promontory Fort
Access : A third of a mile up a laneway, then across 4 fields
A promontory fort consisting of a tongue of land cut off from the adjoining land by a ditch 15 feet deep and inside it a wall 10 feet high, with partial interior and exterior stone-facing at the top. Three huts and a souterrain existed inside. A smaller promontory adjoining the main one has a triangular enclosure on top of it.
JRSAI 40, 1910, 286

Emlagh East (221/46) Ogham Stone
Access : Down mud-track just to left of golf-links. The stone is at the end of the track and just to the left, re-sited above the high-water mark
An Ogham stone, the first to be discovered, re-erected on its present site. It is known as 'The Priest's Stone'. The inscription reads BRUSCCOS MAQQI CALIACI...M...
Macalister, Corpus I (1945) 172, No. 180

Caherdorgan North (221/47-8) Stone Fort and 'The Chancellor's House'
Access : In separate fields beside the road, not far from Kilmalkedar church
A stone fort with three bee-hive huts, two of which were later joined together by the addition of another. Four fields up the road is 'The Chancellor's House', a medieval building consisting of two rooms. The larger one looks almost like a church with a door in the north and south walls. The smaller room has a fireplace and a well-preserved (but later) baking oven. Nothing is known about the Chancellor.

Ballineetig (355) A Standing Stone
Access : Up private avenue, and across wall into field
A large standing stone, known as 'Gallaunmore'. It is about 15 feet high.

Emlagh East (391) Stone Fort
Access : Over wall into field beside road
A circular fort with a ditch, and surrounded by two walls.

Reask (519) Pillar Stone *Fig. 36*

MAP 6 A 18
OS½″ 20Q.37.04

Access : Direct
A beautifully decorated cross-inscribed pillar standing in an old walled monastic enclosure, which also contains two smaller cross-slabs and the foundations of two bee-hive huts.
Henry, Irish Art Vol 1 (1965) 57

DUNLOE (385) Ogham Stones *Fig. 6*

MAP 6 D 19
OS½″ 21V.88.91

Access : Through gap in wall beside road. Signposted
A group of eight Ogham stones removed to their present position in the last century. The one in the centre came from the church at Kilbonane, while those forming a circle came to light in 1838 as forming part of the roof of a souterrain at Coolmagort which contained some human remains. The stone in the centre has on the edges the inscriptions B...AGNI MAQI ADDILONA (B. son of A.) and NAGUNI MUCO BAIDANI (N. son(?) of B.), while on the face the inscription reads NIR... MN. DAGNIESSICONIDDALA AMIT BAIDAGNI. The other stones bear the following inscriptions:
  MAQI-RITEAS MAQI MAQI-DDUMILEAS MUCOI TOICACI
    CUNACENA
  DEGOS MAQI MOCOI TOICAKI
  MAQI-TTAL MAQI VORGOS MAQI MUCOI TOICAC
  MC.... GE... M... Q... D...E
  NIOTTVRECC MAQI ...GNI
  MAQI-DECEDA MAQ
JRSAI 8, 1866, 523; Macalister, Corpus I (1945) 191, Nos. 197-203; 235, No. 241

INNISFALLEN (183) Church and Abbey

MAP 6 D 19
OS½″ 20V.93.89

Access : Transport to island by boat which may be hired at Ross Castle.
The first monastery on this scenically situated island in Lough Leane is said to have been founded by St Finian the Leper in the 7th century. It was twice plundered by the Vikings. Its most renowned monk, Maelsuthain O'Carroll, 'chief doctor of the Western world of his time' and a friend of the High-King Brian Boru died in 1009. It flourished in the 12th century until it was plundered in 1180 by Maoildúin, son of Donal O'Donoghue. However, it survived this shock and remained such a centre of learning that the *Annals of Innisfallen*—a most important historical source for the early history of Ireland—were written here around 1215. In 1320 it adopted the Benedictine rule. A 12th century oratory standing on a low cliff above the shore has a small round-headed east window and a Romanesque doorway decorated with animal heads in the west wall. A small carved cross found in the water nearby stands inside. About 60 feet away are the remains of the Abbey. The western two-thirds of the Abbey church with antae and a (restored) flat-headed doorway belong to an early church. The rest of the church and the domestic buildings to the north of the church were added some time in the 13th century. Excavations brought to light the site of the original kitchen and several pathways lined with flagstones.
JRSAI 22, 1892, 158 and 36, 1906, 337; Journal of the Ivernian Society 1, 1908, 110; 99th Annual Report of Commissioners of Public Works 1930-1, 41; Leask, Churches I, 68, 74, 162; II, 149

MAP 6 D 19
OS½″ 21V.80.93

KILCOOLAGHT EAST (329) Ogham Stones

Access: Through gate south of bridge and across two fields to stones which are fenced in. Not signposted

Six Ogham stones (some of them broken) on the site of an old burial ground. A seventh stone was stolen about 10 years ago. The inscriptions (including the missing one) read as follows:

　(i) ANM VIRR.... ANNI TIGIRN
　(ii) ...CEDDATOQA MAQI VEDELMET(T)
...ECC MAQI L(UGUQ)RRIT
　UMALL
　...GGO MAQI AGILL....
　DUBE....
　RITTUVECC MAQI VEDDONOS (Rethu son of Fiadu)

and two indecipherable inscriptions.

Macalister, Corpus I (1945) 200 Nos. 206-13

Fig. 36. An Early Christian Pillar at Reask, Co. Kerry.

Fig. 6. An Ogham stone from Coolmagort and now at Dunloe, Co Kerry. The Ogham inscription reads 'CUNACENA'. Early Christian period.

KILLAGHA Augustinian Abbey

MAP 6 D 18
OS½″ 21Q.82.01

Access : Through gate to Abbey. Signposted
The Abbey was erected on the site of an older monastery of St Colman some time after 1216 by Geoffrey de Marisco for the Canons Regular of St. Augustine and dedicated to Our Blessed Lady. In 1302 it was the third richest monastery in the Diocese of Ardfert, and its Prior was a Lord of Parliament. Only the church, with a single long nave, remains. The windows, doors and niches of sandstone are of 13th century date, while the limestone work, including the fine east window, was inserted in the 15th century. The Abbey was suppressed in 1576 and leased first to Thomas Clinton, and shortly afterwards to Sir William Stanley, then to Thomas Spring and later again to Major Godfrey. The domestic buildings to the south were destroyed by Cromwell's soldiers.
JRSAI 36, 1906, 285; Leask, Churches III, 124

KILLARNEY Muckross Friary and Ross Castle
Muckross Friary (311)

MAP 6 D 19
OS½″ 21V.98.87

Access : Car park outside gate of Bourne Vincent Park. From there half a mile walk along avenue in park beside Loch Leane to the 'Abbey'. Signposted
The Friary was probably founded by Donal McCarthy in 1448 for the Observantine Franciscans, and completed by about 1475. It is one of the best preserved of the Irish Franciscan Friaries. The eastern part of the church was begun first and the western part later. The south transept was added around 1500. There is a fine set of slender east windows, as well as three windows in the south wall. The sedilia in the north wall is a later insertion. The church contains a number of tombs. The tower, which was inserted after the church was built, is the only Franciscan tower in Ireland which is as wide as the church. The most remarkable part of the friary is the cloister with an old yew tree in the centre surrounded by a cloister arcade different on each side, indicating different building phases. There are buildings on the first floor above it. On the east side was possibly the monks' day room, and above it a dormitory. On the north side lay a store, above which was the refectory with a kitchen beside it. The ground floor on the western side was probably a cellar, while the Guardian lived on the first floor. To the north of the choir of the church is a three-storey building; the ground floor was the Sacristy while the sacristan probably lived in the floor above. The Friary was suppressed in 1541. In 1587 it was leased to the Earl of Clancarty and in 1595 to Captain Collum. The Friary was formally re-established in 1612 after it had been re-occupied and partially restored in 1602. The restoration work was completed by 1626, but the community had to leave again in 1629. Shortly afterwards the friars returned once more, but were finally driven out by the Cromwellians in 1652.
JCHAS 44, 1939, 40 and 45, 1940, 79 and 85; Official Guidebook; Leask, Churches III, 51, 97, 104, 140

Ross Castle

MAP 6 D 19
OS½″ 21V.94.89

Access : Direct. Castle is temporarily closed. Signposted.
A 16th century tower surrounded by a bawn with rounded turrets, parts of which still remain. Attached to the southern part of the tower is a much later extension. The tower was built by one of the O'Donoghue Ross chieftains, and was held by Lord Muskerry and the Royalists in the

Cromwellian wars. A prophecy said that the castle could never be taken except by an attack made from the water by a Man of War. Ludlow, the Cromwellian commander, had a large boat transported overland and launched in the lake, and when the defenders saw this they knew that the prophecy had been fulfilled and they abandoned the castle.
JRSAI 21, 1890-1, 609; Kerry Arch. Mag. 4, 1917, 149

MAP 6 B 19
OS¼" 20V.45.81

LEACANABUAILE (414) Stone Fort
Access : Down a laneway, then left up path to top of hill. Signposted
A round stone fort situated on a hill-top, with the entrance on the east. The wall is about 10 feet thick, and has been reconstructed to a height of about 4 feet. Originally there were three bee-hive huts inside, but only one remains; a square house was added on to it at some time. Inside the door of the round hut is the entrance to a souterrain which led to a chamber in the wall, while a covered drain leads from the square house out to the gate. Excavation brought iron knives and pins, bone combs, whetstones and querns or mill-stones (one still visible) to light, and these helped to date the fort to about the 9th or 10th century A.D.
JCHAS 46, 1941, 85

MAP 6 E 16
OS½" 17R.00.46

LISLAUGHTIN (258) Franciscan Friary
Access : 100 yards up avenue to cemetery. Signposted
In 1478 John O'Connor Kerry founded this Friary for the Franciscans, probably on the site of an older monastery founded by St Lachtin (died 622). It consists of a long church with north transept and some domestic buildings. The west window of the church has an attractive flame-like form. There are two tomb-niches in the nave and a triple sedilia in the choir. Around the cloister can be seen the remains of domestic buildings, including the refectory on the east side, with the dormitory above. At the north end is a tower which housed the lavatories. The gateway leading from the outside to the monastic enclosure is still preserved. In 1507 a Chapter of the Franciscan order was held here. After the Dissolution of the Monasteries, the Friary was granted to Sir William, Walter and Miles Herbert, but some of the friars probably remained on, for we know that in 1580 three friars were strangled in front of the High Altar. The Franciscans formally regained possession again in 1629, but when they finally left no one knows.
Kerry Arch. Mag. 2, 1912-4, 25; Leask, Churches III, 183

MAP 6 D 17
OS½" 17Q.99.34

LISTOWEL (260) Castle
Access : Through garden of house in town square. Not signposted
Of the 15th century castle built by a McGilligan, only one half, consisting of two towers and a connecting wall, remains. The entrance is modern. In its heyday, the castle must have resembled Bunratty. Fitzmaurice destroyed Listowel and took over the castle in 1582, but in 1600 it was taken by Sir Charles Wilmot.
JCHAS 59, 1954, 72 and 64, 1959, 44

MAP 6 B 20
OS½" 24V.53.67

LOUGH CURRANE (Church Island) (60) Church
Access : Trips can be arranged in Summer through Mr Abie Huggard, Bayview Hotel, Waterville (Tel. Waterville 4)
St Finian founded a monastery on this small island, possibly in the 6th century. On the island is a Romanesque church with nave and chancel.

The Romanesque doorway had four orders, but little remains now of the chancel arch. There is a small widely-splaying east window. Built into the wall of the church is a stone of uncertain date showing a man playing an early stringed instrument—one of the very few representations of an instrument other than a harp in early Ireland. To the west of the church are traces of oblong houses, while at the other end of the island from the church is St Finian's Cell, a small stone house. There are eight grave-slabs or pillar-stones on the island, two with old Irish inscriptions: 'A blessing on the soul of Anmchadh' and 'A blessing on the soul of Gilleinchomded O'Buicne'.

JRSAI 38, 1908, 368 and 56, 1926, 43; PRIA 58, 1956-7, 137; Leask, Churches I, 166

RATASS (57) Church

MAP 6 D 18
OS½″ 20Q.85.14

Access : Direct from road to cemetery in which church stands. Signposted
The nave of this church is the oldest part, and the chancel was added in the 12th century. One of the most notable features is the flat-headed west doorway which is surrounded by an architrave or frame in relief. There are antae on the west gable, and the east wall has a round-headed window with Romanesque moulding. The church was much restored around 1700.
JRSAI 21, 1891, 622; Leask, Churches I, 69

RATTOO (55) Church and Round Tower

MAP 6 D 17
OS½″ 17Q.88.33

Access : Three-quarters of a mile up a largely untarred roadway. Access to church direct from roadway ; but it is then necessary to climb over barbed wire to get to the Round Tower. Signposted
This is an old monastic foundation, but little is known of its history. The church in the graveyard was built in the 15th century, though stones from an earlier church are built into its walls. The Round Tower is very well preserved, and has a round-headed doorway with an architrave or frame in raised relief around it. Further to the east is a 15th century Abbey.
Petrie, Round Towers (1845) 395; JCHAS 16, 1910, 182 and 17, 1911, 17

SKELLIG MICHAEL (61) Early Christian Monastery

MAP 6 A 20
OS½″ 20V.
25.61 (inset)

Access : Trips may be arranged through the following :
from Valentia and calling at Renard Point : Des Lavelle (tel. Valentia 24), Dermot Walsh (tel. Valentia 12).
from Derrynane Pier : Joe Roddy (tel. Waterville 93), Seán O'Shea, Caherdaniel (no telephone), Willie Healy (tel. Caherdaniel 3).
Trips are only made in suitable weather
This early monastery is dramatically situated on the slopes of a barren and rocky island which stands sentinel against the Atlantic waves on the south-western coast of Ireland. Tradition attributes the foundation of the monastery to St Finan. The deaths of some of its monks are recorded in 823, 950 and 1044, but the monastery continued till the 12th or 13th century when its monks transferred to the mainland at Ballinskelligs. The monastic remains are sited on a saddle in the rock about 550 feet above sea level. Six bee-hive huts, two rectangular oratories, St Michael's Church and a small area known as 'The Monk's Garden' are sited on a series of terraces below which the cliffs fall steeply to the sea. The bee-hive cells are round outside and square inside, and some have little wall cupboards and may have had two storeys inside. Near this cluster of bee-hive huts is

a rectangular stone oratory, like that at Gallarus (see under Dingle Peninsula above), while further to the north is another one. One of the oratories and one of the bee-hive huts have a cross made of stones above the door. Below the huts are the remains of a church, possibly 12th century in date. There are a number of cross-shaped slabs scattered around the island.
JRSAI 85, 1955, 174

STAIGUE (143) Stone Fort *Fig. 37*

MAP 6 C 20
OS½″ 24V.61.63

Access : (Be careful going up narrow tarred road.) Across bridge and then up field to fort. Key to be obtained beforehand from caretaker in house beside car-park. You are liable to be charged for trespass on your return from the fort. Signposted

Nestling near the top of a peaceful valley, this is one of the largest and finest of the stone forts of Ireland. The circular wall, which is up to 18 feet high, and 13 feet thick, surrounds an area 90 feet in diameter. The interior is reached through a long passage covered with slabs. There are a series of steps like an 'X' in shape leading to the top of the inside of the wall, and there are also two little rooms in the walls. The whole fort is surrounded by a large bank and ditch. Similar in style to Dun Aenghus, Co Galway and the Grianán of Aileach in Co Donegal, it is equally difficult to date, but may have been built in the centuries preceding St Patrick. Parts of the fort were reconstructed in the last century.
Kerry Arch. Mag. 3, 1914-6, 95; JRSAI 27, 1897, 316 and 81, 1951, 144

TONAKNOCK (303) Cross

MAP 6 D 17
OS½″ 17Q.84.27

Access : Directly beside road. Signposted
A simple stone cross about 9 feet high; one arm is broken. It may have had figure sculpture on it originally, but this is so weathered that it is now invisible.

Fig. 37. Staigue Fort, Co Kerry. Probably Early Iron Age period.

ARDRASS Church

MAP 8 P 12
OS½″ 16N.95.31

Access : Through gate into field. Not signposted

A small stone oratory, rectangular in plan, with a south door and two east windows one above the other. It is most unusual in that it is one of the few remaining examples of a stone-roofed medieval church; its stone roof is supported by an interior pointed vault. It was considerably restored in 1888, though it is at present covered in ivy and serves as a store for agricultural implements.

JCKAS 6, 1911, 411

ARDSCULL Motte

MAP 8 N 14
OS½″ 16S.73.98

Access : Over stile. Signposted

Sitting on top of a hill, this is a massive earthwork consisting of a tall round motte about 35 feet high, surrounded by a ditch and a bank. Traces of a bailey can be seen on the north side. It was probably erected at the end of the 12th century, but it is first mentioned in the historical sources when it was burnt in 1286. Bruce's army met and defeated a strong English force nearby in 1315. Stone buildings at the top may have been added just prior to 1654, but these have vanished. Beside the road is a plaque commemorating the 4th Gordon Bennett Memorial Race of 1903—the first motor race to be run over a closed circuit. Ardscull was one of the points on the circuit.

JCKAS 2, 1896-8, 186

CASTLEDERMOT Crosses, Round Tower, Churches and Tower

MAP 8 N 14
OS½″ 16S.78.85

Round Tower and Crosses (471)

Access : Direct to churchyard from road. Signposted

St Dermot founded a monastery here which was plundered by the Vikings in 841 and again in 867. Cormac Mac Cuilleannáin, the famous scholar,

king and bishop of Cashel was buried here after his head had been cut off in battle in 908. Tradition says that an Abbot who died eleven years later erected the Round Tower. The monastery was plundered in 1048, and the last known abbot of the monastery died in 1073. Between the entrance gate and the church is a reconstructed Romanesque doorway belonging to a vanished church. The Round Tower was built with irregular granite blocks, but the top part is medieval. There are two fine granite crosses and the base of a third. On the west face of the South Cross can be seen the Arrest of Christ, the Crucifixion, the Sacrifice of Isaac, Adam and Eve and Daniel in the Lion's Den; other panels on the cross have other less decipherable figures and geometrical decoration. On the North Cross there is the Temptation of St Anthony, Daniel in the Lion's Den, Adam and Eve, David with the Harp, the Sacrifice of Isaac on the west face and the Miracle of the Loaves and Fishes on the south face. In the churchyard, foundations of a medieval church, as well as Early Christian and medieval grave-slabs, can be seen.

Stokes, The High Crosses of Castledermot and Durrow (1898)

Franciscan Friary (200)

Access: Direct from road. Key to be had from caretaker, Mr Hynes, at adjoining house. Not signposted

Near the southern end of the town are the remains of a Franciscan Friary founded in 1302 by Thomas, Lord of Ossory. It was plundered by Bruce in 1317. Originally the church was a long rectangle with a doorway and a pair of lancet windows in the west wall and a tower on the south side. The north transept was added to it later, and this is probably identical with the Chapel of St Mary built by Thomas, Second Earl of Kildare, in 1328. When a part of the south wall of the church fell many years ago it was found to be hollow at the base and enclosed a row of skeletons. To the south of the Friary is a domestic residence, possibly 15th century in date, while to the north some of the retaining wall of the old monastery still exists. The Friary was suppressed in 1541.

JCKAS 1, 1895, 373; Arch. Journal 88, 1931, 382; Leask, Churches II, 125

St John's or The Pigeon Tower (503)

Access: Through private garden. Not signposted

At the northern end of the town is a tower, possibly of 15th century date and of no great interest. It is the only remaining portion of a Friary founded early in the 13th century by Walter de Riddlesford for the Crutched Friars or Trinitarians, and dedicated to St John the Baptist. The Friars got their name from the Latin word 'Crux' (a cross) which they wore on their breast, and they devoted their energies to the care of the sick and the poor, and to the redemption of captives. The Friary was suppressed in 1541, and passed then into private hands.

JCKAS 1, 1895, 371

DUN AILLINNE Hill-fort

MAP 8 P 13
OS½" 16N.82.08

Access: Through gate and up three fields. Signposted

This fort, situated on a hill-top, and enclosing an area of about 20 acres, was probably at one time the seat of the Kings of Leinster. A circular wall, 450 yards in diameter, is up to 15 feet high, and has a ditch inside and not outside it. Recent excavations have shown that it was probably in use from the Bronze Age up till as late as 1800.

JRSAI 100, 1970, forthcoming

FURNESS (394) Church

MAP 8 P 12/13
OS½" 16N.93.20

Access : Up private avenue and garden, over field and into wood. Not signposted
A small nave-and-chancel church founded around 1210 for the Canons Regular of St Augustine of the branch called 'of St Victor' but it may include parts of an older (12th century ?) church. Richard de Lesse granted it and the tithes of a small parish to the Abbey of St Thomas in Dublin. In the north and south walls are round-headed doorways cut in an unusually soft stone called calcareous tufa, and there is a simple round-headed chancel arch. There is a twin-lighted window in the west end of the chancel. A contemporary baptismal font dug up outside the church in the last century now stands near the west end of the church. After the Dissolution the church passed to the Ashe family and later to the Nevills.
JCKAS 3, 1902, 453 and 14, 1969, 457, Leask, Churches II, 149

JIGGINSTOWN Manorial House

MAP 8 P 13
OS½" 16N.88.19

Access : Over gate. Not signposted
This gaunt-looking mansion with a 380-foot long frontage beside the road was begun in 1636-7 by Thomas Wentworth, Earl of Strafford, Lord Deputy of Ireland from 1633 to 1640. He planned it as a summer residence for himself and as a palace which Charles I could live in if and when he came to visit Ireland. It never served either purpose, however, because it was left unfinished when Strafford was called to London and beheaded in 1641. The eastern portion may have been temporarily finished as it appears to have been roofed at one time. The building consists of fine vaulted cellars and a number of tall rooms on the ground floor (which was reached by an outside stairs). The house was one of the first ones built with red-brick in Ireland, and it is interesting to note that the architectural mouldings are made in the bricks. Tradition says that the bricks were of Dutch manufacture, and that a human chain was formed stretching from Dublin to Jigginstown so that each brick passed from hand to hand from Dublin until it reached Jigginstown. Behind the house is a sunken garden, and the gazebo at the south-east corner of the garden still survives.
JCKAS 1, 1, 1892, 19; 12, 1943, 343 and 14, 1969, 375; Leask, in Studies in Building History, ed Jope (1961) 244.

KILDARE Cathedral and Round Tower

MAP 8 N 13
OS½" 16N.73.13

Access : Direct from road. Normally open except on Tuesdays and Fridays. If locked, apply for key at verger's house beside gate to churchyard. Not signposted
The Cathedral was begun by Ralph of Bristol around 1223, but only the south transept and a part of the tower as well as small portions of the rest of the church date from this period. It was partially restored in the 15th century, and heavily restored in the 19th century when the choir was almost totally rebuilt. In the south transepts are preserved some good medieval tombs (particularly that of Sir Maurice Fitzgerald of Lackagh who died in 1575) and some of the medieval floor-tiles, and in the choir is the effigy of (?) Bishop John of Taunton (died 1258). In the churchyard can be seen a plain granite High Cross and a Round Tower. For a small fee you can climb to the top of the Round Tower. It has a fine Romanesque doorway with a pointed hood; the conical cap of the tower was replaced by a stepped parapet in the 18th century. To the north of the nave of the Cathedral are the foundations of a building in which—according to

tradition—St Brigid kept alight the Sacred Fire. To the east of the choir is a small underground cell, probably of 15th century date. The Cathedral probably marks the site of a famous monastery founded by St Brigid in the 5th or 6th century.

Leask, Churches II, 89

KILTEEL (275) Church and Castle

MAP 8 P 12
OS½" 16N.98.21

Access: Through gate and across field to church; down avenue to castle. Signposted

In the medieval church a 12th century Romanesque chancel arch has been partially re-erected. It is unique in that it is the only Romanesque chancel arch in Ireland which has figure sculpture. On the south side can be seen Adam and Eve, a man with drinking horn, two figures embracing, an acrobat and David with the head of Goliath, while on the north side there is Samson and the Lion, two bearded faces, an abbot with a crozier and other figures. Nearby is a granite cross. Not far away Maurice Fitzgerald, Second Baron of Offaly, founded a Preceptory of the Knights Hospitallers before his death in 1257, and dedicated it to St John the Baptist. Chapters of the Order were held here in 1326, 1332, 1333 and 1334. In the following year Robert Clifford was appointed Porter of the Commandery and was ordered to repair the castle (a precursor of the present building). What remains is a 15th century tower and gateway of five storeys, of which the first and fifth are roofed with barrel vaults. A spiral staircase leads to the roof. The castle was suppressed in 1541, and granted in the following year to Sir John Alen. By the end of the 17th century it had passed to Richard Talbot, later Duke of Tyrconnell. In 1703 it was sold to the Hollow Sword Blade Company, and in 1704 to William Fownes. Further parts of the old Preceptory can be seen near the bridge not far from the church.

JCKAS 1, 1892, 34 and 8, 1915-7, 267; JRSAI 65, 1935, 1; Leask, Churches I, 165

MAYNOOTH (485) Castle

MAP 8 P 12
OS½" 16N.94.38

Access: Through gate. Key to gate obtainable from J. Doyle, in lane 150 yards east of the castle on the left hand side, beside O'Neill's butcher shop. Not signposted

The castle was probably begun by Gerald FitzGerald, Baron of Offaly, in 1203. The main tower, one of the largest of its kind, was built in three successive phases, but the vaults on the ground floor were added probably long after the rest of the tower had been completed. Originally the tower was approached by steps leading up to the first floor, where the wooden stairs now stand. The inside of the tower was divided into two main rooms for each floor, as at Trim, Co Meath, and the walls are preserved almost to the top where fragments of the original turret at the north-eastern angle can still be seen. The tower stood in an enclosure which was surrounded by a curtain wall, of which the main entrance gate (present entrance to castle), parts of the south-eastern tower (much restored in 16th-17th century) and the north-eastern tower as well as much of the eastern and northern portions of the wall itself remain. The arches in the east wall mark the site of a large hall which was used up till the 17th century.

In 1328 the castle had two gates; one leading to the tower, the other to the garden. It was enlarged in 1426 by John, 6th Earl of Kildare. In 1521 a College was founded nearby, but it was suppressed at the Reformation,

Fig. 38. A panel from the High Cross at Moone,
Co Kildare, showing the Twelve Apostles. 9th or
10th century.

only to open its gates again in 1795. The College is now a part of the
National University, and houses a Museum of Ecclesiology. In 1535,
during the rebellion of the castle's owner, Silken Thomas (see St Mary's
Abbey, Dublin), the Castle was treacherously taken by the Lord Deputy,
William Skeffington. Until 1540 the Lords Deputy used it as their resi-
dence, but in 1552 the Castle and Estates were restored to Gerald, 11th
Earl of Kildare. The Earl of Cork who was the father-in-law of the 16th
Earl of Kildare, restored the Castle in 1630 and subsequent years. The
Confederate Catholics occupied the Castle in 1641 but the castle was
rendered harmless at the end of the war. The Fitzgeralds abandoned the
castle probably about 1656.
JCKAS 1, 1894, 223; JRSAI 44, 1914, 281; Arch Journ 93, 1937, 155;
Leask, Castles 36

MOONE High Cross and Church Fig. 38

MAP 8 N 14
OS½" 16S.79.93

*Access : Down lane 100 yards to just short of farmyard, then to the right up
steps and along path to churchyard. Signposted*
This High Cross, with its beautiful flat stylized and naive figures, is 17 feet
high, unique and one of the most appealing of all the High Crosses. On
the east face are Daniel and seven lions, the Sacrifice of Isaac, Adam and
Eve, the Crucifixion as well as animals (including what appear to be
dolphins); on the west face are the Twelve Apostles, the Crucifixion,
The Blessed Virgin (?) and St John (?); the north face has The Miracle
of the Loaves and Fishes, The Flight into Egypt, The Three Children
in the Fiery Furnace and various animals, while the south face has a
variety of figures and animals. The cross stands on the site of an Early
Christian monastery allegedly founded by St Columba. An abbot of the
monastery is known to have died in 1014, and in 1040 it was raided by
Diarmuid of the Uí Ceinnsealaigh who carried away many prisoners
from it. In the 13th century the Fitzgeralds founded a new church which
may have formed part of a Franciscan friary. The church has antae, and
unless these belong to an earlier church, they represent one of the latest
survivals of this feature in Irish architecture. The church was repaired
in 1609. Inside it are the remains of another cross built into cement and
decorated with animals and centaurs. Its shaft may have fitted into the
base of a cross standing beside the tall cross.
JCKAS 1, 1894, 286; TRIA 31, 1901, 342

OLD KILCULLEN (71) High Crosses and Round Tower

MAP 8 P 13
OS½" 16N.83.07

Access : Across a field to graveyard
The most important remnant of this old monastery is the fragment of
a High Cross. On the east face are unidentified figures (Apostles?) in
panels; on the north face David and the Lion and a Bishop; on the west
face Samson and the Lion and other unidentified figures. while there is
interlacing on the south face. There is also the shaft of another High
Cross with very worn panels, and the tall thin base of a third. Nearby are
the remains of a Round Tower with round-headed doorway. The monastery was founded by St Patrick, but St Iserninus (died 469) was its first
Bishop and St Mac Táil (died 548) was one of his successors. The Vikings
of Dublin raided the monastery in 932 and again in 944. Rory O'Lorcain
was captured and blinded in the stone church in 1037, and the monastery
was burned once more in 1114. There are the remains of a Romanesque
church built in the 12th century, but many additions were made to it

and the east wall of the chancel was re-built when the church was re-used in the 18th century.
JCKAS 1, 1893, 81 and 2, 1899, 431; JRSAI 71, 1941, 148

OUGHTERARD (190) Round Tower and Church

MAP 8 P 12
OS½" 16N.96.26

Access : Up a path to graveyard. Signposted
A St Bridget (not to be confused with the Saint of the same name from Kildare) founded a monastery or convent here in the 6th century which was burned in 1094. The 34-foot high stump of a Round Tower with round-headed doorway is all that remains of the old monastery. The church is said to have been built in 1609, but may be earlier. It has an intact east window and partially preserved barrel-vaulting. The staircase leading from the church to the roof forms a separate building beside the church (compare Castledermot Friary). After the Suppression, the lands of the monastery were granted in turn to Richard Miles (1577), Thomas Lambert (1590) and Sir Henry Harrington.
JCKAS 1, 1893, 84

PUNCHESTOWN (305) Standing Stone

MAP 8 P 13
OS½" 16N.92.17

Access : About 50 feet across a field. Not signposted
This tall granite stone tapering to a height of 23 feet is one of the finest examples of its type in the country. When it fell and was re-erected in 1930 it was found to have a Bronze Age burial at its base.
JRSAI 67, 1937, 250

RATHCOFFEY (404) Castle

MAP 8 P 12
OS½" 16N.89.32

Access : One third of a mile up lane way and then through field. Not signposted
Remains of a castle built by the Wogans who came to Ireland with Henry II. The castle is mentioned in 1454 when it was attacked by another branch of the Wogan family. It was fortified in 1641, but surrendered to General Mant in the following year, when Nicholas Wogan was outlawed for treason. The main surviving free-standing structure is nothing but the two-storey gatehouse leading to the enclosure in which the castle stood. It has a mullioned window in the east wall. It possibly dates to the 15th century, but has been much mutilated since. At the end of the 18th century Archibald Rowan Hamilton bought the castle, and incorporated a few parts of the original castle into the mansion which he built, but which is now in ruins.
JRSAI 21, 1891, 119; JCKAS 3, 1900, 79

TAGHADOE (70) Round Tower

MAP 8 P 12
OS½" 16N.92.35

Access : Direct to graveyard. Signposted
This Round Tower, without windows on the top, is 65 feet high and it may never have been completed. There is a flat raised moulding around the round-headed doorway, and an indistinguishable head carved above it. The monastery of which the tower is the sole remnant was founded by an obscure saint named Tua who was attached to the nearby monastery of Clane. Little is known of the history of the monastery except that one of its abbots, named Folachtach, died in 765. The church beside the Round Tower was built in 1831.
JCKAS 1, 1893, 91

Admire—but don't destroy.

AGHAVILLER (334) Church and Round Tower

MAP 8 M 17
OS½" 19S.50.35

Access : Over a stile. Not signposted
The Round Tower is the only remnant of the Early Christian monastery here, the history of which is unknown. The tower still stands to a height of 40 feet, but the square-headed doorway at ground level is comparatively modern. The large rectangular tower nearby may have been built first as a church in the 12th or 13th century, but it was probably fortified around 1600 when the vault and the top floor were constructed, and the large windows reduced in size for defensive purposes. Some time later the tower may again have been used as a church. Immediately to the west of the tower there are foundations of a further extension, which may have been the site of the chancel of the original church.

BALLYLARKIN (282) Church

MAP 7 L 15
OS½" 18S.39.64

Access : Over a stile into field. Not signposted
A small but massive rectangular church dating probably from the 13th century. It looks almost military in appearance because of its small north doorway and because it only has one narrow window—in the east wall. The church is noted for the high quality of its carved stonework, such as on the interior and exterior corbels and on the 14th century triple sedilia in the south wall.
Leask, Churches III, 164

BURNCHURCH (321) Castle

MAP 8 M 16
OS½" 18S.48.47

Access : Through gate, and then 100 yards along cart-track. Signposted
This is a 15th or 16th century castle built by the Burnchurch branch of the Fitzgerald family. It is 6 storeys high, and has an unusually large number of passages and chambers inside the walls. There is a 'secret chamber' off the 4th floor and a fireplace and round chimney (the latter possibly a later addition) on the top floor. A walled courtyard was originally attached to the castle, and of this the 41-foot high circular turret near the castle still remains. The castle was last occupied in 1817.
104th Annual Report of the Commissioners of Public Works 1935-6, 8; Leask, Castles 88

CALLAN Friary, Church and Motte

Augustinian Friary (475)

MAP 8 M 16
OS½" 18S.42.44

Access : Over a stile and through field. Signposted
Emonn Mac Risderd Butler of Pottlerath founded this Friary for the Augustinian Observants in 1462, but it was his son James who erected the existing buildings between 1467 and 1470, by which time the church had been affiliated to Santa Maria del Popolo in Rome. The church consists of one long rectangle crowned by a central tower, and it has a decorative doorway and window in the east wall. The sedilia in the south wall of the choir is one of the most ornamental in the country. The sacristy and domestic buildings have long since disappeared.
Leask, Churches III, 164

St Mary's Church (455)

MAP 8 M 16
OS½" 18S.42.43

Access : Direct. Key obtainable from caretaker Patrick Collins at 63 Collins Park. Signposted
The first parish church on this site in the centre of the town is attributed

to Hugh de Mapilton and was built about 1250, but the west tower is the only remaining part of this church. The rest of the church was demolished to make way for the existing structure which was built about 1460. The church consists of a nave and chancel as well as two aisles, and John Tobyn, the rector of the period, added a chapel in 1530. There are fine sculptured details on the north and south door; the carved head of a lady with 15th century head-dress, probably taken from a tomb-effigy, has been inserted in a special frame above the north door. In the nave there is a fine collection of 16th and 17th century tombstones, the most remarkable being that of John Tobyn, carved by Rory O'Tunney. In the chancel, which has been modernly roofed and which is still used for Divine worship, are an old piscina and baptismal font.

Leask, Churches III, 83; Old Kilkenny Review 15, 1963, 14

Motte (372)

MAP 8 M 16
os½″ 18s.41.44

Access : Down lane off Bridge Street and across field. Signposted

This motte, 40 feet high and 46 yards long and which was originally topped by a wooden tower, was probably built in or slightly before 1217, when William Marshal the Elder granted a Charter to the town of Callan. In 1247 it was granted to Isabella Marshal who in turn gave it to her son Richard de Clare, Earl of Gloucester and Hertford. Remains of the bailey can still be seen to the east of the motte. Another motte stood at the other end of the town but this was removed around 1850.

JRSAI 39, 1909, 319

CLARA (274) Castle

MAP 8 M 16
os½″ 19s.57.58

Access : Direct. If locked, key obtainable from James Murphy in nearby house. Signposted

A 15th century tower-house which is one of the best preserved of its type in Ireland. Preceded by a forecourt with small holes beside the gate for early guns, the entrance leads to a hall-way which has a 'murder-hole' above it through which the defenders could drop things on the heads of unwanted visitors. It is one of the very few tower-houses where the original oak floor-beams are preserved, thus giving the visitor an idea of the lowness of the ceilings in such buildings. There is a fine fireplace on the third floor, and there is also a secret room or dungeon which was only reachable from what masqueraded as a lavatory seat on the fourth floor!

JRSAI 67, 1937, 284; Leask, Castles 79

CLONAMERY (77) Church

MAP 8 N 17
os½″ 19s.66.36

Access : Quarter of a mile down a lane, then up into field to church on top of hill. Not signposted

Situated on a hillock in a serenely calm valley, the church probably stands on the site of an old monastery the history of which is unknown. The church consists of a nave and chancel and a small out-building which may have been a sacristy. The oldest part of the church is the west end, and its most notable characteristic is the flat-headed doorway with a Maltese cross standing in relief above it. There are antae in the west gable. The church was extended twice, the Romanesque chancel being added in the 12th century. The out-building may have been added in the 15th or 16th century when a bell-cot was also added to the top of the west gable.

JRSAI 55, 1925, 54; Leask, Churches I, 70; Old Kilkenny Review 9, 1956-7, 27

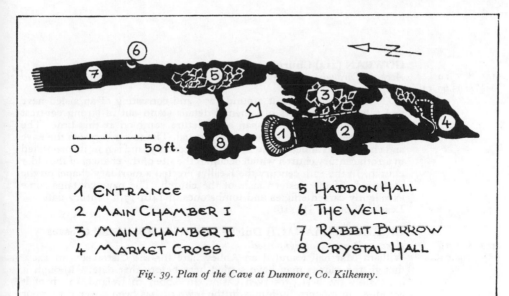

1 ENTRANCE
2 MAIN CHAMBER I
3 MAIN CHAMBER II
4 MARKET CROSS

5 HADDON HALL
6 THE WELL
7 RABBIT BURROW
8 CRYSTAL HALL

Fig. 39. Plan of the Cave at Dunmore, Co. Kilkenny.

DUNMORE (399) Cave Fig. 39

MAP 8 M 15
OS½″ 19S.51.65

Access : Direct. Signposted

Known in Old Irish literature as one of the darkest places in Ireland, and as the place where the monster Luchtigern 'The Lord of the Mice' was slain, this cave was plundered by Godfrey and the Vikings of Dublin in 928. In this raid 1,000 people were killed, and the numerous human bones found in the cave are thought to be the remains of the victims. The cave is divided into three main parts, of which Haddon Hall (No 5) and chambers leading off it are difficult of access. The wide entrance shaft (No 1) leads to the second part (Nos 2 and 3), which is the main chamber. Ahead lies a high chamber which is practically a cul-de-sac, while the portion to the left has a floor of eccentric blocks and a stalagmite on the east wall. From here an ascent leads to the third part (No. 4), the chamber with the 'Market Cross'—a huge stalagmite in the middle of the triangular chamber. To the right and left of the chamber are other dripstone formations, and the blocks forming the floor are covered in stalagmite bosses. JRSAI 11, 1870, 65; PRIA 53, 1950, 15; Coleman, Caves of Ireland (1965) 14

FRESHFORD Church

MAP 8 M 15
OS½″ 18S.41.65

Access : Direct. If locked, key obtainable from Mrs Brigit Delany, of Church Street, next door to a chemist's shop on the left hand side approaching from Kilkenny. Not signposted

The first church here was founded in 622 by St Lachtain whose arm was preserved in a 12th century shrine now in the National Museum in Dublin. The present church was built in 1730, but in the west gable is preserved a fine 12th century Romanesque doorway taken from an earlier church, the rest of which has now disappeared. The doorway, which is deep and has three orders, is covered by a hood moulding, and on the right and left has some unfortunately weathered figure sculpture. An inscription commemorates O'Ceannucain the builder and O'Kerwick the patron, but neither of these names can be identified with historically known persons.

Leask, Churches I, 154; Old Kilkenny Review 21, 1969, 5

GOWRAN (214) Church

MAP 8 N 16
OS½" 19S.63.53

Access : Through gate. Key obtainable from caretaker at 4 Dover Road. Not signposted

A Collegiate church built around 1275 and consisting of an aisled nave and a long chancel. Its ornamental details stand out in strong contrast to the more austere Cistercian architecture common at this time. The windows below the battlements are unusual. The tower between the nave and chancel was added in the 14th or 15th century, and is now incorporated in a 19th century church which occupies the site of the chancel of the older church. In the 17th century the Keallys erected a mortuary chapel on the south side of the western aisle of the church. The nave contains some excellently carved effigies and tombstones of 14th-17th century date.
Leask, Churches II, 116

GRAIGUENAMANAGH Duiske Cistercian Abbey and Crosses

MAP 8 N 16
OS½" 19S.71.44

Access : Direct. Not signposted

William Marshall founded an Abbey here for the Cistercians in 1207, though the monks may have settled here before that date. Although it is possibly the best preserved Cistercian Abbey in Ireland, much of it is hidden in modern buildings in the town or has been covered by poor modern restoration. The church consists of a nave and chancel with an aisle on each side. Although the restorations of 1813 and 1886 have covered much of the walls, the decoration of the capitals and the shapes of the arches can still be seen. The present floor of the church is about 7 feet above its original level. The chancel, the crossing and the east window give the best idea of what the church was like. In the Baptistery off the south aisle is a very fine transitional doorway of early 13th century date. The chapter house and many of the domestic buildings are smothered by modern buildings to the south of the church, but while a visit is not recommended, they contain some fine architectural features. One Richard O'Nolan was besieged in the tower of the Abbey in 1330, and in 1346 the Abbot was fined forty shillings for having harboured outlaws in the Abbey. After the Dissolution in 1541, the monastery passed to the Butlers, and the Agars bought it in 1703. In 1728 the 'Mass House' was erected against the south wall of the transept, and in 1774 the original octagonal tower fell. Much of the church was restored in 1813, and the west end re-roofed in 1886. In the graveyard to the south of the chancel there are two small granite High Crosses which were brought here from elsewhere. One, from Ballyogan, has representations of King David, the Sacrifice of Isaac, Adam and Eve and the Crucifixion on the east face and spirals on the west, while the second cross, from Aghailta, has a Crucifixion and interlacings.
JRSAI 22, 1892, 237; Leask, Churches II, 86

GRANGEFERTAGH (74) Round Tower and Church

MAP 7 L 15
OS½" 18S.31.70

Access : Through gate to graveyard. Signposted

A monastery was founded here probably by St Ciarán of Saighir in the 6th century, and in 861 Cerbhall of Ossory drove off a band of marauding Vikings who were raiding it. The only remnant of the old monastery is the 100-foot high Round Tower with 8 floors, which was burned in 1156. In the 13th century the Blanchvilles founded a monastery close by for the Canons Regular of St Augustine, and its church, dating from various periods, was in use up till 1780, and now forms part of a hand-ball alley!

Joined to the church is the Mac Gillapatrick Chapel containing the tomb of John Mac Gillapatrick (c. 1511) by O'Tunney. In 1566 the church passed into the hands of the Butlers, and in the 19th century the west doorway and east window were removed to Johnstown Church of Ireland church while a baptismal font and the representation of the Crucifixion were removed to the Catholic church there.
Old Kilkenny Review 11, 1959, 23

GRANAGH (253) Castle
MAP 8 M 18
OS½" 23S.57.14

Access : Over a stile. Not signposted
Situated on a good site overlooking the river Suir, this castle was originally built by the Le Poers, but when they lost favour with Edward III, the King granted it in 1375 to James, 2nd Earl of Ormond, in whose family it remained until it surrendered to Cromwellian troops under Axtell in 1650. Although tradition says that it was the Ormonds who built it in the 14th century, the oldest part of the castle dates back to the 13th century. These oldest parts are the three round turrets and their joining curtain wall overlooking the river. These formed part of the outer fortifications of the original castle which surrounded a square enclosure in the centre. The tall square tower was built possibly in the 14th century, but has 15th century additions. The oriel window high up in its south wall was added in the 17th century. To the west of the tower stood a fine two-storeyed hall, one of the upper windows of which is beautifully decorated with sculpted figures including an angel with the Butler arms and also St Michael the Archangel dispensing justice on the Day of Judgment with his weighing-scales. The circular building at the north-western corner of the enclosure may have been a windmill. George Roche, whose family had bought the castle in the 18th century, did some restoration work in 1824, and the castle was again partially restored around 1925.
JRSAI 64, 1934, 50; Old Kilkenny Review 12, 1960, 29

JERPOINT (80) Cistercian Abbey *Figs. 12 and 40*
MAP 8 M 16
OS½" 19S.57.40

Access : Direct. If locked, key obtainable from Edward Wallace, 150 yards down the road, 4th house on left. Signposted
This is undoubtedly one of the finest Cistercian monastic ruins in Ireland. The Abbey was founded by Donal Mac Gillapatrick, King of Ossory, in 1158 for the Benedictines (?), but it was later colonized by the Cistercians from Baltinglass in 1180. Jerpoint, in its turn, became the mother house for the Abbeys of Kilcooly, Co Tipperary and Killenny in 1184. In 1227 it became affiliated to Fountains Abbey in Yorkshire. After the Dissolution of the Monasteries it was leased to the Earl of Ormond. The lay-out is typical of the Cistercian monastery, with a three-aisled church standing on the north side of a quadrangle, on the other three sides of which lay the cloister and the domestic buildings including the Chapter House, refectory, dormitory and kitchen. The eastern end of the church may date to as early as 1160, though the original east window was replaced by the present window in the 14th century. The rest of the church was built about 1180, and although the aisles have bluntly pointed Gothic arches, the capitals are still Romanesque in character, as are also the round-headed windows in the west wall. A low wall was built up between the pillars of the aisle, and against it were placed the wooden choir-stalls. The monks in the eastern part of the church were divided from the lay-brothers in the western part of the church by a cross-wall. In the 15th

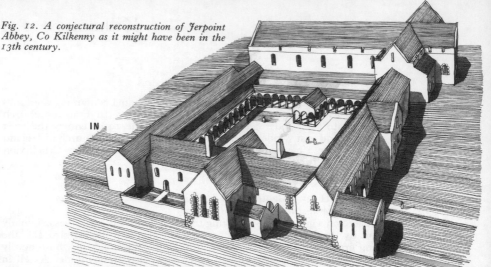

Fig. 12. A conjectural reconstruction of Jerpoint Abbey, Co Kilkenny as it might have been in the 13th century.

IN

century, considerable reconstruction took place: the north wall of the nave was rebuilt, the large square tower was placed above the crossing and the south aisle was extended outwards. The cloister, which has recently been excellently restored to some of its former glory, also dates from the 15th century and displays a fascinating variety of figured sculpture of saints, knights etc. The church harbours some very fine sculptured tombs, the most important of which are those of Felix O Dulany, Bishop of Ossory (1178-1202) in the western niche on the north side of the chancel, Katerine Poher and Robert Walsh (died 1501) and a late 13th century tomb of two knights.

Leask, Churches II, 7 and 29; JRSAI 96, 1966, 59; Official Guidebook

Fig. 40. Plan of the Cistercian Abbey at Jerpoint, Co. Kilkenny.

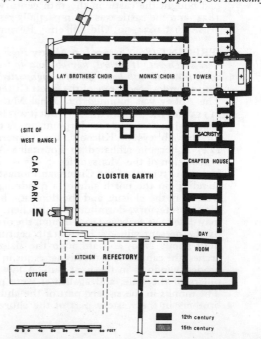

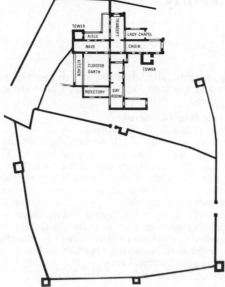

Fig. 41. Plan of the Priory at Kells, Co Kilkenny.

KELLS (180) Augustinian Priory *Fig. 41*

MAP 8 M 16
OS½" 19S.50.43

Access: Over a stile and through field. Signposted

Geoffrey de Marisco brought over four Augustinian Canons from Bodmin in Cornwall to found a new Priory here in 1193. The Prior was a Lord of Parliament. Most of the existing buildings, however, date from the 14th and 15th centuries, and although little known, they form one of the most striking conglomerations of medieval buildings in Ireland. The church consists of a nave and chancel, topped by a central square tower. It has an aisle on the west side and a chapel on the south side of the tower. Another chapel, the large Lady Chapel, opens off the transept. A further tower stands at the north-western angle of the church, and this is presumed to have been the Prior's residence, though it could also have acted as a sacristy. To the south of the church there are remnants of extensive domestic buildings, including a kitchen. The five acres to the south of the church were fortified by two enclosures, thus making it one of the largest monastic enclosures in the country. The inner enclosure is fortified by a wall with two turrets, and the main entrance is to be found in the east wall. The outer enclosure is also surrounded by a wall which is occasionally interrupted by a total of five turrets which are similar in type to tower-houses. Although the monastery was suppressed in 1540 and granted to James, Earl of Ormond, Priors continued to be elected almost until Cromwellian times.

JRSAI 36, 1906, 268

KILFANE (300) Church

MAP 8 M 16
OS½" 19S.59.45

Access: Up laneway 150 yards. Signposted

This uninteresting 14th century church has a castellated building beside it which may have been a sacristy on the ground floor and living quarters on the two floors above. The most important item in the church is the great stone effigy of a warrior with crossed legs. It probably represents Thomas de Cantwell who was described as being very old in 1319, and who may have been either the founder or the re-builder of this church. The over-life-size effigy is one of the most imposing pieces of medieval sculpture in the country. The effigy was buried for a while in the last

century but dug up again, and while the church was being used as a school, bad boys had to kiss the stony lips of 'Long Cantwell' as punishment.
JRSAI 2, 1852-3, 268

KILKEERAN (79) High Crosses

MAP 8 M 17
OS½" 18S.42.27

Access: Down lane to cemetery. Signposted
Three High Crosses, possibly of 9th century date, on the site of an Early Christian monastery about which nothing is known. The west cross is the most important. On the eastern side of the base there are 8 horsemen, while the other sides show interlacing (sometimes irregular) and geometric motifs. The lower part of the shaft of the cross is divided into panels bearing designs including interlaced goose-like animals. The rest of the cross is largely covered with interlacing interspersed with bosses. The east cross is undecorated and may be unfinished. The north cross is tall and thin, has no circle, and bears slight traces of ornament. Near the east cross are some fragments cemented together to form a pillar. The first two crosses have unusual conical caps.
Roe, High Crosses of Western Ossory (1958) 27

KILKENNY Castle, Churches, Round Tower, House etc *Fig. 42*

MAP 8 M 16
OS½" 19S.51.56

Kilkenny is one of the most attractive and quaint of the inland towns of Ireland, and the considerable number of medieval monuments it contains help to preserve its medieval atmosphere. Originally the site of a monastery set up by St Cainnech, its importance really began when William the Marshall built the first stone castle of Kilkenny in the early years of the 13th century. The castle was bought in 1391 by James Butler, 3rd Earl of Ormond, and under his successors the town grew to be one of considerable note, and the seat of the Irish Confederates in 1645.

The Castle

Access: At present accessible only on special occasions. It is hoped that it will be open to the public shortly. Not signposted
Strongbow probably built a motte here shortly after he gained possession of the land in 1172. In 1204 William the Marshall built the first stone castle on the same site. Its shape—square with rounded turrets at the corners—has still been largely preserved despite a number of re-constructions blotting out all view of the original castle. The Castle retained much of its original form until the first Duke of Ormonde altered it in the 1660's, but the present exterior is largely due to a 19th century reconstruction. There is a fine classical gateway in the west wall dating to 1684, and one wing of the present castle is an Art Gallery designed by Woodward in the last century. In the old castle stables on the opposite side of the road is the Kilkenny Design Workshop.
Arch Journal 88, 1931, 391 and 93, 1937, 180; Leask, Castles 57; Lanigan, Kilkenny Castle

Rothe House

Access: Direct. Entrance fee charged. Signposted
Situated in Parliament Street, not far from the fine 18th century Tholsel, this Elizabethan house was built by John Rothe in 1594. Its arcaded front ground floor leads to the tourist office, and the first and second floors, with their mullioned windows, house the museum. The roof of the second floor has recently been expertly restored. A vaulted passage leads from the street into a courtyard (from whence entrance to the museum) and behind this is a second house which was the home of the

Kilkenny Branch of the Gaelic League for some time. Behind this house is a second courtyard and a third house which has not been restored. The front house, which has recently been restored, is one of the best preserved examples of the typical rich merchant's house in an Irish town of the 16th century.
Lanigan, Rothe House

St Canice's Cathedral
Access : Direct. Open 9–1 and 2–6. Signposted
This beautifully kept Cathedral occupies the site of an earlier church which was burned in 1085 and again in 1114. The Cathedral, with nave, choir and two transepts, was begun by Bishop Hugh de Mapilton (1251–6) and was probably finished by 1280. Most of the existing Cathedral dates to the thirteenth century, though the tower was added in the 14th century after the original tower had fallen in 1332 and considerable restorations were carried out in 1863-4. In the chancel are three sets of three lancet windows. An unusual feature of the church is a gallery under the west window; there is also a fine but simple west doorway. The glories of the Cathedral include one of the finest collections of 16th and 17th century tombstones, including that of James Shortal (1508) by O'Tunney. There is also a good 13th century baptismal font. To the south of the church stands the Round Tower which has lost its conical roof. The tower may be climbed on payment of a small fee.
Arch. Journal 88, 1931, 393; Leask, Churches II, 103

St Francis' Friary (72)
Access : Only through Smithwick's brewery. Key obtainable at brewery office.
This Franciscan friary was founded by Richard the Marshal around 1232. It was given a royal grant in 1245, but the only part of the building dating from this period is the choir. However, the choir was further extended in 1321, and during the course of this extension the graceful and unusual 7-light east window was built. The tall and slender tower which includes pleasant sculptural details such as the figures supporting the arches, is one of the earliest of the Franciscan towers in Ireland. There is a Gothic baptismal font in a niche at the base of the tower. A chapel or sacristy, and some remains of the domestic buildings of the Friary were situated to the south of the church and now form part of the buildings of the brewery.
Arch. Journal 88, 1931, 394; Leask, Churches II, 93 and 133

Black Friar's Church
Access : Direct and usually open
This church was founded for the Dominicans probably soon after 1226 and dedicated to the Holy Trinity. Four general chapters of the Irish province of the order were held here. During the Black Death in 1349 eight friars died in one day. It was suppressed in 1541, but was repaired again by the Dominicans in 1643 though abandoned once more shortly afterwards. It now serves as a Catholic church. The chancel of the old church has disappeared, and the present church consists of the nave and south transept of the old church. The nave dates to the 13th century; the transept was added in the 14th century, while new windows were inserted and the tower added in the 15th century. Note the medieval alabaster statue of the Trinity and the crude statue of St Dominic in the nave.
Leask, Churches II, 128

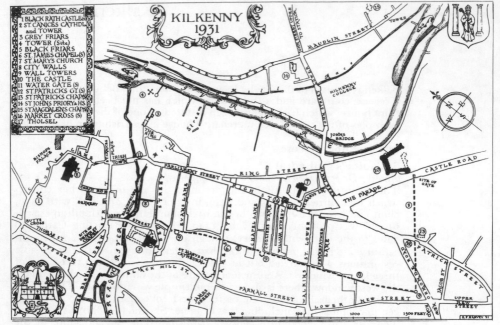

Fig. 42. Plan of the Town of Kilkenny in 1931.

St John's Priory (331 and 344)
Access : Direct

This Priory was founded by William Marshal the younger for the Canons Regular of St Augustine in the first quarter of the 13th century. The choir is the only considerable part of the church remaining; it contains a mutilated double effigy tomb dating from about 1500. It is noted for its twin 3-light windows in the east wall with its capitals carved with heads. The Lady Chapel to the south which was built in the 14th century and re-built in 1817 is still used for Divine Worship, and it had so many windows that it was known as the 'Lantern of Ireland'. In 1780 most of the priory and the church was demolished to make way for a military barracks.
Leask, Churches II, 109

KILLAMERY (75) High Cross

MAP 7 L 17
OS½″ 18s.38.36

Access : Up a lane to cemetery. Signposted

St Goban Find is reputed to have been the founder of the original monastery here. Not far from the modern ruined church stands the fine High Cross which has been dated to the 9th century. Both cross and base are richly ornamented with a variety of geometric motifs. The west face of the cross has a Crucifixion in the centre; to the left a stag-hunting scene, to the right a chariot-procession while above is David playing the harp. The east face is largely decorated with serpents and marigolds. At the end of the north arm of the cross are four scenes arranged in a square, possibly representing Jacob wrestling with the Angel (top left), David killing the lion combined with the Death of Goliath (?) (top right), while the other two scenes have not been identified. On the west side of the expanded butt of the cross is an inscription doubtfully read as OR DO MAELSECHNAILL (a prayer for Maelsechnaill)—a man about whom nothing is known. The cross had a capstone which was used locally as a cure for headaches!
Roe, High Crosses of Western Ossory (1958) 34

KILMOGUE (324) 'Leac an Scáil' Dolmen

MAP 8 M 17
OS½" 19S.50.28

Access : Along a private avenue, over a stile and along a field. Not signposted
This is a fine example of a portal dolmen, consisting of an irregularly shaped chamber closed at the front by a high stone (hence the name 'portal' dolmen). There are traces of a stone cairn around the base. It has not been excavated.

KILREE (76) Church, Round Tower and High Cross

MAP 8 M 16
OS½" 18S.49.41

Access : Over a stile and through field to cemetery. Signposted
A 96-foot high Round Tower, missing its original conical top, dominates this old monastic site whose early history is unknown. Near it stands a ruined church with flat-headed doorway and antae. The chancel and the rounded arch are later additions. The church may have been put to secular use in the 17th century. In the chancel there is a good 17th century tomb. In a field to the west stands a much worn High Cross, possibly of 9th century date. Much of the cross is decorated with geometrical motifs. On the east face are representations of stag-hunting and a chariot, while two of the four figured panels on the end of the south arm of the cross probably represent Jacob and the Angel, and Daniel killing the lion. Daniel in the Lion's Den can be seen on the west face. The cross somewhat resembles that at Killamery (see above), but the decorated bosses which protrude from the centre are peculiar.
Roe, High Crosses of Western Ossory (1958) 39

KNOCKTOPHER (73a) Church

MAP 8 M 17
OS½" 19S.53.37

Access : Through gate to cemetery. Tower locked (key kept at Knocktopher Abbey nearby). Not signposted
The remains of a Gothic church which was largely demolished in 1870. A medieval tower with a probably earlier, 12th century Romanesque doorway and a modern top still survives, together with the north wall of the church with its 15th century window. Below the latter is a fine tomb dated 1622. Locked in the base of the tower is an interesting double-effigy tomb of the 15th century. Knocktopher House nearby (private) incorporates part of the old Carmelite Friary of St Saviour, while on the opposite side of the road to the graveyard is Knocktopher motte, built by Matthew fitz Griffin, seneschal of Leinster, some time around 1200.

RATHEALY (376) Fort

MAP 7 L 15
OS½" 18S.38.60

Access : Across three fields. Not signposted
A fine ring-fort with a raised circular area in the centre and surrounded by a 20-foot deep ditch, outside which lie two concentric banks. In the same field are the scant remains of a medieval chapel.
JRSAI 89, 1959, 97

SHEEPSTOWN (73b) Church

MAP 8 M 17
OS½" 19S.51.37

Access : Over a field to churchyard. Not signposted
A simple rectangular church of 12th century date, with later additions. There is a simple round-headed doorway with Romanesque moulding in the west wall, while the 12th century south door was altered later.
Leask, Churches I, 83

THOMASTOWN (191) Church

MAP 8 M 16
OS½" 19S.58.42

Access : Direct. Key obtainable from Staffords, Pipe Street, the second house on the left leaving Thomastown on the Kilkenny road. Not signposted

The ruins of a 13th century three-aisled church with chancel. The north aisle with its sparse decoration as well as the foundations of the outer wall and a sacristy still remain. Note the fragments of a baptismal font and a piscina near the west doorway. In the cemetery, near the main gate to the town, is the head of an unpierced ringed cross of unknown date mounted on a cement shaft.
Leask, Churches II, 117

TIBBERAGHNY Cross-pillar

MAP 8 M 17
OS½" 22S.44.21

Access: Through gate, 100 yards down through field, then just before bridge over railway line turn right through gate. Pillar is in cemetery beside gate. Not signposted
A pillar (originally forming part of a cross?) standing on the site of an ancient monastery founded by St Modomhnach in the 6th century. On one face is a centaur holding an object looking like an axe in one hand and a dagger(?) in the other, and above him are two animals. On the other face is a circular motif with a Celtic spiraloid pattern. On the two narrow sides are animals, one of which is a stag. The date of the pillar is uncertain, but it could date to the 9th century.
Roe, High Crosses of Western Ossory (1958) 25

TULLAHERIN (161) Church, Round Tower and Ogham Stone

MAP 8 M 16
OS½" 19S.59.48

Access: Through a stile to cemetery. Signposted
The most prominent monument on this old monastic site is the 6-storey high Round Tower. Its door is blocked up, and its top storey may have been built at the same time as the rebuilding of the neighbouring church. The church consists of a pre-Norman nave with antae, which was later extensively re-built, and a chancel was added possibly in the 15th century. Near the south side of the church is a much defaced Ogham stone. A pilgrimage used to be held here in honour of St Ciarán of Saigher, who was probably the founder of the monastery.
JRSAI 23, 1893, 208; Old Kilkenny Review 6, 1953, 47

ULLARD (78) Church and High Cross

MAP 8 N 16
OS½" 19S.72.48

Access: Over a stile into graveyard. Key for vault obtainable from Patrick Gardner, Ullard. Not signposted
A 12th century Romanesque church consisting of nave and chancel. The doorway has been much tampered with (possibly in the 16th century when the innermost order of the doorway was constructed). Over the window above the doorway is a sculptured panel showing the meeting of two people—it may have formed part of the original doorway, as at Freshford (see above). Note the worn heads above the doorway; one is meant to represent St Moling, the founder of the church, and the other is said to be St Fiacre. The chancel also bears some Romanesque features, but was partially blocked up (in the 16th century?). An interesting feature is the vault under the chancel, which was necessary to keep the chancel on the same level as the nave, as the church is built on the slope of a hill. The north wall of the chancel was widened in the 15th century and a staircase built into the thickness of the wall. Behind the church, at the corner of the handball alley, there is a granite High Cross with scenes representing the Crucifixion, David with his harp, the Temptation of St Anthony, Adam and Eve, the Sacrifice of Isaac and six Apostles. A pilgrimage used to take place to a well in the field beside the church.
Old Kilkenny Review 22, 1970, 58; Leask, Churches I, 126

AGHABOE Churches

MAP 7 L 14
OS½" 15S.33.86

Access : Over wall or through gate. Not signposted

The first monastery was founded here by St Cainnech in the 6th century. It was plundered in 913, rebuilt in 1052 and burnt again in 1116. It was once the principal church of the Kingdom of Ossory. In 1234 it was rebuilt again as an Augustinian Priory, but was burnt once more in 1346 by Dermot Mac Gillapatrick, and after 1349 remained in Mac Gillapatrick hands. The tower of the present Protestant church retains original 13th century portions, including the arcade near the top, but the door is probably 15th century. The church, which stands on the site of the Augustinian church, has some windows taken from the nearby Dominican Friary. This friary was founded in 1382 by Mac Gillapatrick, and consists of one long nave with some niches, and a south chapel built by the Phelans. Some of the windows were incorporated into a 'folly' at Heywood House, Ballinakill. In a field to the north is a square motte, possibly built in the 13th century by Adam de Hereford.

DUNAMASE Castle

MAP 8 M 14
OS½" 16S.53.98

Access : Up path from road. Signposted

Originally used as a fort in Early Christian times, this is one of the most superbly and strategically sited castles in the country; it is unfortunate that its state of preservation does not match its siting. On the arrival of the Normans, the site was in the hands of Dermot McMurrough Kavanagh. Through his marriage with Eva, it fell into the hands of his father-in-law, Strongbow, and then through his daughter Isabella to William Marshall. The castle is first mentioned in 1215 when King John ordered Geoffrey Lutterel to hand it over to William. On William's death it came into the possession of William de Braos who enlarged and re-fortified the castle and erected it into a manor around 1250. By 1264 it had passed to the Fitzgeralds; shortly afterwards it was owned by Roger de Mortimer, and on his death it passed by marriage to Theobald de Verdun. In 1335 the King ordered that it be handed over to Fulk-de-la-Freine. The O'Mores, hereditary owners of the area, seized it for two years, but it was then re-taken by Roger de Mortimer who further fortified and garrisoned it. Some time later the O'Mores regained possession, but handed it over to the King in 1538. During the Civil War it changed hands many times before being taken finally by the Cromwellian generals Hewson and Reynolds, who rendered its fortifications harmless. In the 17th century Sir John Parnell partially restored it as a residence, but his son allowed it to fall into its final decay.

On approaching from the road, one passes first the banks and ditches forming the oldest and outermost defences. Then through the bailey one reaches the first gate, of uncertain date. It leads into a triangular area, which in turn leads through a gateway with double turrets in the curtain wall into the innermost area. Here, on top of the hill, stand the remains of a long rectangular tower of 13th century date. It is made of massive masonry and has a square tower on the west face. The door on the west face and the west, north and east windows are probably 15th century insertions.

JCKAS 6, 1909, 161; Arch Journal 93, 1937, 192; Leask, Castles 64

ERRILL (113) Church and Cross

MAP 7 L 15
OS½" 18S.22.78

Access : Direct. Not signposted

In the cemetery is a late medieval church of little interest. The round-

headed south window may have come from an earlier church on the same site. The trunk of a cross with coat of arms and an inscription, put up in 1622 in memory of Florence Fitzpatrick and his wife, has been re-erected near the National School nearby.
JRSAI 54, 1924, 147

FOSSY (114a) Church

MAP 8 M 14
OS½″ 16S.55.90

Access : Over two stiles and through a field. Not signposted
A 15th century church of little interest with arched doorway and small square side windows as well as an east window.

KILLESHIN (115) Church *Fig. 43*

MAP 8 N 15
OS½″ 19S.67.78

Access : Up path to cemetery. Signposted
The site of an old monastery founded allegedly by St Comdhan or Comghan towards the end of the 5th century. The last historical reference to the monastery is in 1082. An oratory here was destroyed in 1041 and the monastery was burned in 1077. The present church was built in the 12th century, and has one of the finest Romanesque doorways in the country. The doorway has four orders, with capitals bearing heads with intertwined hair, an arch with foliage and animal motifs, the whole being topped by a partially modern hood. An inscription on the door which may possibly read 'A prayer for Diarmait (?) King of Leinster' might date the church to the reign of a king of that name who died in 1117. One anta of the original church still remains. The chancel is a later addition and in the north wall it has a window which is round-headed inside and pointed outside. The east window is probably 16th century in date, but may possibly have been inserted in its present position when the church was partially re-built in the 18th century. There is an old font beside the door. A Round Tower, 105 feet high, lay to the north-west of the church, but this was taken down in 1703 because the owner feared that it might fall on his cattle!
JCKAS 6, 1910, 185; JRSAI 48, 1918, 183 and 55, 1925, 83; Leask, Churches I, 101

Fig. 43. The 12th century Romanesque doorway at Killeshin, Co Laois.

LEA Castle

MAP 8 M·13
os½″ 16N.57.12

Access : Through farmyard and 100 yards across field. Signposted
The remnants of a once great Norman castle built either by the Marshalls or the Fitzgeralds. A castle is mentioned in 1203 as already existing, but this probably refers to an earlier castle here. O'More burned the castle in 1346, and in 1422 O'Dempsey captured it from the Earl of Kildare. The O'Dempseys retained the castle until it was taken from them in 1452 by the Earl of Ormond. Silken Thomas Fitzgerald retreated here during his rebellion in 1535. In 1556 it was mortgaged for £500 and 600 ounces of silver plate by the Earl of Kildare to Sir Maurice Fitzgerald of Lackagh, and was leased to Robert Bath in 1618. It changed hands a number of times in the 1640's, and the Confederates used it as a mint before the Cromwellians took it in 1650. Although it passed through various private hands after that, it was never afterwards used as a fortification. The castle itself is square in plan with three-quarters round towers at the corners; it stands within an oval-shaped area, which is still partly surrounded by a wall with wall-walks. The tower consisted of a basement and three storeys, and the entrance was in the first floor. A window in the north side of the tower is still preserved and through its shape the castle can be dated to about 1250. To the east of the castle itself is an open area surrounded by a wall with a gate-building in the south wall with two rounded towers which may date to about 1297. This gate-building was later made residential by blocking the gateway and by the addition of another building. A town which surrounded the castle was destroyed in the 14th century.
JCKAS 4, 1903-5, 325; Arch Journal 93, 1937, 173

SLEATY (116) Church and Crosses

MAP 8 N 15
os½″ 19S.71.79

Access : Through gate and over field to cemetery. Not signposted.
The first monastery was founded by St Fiach, who was a bishop of all Leinster during St Patrick's lifetime. One of its most famous abbots was Aedh who dictated a Life of St Patrick, and who made the monastery a centre for studies dealing with St Patrick. The scant remains include two tall but undecorated granite crosses and a medieval church with pointed side-door.

TIMAHOE (114b) Round Tower and Church

MAP 8 M 14
os½″ 16S.54.90

Access : Over stile to churchyard. Key if necessary from Mr H. Kerr in village nearby. Signposted
The only remnant of the early monastery founded by St Mochua (died 657) is a very well preserved Round Tower, 96 feet high. It is one of the fattest Round Towers in the country. It is unique in that it has a double Romanesque doorway with fine ornamentation including heads with intertwined hair. Bring a pair of binoculars with you to see the detail, as it is high up off the ground. There is also a Romanesque window in the third floor. The deaths of monks in the old monastery are reported between 880 and 1007, and reference is made to a church in 1089. But the Round Tower probably dates to the 12th century. The monastery was re-founded in later medieval times by the O'Mores. After the Suppression, the monastery and lands were granted to Sir Thomas Loftus and later (1609) to Richard Cosby. It was probably one of the Cosby family who transformed what was a medieval church into a castle; only the east wall of the castle, incorporating an arch of the 15th century church, remains. The last friar of the monastery was killed in 1650.
JRSAI 54, 1924, 31; Leask, Churches I, 107

AGHADERRARD WEST (477) Court Cairn

MAP 2 J 6
OS½" 7G.85.54

Access: Down private path, and then through two fields. Visit not recommended. Not signposted
Remains of the chamber and one side of the court of a court cairn.
PRIA 60 C 1960, 99, No 2

CLOONMORRIS Church and Ogham Stone

MAP 4 K 9
OS½" 12N.08.85

Access: Through stile into graveyard. Signposted
A church, built around 1200, which served as an auxiliary to the Augustinian Priory of Mohill. The church has simple but attractive east and south lancet windows. The moulding on the outside of the east window ends with two upturned heads. The plain north doorway was inserted in the 15th century. Beside the entrance to the graveyard an Ogham stone has been re-erected—it is the only one in Co. Leitrim. All that can be read of the inscription is the name of the person commemorated: 'Qenuven'; the other letters have been defaced.
JRSAI 39, 1909, 132

CORRACLOONA (405) Megalithic Tomb

MAP 2 J 6
OS½" 7G.00.43

Access: Across low wall and across 40 yards of boggy land. Signposted
A megalithic tomb consisting of a rectangular chamber and what seems like a forecourt. The forecourt wall is made of dry-stone walling. The unusual feature of this tomb is the stone blocking the entrance to the tomb, at the bottom of which is a 'port hole'—presumably to allow subsequent burials to take place. The whole is surrounded by the remains of a cairn 60 feet long. The tomb was excavated, but the results were never published.
JRSAI 67, 1937, 302

CREEVELEA (69) Franciscan Friary

MAP 2 H/J 7
OS½" 7G.80.31

Access: 100 yards down lane, then turn right to cemetery; alternatively along path from town centre, down by riverside. Signposted
This Franciscan Friary, founded by Owen O'Rourke and his wife Margaret in 1508, was the last Franciscan Friary to be founded in Ireland before the Suppression of the Monasteries. The church has a nave, choir, tower and south transept. The west doorway and the window above it are well preserved, as is also the east window, but the window in the south transept has vanished. The transept has a number of recesses. The tower was converted into living quarters in the 17th century. To the north of the church a number of domestic buildings surround the cloister. The cloister is irregular in shape, and in the centre of the north side there are a number of interesting carvings on the pillars. One of these shows St Francis with the stigmata, and with an inscription crossing his body. Another shows the same saint in a pulpit with birds perched on a tree; legend says that he understood the language of the birds. On the east side of the cloister are three rooms, that nearest the church being a sacristy, and beyond these rooms is a passage joining the cloister with the outside world. In the north wing is the refectory and kitchen; the buildings in the north-western part are later additions. On the first and second floors were dormitories and other rooms. The friary was accidentally burned in 1536, but it was probably impossible to restore it completely before it was suppressed five years later. It was still in use in 1574, but its woodwork was burned when Bingham took it over and used it as a stables in 1590. The friars

took possession again in 1601-2 and the church was repaired again by some Franciscans in 1642, but the Cromwellians forced them to leave. It later fell into the hands of a man named Harrison who, on being paid a fantastic rent, allowed the friars to return once more and roof the church with thatch. But they probably left finally towards the end of the 17th century.

Official Guidebook; Leask, Churches III, 129 and 149

FENAGH (68) Churches

MAP 2 K 8
OS½″ 7H.11.08

Access : Across field. Signposted
Two churches stand on the site of an earlier monastery. The south church has a fine pointed west doorway and a beautiful 14th or 15th century east window. Note the string course with rolled moulding beneath the outside of the window. The north church was probably built in the 15th century, but replaces and partly uses the stones of a pre-Norman church. Both churches have the western part roofed with a vault above which was a gallery. Other buildings and various earthworks are presumably part of the medieval monastery. The old monastery was founded by St Caillin, and it seems to have continued in use till the Dissolution in 1541. It was burned in 1360, and was known to have had a house of public hospitality in 1447.

JRSAI 61, 1931, 44; Leask, Churches II, 148

JAMESTOWN Town Gate

MAP 4 J 9
OS½″ 12M.98.97

Access : Road passes under gate
Jamestown was founded by Sir Charles Coote in 1625 and was occupied by O'Rourke in 1642. Little remains of the town wall except the old town gate which straddles the modern Dublin-Sligo road.

JRSAI 35, 1905, 140

LAGHTY BARR (508) Seán Mac Diarmada's House

MAP 2 J 6
OS½″ 7G.99.42

Access : Along partly untarred road, then up avenue to house. Signposted
A three-roomed thatched cottage, partially surrounded by rhododendrons, and with a fine view over Upper Lough Macnean. It was the house of Sean Mac Diarmada, the patriot who was one of the seven signatories of the Proclamation of Independence in 1916 and who was shot later in the same year. It is now lived in as a private house.

PARK'S CASTLE (390)

MAP 2 H 7
OS½″ 7G.78.35

Access : Direct from road. Key obtainable from Patrick Healy, 200 yards away at Five Mile Bourne. Signposted
Picturesquely situated on the Sligo-Dromahaire road beside Lough Gill, this is a castle built by one of the 'Planters' early in the 17th century. The castle is rectangular in shape, has three storeys with mullioned windows and diamond-shaped chimneys. It forms part of one side of a five-sided bawn with large rounded turrets at two corners. The entrance to the bawn is through a passage-way in the ground floor of the house.

Leask, Castles 140

Admire—but don't destroy

ADARE Churches and Castle

MAP 7 G 16
OS½″ 17R.47.46

Adare is a beautiful village which is situated not far from an important cluster of medieval monuments, and some of these are still in use. The town seems to have come into prominence first in Norman times. Geoffrey de Marisco may have been the first founder of the castle in the early years of the 13th century. Later in the same century, probably around 1230, a monastery was founded for Trinitarian monks of the Order of the Redemption of Captives, and later again Augustinian and Franciscan monasteries were founded.
JRSAI 37, 1907, 24

The following 4 buildings are in the grounds of Adare Manor and may be reached through the entrance to the Manor (Open Tuesdays-Fridays 10.00–1.00 and 2.30–6.00 and Sundays 2.30–6.00; Closed Saturdays and Mondays. Admission fee to Manor and Demesne charged) or through the Golf course.

Castle *Fig. 44*

This is a large square tower standing in a possibly contemporary ringfort. It is surrounded by a strong battlemented rampart with semi-circular bastions and a gate to the south with a drawbridge. Outside the surrounding ditch is another wall with two gates, the southern one being flanked by two towers. Beside the river is the great hall, with early 13th century windows looking on to the river, and nearby is a 15th century kitchen and a bakery. The east gate leads to an enclosed but unwalled space inside the outer ditch; it was originally part of an old bailey belonging to the castle, but when the new wall was built it was left outside the wall. The castle was already in ruins by 1329; it was partially rebuilt shortly afterwards, but was damaged again before 1376. The castle was besieged by the English in 1580 and rendered harmless in 1599. Although it was made harmless again by the Cromwellians, it had ceased to play any important role by then.
Leask, Castles 34; NMAJ 8, 1961, 193

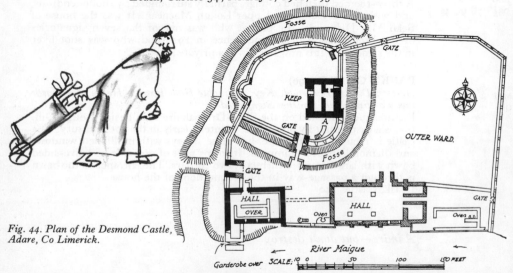

Fig. 44. Plan of the Desmond Castle, Adare, Co Limerick.

Franciscan Friary

Founded for the Franciscans by Thomas, Earl of Kildare in 1464 and completed two years later, this Friary stands in the middle of the golf course—so watch out for golf-balls! It was approached by the 'Kilmallock Gate' which now stands by itself to the west of the church, minus the Geraldine arms which once adorned it. The church consists of a nave and choir, and a transept with side chapels which was added before 1484. The church has a fine sedilia and well preserved windows; the founder and his wife provided the money for glass for the windows. The tower was added before 1492. To the north of the church is a cloister, the west side of which is more ornamental than the other sides. The surrounding buildings include a refectory, and a dormitory which was added before 1502. Other buildings separate from the main building, including an infirmary, were added at about the same time. The Friary was restored by the Earl of Dunraven in 1875.
Leask, Churches II, 147

St Nicholas of Myra Church

North of the castle, also beside the golf course, is the chapel of St Nicholas of Myra which was built and re-built between the 13th and the 16th centuries. To the north of it is a small 15th century chapel with a chaplain's quarters over the east end.

Adare Manor

Opening times given above. This is a fine Gothic mansion owned by the Wyndham-Quins which houses paintings by Canaletto, Ruysdael and Reynolds among others. In the grounds are some Ogham stones. The mansion was built in 1832.

White or 'Trinitarian' Monastery

In the village itself is the White or 'Trinitarian' Monastery which is now the Catholic parish church. Of the original church the tower, south wall and a part of the domestic buildings survive, as well as a low turret which was a bell-cot. This monastery was dedicated to St James and was allegedly founded by Lord Ossory in 1230 and restored in 1275. It is the only monastery of its order known to have survived in Ireland; the monks' full title was Trinitarian Canons of the Order of the Redemption of Captives. The church was extended to its present size in the middle of the last century.

Augustinian Friary

To the east of the village, near the Limerick road, is the Augustinian Friary. Built around 1325, it is now the Church of Ireland parish church. It has a nave, chancel and a south aisle. There are some fine windows and a sedilia. The tower and some of the domestic buildings (partly re-roofed to serve as a school) were added in the 15th century. The stonework of the church is of a high quality, and the church is one of the few examples where we can get an idea of what these Irish medieval churches looked like originally.
NMAJ 1, 3, 1938, 108; Leask, Churches II, 126

ARDAGH (459) Ring-fort

MAP 6 F 17
OS½″ 17R.27.39

Access : Across bank into field. Signposted
A ring-fort with high bank and deep ditch on the north and south sides, but the eastern and western portions appear never to have been finished.

In 1868 the Ardagh chalice and a brooch (now in the National Museum in Dublin) were found in the fort.

ARDPATRICK Church and Round Tower

MAP 7 H 17
OS½" 22R.64.21

Access : 100 yards up lane, then left into field and up track for 300 yards to top of hill. Not signposted

The first monastery here is said to have been founded by St Patrick, and it was the place from where contributions from all Munster were collected for Armagh. All that remains of the old monastery is the stump of a Round Tower (outside the cemetery wall) and a church with antae and a plain round-headed south doorway, built probably around 1200. The monuments are not interesting in themselves, but the climb to the top of the hill is worth it for the panoramic view of Co Limerick.
JRSAI 38, 1908, 75

ASKEATON Castle and Franciscan Friary

MAP 6 F 16
OS½" 17R.34.50

Access : Direct, and down a slight lane in each case. Key for castle from Mr Casey at house beside gate. Signposted

The Castle (201)

The castle was founded on an island in the river Deel around 1199, probably by William de Burgo. The tower on the rock dates to the 15th century, but it replaces an older tower on the site. Only a part of the tower remains, but it still retains some fine windows and a fine fireplace on the third floor. It stands at the corner of a walled bawn, and the whole island was also surrounded by a stout wall. This latter wall on its western side enclosed the Banqueting Hall which was erected by the 7th Earl of Desmond between 1440 and 1459 on the vaulted foundations of an earlier hall. One of the finest medieval secular buildings in Ireland, the hall has finely carved windows as well as a blind arcade in the south wall. There was originally a chapel at the south end. The castle itself had already passed to Thomas de Clare before 1287. In 1318 Edward II granted it to Robert de Welle, and only by 1348 had it passed to the Earls of Desmond who held it for over two centuries. In the Desmond Rebellion of 1579, the Earl defended it against John Malbie, but in 1580 it fell to Pelham and was handed over shortly afterwards to Edward or Francis Berkeley. In 1599 it was besieged by the 'Sugán' Earl of Desmond, but the siege was successfully raised by the Earl of Essex 247 days later, after which Queen Elizabeth granted it to St Leger. The Berkeleys regained possession in 1610. The castle surrendered to the Confederates under Purcell in 1642, and it was rendered harmless in 1652. The early 18th century building near the tower is reputed to have been a 'Hell-Fire Club'.
JRSAI 33, 1903, 28; PRIA 26, 1906, 203; Leask, Castles 123

Franciscan Friary (185)

The friary was founded probably by Gerald 'The Poet', 4th Earl of Desmond in 1389. The Conventual Franciscans for whom it was built changed to the Observantine rule in 1490. Although the church was begun at the time of foundation, much of the present building dates from 1420-40. It has a nave and chancel, as well as a north transept. Noteworthy are the delicately carved windows, the sedilia and the triple tomb niches. One of the best features of the Friary is the excellently preserved cloister which is unusual in being situated to the south of the church. In the north east corner is a representation of St Francis with stigmata, and the buildings above the cloister, including the dormitory, are situated over the cloister in the usual Franciscan manner. To the south of the cloister is the refectory, with a special niche for the reader. The Friary was plundered and wrecked by Sir John Malbie in 1579, and some of the friars were massacred. The Friary was revived again in 1627, and continued to be used by the friars as late as 1714.

JRSAI 33, 1903, 32; Leask, Churches III, 100, 137 and 156

BALLYGRENNAN Castle

MAP 7 H 17
OS½" 18R.63.35

Access: 100 yards along private avenue. Not signposted
Now used as a farmyard, this was a fine four-storeyed tower of 15th century date. The second floor is vaulted, and the castle still preserves a number of mullioned windows. It stands in one of two courtyards adjacent to the castle, and high-gabled houses of a slightly later date also stand within the walls. The castle was originally held by Gerald, Earl of Kildare, but in 1583 it was in the hands of W. ffoxe. In 1621 it was granted to Dr Metcalf and a man named Jones, but by 1657 it was again in ffoxe hands. It was sold shortly afterwards to a man named Evans.

PRIA 26, 1906-7, 171, No. 188; Leask, Castles 122

CARRIGOGUNNELL Castle

MAP 7 G 16
OS½" 17R.50.55

Access: Up untarred lane for a quarter of a mile. Not signposted
This castle is superbly situated on a volcanic rock with a marvellous view overlooking the whole Shannon estuary. It consists of a multi-sided enclosure fortified by a strong wall probably of 15th century date. At the north end, overlooking the Shannon, is a four-storeyed tower, and to the east is a tower of three storeys, with a gabled roof and a fireplace on the first floor. Both of these buildings probably belong to the second half of the 16th century. There are also stout walls of another building within the enclosure. It is a pity that the buildings are not better preserved. Mahon O'Brien surrendered the castle to Grey, the Lord Deputy, in 1536, after which it passed to Donoth O'Brien and his successors. It was later sold to Michael Boyle, afterwards Archbishop of Dublin. In 1691 it surrendered, together with its garrison of 150 men, to S'Gravenmore, and Ginckell had it blown up a month afterwards.

JRSAI 37, 1907, 374

CLONKEEN (84) Church *Fig. 45*

MAP 7 H 16
OS½" 18R.69.55

Access: Over stile into churchyard. Signposted
A small church with antae, and with a well-preserved Romanesque doorway with bulbous capitals, a decorative pillar and a head at the top of the arch. There is a round-headed window, also 12th century in date, in the north wall. The eastern two-thirds of the church date probably to the 15th century. Nothing is known of the history of the church except that it was already in ruins in 1657, and that a vandal carved his initials on the doorway in 1779!

Leask, Churches I, 127

DISERT OENGHUSA (83) Church and Round Tower

MAP 7 G 16
OS½" 17R.49.41

Access: One third of a mile up private avenue with many pot-holes. Signposted
The monastery is first mentioned in history in 1083, when one of its abbots died, but it was probably founded by Oenghus the Culdee, the great reformer who died in 815. The present church is 15th/16th century in date, but it incorporates parts of an older church as can be seen from the many large stones in the walls and the broken lintelled doorway now in

Fig. 45. Twelfth century Romanesque doorway at Clonkeen, Co Limerick.

the south wall. The east gable is a later construction, and the west gable was rebuilt sometime before 1869. The church was in use as a parish church up till at least 1418. Near the church is a Round Tower, 65 feet high, with pellets and moulding above the round-headed doorway. When excavated, the floor of the Round Tower was found to contain human bones and a solid clay floor.

JRSAI 10, 1868, 54; PRIA 25, 1904, 385

DUNTRYLEAGUE (315) Passage Grave etc

MAP 7 H 17
OS½" 18R.78.28

Access: From Galbally up laneway to its highest point, then into field and bog up to the top of the hill. Not signposted
On the top of the hill is a mound which contained 8 smaller mounds, but excavation yielded nothing other than a piece of iron. In a saddle between the two neighbouring hill-tops is a fine megalithic tomb, with a long entrance passage leading to a chamber which expands inwards. The roof-stones rise like steps to the top of the chamber—a system well known in Brittany. The grave was probably surrounded by a round mound.

Journal of the Limerick Field Club 3, 1908, 217; JRSAI 50, 1920, 119 and 66, 1936, 182; PRIA 33 C 1916-7, 477

GLENQUIN (268) Castle

MAP 6 F 17
OS½" 17R.25.26

Access: Through stile. For key, go up road, then first turn right, then second gate on right (with pebble dashing) and up avenue to farmhouse where caretaker, Mr W Deely, lives. Signposted
A fine six-storey castle with two well-preserved barrel-vaulted rooms, and arrow-slits on the top storey. The two entrances on the ground floor are unusual, but one may have been inserted later. According to tradition the castle was built by the O'Hallinans, a family who were all put to the sword by the O'Briens—except for one boy who lived to avenge his family. It is first mentioned in 1569 when it surrendered; in 1587 it was granted to Hungerford and in 1595 to Capt Collum of Glengoune. Mr Furlong, the Duke of Devonshire's agent, restored it in 1840 and lived in it for some time.

PRIA 26, 1906-7, 237

HOSPITAL (194) Church

MAP 7 H 17
OS½" 18R.71.36

Access : Through grounds of Catholic church in village. Key obtainable from Patrick O'Mahoney, Knockaney Road. Not signposted.

Geoffrey de Marisco founded a Commandery of the Knights Hospitallers (hence the name of the village) here in 1215 under the invocation of St John the Baptist, and it continued in use till its dissolution in 1541. The original church still remains, with a door in the south wall and lancet windows. At the west end of the church are two-storey living quarters (possibly part of a belfry-tower), the top part of which has been transformed into a tasteless grotto. Inside the church are three excellent effigy tombs, one possibly being that of the founder, another being that of a Norman knight with helmet. In 1566 the church was leased to John Cockerhan. and in 1578 to W. Apsley.

JRSAI 13, 1874-5, 154; PRIA 25, 1904, 449

KILLALIATHAN (86) Church

MAP 6 F 17/18
OS½" 21R.33.20

Access : Down avenue a few hundred yards then through gate to graveyard on right. Not signposted

A church is first mentioned here in 1209, and was destroyed in 1302. But the present church is scarcely older than the 15th century, and probably served as a parish church. Its most unusual feature is the east window which is divided into three, and the middle part has three further divisions. Note the fine 15th century tomb niche in the north wall, and the baptismal font lying behind the altar in the window niche. There used to be a gallery above the door. Parts of the sacristy still remain.

PRIA 25, 1904, 405

KILLEEN COWPARK (345) Church

MAP 7 F 16
OS½" 17R.39.51

Access : Through gate or across wall into field. Signposted

A well-preserved 15th century parish church. The narrow windows and the turret-like belfry give the church an almost military appearance. There is an unusual water-font in the church.

PRIA 25, 1904, 388

KILLULTA (341) Church

MAP 7 G 16
OS½" 17R.43.54

Access : Along path for about 100 yards, then over wall on right into field. Signposted

Said to be the earliest surviving church in Co. Limerick, being probably earlier than the 12th century. It is a small rectangular church built of large stones and with a triangular-headed window in the east gable. Much of the west gable, including the door, is a reconstruction. Nothing is known of the history of the church.

PRIA 25, 1904, 386; Leask, Churches I, 73

KILMALLOCK Churches, Castle and Town Gate

MAP 7 H 17
OS½" 17R.61.28

Although called after a monastery founded by St Mo-cheallog in the 7th century, the town of Kilmallock was founded by the Fitzgeralds and was fortified in 1375. In 1570 the town was taken and plundered by Sir James Fitzmaurice, the Sweenys and the Sheehys. It contains a number of medieval buildings.

Collegiate Church (408)

Access : Direct to cemetery in which church stands. Signposted
The south-west end of the church includes a Round Tower which may

belong to an earlier monastery on the site. The church itself was probably founded in the 13th century and was dedicated to Saints Peter and Paul. The church has three aisles, a chancel and a north transept, and includes a fine 13th century door in the south wall. The chancel with its five lancet windows served as a Church of Ireland church until recently. The nave and transept were much altered in the 15th century, including the addition of a porch with a richly carved door on the south side of the nave. In 1600 the 'Sugán' Earl of Desmond surrendered to the Queen's representatives, and James, 15th Earl of Desmond, attended a Protestant service in the church thus causing many of his subjects to rebel against him.
Leask, Churches II, 120 and III, 83

Dominican Friary (212)

Access : Over two fields. Key with John O'Donnell at the Abbey Farm nearby. Not signposted

The foundation of this Dominican friary is ascribed to Gilbert, second son of John of Callan, Lord of Offaly, in 1291. It was completed by his son Maurice, the first White Knight, whose family dominated the history of the area for hundreds of years afterwards. The church has a single aisle to which a transept was added in the fourteenth century. Besides the five-light west window—which is one of the most exquisite in the country— the church contains some fine decorative stone-carving of 13th and 14th century date, flower-buds and heads being particularly well executed. The south transept also contains some fine stonework, and a very fine window inserted in the 15th century. The tower is also a 15th century addition. The domestic buildings were built in the 13th century, but were considerably altered and reconstructed in the 15th. A general chapter of the order was held here in 1340. The Friary was granted to Nicholas Miagh in 1594, but was reclaimed by the Queen shortly afterwards for non-payment of rent. The Dominicans may have either remained on here after the Dissolution or may have returned later, for we know that the Cromwellians executed two of them here in 1648.
JRSAI 19, 1889, 210; PRIA 25, 1904, 421; Leask, Churches II, 120 and 130

King's Castle and Blossom Gate (173)

Access : Castle normally permanently locked; key obtainable from the caretaker, Patrick O'Brien, 43 Millmount

The castle is named after King John, but the present castle could not have been built by him as it is probably 15th century in date. It is a four-storey building with mullioned and pointed windows; a part of the ground floor now serves as a thoroughfare. It was granted to H Billingsley in 1588 and to T Browne of Aney in 1604. In 1645 it was used as a chief arsenal by the Irish under Lord Castlehaven. In 1651 it was utilized as a hospital and depôt by the Parliamentary forces. In the last century it served as a forge until it was partly blocked up. Not far away, in Emmet Street, is Blossom Gate, the sole surviving gate of the medieval town wall.
PRIA 26, 1906, 189; Fleming, The Town-Wall Fortifications of Ireland (1914) 43

LIMERICK Castles, Cathedral and Church

MAP 7 G 16
OS½" 17R.58.57

The town was founded by the Norse early in the 10th century, but by the end of the century the Irish under Brian Boru captured it. The O'Briens had already made it their own capital by 1100. In 1175 Raymond Le Gros

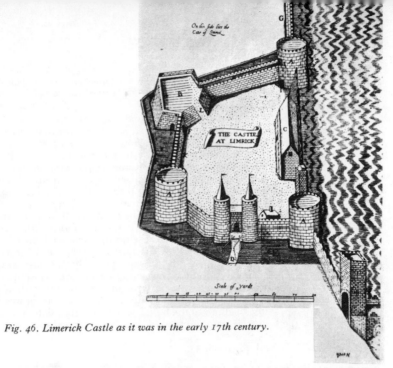

Fig. 46. Limerick Castle as it was in the early 17th century.

took the town for a time, though he had to relinquish it shortly afterwards. But by 1200 the Normans were back again, and with few interruptions held it until the Confederate Catholics captured it in 1642. The Cromwellians took it in 1651. In October 1691 the Williamites delivered a final blow to the Jacobite cause by taking the town and imposing a treaty on the Irish which, if it had been kept, would have granted minimal freedom to Catholics, but when broken, granted them none. After the siege, many of Ireland's nobility fled the country for ever. The town contains a number of interesting old buildings.

King John's Castle (288) *Fig. 46*
Access: Open daily June–September 11 a.m.–1 p.m. and 3 p.m.–7 p.m. If closed contact Mrs A. Moloney, 5 Castle Street, Limerick. Not signposted
The castle was started by the Normans around 1200 and completed by 1202. It was repaired in 1216, and in 1226 was the only castle which was held for the King. It is a five-sided castle, with one of the sides being lapped by the waves of the Shannon. It was fortified by four stout round towers, one of which was replaced by a bastion in 1611; all of them were lowered at some stage to accommodate artillery. On the north side is the entrance, having a pointed arch with traces of a portcullis above it and flanked by two rounded towers which may be slightly later than the original castle. The entrance is now approached by a flight of steps in place of the original drawbridge. The interior of the castle was used as a barracks in the 18th century, and is still cluttered with houses. The castle was taken by the O'Briens and the Macnamaras in 1369, but they were expelled shortly afterwards. The castle was put under the care of the citizens and the Mayor in 1423. In the course of the 17th century it surrendered three times—to the Confederate Catholics in 1641, to the Cromwellian Ireton 10 years later, and to the Williamite forces in 1691.
PRIA 26, 1906, 75; Arch Journal 93, 1937, 178; NMAJ 2, 1941, 95; Leask, Castles 55

Fig. 46,a. Motifs on the oak choir-stalls or Misericords in St Mary's Cathedral, Limerick, carved around 1489.

St Mary's Cathedral *Fig. 46,a*

Access : Open in summer 9 a.m. to 6 p.m., and in winter 9 a.m. to 5 p.m. On Sundays in summer it is open from 3 p.m. to 5 p.m.

The Cathedral was founded by Domhnall Mor O'Brien between 1180 and 1190. Only parts of the Romanesque west doorway (closed), the nave and parts of the aisles and transepts survive from this period. The earliest chancel was built by the first bishop, Donnchadh, who died in 1209, but the present chancel was built in the 15th century. A number of chapels were added to the aisles and one to the south transept in the 15th century. Most of the windows are in the style of the 15th century. The church contains some fine tombs, including those of Donat 'The Great Earl' of Thomond in the wall of the north transept and the Bultingfort-Galway monument in the south transept. Possibly the most unique features of the Cathedral are the black oak misericords or choir stalls which were carved around 1489, and which are the only examples of their kind preserved in Ireland. They show a magnificent collection of figures and animals. It is possible to climb to the belfry where the bells date to 1678. A considerable amount of restoration work has been carried out on the building in the last 150 years.

JRSAI 28, 1898, 35

Fanning's Castle (383)

Access : Through the grounds of the Technical Institute at Barrington's Quay. Not signposted

The somewhat disappointing walls of a four-storey house built by a Limerick merchant named Fanning in the late 16th or early 17th century. It has unusually wide windows. Another building was added to the house later.

Kilrush Church (366)

Access : Through Riverside Guest-house at Barrington's Pier. Not signposted

The church is first mentioned in 1201, but is undoubtedly older, and was incorporated into the north Liberties of the city. It is small and rectangular, with a flat headed doorway, and a round-headed east window. In the south wall is a 15th century window with an obscure inscription of the Quinlinans which was removed from a Franciscan church in St Mary's Lane and preserved for a time by Robert Vere O'Brien before being inserted here probably around 1900.

PRIA 22, 1900, 153, No. 105 and 25, 1904, 363

LOUGH GUR (247) Prehistoric and Early Christian remains *Fig. 47*

MAP 7 H 16
OS½″ 18R.64.41

Some few are signposted

Lough Gur is a small horse-shoe-shaped lake in south-eastern Limerick around whose shores a great number of largely prehistoric monuments remain. The major importance of these monuments lies in the fact that many of them on excavation proved to be Stone Age dwelling-places, and our knowledge of the way of life of the people living around 2,000 B.C. is largely derived from what has been learnt from the excavated sites here. There are also some burial places. Some of the places excavated turned out to belong to the Early Christian period. Not all the monuments are really worthwhile visiting; some of the stone house-foundations excavated within the last twenty years have almost entirely disappeared, or else few indications can be gained from the remains of what was originally

there. The monuments are listed below with the same enumeration as the map Fig. 47, and those which are considered worthwhile visiting are underlined. Access to monuments differs, but many require some walking, including climbing walls etc.

Fig. 47. The National Monuments in the area around Lough Gur, Co Limerick.

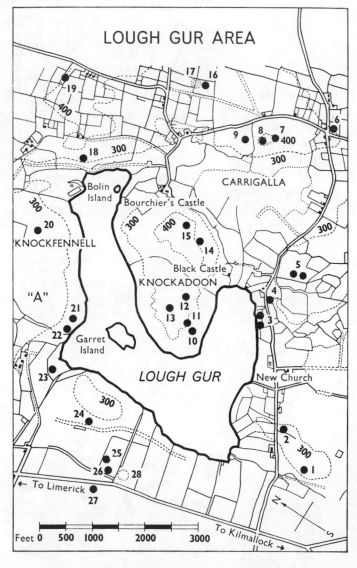

1. Small cairn.
2. 'Leaba na Muice'—'The Pig's Bed'. A partially destroyed megalithic tomb.
3. A number of stones which probably originally formed one or more stone circles.
4. Wedge-shaped gallery grave, at present covered in brambles. JRSAI 85, 1955, 34.
5. Some rather doubtful menhirs or standing stones.
6. A menhir once stood here, but it has been removed.
7. 'Carraig Aille 2'. A stone fort forming an irregular circle. The first houses built inside were curvilinear, the later ones rectangular. Other rectangular structures were found outside. Iron-smelting was practised inside. Probably in use from 8th – 11th centuries A.D. PRIA 52 C 1948, 39
8. 'Carraig Aille 1'. An oval stone fort with remains of rectangular houses built in the Early Christian period. PRIA 52 C 1948, 39
9. Early Christian hut site, of which nothing can be seen.
10. Stone Age habitation site, of which nothing can now be seen.
11. Foundations of a rectangular Stone Age house. PRIA 56 C 1954, 297
12. A Stone Age burial place consisting of a large area enclosed by a double wall, with a small standing stone inside. PRIA 30, 1912–13, 283
13. A large dwelling-enclosure, circular in shape, surrounded by the comparatively well-preserved remains of a double wall. PRIA 56 C 1954, 297
14. An enclosure of stones huddled in on a rock face.
15. Small traces of a stone mound on the top of Knockadoon hill, with traces of the stones which surrounded it.
16. Burial mound with a flat top crowned by a circle of standing stones. It contained burial urns dating from about 1500 B.C. NMAJ 1, 1936–39, 83
17. A fine stone circle with an inner row of stones surrounded by an outer ditch with interior and exterior facing. NMAJ 1, 1936–39, 82
18. 'The Spectacles'. The foundations of huts joined together to look like spectacles, and an adjoining field system. They date from the Early Christian period. PRIA 52 C 1948, 57.
19. A standing stone.
20. A small hill-top cairn.
21. A ring-fort consisting of a raised central area surrounded by a ditch.
22. A small stone circle made of large stones.
23. A lake-dwelling on an island, called a crannóg, consisting of a pile of stones on an islet which is now joined to the land by a strip of marsh, but which originally formed an island.
24. A large standing stone which leans gently.
25. A well-preserved stone circle with fairly large stones.
26. A few remnants of a large stone circle.
27. Scant remains of what was probably a megalithic tomb.
28. One of the most impressive stone circles in Ireland, situated in Grange townland. Its purpose was undoubtedly ritual. Pottery of the Late Stone Age and Early Bronze Age (c. 2000–1500 B.C.) was found inside. It has an almost monumental entrance and has a bank outside the stones. PRIA 54, 1951-2, 37.

For a general survey of the Lough Gur area see NMAJ, 4, 1944-5, 23.

MONASTERANENAGH (171) Cistercian Abbey

MAP 7 G 16
OS½″ 17R.55.41

Access: Over a stile and across field. Signposted

Founded by Turlough O'Brien, King of Limerick, between 1148 and 1151 for the Cistercians who colonized it from Mellifont. The buildings were possibly completed during the reign of Domhnall Mór O'Brien (1170-94). The remains of the long high church are reasonably well preserved, though the east and west windows have suffered much damage. One of the delights of the church are the well-preserved foliate capitals, particularly at the crossing, which, because they were almost blocked up for a long time, have retained much of the freshness which they had when first cut in the warm red sandstone. The screen which divided the church into two parts was possibly built in the 15th century. The Abbot of the monastery was a Lord of Parliament. In the first half of the 13th century the abbots were involved in a number of lawsuits, one involving an abbot who had sold land belonging to the monastery, another about the succession of abbots. In 1365 a great battle took place under the walls of the Abbey when Brian O'Brien and the Macnamaras combined to defeat the King of Thomond. The vanquished took refuge in the monastery, but the victors invaded it and demanded a large ransom. The monastery was dissolved in 1541, and in 1579, after it had been granted to George More, it witnessed another great battle. This time Sir Nicholas Malby, for the English, routed Sir John of Desmond and afterwards turned his cannon on the Abbey where some of the Irish had gone for shelter. As a result the cloister and the refectory were practically destroyed, and the whole of the surviving monastic community was put to the sword. It changed hands a number of times before Elizabeth Norreys was granted it in 1603. The belfry fell in 1807, and in 1874 the chancel vault collapsed, bringing with it much of the fine east window.

JRSAI 19, 1889, 232; Leask, Churches II, 35

MUNGRET (85) Churches

MAP 7 G 16
OS½″ 17R.54.54

Access: Along path and over stile to graveyard. Key obtainable from Office of Public Works, Mallow Street, Limerick. Signposted

The first monastery was founded by St Nessan who died in 551. The Vikings raided it in 834. It was held in such high repute that in 908 King Cormac of Cashel bequeathed three ounces of gold and a satin chasuble to it. It was raided again in 934 and 1080. Eight years later it was destroyed by Donal McLoughlin and a party of Ulstermen, and Murtogh O'Brien plundered it again in 1107. Two churches remain from this early monastery, though tradition tells us that there was a total of six churches and 1,600 religious at one time. The first of these churches is the one near the road which is broad and tall, with flat-headed west doorway and a monumental east window, dating possibly from the 12th century. The second of these is probably the oldest, and is also the smallest. It is a small narrow rectangular church with three small windows, but nothing remains of the original doorway. Some time, probably before 1200, the monastic lands were given by Domhnall Mor O'Brien to Brictius, Bishop of Limerick. It then became a parish church and was granted to William de Wodeford in the first half of the 13th century. This parish church is what is now the largest church, and the chancel dates from this period. In the chancel walls there are stairs which led to a now no longer existing gallery above it. The date of the nave is uncertain, but it was possibly added in the 15th century when the priests' quarters at the west end were presumably

built also. The square tower at the west end is unusual.
JRSAI 19, 1889, 171; NMAJ 4, 1944, 1; 101st Annual Report of the
Commissioners of Public Works 1933, 9; Leask, Churches III, 183

SHANAGOLDEN "Manisternagalliaghduff" Abbey

MAP 6 F 16
OS½" 17R.28.47

Access : Down private lane and across a field. Not signposted
Situated in a secluded valley about 2 miles east of Shanagolden, this
abbey is unusual in that it is one of the very few medieval nunneries known
to us. It is first mentioned in 1298 and presumably continued in existence
up till the time of the Dissolution in 1541. After this it passed to Warham
St Leger, and then changed hands a number of times in the course of the
next few centuries. It consists of a church and cloister, and much of it
seems to date from the 13th century. The church projects from the eastern
face of the cloister; it has a fine double-sided doorway and a piscina.
The east window and north door were inserted in the 15th century. A
room to the south of the church is called 'The Black Hag's Cell' where
tradition says that the last abbess practised witchcraft. There is a refectory
along the south wall of the cloister. At present the Abbey is covered in
trees, giving the impression that Rip van Winkle was asleep inside it!
About 120 yards to the south-west of the abbey are the remains of one
of the few surviving medieval pigeon-houses in Ireland.
JRSAI 34, 1904, 41

SHANID Castle

MAP 6 F 16
OS½" 17R.24.45

Access : Over fence and up steep field. Not signposted
Although only first mentioned in 1230 when it was granted to Thomas
fitz Maurice, the castle is probably slightly earlier. A motte 35 feet high
surrounded by a ditch and an outer bank supports a multi-sided tower
which is round inside. It is about 35 feet high now, and its walls are 11
feet thick. Near the tower are the remains of a curtain wall with battlements, and at a slightly lower level to the east remains of the D-shaped
bailey can be seen. The castle served as the 'chief house' of the Desmond
family who adopted the motto 'Shanid Aboo' as their battle-cry. The
castle surrendered in 1569 and fell into ruin shortly afterwards. It was
given to F. Trenchard in 1611 and was pillaged in 1641. On a neighbouring
hillock to the south is a ring-fort with raised centre and two concentric
banks and ditches outside it. It is a good example of traditional and
Norman fortifications side by side.
PRIA 25, 1905, 243 and 26, 1906, 243; JRSAI 39, 1909, 34; Arch Journal
93, 1937, 163

ABBEYLARAGH Cistercian Abbey

MAP 4 L 10
OS½" 12N.37.79

Access : Through gate and 50 yards along path to cemetery. Signposted
A Cistercian Abbey founded by Richard Tuit in 1211 and colonized from
St Mary's in Dublin in 1214. It was pillaged by Edward Bruce in 1315.
The only surviving parts of the Abbey are the crossing of 1214, and the
tower inserted over it in the 15th century. The tower was approached by
an inserted stairway; the tower had a barrel vault over the crossing.
Arch Journal 88, 1931, 19 and 31; Leask, Churches III, 43 and 45

ABBEYSHRULE Cistercian Abbey

MAP 4 L 11
OS½" 12N.22.59

Access : Through graveyard and through two gates. Signposted
The remains of a Cistercian Abbey colonized from Mellifont around
1150, but the earliest buildings date from around 1200. The oldest part
is the chancel which was much altered in the 16th century to form a separate
chapel by itself, and the tower, which was later blocked by a wall with 3
compartments. Nothing remains of the cloister; the tower at the south-
eastern angle was built in post-Reformation times. In the graveyard
nearby is the shaft of the only High Cross in Co. Longford; on one side
are four incised lines, on the other a plait of 5 strands and a strange
horse-shoe-like device.
Arch Journal 88, 1931, 13 and 27; JRSAI 54, 1924, 171

GRANARD (263) Motte

MAP 4 L 9
OS½" 12N.33.81

Access : Up laneway, then over stile into field. Signposted
The remains consist of a tall motte (said to be the largest in Ireland) and
an extensive bailey, most of it surrounded by a deep ditch and bank.
On top of the motte stands an incongruous statue of St Patrick erected
in 1932.
Teathbha 1, 1969, 19

INCHCLERAUN (91) Early Monastery

MAP 4 J 11
OS½" 12M.99.59

*Access : Boats available during the Summer season from Mr Duffy at Coosan
Point or from Mr Kelly, Elfleet Bay, Lanesborough*
Situated on an island in Lough Ree, this monastery was founded probably
in the first quarter of the 6th century by St Diarmuid, teacher of St
Ciarán of Clonmacnoise. The island is also associated with the legendary
Queen Maeve who is said to have been killed by a stone fired by the sling
of an Ulsterman from the shore one mile away, while she was bathing there.
The earliest church is probably St Diarmuid's, a small rectangular church
with antae and a flat-headed doorway. Twelve feet to the north stands
Teampul Mor, the Big Church, built possibly in the 13th century. It is
a rectangular church with two lancet east windows; the sacristy and community room to the north were probably added in the 15th century.
Nearby is another church with chancel, to which a nave was added later.
The Church of the Dead is a small rectangular church which is now
ruined. To the south of this group of churches is the Women's Church
which may have been dedicated to the Blessed Virgin. On the highest
point of the island is the Belfry Church, a Romanesque church which is
unusual in that it has a square tower at the west end and a stairs with two
doors in the north wall. The island also houses a number of Early Christian
grave slabs. The men of Munster plundered the monastery in 1010, and
it was plundered again in 1057 and 1193.
JRSAI 30, 1900, 69; Leask, Churches I, 50 and 60; II, 72; III, 115

ST MEL'S, Ardagh Church

MAP 4 K 10
OS½″ 12N.20.69

Access : Up steps and through gate. Not signposted
A small but broad early church with antae and flat-headed doorway (partly reconstructed) on a site said to have been founded by St Mel in the 5th century. During the course of excavations in 1967, traces of a timber church, possibly of 8th century date, were found beneath it.

County Louth

AGHNASKEAGH (326) Cairns

MAP 5 Q 8
OS½″ 9J.08.14

Access : Four fields in from the road, down along a path at the edge of the fields. Signposted
Two cairns, 50 yards apart. One is egg-shaped, with three legs of a roofless portal dolmen in the east end, which contained four cremated bodies and some Late Stone Age/Early Bronze Age pottery and a glass bead. The west end contained Early bronze Age burials (c. 1500 B.C.), and many centuries later a furnace was placed beside the north end of the cairn. The other cairn was round in shape and had four box-like graves in the eastern part of the cairn containing Stone Age pottery, and one later burial belonging to the early centuries of the Christian era.
CLAJ 8, 1935, 235 and 9, 1938, 1

ARDEE Castle

MAP 5 P 9
OS½″ 13N.96.91

Access : Direct. Only open 7–8 p.m. on Wednesdays and Sundays in June and every evening in July and August. Otherwise closed. Key from C.A. O'Flynn, chemist about 7 shops up the street on the opposite side of the road. Not signposted
The castle was founded by Roger de Peppard in 1207, but much of the present building does not go back beyond the 15th century. In the 15th and 16th centuries it was used for attacks on Ulster, and two English Lord Deputies, Stanley (1414) and the White Earl of Ormonde (1452) died here on such expeditions. After the Restoration, it was granted to Theobald Taaffe, Earl of Carlingford.
JRSAI 38, 1908, 213

CARLINGFORD Castle and 'The Mint'

MAP 5 Q 8
OS½″ 9J.19.12

King John's Castle (249) *Fig. 48*
Access : Over railway bridge and grass. Signposted
Allegedly founded by King John who stayed here for three days in 1210, it may well have been founded some years previously by Hugh de Lacy. The semi-circular western half of the castle was probably built before King John's visit. This curving wall, which enclosed an open courtyard, had two-storey buildings leaning against its inner face; the entrance, on the west side, was flanked by two rectangular towers (only parts of the northern tower remain) and at the south-western corner there is another rectangular tower. The high dividing wall, and the whole of the eastern half of the castle was added in 1261. Here there are two floors above a basement (now largely filled up). There were a number of rooms on the ground floor; the entrance to this part of the castle was through a door in the first floor, and here was probably situated the great hall of the castle.

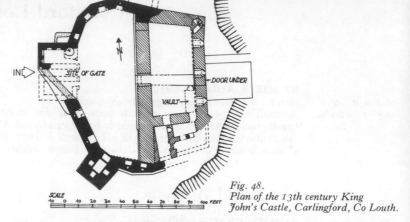

Fig. 48.
*Plan of the 13th century King
John's Castle, Carlingford, Co Louth.*

In 1495 it was decreed that none but an Englishman should be Constable of the castle. Probably taken by Sir Henry Tichbourne in 1642, it was compelled to surrender to Lord Inchiquin in 1649. However in the following year it was delivered to Sir Charles Coote. In 1689 it was fired upon by the retreating Jacobite forces, and General Schomberg later used it as a hospital.
JRSAI 38, 1908, 310; Official Guidebook; Leask, Castles 61

'The Mint' (424)
Access : Direct. Not Signposted
Situated in a narrow street just off the Square, this is a 15th century town tower house with an extended turret over the door. The exterior is remarkable in having mullioned windows which are decorated with some pre-Norman Celtic motifs such as interlacing, as well as a horse and a human head. The stone work has a number of decorative motifs pocked on it. There are three storeys in all, none of which has any fireplaces. It is said to have been the site of a mint which was set up in 1467. Further down the street is an old town gate, above which is a small room, the Tholsel, where the elders of the town met.
JCLAS 11, 1948, 305

CASTLEROCHE (460) Castle
MAP 5 P 8
OS½″ 9H.99.12
Access : Over stile into field. Signposted
Commanding a pass leading into south Armagh, this is one of the lesser known, yet one of the most dramatic of the Norman castles when seen from the plain below. It is said that in 1236 Rohesia de Verdun fortified a castle here on her own lands 'which none of her predecessors had been able to do'. Legend says that she promised herself in marriage to the architect if she liked the castle when it was built. But when he came to claim her hand as a reward, she had him thrown out the window—an explanation for one of the windows which is still called 'the murder window'! But old legend notwithstanding, the castle was probably built by Rohesia's son John, who died in 1274. The castle is almost triangular in shape, with a high wall enclosing the central courtyard. Two semi-circular bastions flank the entrance in the north wall, and the south end of the castle is occupied by a two-storeyed hall with three windows with window-seats in the upper floor. To the north was a bailey, separated from the castle by a rock-cut ditch, and the main approach to the castle was through this bailey. A hosting of all the English forces in Ireland took place at the castle in 1561.
CLAJ 3, 1915, 394; Arch Journal 93, 1937, 181; Leask, Castles 63

CLOCHAFARMORE (474) Standing Stone

MAP 5 Q 8
OS½" 9J.01.04

Access : Across stile and through field. Not signposted
A standing stone which tradition associates with the death of CúChulainn, the legendary hero of the old Irish saga, the Táin Bó Cuailgne. When CúChulainn was dying of his wounds which he got while trying to ward off the army of Queen Maeve of Connacht single-handed, he tied himself to this stone. While he was still alive his enemies kept their distance. It was only when a raven came and rested on his shoulder that they knew he was dead. The scene is commemorated in a statue standing in the General Post Office in O'Connell Street, Dublin.
CLAJ 1, 4, 1904-7, 47

DROGHEDA Town Fortifications and Churches

MAP 5 Q 10
OS½" 13 0.09.75

The town was founded by the Norse in 911, and the Normans made it into one of their important strongholds. A number of Parliaments met here in the Middle Ages. The saddest episode in the town's history was when Cromwell took the town in 1649, massacred 2,000 of its defenders, and sent many captives from it to the Barbadoes. It surrendered to King William after the Battle of the Boyne. There are still a number of medieval remains in the town.

Magdalene Tower

Access : Difficult, as it is surrounded by railings, but it can be easily seen at a short distance from a nearby path. Signposted
This is the only remnant of an old Dominican church founded in 1224 by Luke Netterville, Archbishop of Armagh, and dedicated to St Mary Magdalene. It was in this Priory that Richard II received the submission of four Irish kings in 1394. At the Dissolution it was granted to two Drogheda merchants, Walter Dowdall and Edward Beche. The tower was probably inserted in the 15th century at the place where nave and transepts met. Further south, in Old Abbey Lane off West Street, are the shabby remains of another medieval Abbey, that of the Augustinians which was founded in 1206, though much of the present building is probably 15th century in date.

St Laurence's Gate and Town Fortifications (511)

Access : Road passes underneath. Key not obtainable locally.
This fine building, consisting of two round towers and connecting wall, is a barbican or advance fortification outside the walls of the town. It dates to the 13th century, and gets its name from a friary dedicated to St Laurence which stood nearby inside the walls but which has since disappeared. It is the finest of its type remaining in Ireland. The areas of the town both north and south of the river were separately walled in the 13th century. Parts of the town walls on the south side of the river can be seen in the grounds of St Mary's Church of Ireland church. Not far away is Millmount Fort, possibly originally a Passage-Grave like Newgrange, fortified as a motte in the 12th century, and used as a fortification again around 1800 (recently restored).
Arch Journal 88, 1931, 358; CLAJ 10, 1948, 237; Fleming, The Town-Wall Fortifications of Ireland (1914) 30

DROMISKIN (92) Round Tower, High Cross and Church

MAP 5 Q 9
OS½" 13 0.05.98

Access : Direct to graveyard. Signposted
The church is alleged to have been founded by St Patrick, but it is more

likely that it was his disciple Lughaidh (died 515-6) who founded the monastery. St Ronán, who cursed Suibhne Geilt and caused him to go mad, was abbot here and died of the great plague in 664. The High King, Aedh Finnliath, died here in 876. The monastery was plundered by the Irish in 908, by the Danes in 978 and again by the Irish in 1043. The Round Tower and a High Cross still survive from the old monastery. The Round Tower, which is 55 feet high, has a round-headed doorway which originally had columns supporting the arch. The two rectangular windows at the top as well as the conical roof are modern, dating to 1879. To the east of the tower are the remnants of a High Cross which has been re-erected in modern times on a granite base and shaft. There is a Celtic whirl on the west face of the cross. The east face has a central square panel at the intersection with a wheel out of which grow beasts who devour others; to the left is a hunting scene, to the right a scene showing two men meeting. One of the men would appear to have something behind him or on his back, and behind him is a horse carrying a (dead?) four-legged animal. Nearby are the remains of what was probably a medieval parish church. The east gable of the church probably dates to the 13th century; the present 2-lighted east window was inserted in the 15th century into the earlier 3-lighted window.

JRSAI 27, 1897, 101

Fig. 49. Cistercian Abbey at Mellifont, Co Louth: The Lavabo built around 1200.

DUN DEALGAN (388) Motte and Bailey

MAP 5 Q 8
OS½" 9J.03.08

Access: Through gate and up laneway. Not signposted

Although the site is associated with the legendary hero CúChulainn, the present earthworks are a Norman motte and bailey built possibly by the de Verdons in the last 30 years of the 12th century. The walls of the square bailey are well preserved. The castle on top is a folly built by Patrick Byrne—a well-known pirate—in 1780, and as a wooden tower once crowned the motte, the tower gives some idea of what a motte with a tower must have originally looked like.
JRSAI 38, 1908, 256

GREENMOUNT (144) Motte

MAP 5 Q 9
OS½" 13 0.06.93

Access: Over field and barbed-wire fence. Not signposted

A good Norman motte with well-preserved bailey built on an easily fortifiable position on a slight promontory overlooking a plain. The hole on top of the mound is the result of excavations carried out in the 1860's when a stone-lined passage leading nowhere was found below the top of the mound. A bronze axe of c. 1600 B.C. and a piece of bronze with a Viking inscription also came to light.
JRSAI 11, 1870-1, 471

MANSFIELDSTOWN (480) Church

MAP 5 Q 9
OS½" 13 0.02.95

Access: Direct to graveyard where church stands. Not signposted

The church was built late in the 17th century. The east window, dating from the 15th century, comes originally from another church and was inserted here; the heads above the window on the outside may date to 1691, when the church was built. The other windows were inserted in the 19th century. A baptismal font from this church is now in Ardee.
JCLAS 10, 1942, 107

MELLIFONT (93) Cistercian Abbey *Fig. 49*

MAP 5 Q 10
OS½" 13 0.01.78

Access: Direct. Signposted

St Malachy of Armagh brought a handful of monks with him from Clairvaux and founded the first Irish Cistercian monastery here in 1142, on lands granted by Donogh O'Carroll, Prince of Uriel. St Bernard of Clairvaux sent a skilful architect named Robert to help build the church, and this is reflected in the rounded chapels in the transepts—which are of Continental origin and which are some of the few remaining portions of the original church. In 1157 the church was consecrated with great pomp and glory. However, much of the remaining portions of the chancel, the north transept and the outer walls of the south transept were built about 1225. The monastery was burned early in the 14th century, and as a result, much of the nave of the church was reconstructed in the 14th-15th century. Comparatively little of the church remains, but one unusual feature discovered during excavations about 15 years ago was a crypt under the porch at the western end of the church. To the south of the church lies the cloister, built around 1200. Some of its pillars have been reconstructed, but its most unusual feature is the octagonal two-storey Lavabo in the middle of the south side where there was originally a fountain in which the monks washed their hands before going in to eat in the refectory nearby. On the eastern side of the cloister is the fine vaulted chapter house, built in the 14th century, which now serves as a repository for miscellaneous architectural fragments. Its door was removed in the 18th century. There are a number of other buildings around the cloister, but it is difficult to assign a purpose to them. Within a century after its foundation Mellifont became the parent or grandparent of more than 35 Cistercian monasteries throughout the country. The French monks who were sent over to Mellifont to help found the monastery did not get on well with the Irish monks, and returned shortly afterwards to France. By the first half of the thirteenth century the monks had become lax, and there were many irregularities, including insubordination, both in Mellifont and in its daughter-houses. In 1223 Pope Honorius ordered that all offenders should surrender their office. In 1228 Stephen Lexington came to examine these abuses, and the abbot resigned. Stephen went so far as to ask the Abbot of Clairvaux to move the monastery to another site in order to rid the monastery of the dissension, and he asked the Irish king to protect the monastery. After that there was considerable peace, but in 1494 the local nobles seem to have invaded and plundered the monastery. The church was converted into a residence in 1556, but the monks must have lived on, for the death of the last abbot is recorded in 1743.

JCLAS 8, 1935, 223; 11, 1945, 29 and 13, 1954, 35; Leask, Churches II, 41; PRIA 68 C, 1969, 109

Fig. 8, (4). The east and west faces of Muiredach's Cross, Monasterboice.

MONASTERBOICE (94) High Crosses, Round Tower and Churches
Fig. 8

MAP 5 Q 9
OS½" 13 0.04.82 *Access: Through gateway and up lane to graveyard. Key to Round Tower from Michael Derby who lives nearby. Signposted*
This first monastery was founded by an obscure saint named Buite who died in 521. We know that the monastery remained in existence up till 1122, and the Vikings appeared to have occupied it for a time until they were attacked by Domhnall, King of Tara, in 968. One of its most learned monks, Flann, died in 1056. The importance of Monasterboice lies in the fact that it contains one of the most perfect High Crosses in Ireland— the Cross of Muiredach which has been dated to the early 10th century. It gets its name from an inscription on the base saying that it was erected by one Muiredach who has been tentatively identified with an abbot of that name who died in 922. On the east face can be seen Adam and Eve, and Cain slaying Abel; David and Goliath (?); Moses smiting the rock (?); Adoration of the Magi; Christ in Glory surrounded by good souls, bad souls and the Archangel Michael weighing the souls, and at the top, the meeting of St Paul and St Anthony in the desert. On the west face are the Arrest of Christ (?), Doubting Thomas (?), Christ with St Peter and St Paul (?), the Crucifixion and an unidentified scene. On the north face are SS Paul and Anthony (?) again, the Scourging at the Pillar, the Hand of God (under the arm of the cross) and interlacing motifs, while on the south face there is the Flight into Egypt, Pilate washing his hands (?) and interlacing and vinescroll motifs. On the base are hunters, animals, interlacing and fretwork. Not far away is the Tall Cross of much the same date, on which the following panels may be tentatively identified: East face— David kills the Lion, the Sacrifice of Isaac, the Three Children in the Fiery Furnace, the Arrest of Christ, the Ascension, St Michael spears Satan; West face—soldiers guarding the tomb of Christ, The Baptism of Christ, The Mocking of Christ, The Kiss of Judas and the Crucifixion. Many of the panels with three figures have not been identified. The nearby Round Tower (climbable to the top) was burned in 1097 when it contained the monastic library and other treasures. In the graveyard there are also two churches, neither of great interest. Other items of interest include a High Cross near the north-east corner of the graveyard with a Crucifixion scene on one face; a sundial and a grave-slab with the inscription 'A prayer for Ruarcan'.
Macalister, Monasterboice (1946); JCLAS 10, 1944, 287 and 12, 1951, 123; JRSAI 81, 1951, 1

PROLEEK (476) Dolmen

MAP 5 Q 8
OS½″ 9J.08.11

Access: Best approached along path through grounds of Ballymascanlon Hotel. Signposted
A very fine example of a Portal Dolmen with a capstone of about 40 tons supported by three legs. Legend says that a wish will be granted to those who can throw a pebble on to the top of the capstone so that it stays there. In the same field is a wedge-shaped gallery grave.
CLAJ 1, 3, 1904-7, 46; JRSAI 38, 1908, 316

ROODSTOWN (298) Castle *Figs. 16 and 17*

MAP 5 P 9
OS½″ 13N.00.93

Access: Through gate into field. Key obtainable from Thomas Halpenny, Roodstown. Signposted
A well-preserved tower-house of 15th century date. It has four storeys, and the bottom one is vaulted. There are also some nicely carved trefoil-headed windows. There is a fine 'murder-hole' above the door enabling the defenders to drop things on the heads of intruders. One of the unusual features of the castle are the two turrets, one containing a stairs, the other a lavatory, which project from the sides of two diagonally opposite corners.
Leask, Castles 107

St MOCHTA'S HOUSE, Louth (312) Oratory

MAP 5 P 8
OS½″ 9H.96.01

Access: Along lane for 100 yards, then into field. Signposted
Legend says that the church was built in a night to form a suitable resting place for the founder, St Mochta, who died in 534. The monastery was plundered by the Vikings in 830 and 839, by Muircheartach, King of Aileach in 968 and by Gluniollar (Eagle-Knee) O'Flaherty in 978. The monastery was flattened by a storm in 986, burned in 1075 and again in 1111, 1113, 1148, 1160, 1164 and 1166. The church possibly dates to the second half of the 12th century. It is a rectangular building with a vaulted roof, above which is a chamber with a pointed vault which also serves to prevent the stone roof from sagging inwards and collapsing. The upper storey is lit by a small window, and is reached from below by a narrow stairs. The church has been much restored over the years. Nearby is Louth 'Abbey'—a 14th or 15th century building.
JCLAS 9, 1937, 32; Leask, Churches I, 40

TERMONFECKIN Castle and High Cross

Castle (178)

MAP 5 Q 9
OS½″ 13 O.14.80

Access: Up laneway and through gate. Key with Jack Fowler in thatched cottage opposite gate of castle. Signposted
This is a 15th or 16th century tower-house of 3 storeys, and with good trefoil-headed windows. Its most unusual feature is the excellent corbelled roof (in the same technique as the Newgrange chamber roof, 4,000 years older!) which is on the third storey. The famous antiquarian Ussher lived nearby for some time. It was repaired by Captain Brabazon in 1641. A bawn with rounded turret which belonged to the castle has disappeared.
CLAJ 5, 1921, 58; JRSAI 38, 1908, 298

High Cross

Access: Direct to graveyard. Not Signposted
In the graveyard of St Feckin's Church is a small High Cross with a winged figure above the Crucifixion on the east face, and Christ in Glory on the west face; the rest of the cross is covered in interlacing and geomet-

rical patterns. At the foot of the cross is a slab with a Crucifixion scene (probably 17th century) and nearby is the base of another cross. Built into the porch of the church is a stone with an inscription which reads 'A prayer for Ultan and Dubthach who made this stone fort'. The original monastery here was founded by St Fechín of Fore who died in 664. It was plundered by the Leinstermen and the Vikings in 1013, was plundered again in 1025, and finally in 1149.

TRIA 31, 1901, 560

Fig. 16 & 17. View, plan, section and details of
Roodstown Castle, Co Louth. 16th century.

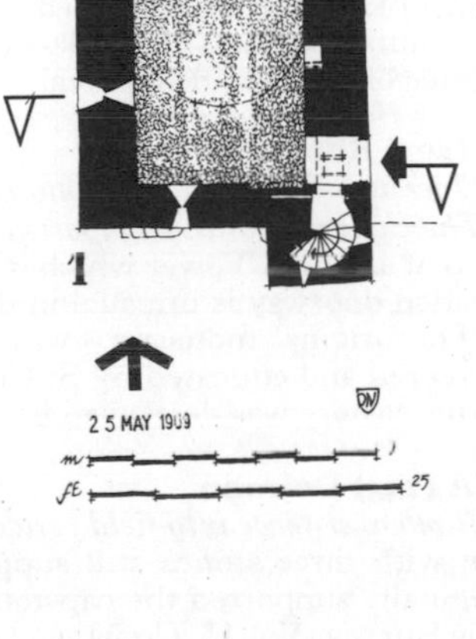

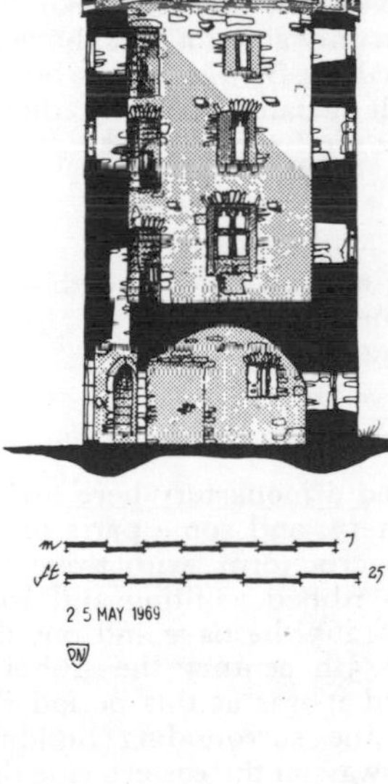

AGHAGOWER (96) Church and Round Tower

MAP 3 E 9
OS½″ 11M.03.80

Access : Direct from road. Not signposted
The founder of the first monastery here was St Senach who was created Bishop of Aghagower by St Patrick. The Round Tower, which is preserved up to the fourth floor, has a round-headed doorway. The present ground-floor entrance is modern, and the roof is said to have been struck by lightning. The nearby church was built in the 15th century, but with fragments of an earlier church.

AGHALARD (243) Castle

MAP 3 E 11
OS½″ 11M.14.57

Access : A quarter of a mile along an untarred road, and then turn right up a similar lane to a farmyard. The castle is in a field behind the farmyard. Not signposted
A 15th century three-storey tower, one half of which has fallen away. The tower stands in a polygonal bawn with square turrets. A building in the south-east of the bawn was apparently added later. The castle was owned in 1574 by the MacDonnells who had been mercenaries in the Burke armies. In 1596 Brabazon, Clanrickard and Darcy captured the castle but evacuated it shortly afterwards on hearing of the approach of Red Hugh O'Donnell. It remained in MacDonnell hands until bought by Sir Benjamin Guinness in the last century.
Neary, Notes on Cong and the Neale, 55

BALLA (403) Round Tower

MAP 3 F 9
OS½″ 11M.26.85

Access : Over two-foot-high wall into cemetery. Key obtainable from Henry Martin, The Square, Balla. Signposted
The stump of a Round Tower which is preserved up to the third floor. The round-headed doorway is unusual in that it is only about a foot above the ground. The original monastery was founded by St Mochua, who was adopted, reared and educated by St Comghall of Bangor and who died in 637. The monastery was destroyed by fire in 1179.

BALLINA (145) Dolmen

MAP 3 F 8
OS½″ 6G.24.18

Access : Climb over fence into field beside road. Not signposted
A dolmen with three stones still supporting a capstone. A fourth stone which originally supported the capstone lies nearby.
Megalithic Survey, Vol II, Co Mayo (1964) 42, No. 49

BALLINTUBBER (501) Augustinian Abbey

MAP 3 E 10
OS½″ 11M.15.79

Access : Direct. Signposted
In 1216 Cathal Crovdearg O'Connor founded a monastery here for the Augustinians on the site of an older monastery, and some parts of the church date from this time. The church is cruciform, with three fine transitional east windows. The chancel has ribbed vaulting and well-carved capitals supporting it. After a fire in 1265 the nave and possibly part of the crossing were re-built. In the 15th century the Abbey is occasionally mentioned in Papal Letters, and it was at this period that the cloisters were built, though some of the surrounding buildings including the chapter house with its fine doorway on the eastern side date from the 13th century. The west doorway of the church was inserted at this period also; it was removed to Hollymount in the 19th century but was restored to its original position in 1964. In 1465 charges were investigated against the abbot for waste and improper use of the properties

and revenues of the abbey, but we do not know what the outcome was. The monastery was dissolved in 1542, and it was subsequently leased to various private individuals. In 1635 the Augustinians petitioned to the Pope for permission to take over the Abbey once again, and they seem to have regained possession as a result. But in 1653 the Cromwellian soldiers destroyed much of the domestic quarters, though the shell of the church remained intact. The church was partially restored in 1846 and in 1889, but the final restoration was carried out from 1963 and was finished in time for the 750th anniversary of the foundation in 1966; a special stamp was issued to commemorate the event. One of the boasts of the Abbey is that Mass continued to be celebrated in the Abbey throughout the 750 years of its existence.

Egan, The Story of Ballintubber Abbey; Leask, Churches, II, 63

BALLYLAHAN (325) Castle

MAP 3 F 9
OS½″ 11M.27.99

Access : Over wall into field. Signposted
The remains of a once fine 13th century castle, built by the Mac Jordans. The curtain wall encloses an area roughly hexagonal in shape which contains the foundations of a number of buildings. The wall probably dates to the early years of the 13th century, but the two rounded gate-bastions, of which only one remains, were built around 1260.

Arch Journal 93, 1937, 190; Leask, Castles 72

BALLYMACGIBBON (251) Cairn

MAP 3 E 11
OS½″ 11M.18.55

Access : 300 yards up pathway, then over stile to right into field. Signposted
A large stone cairn about 100 feet in diameter and about 25 feet high which probably covers a Passage-Grave. In a field on the opposite side of the road is an overgrown fort called Cathair Phaeter ('The Pewter Fort') which consists of a collapsed stone wall with a bank outside it. There is a souterrain in the interior of the fort.

Wilde's Loch Coirib (1938) 221

BREASTAGH (415) Ogham Stone

MAP 3 E 7
OS½″ 6G.18.34

Access : Through gate into field. Signposted
An Ogham stone about 8 feet high which may originally have been a Bronze Age standing stone. The inscription reads LGG........SD.....LE ESCAD on one side, and on the other MAQ CORRBRI MAQ AMLOITT.

JRSAI 28, 1898, 233; Macalister, Corpus I (1945) 13, No. 10

BURRISCARRA (222a) Churches

MAP 3 E 10
OS½″ 11M.18.76

Access : Direct to graveyard. Signposted
An Abbey or Priory of the Carmelites was founded here in 1298 probably by Adam de Staunton of Castlecarra. It is the lower down of two churches in the field and has some 13th century niches, though much of the church was rebuilt in the 15th century when the present windows were inserted and the domestic buildings added. It became Augustinian in 1413 and was burned in 1430. Further up the field, in the graveyard, is a 14th century parish church with the lower part of the walls sloping outwards. In 1608 Oliver Bowen bought the land from John Kinge to whom James I had granted it in 1607. Usurped by the Cromwellians, it was granted by Charles II to Sir Henry Lynch whose family kept it until the last century.

JGAHS 6, 1909-10, 238; Leask, Churches III, 178

BURRISHOOLE (235) Dominican Friary

MAP 3 D 9
OS½″ 11L.97.96

Access : Half a mile down untarred road to cemetery. Signposted
Situated beside an inlet of the sea, this Friary was founded in 1486 by Richard Burke, MacWilliam Iochtair, for the Dominicans. The church consists of a nave, chancel and south transept, the last two of which have well-preserved windows of the period. The stubby low tower is almost more Cistercian than Dominican in character. The eastern wall of the cloister, with its almost rounded windows, is preserved up to first floor level; the other domestic buildings have vanished. A 15th century seal with an illegible inscription was found in the buildings.
JRSAI 46, 1916, 185; Leask, Churches III, 54

CAHERDUFF (244) Castle

MAP 3 E 11
OS½″ 11M.17.56

Access : One third of a mile along a path, then through a thick hazelwood for 300 yards. A visit is not recommended. Not signposted.
The ground floor of a 15th century castle of little interest. The present entrance was made by Lord Ardilaun in the 19th century. In the last century the castle was said to have been seen 'on fire' on summer nights when the fairies, after their game of hurling, held their banquets there. The castle is scarcely worth a visit.
Wilde's Loch Coirib (1938) 218

CARRICKKILDAVNET (458) Castle

MAP 3 C 9
OS½″ 6L.72.94

Access : Direct. Signposted
A small 15th century castle beside an inlet of the sea. It has a vaulted stone roof about half way up its height, and access to the roof must have been by means of a wooden ladder through a hatchway in the vault. Though associated with the famous sea-pirate Grace O'Malley, it was probably built before her time, very probably by one of her ancestors. There are the remains of an old boat-slip outside the castle, as well as traces of the original bawn.

CARROWCASTLE and CARROWCRUM (293) Megalithic Tombs

MAP 3 F 8
OS½″ 6G.32.16

Access : Across field(s). not signposted.
At Carrowcastle there is a standing stone looking in the distance like a human figure, situated a few fields in from the road. Nearby are the possible remains of a megalithic tomb and a later oven (?). Not far away at Carrowcrum is a wedge-shaped gallery-grave in a field beside the road. The tomb, which is covered in gorse, is surrounded by the remnants of a cairn.
Megalithic Survey, Vol. II Co Mayo (1964) 55, No. 60

CASHEL (483) Burial Mound

MAP 3 E 9
OS½″ 11M.08.84

Access : Into field beside road. Not signposted
An insignificant mound of earth and stone, covered by scrub, in which a number of prehistoric objects were discovered during land reclamation. It is scarcely worth a visit.

CASTLECARRA (222b) Castle

MAP 3 E 10
OS½″ 11M.18.75

Access : 1 mile along an untarred road, then across two fields. Not signposted
The castle was built some time between 1238 and 1300 by de Staunton, one of the Anglo-Norman barons in the following of Richard de Burgo. The present remains consist of a three-storeyed tower standing in a strongly fortified bawn with one rounded corner turret. Much of the present building would appear to be of 15th century date, but it undoubtedly

incorporates older fragments. The family who built it later took on the name of M'Evilly, and they held it until at least 1574. Some time after this the castle was surrendered to the crown and it was granted to Captain William Bowen, whose family kept it until the Cromwellian period. After the Restoration in 1660 it was granted to Sir Henry Lynch, in whose family it remained until the last century. The castle is peacefully situated by Lough Carra near the ruins of Moore Hall, home of the author George Moore.
JGAHS 6, 1909-10, 238

CLARE ISLAND (97 and 198) St Bridget's Church and a Castle

MAP 3 C 9
OS½" IOL.
69 and 71.85

Access : Mail boat sails from Roonagh Quay, Louisburgh, every second day, depending on weather conditions. If necessary, contact Chris O'Grady, Bayview Hotel, Clare Island

Nothing is known about the early history of the island, but in 1220 the Cistercians from Knockmoy, Co Galway (q.v.) established a cell here. The 'Abbey' church consists of a nave and chancel as well as a sacristy. There were other buildings to the north of the church, but these have vanished. The church does not appear to date from the period of foundation, but from about 1500. The most unusual feature of the church are the paintings in the chancel, which are some of the very few medieval frescoes remaining in Ireland. The paintings represent a strange mixture of animals and humans, but their meaning is unknown. The only recognizable figure is that of the Archangel Michael with the scales of Judgment. The walls of the chancel appear to have been covered in bands of yellow and blue paint. Down near the harbour is a weather-slated castle which is said to have been built by the famous pirate queen Grace O'Malley. It is a three-storey building with side passages in the third floor, but it was much altered in the last century. Although the island belonged to her father, there is no definite evidence that Grace was the builder of the castle.
PRIA 31, 1911-5, 29; JRSAI 44, 1914, 323

CONG (432) Abbey *Fig. 50*

MAP 3 E 11
OS½" 11M.14.55

Access : Direct. It is beside the entrance to Ashford Castle. Key with John Varley, Abbey Street, Cong. Not signposted

Situated on the site of an earlier monastery founded in the 6th century, this is an Augustinian Abbey founded possibly in the 12th century. It probably replaces a church which was burnt in 1137. The present Abbey may have been built by Turlough O'Connor, King of Connacht, or else by one of the O'Duffys. Of the church itself comparatively little remains, and the fine Romanesque doorway was inserted into the north wall in modern times. This doorway contains some very fine sculpture. Like most of the rest of the building, it probably dates to around 1200, though the church was possibly built slightly later. The best feature is the cloister which was also erected around 1200 but has been reconstructed. Some of the capitals in the cloister were carved in the 19th century. Beside the cloister is a very fine transitional doorway of the same period, which led to the Chapter House, which has also some fine windows. The decorated stonework is exquisitely executed, and is probably the finest work of its type in the west of Ireland. After the Dissolution, the Abbey passed into the hands of the Kings, and later passed to the Binghams, the O'Donnells and finally to the Brownes.
JRSAI 31, 1901, 321 and 35, 1905, 1; JGAHS 19, 1941, 107; Leask, Churches, II, 59; Neary, Notes on Cong and the Neale

EOCHY'S CAIRN (246) Cairn

MAP 3 E 10
OS½″ 11M.16.60

Access : Half a mile up a laneway, then left down another laneway, and then 300 yards across 6 fields and stone walls. Not signposted
A large stone cairn about 150 feet in diameter, which probably covers a Passage-Grave. It stands near one side of an earthwork which may have been erected much later than the cairn.

ERREW ABBEY and TEMPLENAGALLIAGHDOO (307-8)

MAP 3 E 8
OS½″ 6G.17.12

Access : 2 miles along untarred road, then across fields to tip of peninsula. Signposted

Errew Abbey
Errew Abbey was founded by the Barretts for the Augustinian Canons in 1413. The church is a long rectangular building; although much of the dressed stonework has fallen, there are some good trefoil windows remaining, as well as a piscina. The ground floor of the domestic buildings is preserved on the eastern wing of the cloister, but otherwise little of these buildings remain. The church, however, antedates the foundation and is of 13th century date.

Templenagalliaghdoo
Nearby is a small rectangular oratory which probably stands on the site of the earliest monastery founded here by St Tighernan in the 6th century. The name of the oratory—Templenagalliaghdoo or 'Church of the Black Nun'—suggests that this may have been a convent. The present entrance is in the south wall, but as the church has been greatly reconstructed, it may have originally been in the west wall. A small annexe was added later to the north side enclosing what may have been either a well or the grave of the founder.
105th Annual Report of the Commissioners of Public Works 1937, 7; Leask, Churches III, 96

Fig. 50. A 19th century capital in the cloister at Cong, Co Mayo.

FALLMORE (99b) St Dairbhile's Church

MAP 3 C 8
OS½" 6F.62.18

Access : A quarter of a mile down an untarred road to cemetery in which the church stands. Signposted
Nothing is known of the history of this church, but the fact that it is dedicated to a woman saint suggests that it may have been originally a foundation for nuns. The church is rectangular and has a round-headed east window. The round-headed doorway has beaded and interlacing decoration on the inside and outside, and probably dates to the 12th century. At some later stage the south wall was extended outwards and the west wall was rebuilt at the same time. It is possible that the east wall was rebuilt at this period also, as the window and the door are out of line.
Dunraven, Irish Architecture I (1875) 107; Leask, Churches I, 158

GLEBE (146) Stone Circles

MAP 3 E 11
OS½" 11M.16.56

Access : Through stile into fields beside road. Not signposted
A set of four stone circles in three different townlands and three different fields near the road.

INISHGLORA (99a) Early Monastery

MAP 3 C 7
OS½" 6F.62.31

Access : By boat. For transport apply to Ted Sweeney, Blacksod (tel. Blacksod 4) or to Belmullet or Blacksod Post Office
Nothing is known of the history of this monastery beyond the fact that it was founded by St Brendan the Navigator in the mid-6th century. The remains consist of three churches, three beehive huts, part of the old monastic wall and some inscribed crosses. Of the three churches, St Brendan's Oratory is rectangular and has a sloping roof, a flat-headed doorway and a square-headed east window. The Saints Church nearby uses mortar to bind the stones together, and it is probably later than the oratory. Outside the monastic wall is Teampull na mBan ('Nuns Church'). There is also a holy well which is approached by seven steps.
Dunraven, Irish Architecture I (1875) 40

INISHKEA NORTH (379) Early Monastery

MAP 3 B 7
OS½" 6F.56.22

Access : By boat. For transport apply to Ted Sweeney, Blacksod (tel. Blacksod 4) or to Belmullet or Blacksod Post Office
The island is now only occasionally inhabited by fishermen, but in the Early Christian period it supported an apparently flourishing monastery. The most conspicuous thing on the island is the Bailey Mór, a large mound 500 feet in diameter and 60 feet high, on which bee-hive huts and square houses were found. One of these houses contained an Early Christian cross-slab with the Crucifixion on it. A number of cross-slabs have also been found. A great number of purpura shells came to light, with which the monks used to produce a blue dye for manuscript illumination, clothes dyeing etc. On the island there is also a rectangular church dedicated to St Colmcille.
JRSAI 67, 1937, 273; 75, 1945, 127; 81, 1951, 65 and 82, 1952, 145

INISHMAINE (102) Augustinian Abbey

MAP 3 E 10
OS½" 11M.14.62

Access : Through gate, along private path and along stone path. Signposted
The church now stands on a peninsula which was originally an island on which St Cormac founded a monastery. The Church was built in the early part of the 13th century, and consists of a nave and chancel. The church is entered through a flat-headed doorway in the north wall which may have been taken from an earlier church on the same site and inserted

here, or could be one of the latest uses of this type of doorway in Ireland. Although the chancel arch with its four orders is incomplete, it still retains fine sculptured capitals including foliage and imaginary beasts. Other fantastic beasts are found on the end of the mouldings on the inside and outside of the twin east window. Not far away from the church is a gate-house, probably of 15th century date, which gave access to the monastic enclosure. The monastery was burned in 1227 by Hugh, son of Roderic O'Conor, but it probably continued to exist for a long time after that.

JRSAI 10, 1868, 136 and 35, 1905, 1; Wilde's Loch Coirib (1938) 252

KELLY'S CAVE (413)

MAP 3 E 11
OS½" 11M.15.56

Access: Over stile, then 150 yards along path through wood. Key obtainable in Cong village from Mrs John Gibbons in Café in Main Street, Cong. Signposted

A natural cave which may have been turned into a burial place during the Bronze Age.

Antiquity 11, 1937, 348

KILDERMOT (402) Church

MAP 3 F 8
OS½" 6G.28.12

Access: Along an untarred road, then to the left through gate and up two fields. Not signposted

A small 12th century church which consisted of a nave and chancel. Only the foundations of the nave remain, but the chancel is better preserved and contains a rounded east window which splays inwards. It is picturesquely situated beside Lake Ballymore.

KILDUN (423) Pillar-stones

MAP 3 C 8
OS½" 6F.79.06

Access: Along a few miles of untarred road, then over fence into a field in front of a house. Not signposted

Two upright stones, one of them being decorated with a Maltese cross in a circle.

JRSAI 72, 1942, 149

KILLALA (105) Round Tower

MAP 3 F 7
OS½" 6G.20.30

Access: Up lane and through gate. Key from Mrs Catherine Lynnott, Tower Hill, Killala. Signposted

This is a well-preserved Round Tower 84 feet high, standing on a plinth 3 feet high, and with a doorway 11 feet above the ground. The tower was struck by lightning in the last century, but it was repaired around 1840 by Bishop Verschoyle. The original monastic foundation here probably goes back to the 5th century when St Patrick appointed Muiredach as first bishop of Killala.

JRSAI 28, 1898, 274

KINLOUGH (95a) Church and Castle

MAP 3 F 11
OS½" 11M.26.50

Access: 1 mile along roadway then across 2 fields to church, and across bridge and wall to the castle. Not signposted

On one side of the river is a 13th century church incorporating a square belfry at the western end. The remains of three lancet windows can be seen in the east wall. On the other side of the river is a castle which is not in the best of condition but has two corner fireplaces and tall profiled chimney stacks. The castle was built in the 16th century by the Burkes; in 1574 it was in the possession of 'MacWilliam Eighter' (Sir John fitz Oliver Burke). In 1618 it was granted to John Bourke fitz William, but

his son Walter mortgaged the lands to Sir Valentine Blake in 1629. In 1668 Sir Thomas Blake leased the castle to John Darcy.
JRSAI 30, 1900, 164; JGAHS 6, 1909–10, 95

LANKILL (297) Standing Stone

MAP 3 E 10
OS½" 11M.01.79

Access : About 200 yards down lane and then across three fields. Not signposted
A standing stone 7 feet high. On the west face is a cross with a V-shaped ornament beneath it, and on the east face is a cross and four concentric circles. These last have been thought to belong to the art of the megalithic tombs; the stone however probably belongs to the Early Christian period — if it is not a modern forgery!
JRSAI 82, 1952, 68

MEELICK (98) Round Tower

MAP 3 F 9
OS½" 11M.33.97

Access . Direct. Signposted
A fine Round Tower with a round-headed splaying doorway and with flat-headed and pointed windows, but its conical cap is missing. At the foot of the tower is an old Irish grave-stone bearing interlacing ornament and the old Irish inscription OR DO GRICOUR (last two letters doubtful) meaning 'A prayer for Gricour'.
JRSAI 52, 1922, 179

MOYNE (103) Franciscan Friary *Fig. 51*

MAP 3 F 7
OS½" 6G.23.29

Access : Along an untarred road for a considerable distance, then over stiles and through fields. Signposted
The Friary was founded by permission of Pope Nicholas for the Observantine Franciscans in 1460. The founder may have been MacWilliam Burke or one of the Barrett family. The church consists of a rectangular nave and chancel with an eastward extension of the nave which is wider than it. The west doorway was added in the 17th century. There is also a chapel running southwards from the east end of the church. The tower was added later, though apparently planned originally as part of the church. The stairs, leading to the top, are still intact. The well-preserved cloisters

Fig. 51. Plan of the Franciscan Friary at Moyne, Co Mayo.

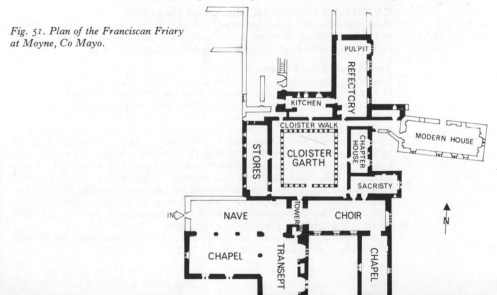

were added towards the end of the 15th century. The various buildings surrounding it include a sacristy next to the church with a chapter house beside it, and on the side opposite the church there is a kitchen and a refectory, under which a stream flows. Provincial chapters of the order were held here in 1464, 1478, 1498, 1504, 1512, 1541 and 1550. The friars remained on long after the Dissolution. Sir Richard Bingham burned the friary in 1590. In 1595 it was granted to Edward Barrett. In 1617 it was in the hands of an unnamed widow who, however, still allowed the friars to remain on. At that time there were only 6 friars left. The last friar probably died around 1800.

JGAHS 29, 1958-9, 43; Leask, Churches III, 109 and 149

MURRISK (196) Augustinian Monastery

MAP 3 D 9
OS½″ 11L.92.83

Access : A quarter of a mile down untarred road then direct to church. Signposted

This was founded in 1457 by Hugh O'Malley for the Augustinian Canons. It is beautifully situated beside a quiet inlet of Clew Bay, and dominated by Croagh Patrick, the Pilgrimage Mountain. The remains consist of a single-aisled church with unusual battlemented walls and a fine east window, as well as the east wing of the domestic buildings. The west doorway was added in the 17th century. The south and west wings may never have been completed. At the west end of the church was a tower, the lower part of which was vaulted, but this had already disappeared by 1800.

JRSAI 73, 1943, 137 and 74, 1944, 87; Leask, Churches III, 53

NEALE PARK (359) Monument known as 'The Gods of the Neale'

MAP 3 E 11
OS½″ 11M.19.59

Access : Through gates of an old estate ; the monument stands about 100 yards to the south-west of the old house. Not signposted

A strange monumental garden ornament incorporating three medieval sculptures (a unicorn, a saint and a lion), and a long and curious inscription of 1757.

RATHFRAN Dominican Friary and Megaliths

MAP 3 E 7
OS½″ 6G.19.33

Access : Half a mile along untarred path and then across a field to monastery ; to reach megaliths, continue along path for a few hundred yards, then up into fields on left of path to near top of hill. Friary signposted

The Dominican Friary (269)

The friary was founded by a de Burgh or a MacJordan for the Dominicans in 1274. The 13th century church is a long rectangular structure with a small crucifixion panel over the west door and the remains of a fine triple lancet east window. Possibly as late as the 15th century some of the lancet windows in the south wall were built up, and at the same time a separate aisle was added with a fine window. The nave was partially rebuilt in the 15th century. To the north of the church there were originally two cloisters, but only the foundations remain to show where they stood. The living quarters to be seen north of the church probably date from the 16th century and incorporate part of the original sacristy. After the Dissolution, the monastery was granted to Thomas Exeter in 1577. Bingham burned it in 1590. The friars remained in the neighbourhood down to the 18th century, though not necessarily in the friary.

JRSAI 28, 1898, 293; 99th Annual Report of the Commissioners of Public Works 1931, 11; Leask, Churches II, 117

Megaliths (389)
As for the megalithic tombs, there is a wedge-shaped tomb with large boulders making up the surrounding kerbstones near the road, and near the top of the hill there are two stone circles.
JRSAI 81, 1951, 180; Megalithic Survey, Vol. II, Co Mayo (1964) 32, No. 35

ROCKFLEET or CARRIGAHOWLEY (454) Castle

MAP 3 D 9
OS½" 6L.93.95

Access: Down one mile of untarred road. Key obtainable from Michael Chambers, Rossyvena, Carrowbeg Post Office, Westport. Signposted
A fine 15th or 16th century tower beautifully situated beside an inlet of Clew Bay. It has four storeys and a corner turret, as well as a fireplace on the top floor. It is said to have been besieged by an expedition sent from Galway in 1574, but the invasion was driven off by Grace O'Malley who lived there after the death of her second husband, Sir Richard Burke, in 1583. She retired to the castle with 'all her own followers and 1,000 head of cows and mares'.
JGAHS 4, 1905-6, 66; Leask, Castles 106

ROSDOAGH (386) Stone Circle

MAP 3 D 7
OS½" 6F.83.39

Access: Quarter of a mile along untarred road, then over ditch to right into field. Not signposted
Beautifully situated overlooking Broad Haven, this stone circle consists of an outer ring of 33 stones with a diameter of 54 feet and an inner ring of 16 stones with a diameter of about 30 feet. One part of the circle may have been adapted for other uses later.

ROSSERK (104) Franciscan Friary

MAP 3 F 7
OS½" 6G.25.25

Access: About a mile along an untarred road. Signposted
One of the finest and best preserved of the Franciscan Friaries in Ireland, this was founded possibly around 1460 by William Gannard. It was probably founded for the Observantine Franciscans. A finely carved west doorway leads to the single-aisled church which has a graceful east window. In the south chapel is another fine window. In the south-east corner of the chancel is a double piscina, unique in that it has a Round Tower carved on one of the pillars. Other carvings on the piscina include two angels and the Instruments of the Passion. The domestic buildings are well preserved, with three vaulted rooms on each side. The dormitory, refectory and kitchen were on the upper floor, where two fireplaces back to back may be seen.
JRSAI 28, 1898, 258; JGAHS 29, 1960, 7; Leask, Churches III, 111

SHRULE (95b) 'Abbey'

MAP 3 F 11
OS½" 11M.28.53

Access: Along tarred path to graveyard. Signposted
A medieval parish church of comparatively little interest with a 15th century south doorway decorated with maeander and chess-board motifs.
JGAHS 6, 1909-10, 104

STRADE (172) Friary *Fig. 52*

MAP 3 F 9
OS½" 11M.26.98

Access: Direct. Signposted
One of the MacJordan sept founded a monastery here in the first half of the 13th century for the Franciscans. But Jordan of Exeter, Lord of Athlethan, transferred it to the Dominicans in 1252 at the request of his wife Basilia, daughter of Meiler de Bermingham. The chancel of the

church, with its 6 slender side-windows in the north wall would appear to date from the 13th century, though much of the rest of the buildings seems to be 15th century work. Its main glory is a 15th century sculptured tomb in the north wall of the chancel which is one of the most beautiful in Ireland. The tomb has a series of figures on it, from left to right: Three crowned figures (The Magi?), Christ showing the five wounds, a man kneeling, taking off his hat, three figures (a bishop with a cross, St Peter and St Paul (?)). Under the east window is another 15th century tomb with a Pietà surrounded by two kneeling figures. In the sacristy there are also some good medieval tombstones.

JGAHS 29, 1958-9, 42; Leask, Churches III, 168

TURLOUGH (100) Round Tower and Church

MAP 3 F 9
OS½" 11M.21.94

Access: Direct. Signposted

A well-preserved Round Tower which is lower and fatter than most examples. It had a round-headed doorway (now blocked up), and flat- and gable-headed windows. The church beside it, although built in the 18th century, incorporates a 16th century mullioned window and a small plaque with the Crucifixion dated 1625. The first church here was founded by St Patrick, and because of this the Archbishops of Armagh long claimed jurisdiction over it. But in 1351 the Pope authorized the Archbishop of Armagh to relinquish his rights over it to the Archbishop of Tuam. After the Dissolution it passed to the Bourkes, but some time after 1655 it came into the ownership of the Fitzgerald family.

JGAHS 8, 1913-4, 39

Fig. 52. Figures on a tomb at Strade, Co Mayo, carved around 1475.

ARDMULCHAN (496) Motte

MAP 5 P 10
OS½″ 13N.92.71

Access : Through gate and over field and fence. Signposted
A motte having an oval platform surrounded by a ditch and bank; it occupies a dominant position overlooking the River Boyne. Its present function is to act as the partial support of a high voltage electricity pylon.

ATHCARNE (322) 'White Cross'

MAP 5 Q 10
OS½″ 13 0.02.65

Access : Directly beside road. Not signposted
A wayside cross erected by Dame Jennet Dowdall around 1600. On the east face is a Crucifixion, and on the west side an attractive Virgin and Child, and the arms of the Bathe and the Dowdall families. The cross may have been inserted into an earlier base, and the baroque cap may be later than the cross. Dame Jennet Dowdall erected a number of wayside crosses (see below under Duleek) in memory of her third husband, William Bathe, who was created Justice of the Common Pleas by Sir John Perrot, the Lord Deputy, in 1581, and who died in 1599. She had previously been married to Oliver Plunket, Baron of Louth, and Nicholas St Lawrence, 21st Earl of Howth. She was born at Athlumney near Navan, and lived until 1619.
CLAJ 2, 1910, 257; JRSAI 46, 1916, 201

ATHLUMNEY (287) Castle

MAP 5 P 10
OS½″ 13 0.02.65

Access : Through a garden. Key obtainable from Convent on opposite side of the road. Signposted
The castle was built in two periods. The tower at the southern end was built in the 15th century, and has four storeys (topped by a ghastly modern water-tank!) In the first floor there is a secret chamber in the wall, reachable down a small stairs. Beside the tower are the remains of a vaulted room, which was probably added later. The rest of the Castle is a Tudor mansion built around 1600 beside the older tower. It had a gabled roof, and still retains a number of its mullioned windows. A number of fireplaces and an oven can still be seen in the inside walls. There is also a fine oriel window in the south wall overlooking the road. When Cromwell was attacking Drogheda in 1649, the castle was held by the Maguires who set it on fire rather than let Cromwell capture it.
JRSAI 22, 1892, 24

BALRATH (356) Wayside Cross

MAP 5 P/Q 10
OS½″ 13N/0.
00.65

Access : Directly beside road. Not signposted
A late 16th century wayside cross with the inscription ORATE-P-AĪA JOHANIS BROIN (Pray for the Soul of John Broin). On the east face is a representation of the Pietà, on the west face there is a Crucifixion and Gothic decoration; the north face bears geometric designs and a head, and there is another head at the end of the south arm. The cross was presumably re-erected in 1727, as the following inscription which was added later suggests 'Sʳ Andrew Aylmer of Mountaylmer Barᵗ and his Lady Catherine Aylmer had this cross beautified A.D. 1727. Pʳ. H. Smith'.
JRSAI 46, 1916, 201

BECTIVE (187) Cistercian Abbey

MAP 5 P 10
OS½″ 13N.86.60

Access : Through gate and field, then over a stile. Key obtainable from Joseph Scully, Bective. Signposted
The Abbey was founded in 1150 by Murchad O Maeil-Sheachlainn, King of Meath, for the Cistercians, and dedicated to the Blessed Virgin. It is one of the earliest Cistercian abbeys in Ireland. The Abbot sat in the

Parliament of the Pale. Hugh de Lacy's body was buried here in 1195, but after a dispute it was later transferred to St Thomas's in Dublin. Of the original 12th century abbey only remnants of the south of the nave arcade, parts of the south transept, the chapter house, part of the west wing of the domestic buildings and some of the doorways in the south wing remain. In the 15th century, the buildings were fortified and great changes took place. The southern arcade of the nave was blocked up, the present cloister and many of the buildings around it (excluding the chapter house) were built. This cloister is the best feature of the abbey; one of the pillars bears a figure carrying a crozier. The tower, and the great hall in the south wing (probably the monks' refectory) were also added in this period. At some later period further alterations took place in the south transept; the oven between the south transept and the chapter house was inserted, and an external entrance to the south range was also added. The monastery was suppressed in 1536. In the following year, the abbey and its lands were leased to Thomas Agarde, and they were bought by Andrew Wyse in 1552. Subsequently it passed to the Dillons and then to the Boltons.
JRSAI 46, 1916, 46; Arch Journal 88, 1931, 362; Leask, Churches III, 27 and 143.

CANNISTOWN (239) Church

MAP 5 P 10
OS½" 13N.88.64

Access : Over stile, along path and through gate to cemetery. Signposted
The first church on the site was founded by St Finian, but the present church dates from the late 12th or early 13th century, and it became the parish church dedicated to St Brigid. The property belonged to Hugh de Lacy when it was built, and later passed to the Nangles, the Prestons, the Ludlows, the Duke of Bedford and to Earl Russell in turn. The chancel is 13th century, and there is a fine chancel arch with foliage capitals, and above them, on the left, three dogs pouncing on a fox (?), and on the right, three figures with the central one holding a staff in his hand. In the wall above the arch, and also lying on the ground nearby, are other sculpted stones bearing grotesque animal masks and a rampant lion. In the 15th century the nave of the church was altered, and windows were inserted which are made of limestone, in contrast to the earlier ones made of sandstone.
JRSAI 51, 1921, 125; Leask, Churches II, 145

CASTLEKEERAN (107) High Crosses

MAP 5 N 10
OS½" 13N.69.77

Access : Through farmyard, across field and then over stile to old cemetery. Signposted
The place is called Diseart Chiaráin, the Hermitage of Ciarán, who was a monk of the monastery at Kells nearby, but who is not to be confused with the founder of Clonmacnoise. The monastery was plundered by the Vikings in 949, and by Dermod McMurrough in 1170. In the 13th century it passed to the Knights Hospitallers and by the 16th century it was owned by the Plunketts. There are three High Crosses with moulding at the edges, but none of them bears figure sculpture. One has bosses at the centre of the arms and another has interlacing at the end of the arms. Beside the insignificant remains of a church there is also an Early Christian grave-slab, and an Ogham stone with the inscription COVAGNI MAQI MUCOI LUGUNI. In the River Blackwater beside the monastery there is another High Cross; tradition says that it was dumped in the river by St Columba when St Ciarán caught him red-handed taking it to his nearby monastery at Kells!

JRSAI 56, 1926, 9 and 87, 1957, 167; Ríocht na Midhe 1, 3, 1957, 17; Macalister, Corpus I (1945) 46, No. 46

CRUICETOWN (264) Church and Cross

MAP 5 N 9
OS½" 13N.79.85

Access : Through gate, 200 yards through field and then over stile to graveyard in the middle of the field. Signposted
A medieval parish church, consisting of nave and chancel, built around 1200. In the nave there is a double-effigy tomb of the Cruice family carved in 1688. In the north-western corner of the church there is an old but undecorated baptismal font. To the south of the church is a cross, also dating from 1688, with the Virgin and Child on the east face, and on the west a primitive but touching representation of the Crucifixion.

DANESTOWN (309) Ring-fort

MAP 5 P 10
OS½" 13N.98.65

Access : Over fence or through gate into field. Signposted
A ring-fort about 150 feet in diameter and consisting of a central round raised platform surrounded by a concentric ditch and bank.

DONAGHMORE (106) Church and Round Tower

MAP 5 P 10
OS½" 13N.88.69

Access : Direct from car-park. Signposted
St Patrick is said to have founded the first monastery here. There is a well-preserved Round Tower, which lacks its top windows. It is to be suspected that these originally existed, but were not included in the res-toration works when the conical cap was replaced about 150 years ago. The tower is unusual in that there is a Crucifixion above the round-headed doorway, and there are heads beside the arch. The nearby church was built in the 15th century, but it replaces a Romanesque church from which a head is incorporated in the south wall of the bell-tower of the church. In the graveyard there are some Early Christian grave-slabs.
Petrie, Round Towers (1845) 406

DONORE (232) Castle

MAP 5 N 11
OS½" 13N.70.50

Access : Across fence and into field. Key obtainable at cottage on opposite side of the road. Signposted
In 1429 King Henry VI promised a grant of £10 to every one of his subjects who built a castle 20 feet long, 16 feet wide and 40 feet high before 1439 in counties Dublin, Meath, Kildare and Louth. As this castle roughly conforms to these measurements, it is quite probable that it is one of these '£10 castles'. There are 3 storeys, of which the ground floor is vaulted. The corners of the castle are rounded, and a projecting tower at the south-western corner contained the spiral staircase.
Leask, Castles 77

DOWTH (147) Passage-grave

MAP 5 Q 10
OS½" 13 0.02.74

Access : Up path with stiles in it. Key obtainable from Mrs Nora White, Dowth. Signposted
Together with Knowth and Newgrange, this mound forms part of the great Passage-grave cemetery beside the lower stretches of the Boyne. The mound has a diameter of 280 feet and is 50 feet high. A number of the stones surrounding the bottom of the mound can still be seen, some of them bearing ornamentation. There are two prehistoric tombs in the western part of the mound, dating from about 2,500–2,000 B.C. One of these is reached by climbing down a ladder in an iron cage; it has a long passage,

with some transverse stones on the floor. This leads to a round chamber
with a large ritual basin stone in the middle, and there are tomb niches
at the back and on two sides of the burial chamber. A further burial
chamber is annexed to the right hand tomb niche. At the entrance to the
passage is an Early Christian souterrain which emerges to the north-east
of the iron cage. Further to the south of the first Passage-Grave is a second
one. This is approached by a short passage which leads to a round burial
chamber (with modern roof), with one recess off to the right. A visit to
the first tomb is only recommended to those who are in good physical
condition, as a certain amount of crawling and climbing over stones is
involved!

PRIA 41, 1932-4, 162; C.O'Kelly, Dowth; C.O'Kelly, Newgrange (1967)

DULEEK Churches and Crosses

MAP 5 Q 10
OS½" 130.04.69

St Patrick placed St Cianán over the first church here in the 5th century.
St Cianán, who is credited with the building of the first stone church in
Ireland, died in 489 and his body was said to have been preserved without
decay. The monastery was plundered at least 10 times between 830 and
1149. The bodies of King Brian Boru and the other heroes slain at the
Battle of Clontarf in 1014 rested here for a night before being brought to
Armagh for burial. Duleek became the centre of a diocese in 1110, but in
the late 12th century Bishop Simon de Rochfort had it merged with the
diocese of Meath. The last skirmish in the Battle of the Boyne took place
nearby, and King William slept here after the battle.

JRSAI 46, 1916, 202; Ríocht na Midhe 3, 3, 1965, 187

The Priory (179)

*Access : Direct from road. If main gate is locked, try the side gate. Key to
tower is not available locally. Not signposted*

The Augustinians may have been introduced to Duleek by 1150, but
Hugh de Lacy founded an Augustinian house nearby in 1182. The present
priory is possibly a part of that monastery. Parts of the arcade of the church
may be 13th century and the south wall of the south aisle may be 14th
century, but the tower is certainly 15th century. In the north aisle is the
tomb of Dr Cusack, the Catholic Bishop of Meath from 1679 to 1688.
In the centre of the nave is the altar tomb of the Prestons and Plunketts,
with representations of SS Katherine, Patrick (?) and Peter at the west end,
the Crucifixion, angels and St Michael at the east end. the instruments of
the Passion on the north side and the Bellew, Preston and Plunkett arms
on the south. In the tower some Romanesque fragments are preserved.
A Round Tower originally stood immediately to the north of the tower,
and the square tower was built around it, but only the impression of the
Round Tower remains in the wall of the square tower. To the north of the
modern church stands a squat High Cross, probably of 10th century date.
On the west face is the Crucifixion and some unidentifiable figures. The
cross is decorated with bosses, interlacing and two Evangelists symbols—
the eagle and the ox.

JRSAI 58, 1926, 4; 102nd Annual Report of the Commissioners of
Public Works 1933-4, 8

St Cianán's Church (199)

*Access : In a field on the opposite side of the road to the graveyard. Key to
field obtainable from Miss A Donnelly, Duleek. Not signposted*

An insignificant medieval church with south doorway, possibly incorporating parts of an earlier church. Built into the north wall is a large stone

Fig. 53. Cross erected by Dame Jennet Dowdall at Duleek, Co Meath in 1601.

Fig. 54. Dunmoe Castle, Co Meath in 1795.

with the rough inscription OR DO SCANLAN (A prayer for Scanlan).

Dowdall Cross (440) *Fig. 53*
Access : On platform beside road. Not signposted
A wayside cross built by Dame Jennet Dowdall (see above under Athcarne) in 1601 and repaired in 1810. The two top pieces may have been added later. On the cross there are a number of figures including an angel with a coat of arms, St Peter, St Patrick and St Keenane (Cianán) on the east face, St George and the Dragon (?), and angel, St Mary Magdalen, St James and St Thomas on the north face; St George, St Andrew, St Katherine and St Stephen on the south face, and an angel and the Bathe coat of arms and an inscription on the west face. The inscription reads THIS CROSS WAS BUILDED BY IENNET DOWDALL WIFE TO WILLIAM BATHE OF ATHCARN JUSTICE OF HER MAJESTIES COURT OF COMMON PLEAS FOR HIM AND HER ANO 1601. HE DECEACED THE 15 OF OCT 1599 BURIED IN THE CHURCH OF DULEEK. WHOSE SOULES I PRAY GOD TAKE TO HIS MERCIE.
CLAJ 2, 1910, 259-60; JRSAI 46, 1916, 202

DUNMOE (482) Castle *Fig. 54*
MAP 5 P 10
OS½″ 13N.90.70
Access : Down lane for about 300 yards, then across fences, through field and over stile to castle. Signposted
Two sides of a four-storey castle which was square in shape with large rounded turrets at the four corners. The two lower storeys were vaulted.

Although built in the style of the 13th century castles, it was probably not built till the 15th century. Cromwell is said to have fired on it from the opposite bank of the Boyne on his way from Drogheda to Athboy in 1649. JRSAI 28, 1898, 274

DUNSANY (489) Church and Cross

MAP 5 P 11
OS½″ 13N.91.55

Access: Only through the private estate of Lord Dunsany, 75 yards along a private avenue and then in to the left. Not signposted
The church was built by Nicholas Plunkett, first Baron Dunsany, in the middle of the 15th century on the site of an earlier church. It has a nave and a very slightly narrower chancel. There are towers at each corner, that on the north-west (locked) being the sacristy. In a niche in the north wall is a fine double-effigy tomb, possibly representing Christopher, Lord Dunsany and his wife Anna Fitzgerald. It was they who had the very fine 15th century font in the church carved. This is one of the finest medieval fonts in Ireland, and has representations of the Crucifixion and of the Twelve Apostles on it. The east window of the church is a 19th century insertion. To the north of the church is the fragment of a 15th century cross with representations of the Apostles on it.
JRSAI 24, 1894, 222; Leask, Churches III, 12; Roe, Medieval Fonts of Meath (1968) 49

DUNSHAUGHLIN (400) Lintel

MAP 5 P 11
OS½″ 13N.97.53

Access: Up path to graveyard. Not signposted
The insignificant remains of the aisle of a medieval church as well as a few 15th or 16th century architectural fragments. The main interest of the place is a slab mounted beside these remains with a representation of the Crucifixion on it. On Christ's right is a man holding a spear, and on his left a man offers him vinegar in a chalice on the end of a pole. It probably formed the lintel over the doorway of a church which has since disappeared. The lintel is probably 10th or 11th century in date.
Henry, Irish Art Vol 2 (1967) 188

FOURKNOCKS (472) Passage-Grave

MAP 5 Q 10
OS½″ 13 O.11.62

Access: Over stile and up path for 100 yards. Key to mound obtainable from Mr T. Connell, at first house on left down the hill eastwards from the stile. Signposted
This is a fine example of a Passage-Grave, differing from other Irish examples in having an inordinately large chamber which takes up most of the area of the mound. The chamber is reached by a passage, and has three side-niches. Stones bearing Passage-Grave art with zigzags etc. were found in the passage and on the stones above the tomb-niches off the main chamber. Two other decorated stones stand on the floor; one of these, on left near the passage, has a very amusing face engraved with a few simple lines—the clearest representation of the human face in prehistoric Irish art. Over 60 burials were found in the passage and the side niches, but none was found in the central chamber. Later burials were found in the mound itself. The central chamber is now covered by a cleverly designed concrete dome, with shafts letting in enough light to see by and creating a suitably eerie atmosphere inside. The original roof was probably of wood, carried on a central pole. The grave was built around 1800 B.C. 150 yards to the east of the Passage Grave is another mound, where the dead were cremated. Another mound, dating to about 1500 B.C., was found nearby.
PRIA 58 C 1957, 197

HILL OF WARD (150) Earthworks

MAP 5 N 10
OS½" 13N.74.65

Access : Across fence into field. Signposted

The earthworks consist of a central raised enclosure surrounded by four banks and ditches, which were much disturbed in 1641. This is Tlachtga, an ancient site said to have been founded by the Celtic god Lug and a place dedicated to the cult of the sacred fire. It was the site of an important Oenach or gathering in pagan times which took place here at Samhain, the beginning of winter, and in which all the men of Ireland took part. Tlachtga was said to be the daughter of a famous wizard Mug Roith who according to tradition is credited with having cut off the head of St John the Baptist! JRSAI 49, 1919, 8; Arch Journal 88, 1931, 371

KELLS High Crosses, Round Tower and 'St Columb's House'

MAP 5 N 10
OS½" 13N.74.76

Frontispiece and Fig. 8

Signposted

The site was granted to St Colmcille for the foundation of a monastery about the middle of the 6th century. But the monastery was possibly re-founded in 804, and a new church was built to honour the event. The reason for the new foundation was possibly the return from Iona—another of St Colmcille's great foundations—of the monks who where fleeing from the onslaught of the Vikings. In 877 reliquaries of the saint were transferred to Kells. The monastery was raided by the Vikings in 919, 950 and 969. The greatest treasure of the monastery—the Book of Kells, now in Trinity College, Dublin—which had possibly been written here in the 8th century or early 9th century, was stolen in 1007 from the western sacristy of the church, but was found two and a half months later without its gold and covered by a sod. The monastery was raided many times in the course of the 11th century—this time by the Irish. It was burned in 1111 and again in 1156. A famous Synod met here in 1152 to finalize the arrangement of dioceses in the country. This Synod raised Kells to a Diocese, but it was later reduced to parochial status. After this Kells became prominent as a Norman fortification, but while the Norman remains have vanished, there are many remnants of the old monastery.

Round Tower and High Crosses (158)

Access : Up tarred path to churchyard

In the churchyard on the top of the hill are found the Round Tower and a number of High Crosses. The Round Tower is about 100 feet high, and has five windows at the top, though the original conical cap is missing. The doorway had heads carved on it, but these have almost entirely weathered away. The tower must date to before 1076, for in that year Murchadh Mac Flainn, who was claiming the High Kingship of Ireland, was murdered in the tower. Near the Round Tower is the South Cross dedicated to Saints Patrick and Columba, which was possibly erected in the 9th century. On the base are interlacings, animals including a deer, and a chariot procession. On the south face are Adam and Eve, and Cain and Abel, then the Three Children in the Fiery Furnace, above that Daniel in the Lions Den; on the left arm is the sacrifice of Isaac, on the right SS Paul and Anthony in the desert, while on top is David with his harp, and the Miracle of Loaves and Fishes. On the west side is the Crucifixion, and above that Christ in Judgment. On the end of the arm on the south side David can be seen killing the lion, while on the end of the north arm he kills the bear. The cross is also decorated with a number of ornamental

Conjectural reconstruction of the monastery at Kells, Co Meath as it might have been c. 1100. (See also frontispiece)

panels, particularly interlacing, and a vine scroll in which animals and birds prance about. About 20 yards to the north-west is the sturdy stump of what must have been a very fine and tall cross. On the base is an inscription OROIT DO ARTGAL—A Prayer for Artgal, but unfortunately we know nothing about the man in question. On the east side can be seen The Baptism of Christ in the Jordan (the flowing together of two rivers), The Marriage Feast at Cana (?or the Adoration of the Magi?), David with his harp, The Presentation in the Temple (?), an unidentified panel and above, the Entry of Christ into Jerusalem (or possibly the Flight into Egypt). On the west face can be seen Adam and Eve, an amusing representation of Noah's Ark and other unidentified panels. Both the narrow sides have various geometrically decorated panels. Beside the modern church is an unfinished Cross with a Crucifixion on one face. It is interesting as it shows the various stages involved in the carving of these High Crosses. To the north of the modern church is the tower of a medieval church, into which various fragments and grave-slabs have been inserted. Beside the tower is the rounded base of another High Cross. In the organ-loft of the modern church is a display of photographs of items associated with the ancient monastery, such as blow-ups of the Book of Kells etc.

The Market Cross
This cross now stands at the crossing of two streets in the town, but it is not certain that this was its original position. The base shows horsemen, a battle scene and various animals. On the east face can be seen Christ in the Tomb guarded by soldiers, Goliath (?), Adam and Eve, and Cain and Abel; in the centre of the head is Daniel in the Lion's Den, on the left arm is the Sacrifice of Isaac. On the west face is an inscription saying that Robert (Ba)lfe erected the cross in 1688; above it is the Adoration of the Magi, The Marriage Feast at Cana (?), the Miracle of the Loaves and Fishes (?); in the centre of the head is the Crucifixion. On the south side is The Slaughter of the Innocents, the Healing of the Blind Man (?) and Moses receiving the Law, while David and the Lion can be seen at the end of the arm.

'St Columb's House' (108)

Access: Direct, but get keys from Mrs Carpenter at first house on right on coming up the hill after the main entrance to the Church of Ireland church. Signposted

This is an ancient oratory with steep stone roof. The present entrance is modern; the vaulted room it leads to was originally divided into two levels, the present ground floor acting as a basement, and the original church proper was entered by a door (now blocked up) in the west wall, and was about 6 or 7 feet above present floor level. Above the vault is a small chamber (reachable by a ladder) which also served the purpose of preventing the roof from collapsing. It is thought by some that this was the building erected shortly after 804 to commemorate the return of the monks from Iona, but it is likely to have been built a few centuries later than this.

Roe, The High Crosses of Kells (1959); Ríocht na Midhe 2, 1, 1959, 18 and 2, 2, 1960, 8; Leask, Churches I, 33

KILLARY High Cross

MAP 5 P 9
OS½" 13N.88.83

Access: 50 yards up path into graveyard. Signposted

Here there is the shaft of a High Cross of about 10th century date. On the east face are Adam and Eve, Noah's Ark, the Sacrifice of Isaac, and Daniel in the Lion's Den. On the west face are two unidentified figures, the Baptism of Christ and the Presentation in the Temple, while on the other sides there are two figures and various geometrical motifs. Nearby are the insignificant remains of a medieval church and in the north-eastern corner of the graveyard is a square base and the arm of a High Cross, possibly belonging to the shaft described above.

JRSAI 56, 1926, 2

KILLEEN (257) Church and Cross

MAP 5 P 11
OS½" 13N.93.55

Access: Half a mile up a private avenue in the estate of Killeen castle. The church is only 100 yards from the castle. For permission to visit the church, please apply in writing beforehand to Mr Charles A. Rogers, Balfstown, Mulhuddart, Co. Dublin. Not signposted

A long 15th century church consisting of a nave and a slightly narrower chancel, with an entrance on the north side. There are towers at each corner, that on the north-east corner housing the sacristy and with sleeping-quarters on the first floor. The church is mainly noteworthy because of of the number of its well-preserved and similar traceried windows, and there is a good triple sedilia in the south wall of the church. There are also a considerable number of gravestones of the Plunkett family in the church, including two fine double-effigy tombs of the late 15th century. To the north of the church two fragments of a 15th century cross with six apostles on the bottom have been re-erected. The church is very similar to that at Dunsany (q.v.).

Leask, Churches III, 12

KNOWTH (147 and 409) Passage-Grave

MAP 5 P 10
OS½" 13N.99.73

Access: Direct from road, but PERMANENTLY CLOSED TO THE PUBLIC UNTIL EXCAVATIONS ARE FINISHED. Signposted

In this great mound about 40 feet high and 220 feet in diameter two great Passage-Graves were discovered in 1967 and 1968. One of the chambers is corbelled, like that at Newgrange, and is round and has side-chambers;

the other has a flat roof and looks like little more than a widening of the passage. Both graves are richly decorated with megalithic art, as are also many of the kerbstones surrounding the base of the large mound. The entrances to the tombs were considerably disturbed in the Early Christian Period by the building of souterrains, which seem to penetrate into the mound like rabbit-burrows. As the Passage-graves have not yet been excavated, no dating evidence has yet come to light, but it is likely that this great mound was raised between 2500 and 2000 B.C. Excavations during the last 8 years have uncovered 15 satellite tombs (smaller passage-graves) and other ritual features dotted around the base of the mound. In the 9th and 10th centuries Knowth was the seat of the kings of Northern Brega, and the Normans used the mound as a motte at the end of the 12th century.
PRIA 66 C 1968, 299; Antiquity 41, 1967, 302 and 43, 1969, 8

MAP 5 M 10
OS½″ 13N.
57-60.77/78

LOUGHCREW (151 and 290) Passage-Grave Cemetery *Fig 55*

Access : Spread over a number of fields on both sides of the road. Through gates, and then a long climb up to the various hill-tops. Key for the locked Cairns L and T is kept by John Balfe, Newtown, to the left of the first left turn below the car park. Signposted
This is a cemetery or collection of Passage-Graves situated on two neighbouring peaks, called Cairnbane East and Cairnbane West. The whole cemetery is sometimes known as Slieve na Calliagh, or the Hill of the Witch. At least thirty tombs are known, but not all have been opened, and, indeed, only a few have recognizable burial chambers. In the westerly group, cairns G and K are the largest. Cairn G is a large mound, but no chamber has ever been found inside it, while Cairn K has a large chamber with five side-chambers and a standing stone inside. Some of its stones are decorated. Near it is cairn H where excavations in 1943 produced bone objects decorated in the La Tène art style of the Iron Age. In the

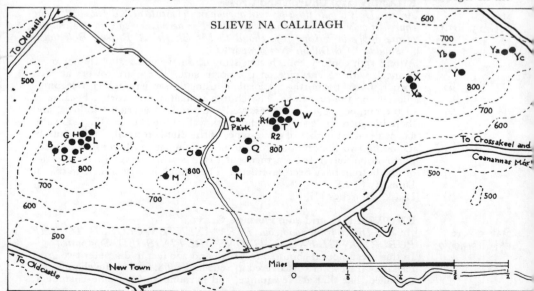

Fig. 55. Plan of the Passage Grave cemetery at Loughcrew, Co Meath.

eastern Group, cairn T is the largest, with a diameter of 120 feet. It has a large chamber with side-chambers, and has many stones bearing decoration such as concentric circles, arcs and flower-motifs, zigzags etc. There are also a number of small satellite tombs around cairn T. The majority of the tombs were probably built in the second half of the third millennium B.C., but Cairn H produced material which could be as late as the 1st century A.D.

JRSAI 55, 1925, 15; O Ríordáin/Daniel, Newgrange (1964) 100 and 122

NEWGRANGE (147) Passage-Grave *Fig. 56*

MAP 5 Q 10
OS½″ 13 0.00.72

Access : Direct. Open daily 10 a.m. to 6 p.m. (June-July, Monday-Saturday open till 7 p.m.), with guided tours in summer. Admission fee charged. Tickets obtainable at the Tourist Office and Display Centre nearby.

Newgrange is Ireland's best known prehistoric monument, and one of the finest Passage-Graves in the whole of western Europe. The almost heart-shaped mound is about 36 feet high and about 300 feet in diameter. Standing upright in the earth outside the base of the mound are large boulders up to 8 feet high, of which 12 out of the original estimated 38 survive. The base of the mound is retained by large stones, lying horizontally, many of which bear geometric decoration. The most famous of these is the stone marking the entrance, where the triple spiral—unique in Newgrange—is found together with normal double spirals, concentric semi-circles and diamond-shaped motifs known as lozenges. The area surrounding the entrance has recently been reconstructed. Above the entrance to the tomb is a decorated stone covering a small box over the passage which may have been used to pass offerings for the dead through a slit in the bottom of the box down into the passage after the grave had been finally blocked up. The passage itself is 62 feet long, and a number of its stones, particularly those in the inner half, bear decoration such as spirals, zigzags etc, and one, on the right, has a number of grooves making the stone look as if it had ribs. The chamber is roughly round, has two side chambers and another at the back, and is roofed by a magnificent corbelled roof reaching to a height 20 feet above the floor. The stones in the side-chambers are richly decorated; note the spirals on one stone and the fern on another in the western chamber, the triple spiral on the right-hand stone of the back chamber and the capstone of the eastern chamber. In the eastern chamber there is a double stone basin on the floor, and there is one each in the other side-chambers; these had some ritual use presumably. Recent excavations have shown up some clever and intricate techniques used in building the mound, particularly the stone packing above the chamber, and also the use of a channel on the upper part of the stones of the passage so that water filtering down from above could be drained off rather than dripping into the chamber—which remains remarkably dry. As at Knowth (see above) some satellite tombs have been found outside the edge of the mound, and traces of both earlier and later occupation of the area have also been discovered there. Radio carbon dating has shown that the tomb was constructed around 2500 B.C. Near the car-park is a small museum displaying plaster casts of some of the stones, as well as details of other Passage-Graves and photographs of other interesting monuments in the area. In the court of the museum is another decorated stone, found nearby.

Coffey, Newgrange (1912); O Ríordáin/Daniel, Newgrange (1964); C. O'Kelly, Newgrange (1967)

RATHMORE (289) Church and Cross

MAP 5 N 10
OS½" 13N.75.67

Access : Over stile, along path for 20 yards, then through gate and field to graveyard in which church lies. Signposted.

A church built probably by Sir Thomas Plunkett in the mid 15th century, and dedicated to St Lawrence. It remained in use until at least 1678. Though the nave and chancel were built separately, they were both built around the same time. At each corner there is a tower; that on the north-east being a sacristy with living quarters overhead, while the belfry is at the south-western corner. There is a fine sedilia and piscina, and a very good east window with sculptures of kings and queens on the outside. The altar has niches containing angels swinging censers, St Lawrence with the grid-iron, bishops, an abbess with a crosier, and the coats of arms of the Plunkett, Fitzgerald, Talbot, Fleming, Eustace, Bellew, Bermingham and Cusack families. There is also a double-effigy tomb of the founder and his wife erected around 1471, as well as a 15th century font. A cross to the north of the church was erected by Sir Christopher Plunkett and his wife Catherine in 1519, and shows St Lawrence (again with grid-iron), St Patrick or an archbishop, an abbess and vine-leaves. The church resembles those at Dunsany and Killeen.

JRSAI 63, 1933, 153; Leask, Churches III, 16; Roe, Medieval Fonts of Meath (1968) 92

NEWGRANGE   CO. MEATH.

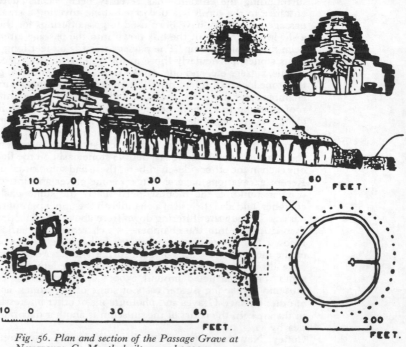

10   0   30   60   FEET.

10   0   30   60   FEET.

0   200   FEET.

Fig. 56. Plan and section of the Passage Grave at Newgrange, Co Meath, built around 2500 B.C.

REALTOGE (495) Ring-fort

MAP 5 P 10
OS½" 13N.94.67

Access : Through private garden into field beside house. Not signposted
A ring-fort with a diameter of about 120 feet and covered in gorse bushes. It consists of a round central area surrounded by a bank, a ditch and another bank. In the centre there are traces of hut foundations, and a souterrain is also said to exist.

ROBERTSTOWN (256) Castle

MAP 5 N 9
OS½" 13N.79.84

Access : Across fence and then 50 yards through field. Key obtainable from Mrs May O'Reilly in house about 200 yards behind the castle. Signposted
A three-storey castle with gabled roof built in the 17th century. The ground floor is a series of vaulted rooms; the first floor is divided into three rooms. Its most unusual features are the two projecting towers on the first floor, which have corbels at the bottom like those in Scottish castles.

SKREEN (109) Church

MAP 5 P 10
OS½" 13N.95.61

Access : Up steps and through gate. Key to tower obtainable at O'Connell's, opposite the entrance. Signposted
An older church existed on the site which was dedicated to St Columba, and there was once a shrine to him here (hence the name, from Latin *scrinium*, a shrine). Around 1175 Adam de Feipo was granted the land and built another church whose tithes he brought with him when he joined the Cistercian Abbey of St Mary's in Dublin around 1185. The present church was founded around 1341. It has a nave and chancel, and a tower at the western end of the church. The north doorway retains some of its architectural decoration, while there is the representation of a bishop over the 14th or 15th century south doorway. The tower, which was probably built in the 15th century, houses the fragments of an undecorated baptismal font and a tomb-slab. To the north-east of the church stands a medieval cross with a crude representation of the Crucifixion on its west face. Nearby is the decorative grave-slab of Walter Marward dated 1611.
JRSAI 24, 1894, 229; and 82, 1952, 145

SLANE (188) Friary

MAP 5 P 10
OS½" 13N.96.75

Access : Through stile and field. Signposted
The site is intimately associated with the lighting of the first Paschal Fire in Ireland by St Patrick in 433, thus symbolizing the triumph of Christianity over paganism. St Erc founded a monastery here in Early Christian times, and there was also a medieval abbey here, but little is known about the history of the place until it was re-built in its present form in 1512 when Sir Christopher Flemmyng founded a small Franciscan friary here. Both it and the College were surrendered in 1540, and in 1543 the lands were granted to Sir James Flemmyng. In 1631 the Capuchins were settled in the monastery, where they stayed until the advent of Cromwell. The church was finally abandoned as a place of worship in 1723. The church has a nave and chancel, and a short south aisle, as well as a tower at the western end. The window on the eastern face of the tower, just above the door, is earlier and is probably taken from an older church on the site. Nearby is the College which was founded by Sir Christopher Flemmyng for four priests, four lay-brothers and four choristers. It is built around an open quadrangle, with the priests' residence on the north side, and a tower on the south side. In the south wall there are some fine windows, forming part of what was probably a refectory or

Fig. 57. Map of the Hill of Tara, Co Mea

reading room. The use of the other rooms is not known, but most of them have fire-places. Built into the west wall of the southern wing is the representation of a dragon. To the east of the college are the remains of a gateway, possibly built after the College went out of use at the Dissolution of the Monasteries in 1541.
JRSAI 31, 1901, 405; Leask, Churches III, 22 and 30

TARA (148) Old Royal Site *Fig. 57*

MAP 5 P II
OS½″ 13N.92.60

Access: Preferably where signpost stands, through stile, up field and across another stile. Signposted

Tara Hill was one of the most venerated spots in early Ireland. From the time of the legendary king Cormac Mac Airt in the 3rd century, it came into the historical limelight, but it probably had a religious significance long before that. The seat of priest-kings going back to a time long before Irish history began, it developed from being a religious-royal site of small local priest-kings to become the seat of the High Kings of Ireland. These kings were not a hereditary line of kings based in Tara, but were chosen to be High King or fought their way to the title, and many of them came from widely differing places in the northern half of the country. The kings were thus not always resident at Tara, but spent a considerable part of their time in the areas from whence they came. When St Patrick visited the site in an effort to convert the High King of his day, Laoire, the king-priests were at the height of their power, but with the advent of Christianity, Tara gradually lost its religious significance and became the nominal seat of the High King, until it was finally abandoned by Mael-Shechlainn in 1022. A skirmish took place here in 1798, and in the last century O'Connell held a mammoth meeting on the Hill to re-inforce his demand for Catholic emancipation. The visitor to the Hill will be disappointed in what he sees; there are no signs of great regal palaces—nothing but simple earthworks remain. The buildings must have been made of wood or wattle and daub, and all have long since disappeared. Indeed the old literary sources suggest that many more buildings existed than there are earthworks on the hill. But the visitor must use his imagination, and create in his mind's eye a number of comparatively small buildings dotting the hill, and he must use his fantasy to see these buildings peopled by the King and his supporters busying themselves with 'old forgotten far-off things and battles long ago'. The most prominent monument on the hill is also the oldest. It is the Mound of the Hostages which on excavation proved to be a small Passage-Grave (locked) having a narrow passage (with a decorated stone) leading to a small chamber. It dates to around 1800. B.C., but was also used in the ensuing centuries for secondary burials. The mound stands in the northern part of a large enclosure surrounded by a bank with a ditch outside it. This enclosure is a Hill Fort, a type of fortification typical of the Iron Age, and therefore much later than the Mound of the Hostages. In the middle of this enclosure stand two linked ringforts known as the Royal Seat and Cormac's House respectively. Cormac's House has two banks and two ditches around it, the outer one making a bend on the north side to include an older burial mound. In the centre of it, beside the atrocious statue of St Patrick, is the Lia Fáil, which originally stood near the Mound of the Hostages but which was re-erected here in honour of those who died in the skirmish in 1798. The Kings were crowned on the stone, and tradition says that it roared when the king was accepted. To the south of the royal enclosure are the remains of another

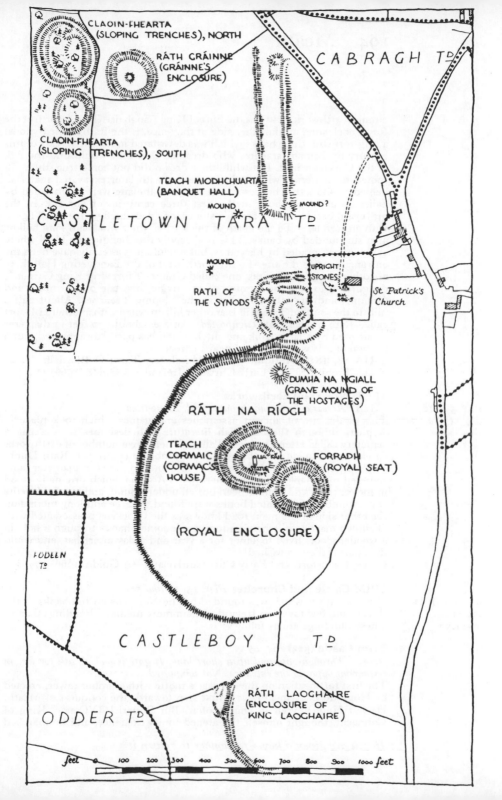

CLAOIN-FHEARTA
(SLOPING TRENCHES), NORTH

RÁTH GRÁINNE
(GRÁINNE'S
ENCLOSURE)

CABRAGH T⁰

CLAOIN-FHEARTA
(SLOPING TRENCHES), SOUTH

TEACH MIODHCHUARTA
(BANQUET HALL)

MOUND   MOUND?

CASTLETOWN TARA T⁰

MOUND

UPRIGHT
STONES

RATH OF
THE SYNODS

St. Patrick's
Church

DUMHA NA N'GIALL
(GRAVE MOUND OF
THE HOSTAGES)

RÁTH NA RÍOGH

TEACH
CORMAIC
(CORMAC'S
HOUSE)

FORRADH
(ROYAL SEAT)

(ROYAL ENCLOSURE)

LODEEN
T⁰

CASTLEBOY   T⁰

RÁTH LAOGHAIRE
(ENCLOSURE OF
KING LAOGHAIRE)

ODDER T⁰

feet   0   100   200   300   400   500   600   700   800   900   1000   feet circular earthwork known as the Fort of King Laoghaire. To the north of the Royal enclosure, on the other side of the fence, is the Rath of the Synods, a ring-fort with three banks which was devastated in the early years of this century by British Israelites who dreamed that they would find the Ark of the Covenant in it. But while their dream did not come true, their dig rooted up material, which taken together with later excavated material, helped to show that houses which stood on the site were surrounded by palisades and were built in the first three centuries of our era. In the graveyard beside it there are two stones, one decorated with a small figure with crossed legs. To the north of the Rath of the Synods is a long hollow area surrounded by banks. This is allegedly the 'Banqueting Hall' where everyone sat, graded by his status, but it could just as easily have been the entrance road to the site. To the north-west of the Banqueting Hall there are other round earthworks, one called Gráinne's fort after King Cormac's daughter who was the heroine of the tragic love tale of Diarmuid and Gráinne, and the others known as the Sloping Trenches. About half a mile to the south of Tara Hill is another hill crowned with another Hill-fort called Rath Maeve (261) (signposted). An area about 750 feet in diameter is enclosed by a large bank and ditch which has partly disappeared, but a portion of it is well preserved near the road.

TRIA 18, 1838, Antiquities, 25; Macalister, Tara; O Ríordáin, Tara; Evans, Prehistoric and Early Christian Ireland—A Guide (1966) 174

TELTOWN (149) Earthworks

MAP 5 P 10
OS½″ 13N.80.74

Access: Across a fence and through field. Signposted
This is the site of ancient assemblies and games which took place in August, although the old Irish literature also describes it as a pagan cemetery called after a goddess Tailtiu. There are a number of earthworks spread over a wide area, but the most probable centre was Rath Dubh, or the Black Fort, a circular earthwork about 50 yards in diameter, surrounded by a bank on the northern part. A stone which originally stood in the centre is said to have been buried underground, and in a field to the east a number of cremated bones were found. A large and long mound on the other side of the main road known as the Crockans is associated with 'Teltown marriages' where young people joined hands through a hole in a wooden door, lived together for a year and a day after that, and could then part if they so wished!

Evans, Prehistoric and Early Christian Ireland—A Guide (1966) 177

TRIM Castle and Churches *Figs. 15, 58 and 58a*

MAP 5 N/P 11
OS½″ 13N.
80-81.57

Trim is a town which was founded by the Normans on the banks of the Boyne, and few towns in Ireland contain more medieval buildings than it. These buildings are as follows:

Trim Castle (514) *Fig. 15*

Access: Through gate and up a short lane. If gate is locked, ask for key in restaurant opposite the entrance. Not signposted
The first fortification on the site was a motte with a timber tower, erected by Hugh de Lacy in 1172 as a first step towards the conquest of Meath. He left Hugh Tyrell in charge of it. But Roderick O'Conor, King of Connacht, thought himself threatened by its existence, and he marched

If you are given a key—remember to return it

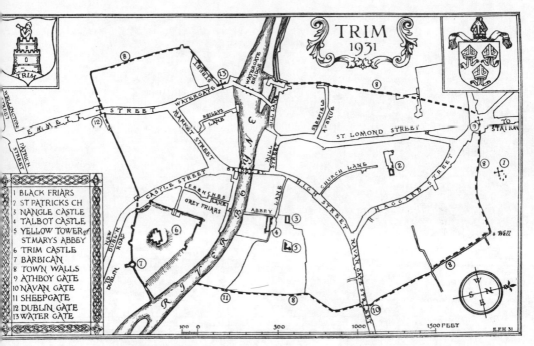

Fig. 58. *Map of the Town of Trim in 1931.*

against it but Tyrell set fire to it and abandoned it before Roderick arrived. However, Tyrell rebuilt it shortly afterwards. King John visited Trim in 1210. Two years later the tower was pulled down, and the present three-storey tower was then built on the same spot, and completed by William Peppard in 1220. This is a massive tower with walls 11 feet thick; it is square in plan with smaller square towers projecting from the middle of each wall (only three out of the original four remain). The main entrance was at first floor level. Inside, the main tower is divided into two parts, the Hall and the Bedroom or Chamber, and there was a chapel in the east tower. Around the time when the tower was completed, the great curtain wall was built. It has 5 D-shaped towers projecting from it on the southern half of the wall, and a square gateway which has a groove for a portcullis on the west. An unusual feature is the slightly later round tower at the southernmost point, which has another building—a barbican—projecting from it which spanned the water-filled moat which originally surrounded the curtain wall. In this building there was a drawbridge which was operated from above. The old town wall was originally joined to the castle near the south-western corner. There were small openings near one of the D-shaped towers, and another at the north-western tower, to allow the defenders to make surprise attacks. In the second half of the 13th century the castle passed through De Lacy's daughter Matilda to the Mortimers,

Fig. 15. Conjectural reconstruction of Trim Castle, Co Meath as it might have been around 1250.

Fig. 58a. The Yellow Steeple, Trim. 14th century.

Earls of the March, who rarely ever visited the castle. When Richard II visited the castle in 1399, he left behind him there two boys as wards, Prince Hal, later Henry V, and Humphrey of Gloucester, later the 'Good Duke', who were housed in the gate-tower with the drawbridge. During the Rebellion of Silken Thomas in 1536-41 repairs were made to the castle, but by 1599 it was in ruins. During the Civil War, Coote and Grenville took the castle in 1642. In 1647 it was strongly fortified by the Parliamentarians under Fennick, but Lord Inchiquin succeeded in taking it in 1649. Ormonde abandoned it to the Cromwellians shortly afterwards, and it does not appear to have been used after that.

Arch Journal 88, 1931, 366 and 93, 1937, 149; The Irish Sword 5, 1961, 94; Leask, Castles 31

On the opposite side of the river are the remains of the Sheep Gate (469) which is the only remaining portion of the town walls erected in 1359 by Roger Mortimer, Earl of Ulster, and consisting of a two-storey tower. Nearby is the Yellow Steeple (186), a very tall but battered tower of the 14th century which formed part of an Augustinian Abbey called St Mary's, where the 'Idol of Trim'—a statue of the Blessed Virgin—was venerated. 125 feet high, it stood on the north side of the now demolished church. Close to it is a farm-shed with corrugated iron roof which was once Nangle's Castle (468).

Leask, Churches II, 153

St Patrick's Church
Access : Direct. Not signposted
In the western part of the town is the 19th century Church of Ireland church to which a 15th century tower (locked) is attached. In the porch of the tower is a very fine (15th century?) baptismal font and an interesting collection of medieval grave stones. The door leading from the tower to the church is 15th century, and at the back of the church is a large baptismal font of around 1200. Behind the modern church are the remains of an older church, into a wall of which a fine triple-light 15th or 16th century window has been inserted.

Newtown Trim (110) *Fig. 59*
Access : Up a path and over stile. Signposted
About a mile downstream from the castle stands the vast ruin of Newtown Trim, peacefully situated on the banks of the Boyne. The episcopal See of Meath was moved here from Clonard by John Cardinal in the late 12th century. Simon de Rochfort, Bishop of Meath (1194-1224) founded a priory here in 1206 for the Canons of the Augustinian Congregation of St Victor of Paris to serve the cathedral. An attempt to substitute secular priests for the canons was made in 1397, but was unsuccessful. The church dates from 1206, and must have been one of the largest churches in Ireland. It originally consisted of a nave, chancel and two transepts, with fine ribbed vaulting over the chancel. But when the nave and transepts fell into decay in the later Middle Ages, the nave was shortened by about 80 feet, and the present west wall was built, so that the original church was much longer than the present one. There were a number of graceful lancet windows in the church, but those in the east wall were later blocked up. In the north wall there is a round-headed sedilia. To the south of the original nave stood the domestic buildings. The refectory, retaining some

of its original windows (though one towards the eastern end was added in the 15th century), stands at the south end of the quadrangle, and had a basement supporting the floor in order to keep it at the same level as the surrounding buildings. There are the remnants of a fine 13th century doorway near a stile at a point where the east wing of the cloister stood; it was the door to the chapter-house. A kitchen was added to the western wing in the 15th or 16th century. To the east of this complex is another smaller 13th century parish church, with a north and south doorway, into which a 15th century window has been inserted. 15th century fragments have been built into the south wall of the church, and inside is a fine late 16th century double effigy tomb of Sir Luke Dillon and his wife. The buildings on the far side of the ancient bridge are the remnants of the 13th and 15th century Friary and Hospital of St John the Baptist. From a gate beside the road on the opposite side of the river to the refectory of the monastery mentioned above, there is a remarkable echo.
Arch Journal 88, 1931, 364

NEWTOWN. TRIM
CATHEDRAL OF SS. PETER AND PAUL

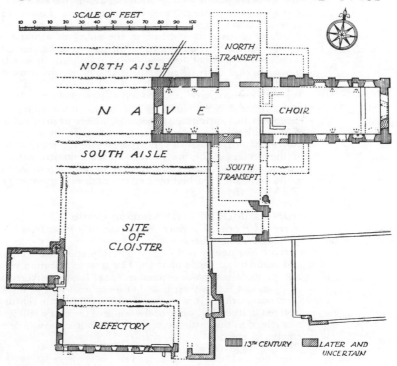

Fig. 59. Plan of the Cathedral of SS Peter and Paul at Newtown, Trim, Co Meath, founded in 1206.

CAIRNBANE (367) Court Cairn

MAP 5 N 7
OS½″ 8H.60.27

Access: Up lane 300 yards, through gate straight ahead, then 100 yards left across field. Not signposted. A visit is not recommended
An ill cared-for court cairn with reasonably well-defined court, and one capstone remaining. It was covered by an oval-shaped mound.
PRIA 60 C 1960, 123, No. 3

CLONES (111-2) Round Tower, High Cross and Church

MAP 5 M 7
OS½″ 8H.50.26

Access: High Cross stands in the middle of the town, the Round Tower and the church in separate graveyards. The graveyard with the church is open; the key to that with the Round Tower is obtainable from Patton's public house near the entrance, while the key for the Round Tower is obtainable from the Garda station. Signposted
An old monastery was founded here by St Tighernach in the 6th century. The High Cross probably stood near the Round Tower originally and was later moved to its present position in the Diamond. The cross (10th century?) is in two parts which may not have belonged together originally. On the west face are Adam and Eve, Cain and Abel, Daniel in the Lion's Den and the Arrest of Christ (?), while on the east face are the Adoration of the Magi, the 12 Apostles (?), the Last Supper and the Crucifixion, and there are panels with geometrical decoration on the other side. Further down the town is the graveyard with the Round Tower. The Round Tower is retained to a height of about 75 feet, and has a square-headed door and windows. Nearby is a shrine in the shape of a house, with interesting finials, called St Tighernach's Shrine. It is carved out of one stone. Tradition says that there is a vault underneath it, in which bodies were placed having been taken from their coffins which were later destroyed beside the shrine. In a churchyard not far away is 'The Abbey' which is the 12th century nave of a nave-and-chancel church. It has a chancel arch and a round-headed window. The stones of the arch have been removed except for two springing stones which were probably shaped in the form of animal heads. In both of these graveyards there are a number of most individual 17th and 18th century gravestones, some giving an indication of the profession of the person buried beneath, others having skulls, crossbones, hour-glasses etc. On the north-western side of the town is a motte and bailey reached by a tarred pathway *(signposted)*.
JRSAI 13, 1874-5, 327

DONAGHMOYNE (382) 'Manaan Castle'

MAP 5 P 8
OS½″ 8H.85.08

Access: Up private avenue, then across two fields from house up to the top of a hill. Not signposted
A motte, causeway and bailey possibly started by Pipard around 1193 and made into a castle in 1197. The first fortification was made of wood, but the stone castle was erected in 1244. It was delivered up to the Crown in 1302, and it was then leased at a nominal rent to the Clintons and the Gernons in turn. It was abandoned in the 15th century. The motte is covered in trees, but some of the walls of the castle still remain. The motte was joined to the castle by means of a stone causeway or bridge, probably erected in 1244.
CLAJ 2, 1908-11, 262

If you open a gate—then close it too

INISHKEEN (208) Round Tower

MAP 5 P 8
OS½" 8H.93.07

Access : Direct to graveyard. Signposted
The first reference to the existence of a monastery here is in 685, and the death of the last recorded monk took place in 1085. The monastery, however, was founded in the 6th century by St Dega who studied under St Ciarán at Clonmacnoise, and St Colmcille is said to have been present at the foundation, and blessed the monastery. There remains the stump of a Round Tower now 42 feet high, with a doorway 14 feet above the ground. A road contractor made a hole in the tower in the last century, but he was mercifully stopped in time from doing any further damage. Some fragments of an older church have been built into the wall of the ruined modern church nearby.
UJA 5, 1857, 116 and 2nd Ser. 3, 1896-7, 173

County Offaly

CASTLETOWN and GLINSK (510) High Cross and Church

MAP 4 L 13
OS½" 15N.20.06

Access : Up tarred avenue to 19th century castle. Signposted
In the garden of Castle Bernard, now a Forestry Training Centre, is a 10th century High Cross with the Presentation in the Temple (?) and the Crucifixion on the east face, and Adam and Eve, intertwined birds, interlacing and other geometric motifs on the west face. There is an unidentified figure, interlacing and other geometric patterns on the north and south faces. The south wall of the courtyard behind the castle formed part of a 15th century church, of which some windows remain. The original monastery was founded by St Finian Cam, a disciple of St Brendan of Clonfert, in the second half of the 6th century. One of its abbots died in 850, another in 884, and yet another, Colmán, was killed at the battle of Ballaghmoon in 908 when supporting Cormac Mac Cuileannáin, King-Bishop of Cashel, to become High King.
JRSAI 47, 1917, 185

CLONFINLOUGH (336) Decorated Prehistoric Stone

MAP 4 K 12
OS½" 15N.04.30

Access : Along a path between the church and the curate's house to a field behind, and then into another field to the right. Not signposted
A large boulder lying flat on the ground in the middle of a field, decorated with a number of motifs including crosses, and something resembling the Greek letter Φ which have been interpreted as being representations of human figures. It has recently been shown that only the circular parts of the Φ are artificial and the rest of the 'decorations' are natural, resulting from the effects of natural chemical solution. Similar signs have been found on stones in North-western Spain where they are dated to the Bronze Age.
Jackson in North Munster Studies (ed. Rynne) 1967, 11

MAP 4 K 12
OS½″ 15N.01.31

CLONMACNOISE (81) Churches, High Crosses, Round Towers, Castle etc. *Figs. 9, 60, 61 and 62*
Access : Direct. Signposted

This great monastery was founded in 548-9 by St Ciarán, who sought peace here when he abandoned his cell on Hare Island in Lough Ree. Dermot, a local prince, helped him erect the first posts for his church, and when Dermot was elected High King shortly afterwards he richly endowed the monastery. Although St Ciarán did not live long after the foundation, the monastery grew rapidly. It was plundered six times between 834 and 1012, and burned 26 times between 841 and 1204. In 845 Turgesius, a Viking leader who was trying to stamp out Christianity in Ireland, placed his wife on the high altar at Clonmacnoise, from whence she gave forth oracles. Clonmacnoise was a great centre of learning, and many manuscripts, including the Annals of Tighernach (11th century) and the Book of the Dun Cow (12th century), were written here. The Normans attacked Clonmacnoise in 1179, and burned 105 houses, and for the next four hundred years the monastery was often plundered. In 1552 the English garrison from Athlone took all the monastic valuables away, and after that it never recovered.

On entering the enclosure, a great number of Early Christian grave-slabs are seen, re-erected along a wall on the left. They are exhibited in groups, denoting the various types of grave-stone used from about the 8th century until the 11th or 12th century. Many of the stones have old Irish inscriptions on them, usually using the formula OR DO . . . (A prayer

Fig. 60. Plan of the monastic remains at Clonmacnoise, Co Offaly.

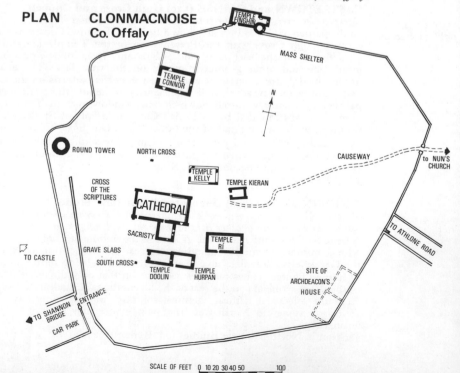

SCALE OF FEET 0 10 20 30 40 50   100

for ...). At the end of the gallery where these stones are exhibited is a Round Tower, said to have been built by Fergal O'Rourke who died in 964, and restored after it had been struck by lightning in 1134. In front of the Cathedral is the famous High Cross known as 'Flann's Cross' or 'The Cross of the Scriptures', which is dated to the first half of the 10th century. On the west face there are the Soldiers guarding the Tomb of Christ, the Arrest of Christ, the Betrayal of Christ (?) and the Crucifixion. On the east face are Diarmuid helping Ciarán to set up the first corner-post of the church, Christ in Glory with the good souls on the right playing instruments, and the bad souls being banished to hell on the left, and various other unidentified figures. On the south face there is a bishop, and David playing the harp, and on the north face are a bishop, a man playing the pipes of Pan and a figure with a falcon. On the base of the cross there are remains of men hunting on horses and on chariots, as well as various animal figures. To the south of this cross is another cross known as the South Cross, which has a Crucifixion below the ring on the west face and also panels of interlacing interspersed with animals. It may date to the 9th century. To the north of the Cathedral is the shaft of another cross, possibly of around the same date.

Fig. 61. Decorated Stone at Clonmacnoise, Co Offaly.

Fig. 62. The Cross of the Scriptures at Clonmacnoise, Co Offaly. 10th century.

The Cathedral was restored by Abbot Colman Mac Aillel and the High King, Flann, around 910 and again by Cormac son of Conor and Flaherty O'Lynch between 1080 and 1104. The building has antae and parts of a Romanesque west doorway which was later replaced by another doorway in the 15th century. The chancel was divided into three vaulted chapels probably in the 15th century. Roderick O'Conor, last High King of Ireland, was buried in the sacristy in 1198, but the present sacristy was not built until about the 17th century; it is at present locked, and contains miscellaneous architectural fragments. The church was repaired in 1330, and in 1460 Dean Odo inserted the fine north doorway with the figures of St Francis, St Patrick and St Dominic. In 1552 the English from Athlone invaded it, but it was repaired again in 1647 by the then Vicar-General, Charles Coghlan. There are two churches to the south of the Cathedral. The western church is divided into two; the western part, known as Temple Doolin, had antae and a round-headed east window, and was restored in 1689 by Edward Dowling who inserted a new door. Temple Hurpan was added to the eastern end of Temple Doolin in the 17th century. To the east of this church lies Teampull Rí or Teampull Melaghlin, a fine church built around 1200, with fine lancet east windows and a gallery at the western end. The south door was inserted later, possibly in the 16th century. Retracing our steps to the Cathedral, the traces of the 12th century Temple Kelly can be seen to the north-east of it, and to the east-north-east lies the smallest church at Clonmacnoise. This is a diminutive oratory with antae which is much mutilated; St Ciarán is said to have been buried in the north-eastern corner. Two croziers were found in the oratory. Further down the slope is Teampull Connor, said to have been built in 1010 when it was endowed with lands by Cathal O'Connor. The west doorway and south window are original; it is locked, and is occasionally used for Church of Ireland Divine service. Further to the north-east, at the edge of the cemetery, is Teampull Finghin, a fine nave and chancel church with traces of a Romanesque south doorway and a fine Romanesque chancel arch beside which a small but well-preserved Round Tower was built as part of the church. To the east of the church is a new Catholic altar built in 1969.

From the Cathedral an 11th century stone-lined causeway leads eastwards out through the east gate of the cemetery, and by following an untarred road further eastwards for about 300 yards the visitor can go over a stile to the right and reach the Nun's Church (250). A church stood on the site before 1026, but the present church was completed in 1166. It is a fine nave-and-chancel Romanesque church with decorative doorway and chancel arch. The doorway has four orders with the capitals adorned with a number of terrifying beasts. The chancel arch is of three orders and is heavily decorated with heads, interlacing etc. The church was restored in 1867. Dervorgilla, wife of Tighernan O'Rourke of Breffny, who was carried off by Dermot McMurrough and thus became indirectly responsible for the Norman invasion, retired here as a penitent in 1170 and was buried here. In a field to the north of the car-park is a Norman castle built around 1212 on the site of an Abbot's house which had been burned in 1135, and the abbot was given compensation for damage done to his lands and gardens by the construction of the castle. The remains consist of a gateway, a courtyard and a tower which fell over as a result of an explosion.

JRSAI 37, 1907, 277; Macalister, Clonmacnoise; Macalister, Memorial Slabs of Clonmacnoise (1909); Leask, Churches I, 61, 72, 146; III, 74

CLONONY Castle

MAP 4 K 12
OS½″ 15N.05.20

Access : Direct. Signposted

A 16th century castle picturesquely situated beside the road. The tower has four storeys, the second being vaulted, but access to the upper floors is dangerous. The interior is disappointing—the 19th century wall-plaster being a fertile ground for the modern graffitist. The tower is surrounded by a bawn which was repaired in the 19th century.

DURROW (313) High Cross and Grave-slabs *Fig. 63*

MAP 4 L 12
OS½″ 15N.32.31

Access · Only through the west gate of a private estate to the old churchyard. Signposted

The monastery was founded here by St Columba about 553 on lands given by Aedh, son of Brendan, a local prince. The earliest known object from the monastery is the mid-7th century illuminated manuscript known as the Book of Durrow (now in the Library of Trinity College Dublin)— and which was at one time used by a local farmer who poured water on it

Fig. 9. A lost grave-slab of Suibine Mac Mailae Humai from Clonmacnoise, Co Offaly. 887 A.D.

Fig. 63. High Cross at Durrow, Co Offaly. 10th century.

as a cure for cattle! The monastery was plundered and burned a number of times. A stone church is mentioned as having been broken into in 1018. Around the middle of the 12th century the monastery became Augustinian, but it was desecrated in 1186 by Hugh de Lacy who was then murdered nearby. Shortly after the death of the last known abbot, Dermot O'Rafferty, in 1190, the Augustinian Abbey was reduced to priory status. After 1541, the church was turned into a parish church, and was still in use up till 1582. The church was restored and re-used in the 18th century and again restored in 1802. The present church is thus modern, but may preserve parts of the older church. The main relic of the old monastery is the fine 10th century High Cross to the west of the church. On the east face are three figures, the Sacrifice of Isaac, Christ in Glory with David and his harp on the left, and David killing the Lion on the right. On the west face are Soldiers guarding the tomb of Christ, the Scourging at the Pillar (?), the Arrest of Christ, and the Crucifixion surrounded by unidentified figures (Denial of St Peter? on the left). On the south face are Adam and Eve, Cain slaying Abel, a warrior and a horseman, while on the north face are two groups of two figures, one being the flight into Egypt (?). Nearby are some 9th-11th century (?) tombstones, one with an inscription OR DO AIGIDIU (A prayer for A.) and another with OR DO CHATHALAN (A prayer for C.). Close by is a fragment of another cross with interlacing, and near the north-eastern corner of the church is a (12th century?) cross fragment with a Crucifixion on one side and a bishop on the other.
JRSAI 27, 1897, 134 and 93, 1963, 83; Stokes, The High Crosses of Castledermot and Durrow (1898)

GALLEN (504) Priory and Grave-slabs

MAP 4 K 12
OS½″ 15N.12.24

Access: Up private priory avenue to near convent, where remains stand fenced off in a field. Not signposted
A monastery was founded here in 492, and having been burned in 820, was restored by a party of monks from Wales who founded a successful school here. The church was probably built in the 13th century. In 1548 it was taken from the local chieftain by O'Melaghlin and Edmund Fay, but by this time it must have been rather insignificant, for in the previous century it had consisted of only one prior and three canons. The site is noteworthy because of its collection of Early Christian grave-stones, one bearing an inscription OR DO BRALIN. Many of these are now attached to the rebuilt gables of the church, and one very unusual one stands in the middle of the church and has interlacing, fretwork and deer on it. Another stone has a ringed cross on it, with a figure standing just below the cross. These stones are probably largely 8th-11th century in date.
JRSAI 69, 1939, 1; PRIA 46 C 1941, 103

RAHAN (82) Churches

MAP 4 L 12
OS½″ 15N.26.25

Access: Through gate and 150 yards through field. Key obtainable from John Monahan, Tullabeg, Rahan. Signposted
St Carthach or Mochudha founded a monastery here around 580. A King of Cornwall, named Constantine, is said to have abandoned his throne to retire here as a monk. Carthach was one of the four great monastic founders of Early Christian Ireland, but he was expelled in 636 by King Blathmac, and he retired to Lismore in Co Waterford (q.v.) where he founded a See and died a year later. The monastery was refounded around 760 by Fidhairle Ua Suanaigh. The monastery flourished in the 12th century, and around 1200 turned over to the Augustinian rule. There are two important

churches on the site, both of which have been much altered in the course of time. The roofed church, now unfortunately pebble-dashed, was begun in the 12th century. It was originally in the shape of a cross, but the two transepts have largely disappeared. There is a fine chancel arch decorated with heads, and the north, south and parts of the east wall of the chancel are also Romanesque. The east window was inserted in the 13th century (though the present window is modern), and the vault above added possibly in the 15th century. Near the altar was a small doorway leading to a chamber above the vault; the doors leading to the transepts have now been blocked up. The nave was built in 1732, but the lower parts are probably 15th century. The fine window on the north side, decorated with a bird, a griffin and a dragon eating its tail, probably belonged to the 15th century nave. The most unique feature of the church is the round Romanesque window high up in the exterior wall of the east gable of the church; it bears excellent Romanesque decoration and may have once stood in the original west gable of the church above the door. About 100 yards to the east of this church is another church with a good Romanesque doorway which originally had a pillar on each side of it. This church was possibly rebuilt in the 15th or 16th century, but incorporated the Romanesque doorway, some of the windows and also some of the square blocks from the nave of the larger West church described above. In the east corner of the cemetery to the south of the main church are the uninteresting ruins of another church.

JCKAS 12, 1935-45, 111; Leask, Churches I, 88, 142, 145

SEIRKIERAN (497) Old Monastic Site

MAP 4 K· 13
OS½" 15N.14.02

Access : Through gate into field. Signposted

St Ciarán the Elder, a contemporary of St Patrick, founded a Bishopric here which was later transferred first to Aghaboe, Co Laois (q.v.) in 1052 and then to Kilkenny (q.v.). The monastery was raided by the Vikings in 842. The present church is modern but probably incorporates part of an older church believed to have been founded by the Canons Regular of St Augustine. Some figures have been inserted in the east gable of the church, and beside the church is a small cross and an old grave-slab. There are also the remains of a Round Tower, and a church to the west of which there is a decorated cross-base. The churchyard stands in a 10-acre area which is still surrounded by traces of the old monastic wall with a ditch outside it.

JRSAI 68, 1938, 285

TIHILLY Church and High Cross

MAP 4 L 12
OS½" 15N.30.29

Access : Along a laneway (if gate is locked, then jump over the wall !), past a ruined house, and then through two fields to old church. Not signposted

The monastery was founded here by St Fintan, though he later gave it over to a nun, Cera, who died in 670, while he moved to Slieve Margy. The monastery was burned in 670, and the last known abbot, Robbartach, died in 936. The church seems to have been a dependant of Castledermot, Co Kildare (q.v.). The site is marked by a medieval church of little interest, which probably used stones from an earlier church. But the main item of interest is a High Cross standing near the church on a round base. Adam and Eve, and a Crucifixion can be seen on the west face, and many of the other panels are filled up with good interlacing, geometrical and animal motifs. Nearby is also an Early Christian grave-slab.

JRSAI 27, 1897, 129 and 29, 1899, 65

ARDCARN (488) Mound and Ring-fort

MAP 4 J 8
OS½" 7G.87.02

Access : Up grassy path, across fence and into field. Not signposted
A large burial mound, probably a Passage Grave, situated on top of a hill.
Not far away is a triple-walled stone ring-fort.

BALLINTOBER Castle

MAP 4 H 10
OS½" 12M.73.75

Access : Direct from road. Not signposted
Shortly after the Norman invasion, Ballintober became the chief seat of
the O'Conors of Connacht, but the castle was probably not built till
around 1300. The castle is nearly square in plan, with an open courtyard
in the centre and a strong polygonal tower at each corner. In the east wall
there are two projecting turrets which guarded the entrance. The whole
castle was surrounded by a water-filled moat. The castle was taken by
another branch of the O'Conors in 1315, and was besieged and burnt a
number of times again before 1500. In 1627 the north-western tower was
partially re-built, as an inscription on a fire-place on the second floor shows.
The castle was held by the O'Conor Don until 1652 when it was taken by
the Cromwellians. But it was restored in 1677 and lived in until the last
century.
JRSAI 19, 1889, 24; Arch Journal 93, 1937, 187; Leask, Castles 69

BOYLE (167) Cistercian Abbey *Fig. 64*

MAP 4 J 8
OS½" 7G.80.03

*Access : Through gate. If locked, key is obtainable from Mr McDermott, 400
yards east of entrance, in Abbeytown. Signposted*
One of the best preserved in Ireland, this Cistercian Abbey was colonized
from Mellifont in 1161. The building of the chancel, and the transepts with
their side-chapels, must have begun shortly after this date, though the
lancet windows in the east gable were inserted in the 13th century. There
is an interesting combination of rounded and pointed arches in the transepts
and crossing. The large square tower formed part of the church from the
beginning, though it was raised in height at a later stage. The five eastern
arches of the nave and their supporting pillars were built at the end of
the 12th century, and have well-preserved capitals typical of the period.
Although built at the same time, the arches of the northern side of the
nave are different in type, and have differently shaped columns and capitals.
The three westernmost arches in the south arcade, with their attractive
leafed and figured capitals, and the west wall were built after 1205 but
before the church was finally consecrated in 1218. Nothing remains of
the cloister, but on the eastern side there are two doorways of c. 1200, now
blocked up, while on the west side there is a gate containing some features
of about the same date. The rest of the buildings surrounding the cloister
are largely 16th or 17th century in date. The Abbey was one of the most
important in Connacht, and was invaded by Richard de Burgo and Maurice
Fitzgerald, the Justiciar, in 1235. In 1659, the Cromwellians occupied the
monastery and did a great deal of destruction.
Leask, Churches II, 32 and 61

CARNAGH WEST (487) Ring-fort

MAP 4 J 11
OS½" 12M.98.52

Access : Across wall into field. Not signposted
A ring-fort with foundations of round and rectangular huts inside. Because
of the double-walling of the outside, it is thought by some to be Stone Age
in date.

CASTLESTRANGE (320) Decorated Stone

MAP 4 J 11
OS½" 12M.82.60

*Access : About 150 yards up private avenue ; stone is in a round fence beside
avenue. Signposted*
A small, rounded stone decorated with incised curvilinear ornament in

the Celtic La Tène style. It probably dates to the last few centuries B.C. and was probably ritual in purpose. Together with the stone at Turoe, Co Galway (q.v.), it is one of the best of the Celtic decorated stones of Europe.
PRIA 24, 1903, 260; JRSAI 37, 1907, 346

EMLAGH (397) Cross

MAP 4 H 10
OS½″ 12M.70.78

Access : Over stile into field. Signposted
The shafts and head of one or two crosses, possibly of 11th century date. The decoration is well executed, and presents a fine study in loosely-knit geometrical interlacing patterns.

RATHCROGHAN and GLENBALLYTHOMAS (294 and 473) Earthworks and Megalithic Tombs

MAP 4 H/J 9
OS½″ 12M.80.84

Access : Over fence and into fields. Signposted
This place is tentatively acclaimed to have been the inauguration place of the Kings of Connacht. The site covers an area of about 2 square miles, and consists of a great number of earthworks of different kinds, varying from a large mound (possibly a Passage-Grave which, like the Mound of the Hostages at Tara, Co Meath (q.v.), is much older than the royal site) to square, round, oblong and irregularly-shaped enclosures. One of these is called the Cemetery of the Kings, and there is also a 7 foot high standing stone said to mark the grave of King Dathi, the last pagan king of Ireland who was killed by lightning in the Alps. The stone is situated in the middle of a ring-fort. Not too far from the cross-roads in various directions are a number of ring-forts. To the south of the main group of monuments, and also spread over a wide area, are a number of degenerate megalithic tombs.
PRIA 15, 1872, 114; JRSAI 44, 1914, 6 and 48, 1918, 157; Dillon and Chadwick, The Celtic Realms (1967) 343 Map 8

Fig. 64. The 12th and 13th century nave of the Cistercian Abbey at Boyle, Co. Roscommon.

RINNDOWN Castle and Fortifications

MAP 4 K 11
OS½″ 12N.00.54

Access: About half a mile along an untarred path towards the point of a peninsula. Not signposted

Although the Normans had used this peninsula as early as 1201, it was not until 1227 that Geoffrey de Marisco first fortified it. In 1251 the Justiciar was ordered to levy tolls for the purpose of enclosing the vill or town, and repairing the castle. Between 1273 and 1279 large sums were spent on repairing the castle, and between 1299 and 1302 the Sheriff allowed £113 for the construction of a new hall. About half a mile from the end of the peninsula a wall, with a fortified gateway and three square turrets projecting westwards, stretches across the whole peninsula. This wall was probably erected with the tolls levied in 1251, and it protected the vill or town around the castle from attacks from the landward side. However, Felim O'Conor once successfully stormed its walls in 1236. About 800 yards east of this wall, a wide moat, once filled with water, again cuts right across the peninsula. An arm of the moat encircles the castle, but unfortunately undergrowth helps to hide the grandiose fortifications of the castle. This arm encloses a roughly triangular-shaped area which is surrounded by a high curtain wall. The tower, which originally must have had three or four storeys, is a long rectangular building built up against the northern side of the curtain wall; the lower storey has a barrel vault. Beside it is the gateway which has a round-headed arch and grooves for a portcullis, and on the opposite side of the fosse to it is a building which was probably a barbican; the main part of the castle was thus reached by a drawbridge which no longer exists. Most of these buildings date to the years after 1227, but near the north-eastern side of the curtain wall are the remains of a building which is probably identical with the 'new hall' erected by Robert of Oxford in 1299-1302. About 250 yards to the south-east of the castle, towards the end of the peninsula, a round tower of uncertain use and date stands in a circular earthwork. Near a farmhouse where the peninsula is attached to the surrounding area there is a 13th century church, modified later, which may have been erected by the Knights Hospitallers, and which stood outside the walls of the vill.

JRSAI 37, 1907, 274 and 65, 1935, 177; Arch Journal 93, 1937, 159

ROSCOMMON Castle and Friary

MAP 4 J 10
OS½″ 12M.
88.64-65

The Castle (181)

Access: Along path for 100 yards; then across stile, and through field to castle. Signposted

This Norman castle was built by Robert de Ufford, Lord Justice of Ireland, in 1269. But it passed into Irish hands seven years later when it was taken by Hugh O'Conor, King of Connacht. It was restored in 1280. The O'Kellys gained possession of the castle in 1308 when Donogh O'Kelly slaughtered many of the inhabitants. But the O'Conors took it again in 1341. Taken by the Earl of Kildare on an expedition to Connacht in 1499, it was granted to Mac William Bourke in 1544, and taken once again in 1569, this time by Sir Henry Sidney. Sir Nicholas Malby, Governor of Connacht, probably took it over in 1578. The castle surrendered to the Confederates under Preston in 1645, but they in turn had to surrender it to the Cromwellians under Reynolds in 1652. The castle is quadrangular in shape with rounded bastions at the corner, and a double-towered

entrance gate, as well as a rectangular gate tower in the west wall. After 1578 Sir Nicholas Malby carried out extensive alterations and inserted a number of mullioned windows as well as adding a number of buildings on the north side of the castle.
JRSAI 21, 1891, 546; Arch Journal 93, 1937, 185; Leask, Castles 67

Dominican Friary (362)

Access: Through gate and across field. Before going through the gate, the key should first be obtained from Mr Hughes at the first house up the road from the gate on the same side of the road. Signposted

The Friary was founded for the Dominicans by Felim O'Conor, Lord of Roscommon, in 1253 and was consecrated in 1257. The church originally consisted of one long aisle. The original lancet windows in the east and west walls were replaced in the 15th century by traceried windows which have largely disappeared, but those in the south wall are still preserved. The north transept was added in the 15th century. The most remarkable feature of the Friary is the effigy of Felim O'Conor in a niche in the north wall near where the altar stood. The effigy, carved between 1290 and 1300, has been placed upon a later 15th century tomb with 8 mail-clad warriors (7 with swords, and one with a gallowglass or battle axe) in niches with angels above them. On the opposite wall are traces of another 15th century tomb.
JRSAI 54, 1924, 89; Leask, Churches II, 114

County Sligo

ARDNAREE Ballina Augustinian Friary

MAP 3 F 8
OS½" 6G.25.19

Access: In graveyard beside road. Not signposted

The Friary was founded in 1427 by the O'Dowdas, princes of Hy Fiachrach, for the Eremites of St Augustine. The church dates to shortly after the foundation, and has a finely ornamented west doorway with 2 human heads, and a window above it.
JRSAI 28, 1898, 286

BALLINAFAD (342) Castle

MAP 4 H 8
OS½" 7G.78.08

Access: Up a small path and then through a stile. Signposted

Known as the Castle of the Curlews, this castle was built around 1590 to protect the pass over the Curlew Hills. It was garrisoned by a Constable and ten wardens from 1610 to 1626, and after a stout resistance, had to surrender in 1641 due to lack of water. The plan of the castle is modelled on those of 13th century castles, with a small central square block dwarfed by four massive towers at the corners which are round outside and square inside.
Leask, Castles 140; Waterman, in Studies in Building History ed. Jope (1961) 270

BALLINDOON Dominican Friary

MAP 4 H 8
OS½" 7G.79.14

Access : Through gate, and 100 yards down through field. Not signposted
The Friary was founded in 1507 by the McDonaghs. The unusual church has almost identical windows at each end. The church was entered by doors in the north and south walls. The most remarkable feature of the church is the central tower and belfry, which also acted as a rood-screen, with a narrow passage and two rooms on the ground floor, and an arrangement of three arches (the central one being taller than the other two) on the first floor which is only reachable by a dangerous set of steps on the outside. The Friary is pleasantly situated on the shores of Lough Arrow.
Leask, Churches III, 54

BALLYMOTE Castle

MAP 4 H 8
OS½" 7G.66.15

Access : Through St John of God's Nursing Home. Castle seen to best advantage from the nearby railway bridge. Not signposted
Probably built by Richard de Burgo in 1300, this was possibly the strongest castle in Connacht. It has been mutilated somewhat, and is now covered in ivy. The castle was probably captured by the O'Conors in 1317, but was taken from them in the course of local struggles by Mac Diarmada in 1347. By 1381 it had passed to the MacDonaghs. Although attached to Tadhg MacDiarmada in 1561, it had apparently passed to O'Conor Sligo by 1571, at which time he surrendered the castle and had it regranted to him by the English. In 1577 the castle fell into English hands for a few months, and then more permanently in 1584 when it was taken by Richard Bingham. The O'Conors, O'Hartes and O'Dowdes burned it in 1588. The English surrendered it in 1598 to the MacDonaghs who sold it shortly afterwards to the O'Donnells. It was from here that O'Donnell marched to the disastrous Battle of Kinsale in 1601. When the O'Donnells surrendered it to the English in 1602, it was already in a bad state of repair. By 1633 the Taaffes owned it, but they had to surrender it in 1652. In the Williamite wars, the castle was held by Captain Terence McDonogh for James II, but he had to surrender it to Lord Granard in the face of an artillery attack in 1690. Soon afterwards the fortifications were made harmless, the moat was filled up and the castle fell into ruin. The castle is square in plan, with three-quarters round towers at each corner and in the centre of the east and west curtain walls there are D-shaped towers. The double-towered entrance gate is in the north wall, partly disfigured by a modern grotto of Our Lady of Lourdes. Projecting from the southern curtain wall was a small rectangular tower. All the towers rose to a height above the curtain wall.
JRSAI 57, 1927, 81; Arch Journal 93, 1937, 188; Leask, Castles 69

BALLYSADARE Church

MAP 4 H 7
OS½" 7G.66.30

Access : 200 yards along a poor laneway to graveyard on the west bank of the river below the bridge. Not Signposted
Situated on the site of an older monastery founded by St Feichín of Fore in the 7th century, this is a 13th century or later church incorporating 12th century features including a doorway and mouldings at the corners. The doorway has an arch of heads covered by a hood moulding, and there may have been a tympanum. The capitals have rather worn representations of imaginary beasts. The monks later moved to a spot 300 yards westwards, below the present quarry, where a church with an inserted 15th century tower with well-sculpted details remains.
JRSAI 22, 1892, 4

CARRICKNAGAT (277a) Gallery Grave

MAP 4 H 7
OS½" 7G.74.26

Access : 200 yards across field. Not signposted
Known as 'Diarmuid and Gráinne's Bed' this is a gallery grave of which some of the chamber stones, roof and kerbstones are still visible. In the same field are remnants of two presumably similar tombs.

CARROWKEEL (518) Passage-Grave Cemetery *Figs. 1 and 65*

MAP 4 H 8
OS½" 7G.76.11

Access : For some miles up an untarred road up to the top of the hill. Not signposted
This is a Passage-grave cemetery situated on an eerie hill-top in the Bricklieve mountains overlooking Lough Arrow. The mounds are largely round, except cairn E (a court cairn) which is a long oval in shape, and the plans of the graves underneath them vary considerably. Cairns A and P contained nothing, while cairns H and O had only some box-like cists. Most of the others represent variations on the classic Irish Passage-Grave form: a long passage leading into a chamber which has small chambers at each side and another at the back. This is the case at Cairn E, G and K, and probably also C, M and N, while Cairn F, one of the best, has two chambers on each side. Cairns B and O have the passage widening out into a square or wedge-shaped chamber with no side chambers. Cairn D is so ruined that its shape could not be reconstructed; Cairn L was not excavated but is much ruined. The material found in the course of excavations included mushroom-headed bone pins, stone hammer pendants and beads, and pottery with jabbed ornament typical of Irish Passage-Graves, and shows that the tombs belonged to the Late Stone Age of about 2,500–2,000 B.C., though some of the tombs were used up till about 1,500 B.C. On a neighbouring ridge below the level of the Passage-Graves are a series of almost 50 round huts which may or may not have been inhabited by those who built the graves.
PRIA 29 C 1911-2, 311 and 60 C 1960, 93, No. 34

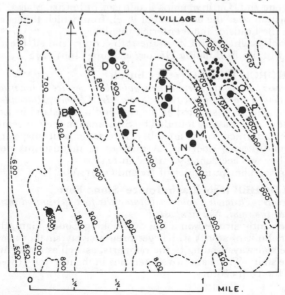

Fig. 65.
Plan of the Passage Grave cemetery at Carrowkeel, Co Sligo.

CARROWMORE (153b) Megalithic Cemetery *Figs 1 and 66*

MAP 4 H 7
OS½" 7G.66.33

Access : Over wall into fields. Signposted
The largest cemetery of megalithic tombs in Ireland; the tombs are spread over a number of fields and townlands, most of them situated near the road. Due to modern gravel quarrying, a number of the monuments have been disturbed, and the cemetery is but a shadow of its former self. The majority of the tombs are a mixture of small Passage-Graves and dolmens, usually surrounded by a stone kerb, but most were probably originally covered by a stone mound. Often, either the tomb itself or the kerb-stones have disappeared. In the area there are also a number of forts and standing stones, as well as a stone with a hole in it.

CARROWREAGH (479) Court Cairn

MAP 3 F 8
OS½" 7G.38.12

Access : Up laneway, then across three-quarters of a mile of bog along the north bank of a rivulet. The tomb is situated just above a lonesome tree about 200 yards from the stream. Because it is difficult to find, and because the bog is treacherous, a visit is certainly not to be recommended
A court cairn with a chamber which expands towards the middle. A few stones of the front court survive, as well as remains of the earthen mound. The whole is surrounded by a modern stone wall.
PRIA 60 C 1960, 92, No. 28

CASHEL BIR (277) 'Cashelore' Stone Fort

MAP 4 H 7
OS½" 7G.76.29

Access : Across stream and fields. Not signposted
A fine but neglected stone fort which is oval in shape and uses uncommonly large stones in its walls.
JRSAI 24, 1894, 278

CASTLEBALDWIN (373) Castle

MAP 4 H 8
OS½" 7G.76.14

Access : Over partly boggy fields. Not signposted
A 17th century fortified house, rectangular in plan, with a square turret at one end. Little remains inside except for fire-places. There is a machicolation over the door at roof level, from which things could be dropped on the heads of those entering the door.
MacLysaght, Irish Life in the 17th century 2nd ed. (1950) 96; Waterman, in Studies in Building History ed. Jope (1961) 272

CHURCH ISLAND (118) Church

MAP 4 H 7
OS½" 7G.75.34

Access : By boat. There is no regular boat service to the island, but boats with outboard motors may be hired from Mr P Henry, Riverside, Sligo
The church is situated at the east end of an island in Lough Gill, on the site of a monastery founded by St Loman in the 6th century. The church, which formed part of an abbey, is rectangular in shape and has an unusual round-headed doorway. A number of manuscripts perished when the abbey was accidentally burned in 1416.
Grose, The Antiquities of Ireland (1791) Vol. I, 58

CLOGHER (159) 'Cashelmore' Stone Fort

MAP 4 H 9
OS½" 12M.66.99

Access : Through Coolavin Estate ; the fort is situated inside the estate wall near the road. Not signposted
Pleasantly situated on a hill overlooking Lough Gara, this is a fine stone fort built of stones which get progressively smaller near the top. Inside are stairways leading to the ramparts, as well as a wall niche under one of the stairs. There are two souterrains in the interior. It was partially rebuilt in the 19th century.

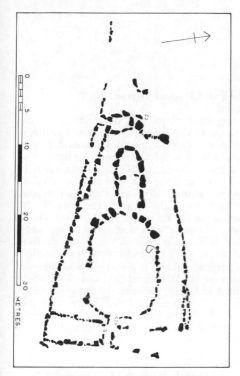

Fig. 67. Plan of the central court cairn at Creevykeel, Co Sligo. 3rd millennium B.C.

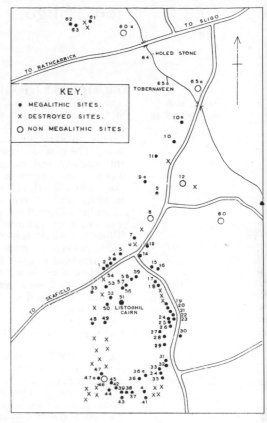

KEY.

- MEGALITHIC SITES.
- X DESTROYED SITES.
- ○ NON MEGALITHIC SITES.

Fig. 66. Plan of the megalithic cemetery at Carrowmore, Co Sligo.

0   ¼   ½   MILE

CREEVYKEEL (338) Court Cairn *Fig. 67*

MAP 2 H 6
OS½″ 7G.72.54

Access : Along a short path. Signposted

One of the finest court cairns in the country. It consists of a wedge-shaped
mound in which an open court occupies the central position. Behind it
is a burial chamber divided into two separate parts. Behind this again, but
entered from the side of the mound, are two further burial chambers
(possibly Passage-Graves inserted at a later stage), while the remains of
another were found in the north-west of the mound. On the south side
there is a double row of stones surrounding the stone mound. The oldest
finds point to a date in the Late Stone Age (c. 2500 B.C.) for the building
of the tomb. In the Early Christian Period, iron smelters built a small
structure in the north-western corner of the court.
JRSAI 69, 1939, 53

CUMMEEN (433) Megalithic Tombs

MAP 4 H 7
OS½″ 7G.65.37

*Access : Up a private avenue, then across three fields to the west of the house
at the end of it, then through gates and fields. Scarcely worth a visit. Not
signposted*

Two twin megalithic tombs, probably court cairns, with entrances facing
each other. They are situated in an earthen fort which was probably
built around them at a much later date. They are near the strand, dominated
by Knocknarea (q.v.) and with a fine view of Ben Bulben.
PRIA 60 C 1960, 88, No. 11

DRUMCLIFFE (119) High Cross and Round Tower *Fig. 8*

MAP 4 H 6
OS½" 7G.68.42

Access : Direct from road. Signposted
St Colmcille founded a monastery here about 575 on lands given by
King Aedh Ainmire. Nor far away, at Culdreimne, the saint had been
heavily involved in a battle in 561 in a dispute over the ownership of a
book! The monastery seems to have been well known from the 9th to the
16th century, and was plundered by Maelseachlain O'Rourke in 1187. It
was plundered again in 1267 and 1315, and the last known abbot died in
1503. The Church of Ireland church stands on the site of an older church
of which nothing remains, and in front of this church the poet W. B.
Yeats lies buried. Beside the road is the stump of a Round Tower which
was struck by lightning in 1396. Tradition says that it will ultimately
fall on the wisest man who passes it (so, if it falls on you, your wisdom
will have been recognized—but too late!). To the right of the path leading
from the road to the Church of Ireland church is a High Cross, erected
possibly around 1000. On the east face are Adam and Eve, Cain kills Abel,
Daniel in the Lion's Den and Christ in Glory, while on the west face there
is the Presentation in the Temple (?), two unidentified figures and the
Crucifixion. There is also a considerable amount of interlacing covering
the surface of the cross, and there are also some imaginary animals.
TRIA 31, 1895, 551; JRSAI 26, 1896, 302

HEAPSTOWN (152) Stone Cairn

MAP 4 H 8
OS½" 7G.78.16

*Access : Over wall into field, where monument is only about 30 yards from the
road. Signposted*
A fine burial mound about 20 feet high, consisting almost entirely of
stones piled on top of one another. Many of the large stones surrounding
the base of the mound can still be seen. The mound presumably harbours
a Passage-Grave underneath it which has never been opened.

INISHMURRAY (117) Early Monastery *Fig. 68*

MAP 3 G 6
OS½" 7G.57.54

*Access : By boat. There is no regular boat service but transport may be arranged
by telephoning Mr P. O'Connell, Beach Hotel, Mullaghmore (tel. Sligo
76103) or Mr C. Herity, Carns, Moneygold Post Office*
Situated on an island in the Atlantic about four miles off the coast, this is
a very interesting old monastery because its good state of preservation
gives us some idea of what the Early Christian monasteries must have
looked like. The monastery was founded by St Molaise or Laisrén in the
early 6th century, and was plundered by the Vikings in 802. The old
monastery is surrounded by a stone wall up to 13 feet high which has five
entrances leading into the central area measuring 175 × 135 feet. It is not
certain whether this wall existed before the monastery was founded or
not. The central area is divided into 4 enclosures, the largest of which
contains Teampull na bFhear (The Men's Church), a church with antae
and with a flat-headed doorway. In the north-west corner is Teach
Molaise, a small and more primitive church with a stone roof, flat-headed
doorway and a round-headed east window. There is an equal-armed cross
on the outside of the lintel-stone above the door; a wooden statue of St
Molaise which stood in the church has now been removed to the National
Museum of Ireland in Dublin. Three square 'altars' with cross-decorated
stones and a number of pillar-stones stand in the main enclosure also.
In the north-western enclosure is Teampull na Teine (The Church of
the Fire) and the 'school-house'—a bee-hive hut. To the north-west of

the monastic wall stands Teampull-na-mBan (Women's Church). About 50 cross-slabs, some of them used as 'stations' for pilgrims, are scattered both inside and outside the monastic wall.
JRSAI 17, 1885-6, 175; Leask, Churches I, 12 and 14

KNOCKNAREA (153a) Passage-Grave

MAP 4 H 7
OS½″ 7G.63.35

Access : Up a path, and then 45 minutes walk up hill (at times steep). It is a good idea to bring a strong pair of shoes. Signposted
Queen Maeve, the famous and fiery legendary Queen of Connacht, is said to have been buried in this great mound of stones 35 feet high and 200 feet in diameter which is situated on the top of a hill with a magnificent view all around Co Sligo. The mound probably hides a Passage-Grave underneath. Nearby are a number of rather ruined 'satellite' tombs, like those in the Boyne Valley.
JRSAI 18, 1887, 84 and 77, 1947, 140

MAGHERAGHANRUSH or DEERPARK (377) Court Cairn

MAP 4 H 7
OS½″ 7G.75.37

Access : 10 minute walk along path up hill to top ; tomb is in an area recently planted with trees. Signposted
Magheraghanrush is one of the finest court cairns in Ireland, and stands on a hill with a beautiful view over Lough Gill. The tomb has a 50-foot long oval central court from which two burial chambers open off at one end, and one chamber at the other end. In the field below is what appears to be a wedge-shaped gallery grave, and nearby there is also a fort with a souterrain, a stone circle, remains of a hut and a small cairn etc.
JRSAI 18, 1887, 136; Antiquity 5, 1931, 98; PRIA 60 C 1960, 88, No. 9

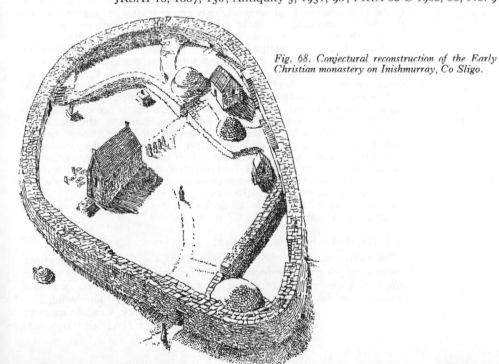

Fig. 68. Conjectural reconstruction of the Early Christian monastery on Inishmurray, Co Sligo.

MAP 4 J 8
OS½" 7G.81.14

MOYTIRRA EAST (465) Court Cairn *Fig. 1*
Access: Up laneway, and 30 yards across field. Signposted
A Stone Age megalithic tomb built possibly around 2500 B.C. consisting of a 'court' at the eastern end and a burial chamber which is divided into four parts.
JRSAI 77, 1947, 142; PRIA 60 C 1960, 93, No. 35

MAP 4 H 7
OS½" 7G.69.36

SLIGO (189) 'Abbey'
Access: Direct from street. Normally locked—key from James McLaughlin, Abbey Street. Signposted
Founded in 1252 or 1253 for the Dominicans by Maurice FitzGerald, 2nd Baron of Offaly, who was also founder of the town. Having escaped the ravages suffered by the now destroyed Sligo Castle in the 13th and 14th centuries, the Friary was accidentally burned in 1414, but was rebuilt two years later by Friar Bryan MacDonagh with assistance from (the other) Pope John XXIII. In 1568 O'Conor Sligo made a petition to Queen Elizabeth not to dissolve the Friary, and this was granted on the condition that the friars become secular clergy. When George Bingham was besieging the castle nearby, he occupied and badly damaged the buildings. The Friary was burned in 1641 by Sir Frederick Hamilton, and it was afterwards granted to Sir William Taaffe. The church has a nave with side aisle and a south transept. The choir, with its eight lancet windows, is the oldest part of the church and dates to shortly after the foundation. The 15th century east window replaced the original three lancet windows. The altar, with carvings of a rose and a bunch of grapes, is also 15th century, as is presumably also the tower. An unusual feature is the 15th century rood-screen (partly reconstructed) which ran across the church separating the choir from the nave. The transept was added in the 16th century. In a recess in the north wall of the nave is the O'Crean tomb dated to 1506, bearing panels in front with the Crucifixion in the centre, the Virgin Mary and St John on either side; other figures are probably to be identified with St Dominic (in friar's robes), St Katherine (with remains of a wheel), St Peter (with keys), St Michael (with shield and raised sword), and there are other unidentified figures. The easternmost lancet window in the south wall was blocked up to accommodate the O'Conor Sligo monument of 1624, with a Crucifixion on the top, below it SS Peter and Paul (?), and below them Sir Donagh O'Conor and his wife Elinor. The sacristy and the chapter house beside the cloister are both 13th century buildings, but the cloister itself and the other buildings around it were built in the 15th century. Note the head on the pillar in the north west corner, and the window in the north wall of the first floor where the reader in the refectory had his desk.
JRSAI 51, 1921, 17; Leask, Churches II, 115 and III, 143 and 162; Official Guidebook

VANDALS—EVEN IN 1797!

"I'm vexed to see it their ambition to destroy and desolate every remains of former grandeur and to level in the dust those venerable piles, with the erection of which our progenitors spent their lives and fortunes and in the defence of which they nobly shed their blood."

—Harden, writing on vandals in 1797
(quoted in JCHAS 58, 1953, 32)

AHENNY (124) High Crosses *Fig. 8*

MAP 8 M 17
OS½″ 18S.41.29

Access : Over stile, then 100 yards down through field to graveyard. Signposted
Two very finely ornamented High Crosses which are credited with being
among the earliest in the country. Each is filled with a number of well-
carved geometrical motifs, such as interlacing, spirals etc. which are so
similar in style to the Book of Kells that they have caused the cross to be
dated to the 8th century. The crosses have unusual 'hats' on them. Figures
only occur on the bases; on the base of the north cross there is a strange
procession showing a cleric carrying a ringed cross (presumably of wood),
a pony carrying a headless man and horses and a chariot with riders. On the
base of the north cross there is also a panel with 7 ecclesiastics with
croziers as well as various animals.
Roe, High Crosses of Western Ossory (1958) 13

ARDANE St Berrihert's Kyle (396) Cross-slabs

MAP 7 J 17
OS½″ 18R.95.29

Access : Across two somewhat marshy fields. Signposted
A small oval area, originally a graveyard, into the wall of which a number
of decorated stones have been built. Many of the stones have crosses in
relief, either plain or with a ring. One larger stone is the head of a High
Cross with, on top, a scene showing one man surrounded by two others
(the Arrest of Christ ?). The shaft of the cross has disappeared, but the
base still rests under the head. Pilgrimages still take place to the spot, and
some of the stones may not be grave-slabs but votive offerings—the
ancestors of the more gaudy ones found there today.
JRSAI 39, 1909, 60; Ó hEailidhe in North Munster Studies (ed. Rynne)
(1967) 102

ATHASSEL (120) Augustinian Priory *Figs. 69 and 70*

MAP 7 K 17
OS½″ 18S.01.36

Access : Through gate and along two fields. Signposted
This, the largest medieval priory in Ireland, was founded for the Canons
Regular of St Augustine by William FitzAdelm de Burgo at the close of
the 12th century and dedicated to St Edmund. The abbot was a Peer of
Parliament. The priory was dissolved in the time of Edward VI, and in
the reign of Philip and Mary was granted to Thomas, Earl of Ormond.
The remains of the monastery cover four acres. The church is 210 feet
long and has two transepts, with a square tower in the centre of the crossing
and another smaller one at the north-western end of the church. The nave
had two aisles which were probably vaulted, and was probably not built
till about 1280. The choir was built about 50 years earlier, though its
east windows were replaced in the 15th century. The tower at the crossing
seems to have been planned from the beginning; there is a very fine doorway in the west wall; above it is a recess (blocked up in the 15th century)
which may have contained the Rood or cross. The tower was rebuilt
probably after the church had been devastated and burned in 1447, and
after this date the nave was probably left roofless. In the south wall of
the chancel is a late 13th century tomb with figures of Norman knights
on it. To the south of the church lay the cloister, of which little remains,
but a number of 13th century buildings surrounding it remain. To the
south of the transept lay the sacristy, and beyond a covered passage lay
the chapter house and other vaulted rooms. The refectory was situated
on the first floor of the south wing, and leading to it is a fine doorway.
The monastery was surrounded by a high wall, and beyond the gate-house
is a bridge connecting the monastery with the surrounding area. Outside

the walls of the monastery there was once a thriving town which was burned in 1319 by Lord Maurice FitzThomas and again in 1329 by Bryan O'Brien—and nothing now remains of it.

JRSAI 39, 1909, 279 and 76, 1946, 215; Leask, Churches II, 95 and III, 134; Journal of the Proceedings of the Clonmel Historical and Archaeological Society I, 4, 1955-6, 61

BALLYNAHOW (234) Castle

MAP 7 K 15
OS½″ 18S.08.60

Access : Up private avenue into farmyard. Signposted

This is one of the few castles in Ireland which is round. It was built by the Purcells in the 16th century. The walls splay at the bottom. Of the two ceilings which are preserved, one is a flat corbelled ceiling, the other is vaulted. The castle has 5 storeys, turrets, a broken fire-place in the 3rd storey, a 'murder hole' above the door to drop things on unwelcome intruders, and a small hole for muskets at one window.

Leask, Castles 108

BALLYNORAN (123) Church

MAP 7 L 17
OS½″ 22S.35.23

Access : Across two fields and a railway line. Not signposted

A small uninteresting parish church which is scarcely worth a visit, as it is covered in ivy. It was built in the 15th century and has a small two-light window.

Fig. 69. Plan of the Augustinian Priory at Athassel, Co Tipperary. This was one of the largest medieval priories in Ireland.

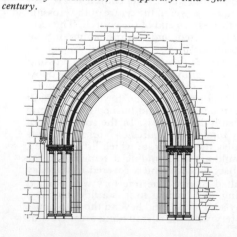

Fig. 70. West doorway of the Choir of the Augustinian Priory at Athassel, Co Tipperary. Mid-13th century.

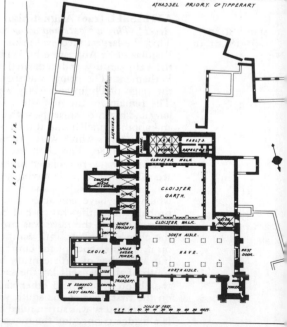

Fig. 71. Burncourt Castle, Co Tipperary in 1795.
The castle was built in 1641.

BURNCOURT (370) Castle *Fig. 71*

MAP 7 J 18
OS½″ 22R.95.18

Access : Through farmyard and across a field. Not signposted

The castle consists of a long main block with a square tower at each corner. The door is of good workmanship, and the interior, which is now empty, was lighted by a myriad of two- and three-mullioned windows. In the interior walls there are a number of fire-places which are no longer in a good state of preservation. Parts of the bawn, with a corner turret, can still be seen nearby. The castle originally had 26 gables and 7 tall chimney stacks. A stone once over the doorway and now built into a wall at the entrance to the nearby farmyard bears the date 1641—the year the castle was built by Sir Richard Everard who occupied it until it was burned by Cromwell in 1650 (hence the name). After Sir Richard was hanged by Ireton in the following year, the castle seems to have remained a ruin. An old rhyme says that 'it was seven years in building, seven years living in it, and fifteen days it was burning'.

JCHAS 4, 1898, 72; JRSAI 37, 1907, 74; Leask, Castles 126

CAHIR (507) Castle

MAP 7 K 17
OS½″ 22S.05.25

Access : Direct from road. Open May–August 10 a.m.–8 p.m.; September 10 a.m.–6 p.m.; October–April weekdays 11 a.m.–1 p.m. and 2 p.m.–4 p.m., Sundays 2 p.m.–4 p.m. Closed Mondays during winter. Not signposted

Cahir passed into the hands of James Butler, Earl of Ormond in 1375, and it was probably his son James who started the building of the castle on a rock beside the river. Although thought to be impregnable, the castle was taken by the Earl of Essex in 1599 after a ten-day siege. However, through the influence of the Earl of Ormond, it remained in Butler hands. It surrendered to Cromwell in 1650, but was restored to the Butlers once more in 1662, though they were deprived of it again in the years 1691-3. It has recently been restored. It is one of the most extensive castles in the south of Ireland. There is a strong outer wall with massive square or rounded turrets. The area within is divided into two enclosures. In the middle stands a strong three-storey tower with a large hall with fireplace on the first floor. In the inner enclosure is a hall renovated in 1842 to act as a church.

JRSAI 39, 1909, 272; Leask, Castles 123

CARRICK-ON-SUIR (447) Castle

MAP 8 M 17
OS½" 22S.40.22

Access: Through public park. If locked, knock on the left-hand door of the entrance passage for caretaker, who has the key. Signposted

The castle originally consisted of two or possibly four square towers surrounding a square enclosure built around 1450 beside the River Suir. Thomas, Earl of Ormond, added on a mansion on the north side for Queen Elizabeth in 1568 and subsequent years. It is the best example in the country of an Elizabethan mansion. Portraits of Queen Elizabeth and Ormond may be seen above the side doors of the entrance passage. On the western portion of the ground floor there is a room with stucco medallions of heraldic motifs of the Ormond family (lion, eagle etc.). Above this room on the first floor are similar stucco panels with the arms of T(homas) Earl of O(rmond) and his motto 'Come les Trouve'. Beside this room is the great hall stretching almost the whole length of the building and decorated in stucco all around the top with representations of Queen Elizabeth flanked by Equity and Justice. A reconstructed section of the ceiling shows what the whole must have originally been like. In the south wall is a fine mantelpiece dated 1565 bearing a Latin inscription saying that it was made by Thomas Butler, Earl of Ormond and Ossory. On the eastern portion of the first floor is a room with stucco panels bearing the motto 'Plues Pense que Edere'. From here entrance is gained to the attic storey and also to the original 15th century castle, on the third floor of which a 15th century window with decoration of angels has been inserted. The older part of the castle was partly destroyed by Cromwell.

Leask, Castles 146; Waterman, in Studies in Building History, ed. Jope (1961) 252

CASHEL Churches and Abbeys

MAP 7 K 16
OS½" 18S.07.41

The Rock of Cashel, rising out of the surrounding plain, is the most dramatic of all Irish monuments. It first appears as a fortification of the Eoghanachta kings of Munster in the 4th century. It was visited by St Patrick who converted Aenghus, the king of the time; by mistake, St Patrick stuck his crozier through the king's foot during the baptism, and the king bore it with fortitude thinking that it was part of the ceremony. St Patrick made Cashel into a bishopric; its best known bishop was Cormac Mac Cuilleannáin, king, bishop and scholar who was killed in the Battle of Ballaghmoon in 908 in an attempt to make himself High King of Ireland. Brian Boru, the famous king killed at the Battle of Clontarf, was crowned here in 977; he made Cashel his capital, and his descendants ruled there for over 100 years afterwards. In 1101 Muircheartach O'Brien granted the Rock to the Church, and shortly afterwards (1127) the bishop, Cormac MacCarthy, began the building of Cormac's Chapel which was consecrated in 1134. In 1152 the bishop of Cashel was raised to the dignity of Archbishop. In 1169 Domhnall Mór O'Brien founded a Cathedral, which was superseded in the 13th century by the present structure. The Cathedral was apparently burned (but not extensively) in the late 15th century by Gerald FitzGerald, and when asked by Henry VII why he had done this, he explained that he did it because he thought that the archbishop was inside! After the Reformation, Queen Elizabeth appointed the Archbishops of Cashel, and the most notorious of these was Miler MacGrath who held three other bishoprics as well and who, after he had died at the age of 100, was buried in the Cathedral. In 1647 Cashel was the scene of terrible fighting in the Confederate wars. The Cathedral was already ruined by the 18th century.

The Rock of Cashel (128) *Figs 11, 72 and 73*
Access: Direct: Open July–August 10 a.m.–8.30 p.m.; September 10 a.m.–
7 p.m. Opening hours shorter in winter. Admission fee charged.
A very striking cluster of buildings, entered through the Hall of the Vicar's
Choral, a 15th century building which housed the clergy of the Cathedral.
It is a two-storey building with a fire-place in the main room, and a dormitory at the eastern end. A cross stands in front of it with the Crucifixion
on one side and St Patrick in high relief on the other. The base of the cross
has geometrical motifs such as animal interlacing and concentric circles
which are much faded but which can be seen best in oblique light. On the
right is Cormac's chapel built in 1127-34, and the most remarkable
Romanesque church in Ireland. Seven years before it was built Dionysius,
abbot of the Irish church at Ratisbon in Germany, had sent four men to
Ireland to collect money for his church, and through this, Cormac's chapel
was influenced by German Romanesque architecture, particularly in the
two square towers which flank it. It also shows the influence of English
Romanesque architecture. The church has a nave and chancel with blind
arcades on the walls, a barrel-vault and a fine chancel arch. The church
was entered by two doors, in the north and south walls respectively. The
main door was in the north wall (now leading to a cul-de-sac); in the
tympanum, it has a very unusual representation of a centaur with bow-and-
arrow killing a large lion, and the whole is topped by a hood. The stonework
of the church is profusely decorated, particularly in the interior, with a
number of motifs, including human heads found both separately and as
part of the capitals. The church has a well-preserved stone roof which is
supported by a small chamber above the barrel vault of the nave. At the
west end of the church is a 12th century tomb with a type of interlacing
consisting of thin and fat serpents which are influenced by Scandinavian
ornamental motifs.
Leask, Churches I, 113; L. de Paor in North Munster Studies ed. Rynne
(1967) 133

*Fig. 72. Interior and exterior views of Cormac's
Chapel, Cashel, Co Tipperary, 1127–34.*

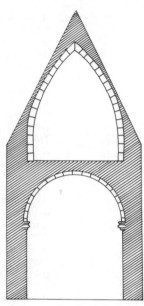

Fig. 73. North doorway of Cormac's Chapel, Cashel, Co Tipperary, 1127–34.

Fig. 11. Schematized cross-section through the roof of Cormac's Chapel, Cashel, Co Tipperary, finished in 1134.

On the other side of the chancel of the Cathedral is a Round Tower which was built at about the same time as Cormac's chapel; it has been repaired recently after it had been struck by lightning. The largest building on the Rock is the 13th century Cathedral, which superseded the 12th century structure of which nothing remains. The Cathedral has a nave, chancel, two transepts, a tower at the crossing and a residential tower at the western end. The choir was built first, and was erected probably by Archbishop Marianus O'Brien around 1230. The east windows have gone, but there are five lancet windows in the south wall. The south transept was probably added by Archbishop MacKelly who died in 1252, while the north transept, the crossing and the nave were probably built by Archbishop MacCarwill around 1260. The tower above the crossing was probably added in the 14th century. Archbishop O'Hedigan built residential quarters for himself in the form of a strongly fortified tower at the western end of the church. Small turrets at the junction of nave and transepts give access to the tower and to the battlements at the top of the walls of the church. The shortness of the nave of the church suggest that it was never completed to its intended length. There are a number of fine tombs in the north transept including a Hacket-Butler tomb of the late 15th century with figures of the Apostles and other saints including St Thomas à Becket, and that of Archbishop Edmund Butler (died 1533), and in the choir is the tomb of Miler MacGrath.

Leask, Churches II, 88

St Dominick's Abbey (193)

Access: Direct. Key obtainable from William Minogue at the cottage at the foot of the Rock of Cashel

This was probably one of the first Dominican churches to be built in Ireland. It was founded by Archbishop David MacKelly whose seat was on the Rock immediately above the abbey. General chapters of the Dominican order in Ireland were held here in 1289 and 1307. Around 1480 Archbishop John Cantwell rebuilt the church after it had been accidentally burned. The church has a number of 13th century lancet windows (some of them blocked up), and others were replaced by windows with flowing tracery in the 15th century. The cloisters have disappeared. A south wing was added to the church around 1270.

Leask, Churches II, 93 and III, 54 and 123

Hore Abbey (127)

Access: Across concrete causeway through field. Signposted

The Benedictines were settled here from Glastonbury by Philip de Worcester at the end of the 12th century, but Archbishop David Mac-Carwill took it from them, and brought Cistercians from Mellifont to found a new Cistercian Abbey here in 1272. It was to be the last Cistercian foundation in Ireland before the Reformation. The Abbey was well endowed at first, but had become impoverished when the Abbot of Athassel (q.v.) was made Abbot of Hore in the 15th century. The Abbey had a leper house in the town of Cashel. Much of the church is 13th century in date, and many of the masons employed in its construction also worked in building the Cathedral on the Rock which dominates it. The plan of the abbey conforms to the usual Cistercian lay-out except that the cloisters lie to the north of the church, which is unusual. The church consists of a nave and chancel and two transepts which each had two chapels originally (though only those in the north transept survive). The domestic buildings are also 13th century, but the chapter house is one of the few parts which have remained in any way intact. In the 15th century the tower was added, some smaller windows were inserted to replace the 13th century lancet windows, alterations were made to the wall of the choir, and a new wall was inserted in the church to act as a rood-screen.

Leask, Churches II, 115 and III, 45

CLONMEL St Mary's Church and Town Walls

MAP 7 L 17
OS½" 22S.20.23

Access: Direct. Key obtainable from the sexton, Mr Reid, in Peter Street. Not signposted

St Mary's was a 13th century parish church which was associated with and possibly dependent upon Athassel (q.v.) prior to the Reformation. The church was heavily repaired in the 15th century, and again in 1857. The east and west windows, the chancel arch, the walls of the aisles, the west window in the porch and the lower part of the tower survive from the 15th century church. The church houses a number of 16th and 17th century tombs. The churchyard is partly surrounded by the old medieval town walls (15th century?), including the tower at the north-western angle, and two other towers.

JRSAI 39, 1909, 252; Fleming, The Town-Wall Fortifications of Ireland (1914) 49; Leask, Churches III, 129; Journal of the Proceedings of the Clonmel Historical and Archaeological Society I, 3, 1954-5, 20

DERRYNAFLAN (335) Church

MAP 7 K 16
OS½″ 18S.18.50

Access : About a mile along scarcely defined paths in the middle of a treacherous-looking bog. A visit is only advisable for the intrepid. Not signposted

This 13th century church stands on an island in the middle of a bog where St Ruadhán of Lorrha founded a monastery in the 6th century. The church, which may incorporate parts of an older church, has a nave and chancel with lancet windows, and a decorative piscina. The west wall of some (15th century ?) domestic buildings remain.

Leask, Churches II, 147

DONAGHMORE (122) Church

MAP 7 K 17
OS½″ 18S.19.29

Access : Over gate into graveyard. Key of church obtainable from John Burke, who lives 50 yards south of the church. Signposted

Little is known of the history of this church other than that it was dedicated to St Farannán. The saint exiled himself from here to the Continent where he died at Waser on the Meuse in 982. The church consists of a nave and chancel, with finely ornamented west doorway and chancel arch. The door has good Romanesque decoration, a hood above it, and is said to have contained a tympanum with a cat with two tails (probably a lion). Above the chancel arch, which has well-preserved capitals, is the entrance to a small room above the chancel which was enterable from the nave of the church. The gables of the church are unusually complete, but the upper portions of the north and south walls were probably restored in the 16th century.

Journal of the Waterford Archaeological Society 2, 1896, 23; JRSAI 39, 1909, 261; Leask, Churches I, 136; Journal of the Proceedings of the Clonmel Historical and Archaeological Society I, 4, 1955-56, 64

FETHARD Churches and Town Walls

MAP 7 L 17
OS½″ 18S.21.35

Access : Direct. Church of Ireland church often closed (key obtainable from Major Hugh Delmege, The Green Farm, on the outskirts of Fethard). Not signposted

Fethard is a small town which retains a remarkable number of medieval remnants. The exterior of Holy Trinity Church off the main street incorporates parts of a 15th century church, including windows, the west tower and part of a transept. In the wall of the churchyard are some tower houses (15th century ?); in all about 4 tower houses (none really accessible) are preserved in the town. In the fire-depot beside the entrance to the church, remnants of a 16th century house can be seen, and coats of arms and a 17th century Crucifixion have been built into its walls. Parts of the old town wall are preserved; a gate in the wall can be studied where the road to Moyglass passes underneath it. The wall can also be seen at other points in the town. They were not strong enough to prevent Cromwell taking the town in 1650. At the east end of the town is an Augustinian Abbey founded around 1306 on lands granted by Walter de Mulcote. The best preserved portion is the north transept. As the church is still in use, it gives some idea of the atmosphere of the original medieval Augustinian church. In the wall of the abbey are a number of 16th and 17th century tombstones, and also a sheela-na-gig. The Abbey was dissolved in 1540 and granted to Sir Edmund Butler in 1545.

JRSAI 39, 1909, 290; Fleming, The Town-Wall Fortifications of Ireland (1914) 34; Leask, Churches III, 56

GRALLAGH (407) Castle

MAP 7 K 16
OS½″ 18S.15.49

Access : Through farmyard. Not signposted

A 16th century tower house of 4 storeys, with vaults over the ground and second floors. The fireplaces and chimneys are later insertions. About 100 feet of the wall of the bawn are still visible.

HOLY CROSS (121) Cistercian Abbey *Figs. 74, 75 and 76*

MAP 7 K 16
OS½″ 18S.09.54

Access : Direct. If locked, key obtainable from Mr P. Kelly, third house on the left on Cashel Road. Signposted

The church of this Cistercian Abbey is shortly going to be re-roofed, and it is hoped that this will restore one of the finest of Irish 15th century churches to its former glory. The foundation was originally Benedictine (1169), but in 1180 Cistercian monks were brought by Donal Mor O'Brien from Monasteranenagh, Co Limerick (q.v.) to re-found the monastery and the Charter of the Abbey was confirmed in 1186. Little remains of the original abbey building, though the processional door leading from the south aisle to the cloister is late twelfth century (but reconstructed later). The west gable, the south aisle and the four western bays of the nave (the lay brothers choir) are thirteenth century work, but the finest parts of the building were constructed in the period 1450-75. This great re-building is probably due to the fact that the Abbey became a very popular place of pilgrimage in the 15th century because it had a relic of the True Cross (hence the name). The church consists of a nave, chancel and two transepts. The chancel is possibly the finest piece of 15th century architecture in Ireland, with a beautiful east window and exquisite ribbed vaulting which is also found in the transepts and the crossing. In the chancel is a fine sedilia with the English royal arms and those of the Earls of Ormond. The north transept is of interest because on its west

Fig. 74. Plan of Holycross Cistercian Abbey, Co Tipperary.

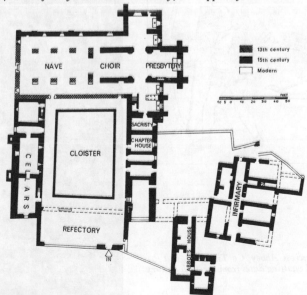

Fig. 76. A 15th century fresco of a hunting scene in the north transept of Holycross Abbey, Co Tipperary.

wall is preserved one of the few medieval wall paintings surviving in Ireland. It depicts two hunters with bows and arrows, and another with a horn in his mouth and a dog on a leash, hunting a deer which is hiding behind a tree. The figures are coloured brown, red and green. In between the two chapels of the south transept is a unique structure with columns and arches; it is known as 'The Monks Waking Place' but it may have been utilised to house the relic of the True Cross. Also in the south transept are stone stairs leading to the first floor of the domestic buildings, by which the monks retired to bed at night. There is fine ribbed vaulting under the tower; note also the owl carved under one of the corbels. What little remains of the cloister built by Dionysius O'Congail around 1450 has been reconstructed recently. On the eastern side of the beautifully kept cloister is a very unusual doorway which led to what must have been the chapter house (locked); nothing but the foundations of the refectory on the south side remain, while the use of the buildings on the west side is unknown. To the east of these buildings are further structures, that nearer the river having been probably an infirmary while the one abutting

Detail of Fig. 76 above.

Fig. 75. Holycross Abbey, Co Tipperary in 1791. The beautiful vaulting dates from the 15th century.

on to the road was probably the abbot's quarters. The Abbey was not suppressed until 1563, but the dispossessed monks returned to the Abbey at intervals throughout the 17th century except during the Cromwellian period and after 1691.

Arch Journal 88, 1931, 384; Leask, Churches III, 59; Oibre 7, 1969, 15

KILCOOLY (218) Cistercian Abbey *Fig. 13*

MAP 7 L 16
OS½″ 18S.29.58

Access: Up avenue, then along path for 200 yards, into field. Signposted
A Cistercian Abbey founded from Jerpoint by Donal Mór O'Brien in 1182 and dedicated to the Virgin Mary and St Benedict. The church, built around 1200, had a nave and two aisles, but after the almost complete destruction of the monastery in 1445, great reconstruction took place within the monastery and the church lost its two aisles. In the course of rebuilding, a new north transept and a tower were also added. The quality of the stonework in these additions is good, as attested by the carving on the two unusual seats at the top of the nave (one for the abbot, the other, possibly, for his deputy), and—even more unusual—the sculptures on the wall leading into the sacristy. Here there are carvings of the Crucifixion, St Christopher, a bishop or abbot (probably St Bernard) as well as a mermaid holding a mirror and accompanied by fish, and also the arms of the Butler family. There is a fine traceried east window in the chancel, and good vaulting in the north transept. Some fine tombs adorn the choir, including that of Piers Fitz Oge Butler (c. 1526) signed by Rory O'Tunney (*Roricus O Tuyne scripsit*), and, on the floor, Abbot Philip (died 1463) who was probably largely responsible for the rebuilding. Little or nothing remains of the domestic buildings, but a two-storey building standing not far from the church was probably an infirmary. In the field approaching the abbey there is one of the few remaining examples of an Irish columbarium—a dove-cot.

JRSAI 21, 1891, 216 and 74, 1944, 219; JCHAS 43, 1938, 96; Leask, Churches III, 69

Fig. 13. The tomb of Piers Fitz Oge Butler at Kilcooley Abbey, Co Tipperary, carved by Rory O Tunney circa 1526.

KILLODIERNAN Church

MAP 7 J 14
OS½″ 15R.83.89

Access : One mile up untarred road, then through two gates and 20 yards along path to graveyard. Not signposted

A rectangular church with doors on three sides. The north door is flat and insignificant, the south door is a simple 15th century entrance while the west door and the east window are both Romanesque. There is interesting scrollwork, and also spirals, on the door which was presumably taken from an earlier church on the site and built into this later medieval church. Some of the stones of the doorway have, however, been wrongly fitted in the course of re-construction.

KNOCKGRAFFON Motte and Church

MAP 7 K 17
OS½″ 18S.04.29

Access : Over wall and field. Not signposted

An interesting collection of medieval monuments comprising a fine motte and bailey, a church and a castle. The motte was built by the English of Leinster beside the River Suir when they were on a raid against Donal Mór O'Brien, King of Thomond, in 1192. It was given by the King to William de Braose, but later taken from him and granted to Philip of Worcester. Nearby is a ruined 13th century nave-and-chancel church with an east window inserted in the 15th century. A few hundred yards further away is a 16th century tower built by the Butlers.
JRSAI 39, 1909, 275

KNOCKKELLY Castle

MAP 7 L 17
OS½″ 18S.23.38

Access : Through gate and up avenue. To respect the privacy of the owner, the castle should only be visited by small groups. Not signposted

A late Elizabethan or early Jacobean tower house (now used as a cow-house), surrounded by one of the most extensive and best preserved bawns in the country, with massive towers at the corners. Little is known of its history, other than that a man named Keating acquired it in the mid-18th century, but on non-payment of rent, he was forcefully evicted by the owners, the Everards. Later a family called Jolly lived in it.
JRSAI 36, 1906, 145; Leask, Castles 122

LACKEEN (378) Castle

MAP 4 J 13
OS½″ 15M.95.04

Access : Through one field. Not signposted

A four-storey tower-house standing in a bawn with a round-headed doorway. The second storey has a good fire-place, and the third floor is vaulted. An unusual feature is the window with remains of tracery on the third floor above the doorway. The ground floor is at present used as an agricultural storage place. The castle belonged to Brian Ua Cinneide Fionn, chieftain of Ormond, who died in 1588. His son, Donnchadh, the last Ua Cinneide chief of lower Ormond, forfeited it to the Cromwellians in 1653.

LIATHMORE (266) Churches

MAP 7 L 16
OS½″ 18S.22.58

Access : Through gate and across two fields. Signposted

Two churches still standing on an old monastic site founded by St Mochoemóg who died in 655. The smaller church is the older of the two, though its date is unknown. The west doorway and the east window have been restored, but the door was probably flat-headed. The church has antae. The larger church was begun in the 12th century, but this church was later considerably altered. The north and east walls of the chancel are the oldest parts of the present church, and they formed part of the original church which had antae at the east end. A chancel was added to this, but nothing remains of it except the foundations to the east of the present church (though remains of the chancel arch can be seen in the exterior of the east wall of the church). Around the 15th century, the old nave was made into a new chancel (and the old chancel probably knocked down), while a totally new nave was built which may never have been completed. The stones used in the new chancel arch were probably brought from elsewhere. At the same time the south wall, the vault and the living quarters over the chancel were built. Some 12th century fragments are built into the wall. In the field surrounding the churches are a number of earthworks, which represent occupation (though not necessarily entirely monastic) from 1000–1700 A.D., some overlain by 17th century houses.

PRIA 51, 1945-8, 1; Leask, Churches I, 62 and 64; Old Kilkenny Review 22, 1970, 29

LISMACRORY (348) Burial Mounds

MAP 7 J 14
OS½″ 15R.98.98

Access : Through gate into two separate fields. Not signposted
Two burial mounds, probably of Bronze Age date. They are both about 7 feet high and 20 feet in diameter. The more northerly mound still retains traces of the stones which surrounded the base.

LORRHA Churches

MAP 4 J 13
OS½″ 15M.92.05

Access : Direct. Signposted

Dominican Priory (361)

Founded around 1269 by Walter de Burgo, Earl of Ulster, for the Dominicans. The church has a nave and chancel of almost equal width, with the remains of a five-light east window. The north and south walls have a number of lancet windows, and there is a good doorway in the north wall. The door in the west gable was mutilated when the Catholic church was built near it in 1812, and an angel and heads from the priory were built into the west wall of the Catholic church. The church houses among others the tombs of the O'Kennedy family and that of the MacEgans sculpted by Patrick Kerin. A tower standing on the modern church side of the old church was probably linked by other buildings to the older church.

NMAJ 6, 1949-52, 9 and 102; Leask, Churches II, 115

St Ruadhán's Church (357)

Normally kept locked : key not kept locally
A 15th century church with fine east and west windows. It is entered by a very ornate west doorway. There is a vaulted sacristy attached to the church.

Church of Ireland Church

Key from Mr Alfie Dyer living opposite the entrance to the church
To the south of the previous church is another, a part of which is still used. It has antae, and a 13th century doorway into which a 15th century doorway was inserted. The 15th century doorway has floral designs, and a pelican cutting its breast to allow blood to flow from it to provide nourishment for its young—a symbol of the church feeding its flock. The church probably stands on the site of an ancient monastery founded by St Ruadhán, who was a disciple of St Finian of Clonard and who died in 584. The monastery was plundered by the Viking Turgesius in 845, and was burned in 1154, 1157 and 1179. In 1589 it was granted to John O'Hogan who later forfeited it because of non-payment of rent. There are remains of 9th century (?) crosses in the churchyard.

NMAJ 6, 1949-52, 102

LOUGHMOE Castle

MAP 7 K 15
OS½″ 18S.12.67

Access: Through two gates and fields. Not signposted
The south end of the castle is a 15th or 16th century tower house with rounded corners. It has 4 storeys, with vaults on the first and third storeys. In the 17th century, windows and a fine fireplace with initials of one of the Purcell family were inserted. In the first half of the 17th century the Purcells added the northern part, with towers at opposite corners. It was lighted by mullioned windows, and a number of fireplaces are still retained in its walls. Col Nicholas Purcell, the last of his line, fought at the battles of the Boyne and Aughrim and also at Limerick with Sarsfield, and died here in 1722.
JRSAI 39, 1909, 70 and 284; Leask, Castles 132; Waterman, in Studies in Building History, ed. Jope (1961) 254

MARLFIELD Church

MAP 7 K 17
OS½″ 22S.17.22

Access: Down an untarred lane and then left along tree-lined avenue. Key of church from Mrs Corrigan at entrance to church avenue. Not signposted
The 19th century church stands on the site of the Cistercian Abbey of Inishlounaght which was founded by Donal Mór O'Brien, King of Limerick, in 1187 and whither a fresh colony of Cistercians were brought from Furness in Lancashire in 1238. Some interesting fragments of the older church are preserved in the modern church. Particularly noteworthy is the transitional doorway of about 1200 which is now high up in the west wall of the church and which was probably the processional doorway leading from the aisle of the old church out into the cloister. In the south wall of the church is a window whose surrounds may have formed a 13th century window or tomb niche of the old church, while the east window of the church is probably the east window inserted in the old church in the 15th century.
JRSAI 39, 1909, 267; Arch Journal 88, 1931, 13; Leask, Churches II, 150; Journal of the Proceedings of the Clonmel Historical and Archaeological Society I, 4, 1955-6, 3

MONAINCHA (125) Church

MAP 7 K 14
OS½″ 15S.17.88

Access: 50 yards along untarred road, then through gate and then a quarter of a mile along untarred road. Signposted
The church is situated on what used to be an island in a bog. It was probably founded by St Cainnech of Aghaboe, Co Laois (q.v.) in the 6th century, though it is also associated with St Cronán of Roscrea (see below). The deaths of abbots are recorded for the years 807, 1120, 1138 and 1143, and the monastery seems to have experienced a revival in the 12th century. Giraldus Cambrensis, the historian of the Norman invasion, describes the place as an island where no woman or animal of the female sex could enter without dying immediately. The monastery became Augustinian at the end of the 12th century. In 1568 it was granted to Sir William Carroll and in 1586 passed to Sir Lucas Dillon. The nave-and-chancel church has a finely decorated 12th century west doorway and chancel arch constructed in a warm sandstone. In the first half of the 13th century new east windows were inserted, as were also two large windows in the south wall of the nave with attractive capitals surrounding them. The window above the doorway is 12th century, but with 15th century insertions. The pilasters on the outside wall of the chancel are unusual. The small sacristy to the north of the chancel was added probably in the 15th or 16th

century. Outside the church are High Cross fragments which originally stood to the south of the church but were re-erected (with the aid of cement) to the west of the church. On the base (9th century?) are sunken crosses and riders on horseback, but the upper part of the cross, with a Crucifixion on one side and interlacing on the other, is 12th century.

JRSAI 50, 1920, 19; Leask, Churches I, 129

MOOR ABBEY (292) Church

MAP 7 J 17
OS½" 18R.81.28

Access: Direct. Not signposted

Donough Cairbreach O'Brien, King of Thomond, founded a friary for the Franciscans here early in the 13th century, but the present church was probably not begun until 1471, only to be burned the following year. After the Suppression in 1541, it was sold to John of Desmond for a fine of £15 and an annual rent of 4d. Sir Humphrey Gilbert's horsemen burned the church once more in 1569, and the friars who had stayed on were massacred in 1570. It suffered little damage when police tried to blow it up in 1921. The church is a simple nave-and-chancel church with a tall slender tower which besides a sedilia and some windows contains little of interest. Nothing remains of the domestic buildings or the cloister.

Official Guidebook

NENAGH (513) Castle *Fig. 77*

MAP 7 J 15
OS½" 18R.87.79

Access: Through Catholic church grounds into field. If locked, key is with church sacristan. Not signposted

The present massive tower, or donjon, was originally one of three towers interspersed in the curtain wall of a strong Norman castle which was also guarded by two semi-circular towers and a gate-house (parts of which remain to the south of the tower). The tower has 5 storeys, and the walls are up to 20 feet thick. A southern window-niche opening off the second floor has Romanesque decoration on the inside, while there is early Gothic decoration on a chimney piece in the floor above. The castle was founded by Theobald Walter (nephew of Thomas à Becket) in the first twenty years of the 13th century. The Butlers resided here continuously till towards the end of the 14th century when they moved to Gowran, in Co Kilkenny. During the 15th century it was in the hands of the MacIbrien family, but by 1533 Sir Piers Butler, Earl of Ossory, had returned to

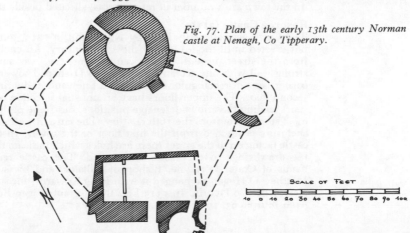

Fig. 77. Plan of the early 13th century Norman castle at Nenagh, Co Tipperary.

SCALE OF FEET
10 0 10 20 30 40 50 60 70 80 90 100

regain possession. However, in 1548 the Irish, under O'Carroll, burned it. By the latter half of the 16th century the Butlers had fully regained possession, but James I granted the castle to Lady Dingwall. It changed hands many times during the Cromwellian wars, but was taken from the Cromwellians in 1660. It also changed hands a number of times during the Williamite wars, being taken first by O'Carroll and then by Ginckel. It was afterwards rendered harmless. In order to rid the tower of sparrows who were ruining his crops, a farmer put gunpowder in the wall in 1760, but only succeeded in blowing a hole in the wall. The topmost part of the tower was added in the 19th century. A few hundred yards away, in Abbey Street, are the remains of a 13th century Franciscan friary which was one of the most important of its order in Ireland before being partially destroyed by Cromwell.

JRSAI 66, 1936, 247; Arch Journal 93, 1937, 163; Leask, Castles 43

PORTLAND (451) Church

MAP 4 J 13
OS½" 15M.89.04

Access : Up avenue for about a quarter of a mile to farmyard, then into field. Signposted

A late medieval small parish church of little interest except for the vaulted west end which was probably the priest's house. The graveyard is now used as a burial place for unbaptized children.

NMAJ 6, 1949-52, 105

RATHURLES Church and Ring-fort

MAP 7 J 14
OS½" 18R.90.80

Access : About half a mile up avenue, then over fence to right into field. Not signposted

A ring-fort with three concentric banks which may have been a meeting-place and the site of an ancient fair. Two massive stones which once formed the gates of entry to the fort are lying in a field outside the north-eastern part of the fort. In the interior of the fort is a simple 15th century church, choked in undergrowth, and possibly built by the O'Kennedys.

Evans, Prehistoric and Early Christian Ireland—A Guide (1966) 195

ROSCREA Castle, Church, High Cross and Round Tower

MAP 7 K 14
OS½" 15S.14.89

Access : Direct. Key of castle in Co. Council building in courtyard of castle. Signposted (Round Tower)

In the town are a number of monuments, situated beside the road.

Roscrea Castle (211)

The Castle was allegedly built by King John in 1213, but was probably not erected until the middle of the 13th century. An enclosure, reached from the street through a 19th century gateway, was surrounded by a strong wall with one rectangular and two D-shaped towers in it. At one corner is a tall rectangular tower with a fine vault and a fire-place on the second floor. The upper floors have an unusual selection of passages and stairs leading to various defensive positions, but some parts of the upper-most storey date from the 16th century. The curtain wall surrounding the enclosure is reached from the first floor of the tower. In the wall of the castle facing on to the street there are holes which indicate the place where the drawbridge to the castle once stood. The castle remained in the hands of Conor O'Heyne, Bishop of Killaloe, and his successors until Matthew O'Hogan exchanged it with King Edward I for some lands near Newcastle, Co Dublin. In 1315 Edward II granted it to Edmund Butler.

Arch Journal 93, 1937, 180; Leask, Castles 57

St Cronan's Church and Round Tower (126) *Fig. 78*

The modern road cuts through a monastery founded by St Cronan who died between 600 and 620. The monastery was active during the 12th century during which it was, however, either plundered or burned four times. Of the 12th century Romanesque church only the west façade remains, beside the road. Above the round-headed doorway is a hood-moulding enclosing the figure of a bishop or abbot, probably St Cronan, and on each side of the door there is a series of blind arcades. The rest of the church was demolished in 1812 and was replaced by the church in the churchyard. Just to the north of the church is a 12th century High Cross with Christ and interlacing motifs on the west face, and a bishop (St Cronan) on the east face. The cross is unusual in having two figures (one male and one female ?) at the bottom of the north and south faces of the shaft. On the opposite side of the road is a Round Tower which has the representation of a ship on the inner face of a window about 25 feet above the ground. The Tower was originally 20 feet higher, but was reduced to its present height by the English in 1798 after one of their sentinels was shot from the top of it by a sniper.

Leask, Churches I, 125

Franciscan Friary

The gateway to the present Catholic parish church is part of a Franciscan friary founded by Maelruanigh O'Carroll before 1477. Only the east and north walls of the chancel, the bell tower and parts of the northern nave arcade remain, and some other pieces have been built into the walls. Near the west end of the modern church is a pillar with the carving of an animal which was removed here from Timoney Park, 5 miles away, and which may date to the 8th century.

Leask, Churches III, 49; Roe, in North Munster Studies (ed. Rynne) (1967) 127

Fig. 78. West façade of St Cronan's Church, Roscrea, Co Tipperary. 12th century.

St PATRICK'S WELL Church and Cross

MAP 7 K 17
OS½" 22S.17.22

Access : Down path. Signposted
A number of wells rise up at this eerie spot where one could imagine that people in times past could have wondered at the primeval power of nature. St Patrick is said to have visited the place, and the water is said to cure 'sore lips, sore eyes, the scrofula and several other chronic diseases'. In the middle of a pond is an Early Christian cross, and beside it is a church which was built on the site of a 12th century edifice, but which in its present mutilated form dates probably from the 16th century. The church was dependent on the Cistercian Abbey of Inishlounaght. In 1619 Pope Paul granted a plenary indulgence valid for 30 years to all who visited the church on St Patrick's day and on the feast of Pentecost. In the church are remnants of a number of tombs, one of which, that of Nicholas White who died in 1622, was brought here from St Mary's Church, Clonmel, in 1805
O'Connell, St Patrick's Well, Clonmel, Co Tipperary (1956)

TERRYGLASS (363) Castle

MAP 4 J 13
OS½" 15M.86.01

Access : Down private avenue and through private garden. Signposted
The castle was probably built by Theobald Walter Butler some time early in the 13th century, and the Butlers still owned it in 1640. The castle is square in plan with rounded turrets at the corner, but only one storey of the original three or four remain. The tower on the north-east is only enterable by steps up from the outside. The interior of the castle was divided into two apartments by a dividing wall. In the nearby village is an Early Christian church, modified in the 15th century, standing on the site of a monastery which was famous for its ascetic monasticism during the so-called Culdee movement in the 8th century.
JRSAI 73, 1943, 141; Arch Journal 93, 1937, 175; Leask, Castles 51

TIMONEY HILLS (353) Standing Stones

MAP 7 K 14
OS½" 15S.20.84

Access :Quarter of a mile up lane, then into fields on either side. Not signposted
A number of standing stones, spread over a number of fields, but they do not form any apparent plan.
O Ríordáin, Antiquities of the Irish Countryside (1953) 84

TOUREEN PEAKAUN (332) Church, Crosses and Slabs

MAP 7 K 17
OS½" 18S.01.28

Access : Up a long, untarred road, over the railway line (gate closed— anyone leaving it open is liable to be fined !), through farmyard, across bridge and into field. Not signposted
St Alban founded the first monastery here around 650, but the site is named after his successor, St Beccan. A 12th century Romanesque church has a flat-headed doorway, and two unusual decorated windows. A number of crosses and Early Christian grave-slabs are either standing free around the church or have been built into its interior or exterior walls.
JRSAI 74, 1944, 226; PRIA 61 C 1961, 154

County Waterford

ARDMORE (131) Church and Round Tower *Fig. 10*

MAP 7 K 20
OS½" 22X.19.77

Access : Over stile to graveyard. Signposted
The earliest monastery was founded here by St Declan who is alleged to have been a bishop in Munster when St Patrick arrived, and who is one

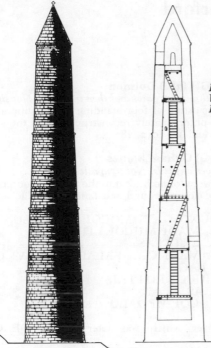

Fig. 10. The Round Tower at Ardmore, Co. Waterford together with a cross-section. Probably 12th century.

of the main supports for the belief in the existence of Christianity in the south of Ireland before St Patrick. Ardmore was recognized as a Cathedral and had its bishop in 1170. In 1591 it was leased to Sir Walter Raleigh who only held it for 2 years. In 1642 the Confederate army hiding in the Church and Round Tower were besieged by the English. When they surrendered, 117 out of 154 of them were hanged on the spot. The Round Tower rises in three steps to a height of 95 feet, and is one of the best preserved examples in Ireland. The church, known as the 'Cathedral', was erected by Moel-ettrim O Duibh-rathra sometime before his death in 1203. It is probable that he utilized the remainder of an older church in the lowest portion of his church. The church has most unusual features: the recessed Roman-esque west window, the arcades on the interior wall, and a pointed chancel arch. Two Ogham stones have been placed in the church for safety. One of these stones has two inscriptions (1) LUGUDECCAS MAQI....COI NETA-SEGAMONAS and (2) DOLATI BIGA ISGOB (a stone commemorating Lugaid, son or grandson of Nia-Segmon) and the other reads simply AMADU (the loved one). The most unusual feature of all in the church are the Romanesque sculptures on the exterior of the west wall which are all arranged in a series of arcades, a row of small ones on the top, and two larger arches containing smaller ones on the bottom. Many of the scenes in the upper arches are much worn, but the Archangel Michael weighing the souls can be made out. Below Adam and Eve, the Judgment of Solomon and the Adoration of the Magi are visible. To the east of the church is a small building, St Declan's oratory, which was re-roofed in 1716. The Lugudeccas Ogham stone was found in the gable. It is traditionally taken to be the burial place of St Declan, and a hollow in the south-east corner is pointed out as his grave.

JRSAI 33, 1903, 353; Macalister, Corpus I (1945) 257, Nos. 263-5; Leask, Churches I, 164 and II, 39

BALLYNAGEERAGH (384) Dolmen

MAP 8 M 18
OS½" 22S.49.03

Access : Along lane, through 2 gates and then into field. Not signposted
A portal dolmen consisting of four standing stones supporting two cap-stones. It has been unfortunately reconstructed with the aid of cement.
JRSAI 8, 1866, 480 and 42, 1912, 283

DRUMLOHAN (154) Ogham Stones

MAP 7 L 18
OS½" 22S.37.01

Access : Over a number of fields. Not signposted
The Ogham stones were found built into the roof of a souterrain, and have now been re-erected above ground and fenced off. The inscriptions are as follows:

> MANU MAGUNO GATI MOCOI MOCORBO
> CALUNOVIC. MAQI MUCOI LIT...
> MAQI-INI.... ....TTEAS
> CUNALEGEA MAQI C.... SALAR CELI AVI QUECI
> BIGU MAQI LAG
> BIR MAQI MUCOI ROTTAIS
> MAQI NE.....AS
> DENAVEC.... COI MEDALO
> BRO...AS
> SOVALINI over which was later written DEAGOS MAQI MUCO.... NAI

JRSAI 10, 1868, 35; Macalister, Corpus I (1945) 267, Nos. 272ff

GAULSTOWN (398) Dolmen

MAP 8 M 18
OS½" 23S.54.06

Access : Up a path and over a stile. Not signposted
A portal dolmen with a chamber of six upright stones (the two in front forming a porch), and all covered by one large capstone.
JRSAI 8, 1866, 479; 42, 1912, 279 and 71, 1941, 18

KILTERA (330) Ogham Stones

MAP 7 K 19
OS½" 22X.10.91

Access : Over wall into field beside road. Signposted
Two Ogham stones standing in an enclosure composed of an earthen ditch which also contained an iron-smelting pit. The inscriptions on the two stones read:

> COLLABOT MUCOI LUGA MAQI LOBACCONA (Collabot son of Lug son of Lobchu)
> MEDUSI MACI LU (later corrected to) MUCOI LUGA.

A third stone with the inscription RITUVVAS has been removed to the National Museum of Ireland in Dublin.
PRIA 43, 1935-7, 1; Macalister, Corpus I (1945) 261, Nos. 262ff

KNOCKEEN (421) Dolmen *Fig. 79*

MAP 8 M 18
OS½" 23S.57.07

Access : Through gate and across field. Signposted
A very fine portal dolmen with a rectangular chamber roofed by two capstones—one partly supporting the other. The two front side stones project so as to form a porch.
JRSAI 8, 1866, 479; 42, 1912, 279 and 71, 1941, 18

LISMORE St Mochuda's or Carthage's Cathedral

MAP 7 K 19
OS½" 22X.05.99

Access : Direct. Signposted
Much of the Cathedral dates from 1633 when Richard Boyle, the Earl of Cork, built it. However, the chancel arch and the south transept windows

Fig. 79. Knockeen Dolmen, Co Waterford. Built circa 2000 B.C.

go back as far as the 13th century. The church contains a fine tomb of the Mac Grath family dated 1557, and showing the Crucifixion, Ecce Homo, St Gregory the Great, St Carthage, St Katherine of Alexandria, St Patrick and some Apostles. It is one of the few cases where the figures are named on Irish medieval tombs. Not far from the tomb, and also at the west end of the church, are some early grave-slabs and a Romanesque head which formed a corbel.
JRSAI 27, 1897, 349

MATTHEWSTOWN (237) Wedge-shaped Gallery-Grave

MAP 8 M 18
OS½" 23S.53.03

Access : 1 mile up untarred road, then over fence to right. Not signposted
A wedge-shaped gallery-grave with a long rectangular chamber still consisting of ten upright stones covered by three capstones. Portions of the original kerb-stones surrounding the mound of covering stones still survive, though nothing remains of the mound itself.
JRSAI 42, 1912, 280

MOLANA—See under Youghal, Co Cork

MOTHEL (132) Abbey

MAP 7 L 18
OS½" 22S.40.16

Access : Through gate into cemetery. Signposted
The original monastery was founded in the 6th century by St Cuan or St Breoghan, but was re-founded for the Augustinians by the Power family, presumably in the 13th century. It was closely associated with St Catherine's Abbey in Waterford. After the Suppression of the Monasteries in 1537, it passed to the Powers, but they were dispossessed half a century later. Some few medieval wall fragments remain, but the best surviving feature is a tomb by Roricus O'Comayn, with the following panels: Christ holding orb and sceptre, Virgin and Child, a monk, St Michael with the Scales of Judgment, Saints Peter and Paul, Saints James and

John of Jerusalem, John the Baptist and (?) Thomas of Canterbury, St Margaret of Antioch with dragon and St Katherine of Alexandria with the wheel.
Journal of the Proceedings of the Clonmel Historical and Archaeological Society I, 2, 1953, 31; NMAJ 8, 1959, 91

MAP 8 N 18
OS½″ 23S.61.12

WATERFORD Church and Tower

Waterford was founded by the Vikings around 914 and initiated its own episcopal See in the 11th century. It was taken by Diarmuid MacMurrough Kavanagh, and later fell to Strongbow who married MacMurrough's daughter in the now no longer existing Cathedral in the town. In medieval times it was a flourishing port, loyal to the English crown. However, it lost status by remaining Catholic, and submitted to Cromwell's son-in-law in 1650. In the 18th and early 19th century, the town had a famous glass industry which was re-established in 1947.

'The French Church' (205)

Access: Locked: Key with the Office of Public Works, Catherine Street. Signposted
The church was founded as a convent for the Franciscans by Hugh Purcell about 1240. In 1395 the O'Conor Don, de Burgo, O'Brien and O'Kennedy submitted to Richard II in the Friary, and Chapters of the Order were held here in 1317, 1469, 1615 and 1834. Of the original buildings a nave, chancel and north aisle remain. There is a triple-light east window in the chancel. In 1545 Henry Walsh was granted a charter by Henry VIII to make the Friary, by then dissolved, into a hospital, and the area over the nave of the church was used as such for hundreds of years, while the chancel and the Lady Chapel were used for the burials of members of illustrious Waterford families such as the Powers, Waddings etc.
JRSAI 42, 1912, 260; JCHAS 69, 1964, 73; Leask, Churches II, 94

Reginald's Tower

Access: Direct. Open Monday-Saturday 9 a.m.–9 p.m. and Sunday 2 p.m.– 8 p.m. in Summer. In Winter it is open 9 a.m. – 5.30 p.m. Monday-Friday, but closed on Saturday and Sunday. Signposted
The tower was allegedly founded by Reginald the Dane in 1003, but it is probably a 13th century Norman tower. In 1463 a mint was established in it. In the 19th century it was used as a prison. The City Museum, displaying the City Regalia etc. is housed on the upper floors.
JRSAI 42, 1912, 267; Fleming, The Town-Wall Fortifications of Ireland (1914) 16; Leask, Castles 111

ATHLONE (520) Castle

MAP 4 K 11
OS½″ 15N.04.41

Access : Direct, up a ramp to top. Not signposted
The Normans had probably erected a motte beside this important ford over the Shannon before John de Grey, the Justiciar, built a castle and a bridge here in 1210. The tower fell in the following year, but the many-sided keep in the centre of the castle is, except for its top, the oldest part of the castle. The castle was repaired around 1251, and again between 1273 and 1279. To this latter period the three-quarter round towers at the angles down near the river may be assigned, but little of the original towers can be seen as they were heavily altered in the 19th century when heavy guns were placed on them. The original entrance was near the south end of the east curtain, but the ramp forming the present entrance is modern. The present castle owes much of its shape to the considerable alterations carried out on the castle in the 17th and 19th centuries. The castle took a heavy battering during the siege of Athlone in 1691.
JRSAI 37, 1907, 257; Arch Journal 93, 1937, 167; Journal of the Old Athlone Society I, 1, 1969, 45

BEALIN Twyford (223) High Cross

MAP 4 K 11
OS½″ 12N.10.43

Access : 150 yards up laneway, then up to top of hillock on left. Not signposted
The cross was originally found at Bealin but it has been removed to its present site in Twyford Demesne. On the east face are three animals above one another with bird-like heads, and a lion at the bottom. On the north face is a hunter with a spear, and above him a dog bites a deer's leg. There are also interlacing and geometric patterns on the cross. On the bottom of the west side there is said to be an inscription to the effect that the cross was erected by one Tuathgal and as there is an abbot of Clonmacnoise of this name who died in 811, it has been assumed that this cross must date from around 800.
JRSAI 57, 1927, 2

DELVIN (481) Castle

MAP 5 M/N 10
OS½″ 13N.60.63

Access : Through back yard of shop. Not signposted
The castle is said to have been built in 1181 by Hugh de Lacy, Lord of Meath, for his brother-in-law, Sir Gilbert de Nugent, who resided in it for some time before building the neighbouring castle of Clonyn. But the castle was probably built in the early 13th century. It was originally square in plan with four rounded turrets at the corner, but only the western half of the castle remains, with two of the rounded turrets. The lower portion is now used as a shop store; the upper portions are inaccessible without a ladder.
Lewis, Topographical Dictionary (1837) 310

FORE (215 and 220) Abbey, Church and Town Gates

MAP 5 M 10
OS½″ 13N.51.70

Access : Down lane and across field to Abbey, up path to church, and over field to town gate. Signposted
An Early Christian monastery was founded here around 630 by St Feichín who died of the plague in 664-5. At one time there were 300 monks in the monastery. It was burned in 771, 830 and again in 870, and a number of times in the course of the 11th and 12th centuries. From this old monastery one church—St Feichín's—survives, standing in a graveyard above the road. Originally it was a simple rectangular building with antae, and with a Greek cross in relief over the flat-headed doorway. A chancel was added

around 1200. There is the small carved head of a monk on the north side of the chancel arch. The two east windows were inserted in the 15th century. A font and the remains of an altar are preserved inside. Around 1200 a Priory was founded by the De Lacys for the Benedictines down on the plain, and dedicated to St Feichín and to St Taurin—the patron saint of the monastery in Normandy from whence the Benedictines were brought. Because it was dependent on a French monastery, it was confiscated by the King when the English were at war with France in 1340. It was then granted to William Tessone, who pocketed the revenue for himself. It was taken over by William Englond who was appointed abbot by Pope Martin V in 1418. It was he, or his successor, William Croys, who turned the monastery into a fortification. When the monastery was suppressed around 1540 it was leased to Christopher, Baron of Delvin, and remained in the hands of the Greville-Nugent family until early this century. The rectangular church was built early in the 13th century; it has three round-headed east windows, but the north wall is largely a modern reconstruction. At the western end is a tower erected as a fortification in the 15th century. Over the sacristy to the south end of the church is another tower of the same date, and each tower formed a residence in itself. The eastern and western sides of the domestic buildings around the cloister have been much modified, and portions of the 15th century cloister were re-erected in 1912. About 40 yards to the north-east of the church are the remains of a columbarium or dove-cot, while remains of an old earthwork, possibly attached to the monastery, can be seen beside the nearby hill. In fields not far away are gates which formed part of the medieval wall of the town **(220)**.

Official Guidebook; Leask, Churches I, 69; II, 47 and III, 26

INCHBOFIN (213) Early Christian Monastery

MAP 4 K 11
OS½" 12N.06.55

Access: Boats available during the summer season from Mr Duffy at Coosan Point or from Mr Kelly, Elfleet Bay, Lanesborough

The monastery was founded by St Ríoch around 530. It is mentioned in the Annals in 750, 809 and 916, and it was raided by the Munstermen in 1015 and 1089. Two churches still remain. The more southerly church is a nave-and-chancel building with round-headed windows in the chancel, and a pointed door in the south wall of the nave. Near the north-eastern point of the island is the other church consisting of a nave, and a transept of almost equal size as well as a sacristy. To the north of the altar is a fine Romanesque window, and opposite it is a piscina which stands out from the wall. The transept is a later addition and has two 15th century windows, one with a bishop's head on the outside. The sacristy, which has a small chamber above it, is also a later addition. The church was surrounded by an irregularly-shaped monastic wall. Outside this wall to the south is an old stone building of uncertain use. There are also a number of fine Early Christian grave-slabs to be seen on the island. A piece of 10th century Viking bronze-work was found on the island which is possibly to be connected with a Viking raid on the island in 922.
JRSAI 37, 1907, 326; 47, 1917, 139 and 92, 1962, 187; Leask, Churches I, 100 and 102

KILLUCAN Wayside Crosses

MAP 8 M 11
OS½" 13N.57.51

Access: Direct. Not signposted

Three 16th and early 17th century wayside crosses erected in a grove just outside the village of Killucan. The first has an inscription 'This stone was for Tir: McKin: and Alson Pluncket his wife in the year 1531'. Those commemorated, Tirlogh McKenny and his wife, died in a coaching accident (it happened even then!). The cross originally stood beside the Dublin-Athlone road. The second cross says 'Arthur Darcy et K. Fitzgerald me feri na Dni 1604'—Arthur Darcy and K Fitzgerald made me in the year of the Lord 1604. The rest of the Latin inscription is from the Service for the Dead. The cross was removed here from the centre of the village of Killucan. The third cross bears the inscription 'Pray for John O McLaghlin and his wife Jovan Hughes died 1601'. This is the only cross of the three standing in its original position. It was erected to commemorate a couple who were killed by a runaway horse. In the village of Killucan not far away is a Protestant church containing a finely carved 13th century baptismal font inside, and with the remains of a 15th century church at its east end. Up the road from the crosses is a motte called Rathwire, with a castle said to have been built by Hugh de Lacy for his brother Robert, and where King John met Cathal Crovderg, King of Connacht, in 1210.

MULTYFARNHAM Franciscan Friary

MAP 4 M 10
OS½" 12N.40.64

Access: Direct from private avenue. Not signposted

In the present friary church parts of a 15th century church survive, including the nave, south transept and tower, as well as the south window (though not its glass). Nothing remains of the chancel or of the original domestic buildings. The church was given its present form in 1827 when the Franciscans returned to their old monastery.
Leask, Churches III, 183

TAGHMON (265) Church

MAP 4 M 10
OS½″ 12N.49.61

Access : Direct to graveyard in which church stands. Key to church obtainable from caretaker in cottage opposite entrance to graveyard. Signposted

A monastery was founded here by St Fintan Munna but little is known of its history. A church appears to have been in existence here in the 14th century (though the present church was probably built in the 15th century) and was plundered by Farrell Macgeoghan in 1452. By 1587 it belonged to the Nugent family, but the church was ruined by 1622. Cromwell is said to have slept here. The church was being used in 1755, and was restored in 1847 and again in 1927. It has a nave and chancel, and its castle-like tower and battlements as well as its small windows suggest that it was used as a fortified building. The tower, which has four storeys, including living quarters, was probably added to the already existing church in the 15th century. Note also the two sculpted figures—one grotesque, the other the head of a bishop—in the outer face of the north wall, and another, older-looking head, in the west wall.

JRSAI 58, 1928, 102; Leask, Churches III, 19

TWYFORD—See under Bealin, above

USHNAGH (155) Earthworks

MAP 4 L 11
OS½″ 12N.29.49

Access : Through gate and up lane to field. Signposted

The site is said to have been an important meeting-place in the days of old where the men of Ireland assembled on May Day. It is also said to have been the seat of King Tuathal Techtmhar who crossed the Shannon from Connacht in the second century A.D. There are a number of monuments on the hill including burial mounds and a fort. The fort was an area (surrounded by a ditch) on which a house was built, and a house surrounded by an elliptical ditch was added to this later. On the western side of the hill is a natural stone, called the 'Catstone' because it resembles a cat watching a mouse; it was said to mark the spot where the five provinces of Ireland converged.

PRIA 38, 1928, 69

BALLYHACK (516) Castle

MAP 8 N 18
OS½" 23S.71.11

Access : Difficult ; through private garden. Not signposted
There was formerly an establishment of the Knights Templars here
beside this peaceful inlet, but the present 5-storey castle is 15th or 16th
century in date and probably has nothing to do with the Knights. The
ground floor is vaulted and has a number of deep recesses, and the second
floor is also vaulted. There are also a number of recesses on the third
storey; that on the east wall was once a chapel. On the same floor is a now
inaccessible prisoners' cell.
JRSAI 27, 1897, 343

BALLYMOTY (375) Motte

MAP 8 Q 16
OS½" 19T.04.40

Access : Across fields. Not signposted
A motte which, because it is difficult of access and covered in undergrowth,
is scarcely worth visiting.
JRSAI 42, 1912, 280

CLONMINES Churches and Castles

MAP 8 P 18
OS½" 23S.84.13

Access : ¼ mile along private avenue. Visitors not encouraged. Not signposted
Once a flourishing medieval town, Clonmines still contains the remains
of some of its old buildings. The town was given a charter by William
Marshall, Earl of Pembroke, early in the 13th century, and the Kavanagh
family founded an Abbey here for the Augustinian Eremites which was
'beautified' and enlarged in 1385. The town was destroyed in 1400, but
rose again. Although it scarcely survived the 17th century, it continued
to send members to Parliament up till 1800. Nevertheless, as late as 1794
the Augustinians still had a prior and brethren attached to their house
here, though they may have lived on the other side of the river. The
prosperity of the town probably depended on the silver and leadmines
nearby which were worked up till Elizabethan times. On the left of the
entrance avenue is one of the old town gates which was later turned into
a lime-kiln. Passing through a gate, one comes on the right to a tower,
known as the Town Hall, a two-storey castle-like building of around 1400
used as a church and a council chamber, and the seat of an ecclesiastical
court. The ground floor is unusual in that half of the ceiling is vaulted
with ribbed arches, and half is barrel-vaulted, and also in that it has two
entrance doorways. There was once a gallery on the ground floor. Beside
the tower is a 15th century nave-and-chancel church with remnants of
a tower at the western end. Further down the avenue, to the left, are
(*i*) ruins of the Augustinian church, built around 1400, (*ii*) a strip of
curtain wall with a tower at the northern end, which seems to have been
used as a fortification though it may have been attached to the Augustinian
church, (*iii*) remains of another church and (*iv*) a tower house built
probably by the Suttons or by the Fitzhenrys in the 15th or 16th century.
The old port sanded up probably around 1600, but remains of the harbour
wall, built of large stones, can still be seen at the river's edge. A private
house nearby incorporates another tower house.
JRSAI 26, 1896, 192 and 52, 1922, 24; Leask, Churches III, 180; Journal
of the Old Wexford Society 1, 1968, 35

DUNBRODY (192) Cistercian Abbey

MAP 8 N 18
OS½" 23S.71.15

*Access : Across field. Before crossing field, get key from William Ryan, who
lives 150 yards away—first turn right from the Abbey in an easterly direction.
Signposted*

The Abbey was founded for the Cistercians between 1175 and 1178 by Hervey de Montemarisco, uncle of Strongbow and Marshal of Henry II, and he became its first abbot. But the work of building was largely carried out by Hervey's nephew, Herlewin, Bishop of Leighlin. The ownership of the Abbey was much disputed throughout the 14th century, but in 1342 it was finally decided that it belonged to St Mary's Abbey in Dublin from whence the original Cistercian monks had probably come to Dunbrody. During the course of this dispute, Philip de Churchill, the abbot, was deposed because of insubordination, and because he refused to submit to an inspection of his monastery by monks from St Mary's Abbey in Dublin. Edward III seized the Abbey and its possessions in 1348 because the monks refused to exercise hospitality or give alms. Shortly afterwards it was made independent of St Mary's, and in 1374 Gregory XI allowed the abbot wear a mitre and raised him to the dignity of being a Lord of Parliament. In 1537 the Abbey was taken over by Henry VIII, and in 1544 formally surrendered to Alexander Devereux, the first Reformation bishop of Ferns. In 1546 Henry VIII granted the Abbey to Sir Osborne Itchingham. The church is one of the longest Cistercian churches in Ireland—195 feet, but it is austere in its ornamentation. The church has a nave, choir and transepts, and there are three large and two small windows in the east wall. Round arches leading to the transepts were partially blocked up when the tower was added in the 15th century. The nave and side aisles were probably built some time after the chancel and transepts, and the south wall of the nave fell in 1852. The corbels at the bottom of the arches of the nave are some of the few decorated stones in the church. Some of the domestic buildings survive, including a book-store and chapter room on the east side and the refectory and kitchen on the south side.

JRSAI 26, 1896, 336; Leask, Churches II, 83

ENNISCORTHY Castle *Fig. 80*

MAP 8 P 17
OS½" 23S.97.40

Access: Direct. Open June–September 10 a.m.–9 p.m. and October–May 2 p.m.–5.30 p.m. Signposted. Entrance fee charged.

The original castle was founded either by a Prendergast or, less likely, by a Rochford some time between 1232 and 1240. This castle was later replaced by the present structure, which probably uses the same ground plan as the older castle, and which was built by Sir Henry Wallop between 1586 and 1595. The poet Edmund Spenser held a lease of the castle for three days in 1581. The castle has four storeys, and rounded turrets at the corner (one of which starts above ground). It now contains a museum displaying a collection of local items of interest from the Stone Age up to the present, as well as showing the crafts of the region and the role of the people of the area in the famous rebellion of 1798.

JRSAI 34, 1904, 380 and 35, 1905, 74 and 177; Arch Journal 93, 1937, 176
Collier, The Castle Museum, Enniscorthy

FERNS (133 and 521) Churches and Castle

MAP 8 Q 16
OS½" 19T.01.50

Access: Through stile or over wall into field in each case. Partially signposted

The Churches

The modern road runs through the area comprising the old monastery founded by the King of Leinster for St Maedhog in the 6th century, and which was plundered by the Vikings in 930. In 1152 the ill-starred Dermot

Fig. 80. Enniscorthy Castle, Co Wexford, rebuilt around 1586. It now serves as a museum.

MacMurrough Kavanagh founded an Abbey, but it was burned down two years later. He rebuilt it in 1160 and handed it over to the Augustinians. Portions of this church still survive; they are the ruins furthermost from the road, and can be recognized by the characteristic tower at the west end of the church which is square at the bottom and becomes round higher up. The north wall of the church still stands, and the chancel once had barrel vaulting as at Cormac's Chapel in Cashel. To the north of the chancel is the sacristy, from where a stairs rises to a room where the sacristan lived and to another room over the chancel. Only the foundations of the cloister remain to the south of the church. The present Church of Ireland church incorporated parts of the Cathedral which was probably built by John St John, the first Anglo-Norman bishop of the Diocese (1223-43) and which was burned in 1577. Seventy five yards to the east is another 13th century building which may have acted as the monks choir. In the churchyard of the present church there are some plain High Crosses, and a fragment of a thin cross-shaft which is supposed to mark the grave of Dermot MacMurrough Kavanagh. Standing on a ledge just to the north of the road is St Peter's Church, a nave-and-chancel church whose original nave extended much further westwards. As the church was not mentioned in a list of the major buildings in Ferns in 1537, it is suspected that the present church was built after that date, but incorporated parts of other churches. The Romanesque window on the interior of the south wall may have come from the Augustinian church, while the pointed external part may have come from the Cathedral.

78th Annual Report of Commissioners of Public Works 1909-10, 11; Leask, Churches I, 163 and II, 99

The Castle

The castle was probably built by one of the sons of Maurice Fitzgerald or by William, Earl Marshall, the Justiciar, around 1200, though the earliest reference to it is 1232, and some of the architectural details would even suggest a building date around the middle of the 13th century, when William de Valence owned it. The O'Toole clan took it in 1331, but it was re-taken shortly afterwards by Bishop Charnell. By 1359 it was held

by the Countess of Athol, and probably some time during the 15th century it was taken by the Irish. Lord Grey took the castle during the Rebellion of 'Silken Thomas' in 1536, but the MacMurroughs remained wardens of the castle until John Travers took it over in the name of the King in 1550. In 1583 the Mastersons became Constables of the Castle, but they became sufficiently friendly to the native Irish to hold it for the Confederate Catholics in 1641. The castle surrendered to Cromwell in 1649, but after the Restoration of Charles II it was sold to Thomas Kiernan of Dublin who bequeathed it to the Donovans, who kept it till recent years. Originally the castle formed a square, with large rounded towers at each corner, but only half of the castle still survives. There were three storeys inside, and some 13th century trefoil-headed windows are still preserved. On the first floor there was a circular chapel lighted by two of these windows and covered by a vault supported by corbels in the shape of capitals.
JRSAI 40, 1910, 297 and 360; Arch Journal 93, 1937, 170; Leask, Castles 49

NEW ROSS (443) St Mary's Church

MAP 8 N 17
OS½″ 23S.72.27

Access : Direct to graveyard. Key obtainable from the sexton, Mr James Condell who lives in the house beside the church gate. Not signposted
St Mary's church was founded probably by William, Earl Marshall and his wife Isabella between 1207 and 1220, and is possibly the largest medieval parish church in Ireland. It had a nave, chancel, and two transepts, but a 19th century church now occupies the site of the nave and the crossing. The south transept may have been built later than the other parts of the church. There are three graceful lancet windows in the east gable, and a number of other lancet windows still survive in other parts of the church. Bishop Patrick Barrett who restored the south transept in the 15th century moved from Ferns and established St Mary's as the diocesan church. The original tower of the church fell in 1763. In the church is a slab bearing a mask and a cross with the inscription 'ISABEL: LAEGN...'—Probably Isabel of Leinster; as Isabel was buried in Monmouthshire, this may be a cenotaph. There are other medieval tombs both in the graveyard and inside the modern church.
Leask, Churches II, 85

RATHMACKNEE (434) Castle

MAP 8 Q 18
OS½″ 23T.03.14

Access : Up a lane and then along a path. Signposted
A castle probably erected by John Rosseter who was made Seneschal of the Liberties of Wexford in 1451, and whose family remained Catholics although they recognized Henry VIII in the 16th century. The tower stands in the south-eastern corner of a well-preserved bawn. The tower is five storeys high, and has battlements which are typical of the 15th and 16th centuries in Ireland. The bawn wall is about 4 feet thick and 24 feet high, with a round turret at the north-eastern corner and a less prominent square one at the north-western corner. It is almost complete, and gives a very good idea of what the tower-houses and bawns of the 15th and 16th centuries in Ireland looked like.
JRSAI 83, 1953, 37; Leask, Castles 101.

RATHUMNEY (229) Castle

MAP 8 N 18
OS½″ 23 S.77.16

Access : Along private path to farmyard which stands beside the castle. Signposted
Rathumney is a hall-castle of a type common in the 13th and 14th centuries. The centre of the building was occupied by a hall, two storeys high, off which opened living rooms with fireplaces. There is a tower at the south-eastern corner of the castle. Practically all the decorated stonework has been removed, but gently-rounded arches still span the larger door and

window openings. Little is known of the history of the castle other than that it was probably built by the Prendergasts.

SLADE (429) Castle *Fig. 81*

MAP 8 N 19
OS½″ 23X.75.98

Access: Direct. If locked, key is obtainable from Mr Rice who lives around the corner. Signposted

Situated beside a little fishing harbour, Slade castle was built in two stages. The first was the tower at the northern end, built probably by one of the Laffan family in the late 15th or early 16th century. The tower is 56 feet high and is battlemented, and there is a fireplace and a cupboard in a room on the third storey. The second stage was the addition of a house in the 16th or early 17th century. The house is not as high as the tower and has simple moulded windows on the first floor. At the east end of the house is an annexe with a corbelled roof, possibly associated with the manufacture of salt in the 18th century.
JRSAI 81, 1951, 198

TACUMSHANE (457) Windmill

MAP 8 Q 18
OS½″ 23T. 08.07

Access: Up laneway beside shop. Key obtainable from Michael Meyler in the nearby shop

This is one of the last two intact windmills in Ireland. It was built by the millwright Nicholas Moran in 1846, was re-thatched in 1908, used up till 1936 and was reconstructed in 1952. The cap of the windmill, which is thatched, could revolve, and the arms of the mill turned two mill-querns. The windmill is not worked at all nowadays.

Fig. 81. Slade Castle, Co Wexford. 16th/17th century.

TINTERN (506) Cistercian Abbey

MAP 8 N 18
OS½" 23S.79.10

Access: Through gate and half a mile up avenue. Church is not accessible at present because of its dangerous condition. Signposted

During a stormy crossing to England once, William, the Earl Marshall, made a vow that he would found a church in Ireland if he survived the voyage. He survived, and fulfilled his vow around 1200 by founding Tintern Abbey, called after its more famous counterpart in Wales from whence its first monks came. The church consisted of a nave and aisles, a chancel and transepts. The aisles have disappeared though a chapel on the east wall of the south aisle is still preserved and contains some nice sculptural details. The chancel was converted into living quarters after 1541, and a number of mullioned windows were inserted. The tower, which had been added to the church in the 15th century, was also converted into residential quarters. The nave and tower were occupied up to a few years ago, and the job of removing the later work in order to reveal the original state of the church has already started.
Leask, Churches II, 121

VINEGAR HILL (392) Windmill

MAP 8 P 17
OS½" 23S.99.40

Access: Up path to top of hill. Signposted

The stump of an old windmill on top of a hill overlooking the town of Enniscorthy and the surrounding countryside. During the Rebellion of 1798, the Irish insurgents encamped on the hill and flew their banner from the windmill. But General Lake stormed the hill on June 21st with 13,000 men; the flag was torn down and replaced by the English Royal Standard. Only the shell of the windmill remains.

WEXFORD (445) St Selskar's Church

MAP 8 Q 17
OS½" 23T.05.22

Access: Through graveyard. Key with lavatory attendant (!) nearby. Not signposted

St Selskar's church was founded possibly by the Roche family for the Canons Regular of St Augustine and dedicated to SS Peter and Paul. The name may be a corruption of the word 'Sepulchre' as tradition says that the church was founded by a lady who thought that her betrothed had been killed on a Crusade to the church of the Holy Sepulchre in Jerusalem, and who joined the monastery she had founded. When her intended returned from the wars alive, he found his bride already a nun, and retired to a monastery himself. John, Bishop of Ferns, held a synod here in 1240. In 1418 John Talbot granted the chapel of St Nicholas of Carrig to the Priory. While founded in the 13th century, the parts of the nave which survive are of 15th century date, though the tower may have been built in the 14th century. The ruined church beside the tower was built in the 19th century.
JRSAI 25, 1895, 369; Leask, Churches III, 56;
Journal of the Old Wexford Society 2, 1969, 11

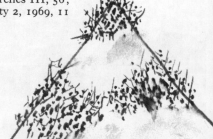

AGHOWLE (137) Church

MAP 8 P 15
OS½" 19S.93.69

Access : Quarter of a mile down lane to cemetery. Signposted

A long rectangular 12th century church. The west doorway is flat-headed but has Romanesque moulding on the outside and a round arch inside, and also holes which held the bars to lock the door. Two round-headed windows in the east wall have hood-mouldings on the outside supported by pillars. There are also some old gravestones, a water font and an unfinished granite cross. Little is known about the history of the place other than that the monastery was possibly founded in the early 6th century by St Finian of Clonard.

JCHAS 18, 1912, 75; JRSAI 55, 1925, 66; Leask, Churches I, 85

BALTINGLASS (203) Abbey

MAP 8 P 14
OS½" 16S.87.89

Access : Through parish church grounds. Signposted

In 1148 Dermot MacMurrough brought Cistercian monks here from Mellifont to found a new monastery which he called 'The Valley of Salvation', and Baltinglass in turn was the mother-house of a number of other Cistercian foundations including Jerpoint, Co. Kilkenny. The monastery was the centre of a number of disputes in the 13th century, one with the Archbishop of Dublin, and another in which the monks were accused of harbouring 'felons against the English'. In 1377 Abbot Peter was awarded damages because two men had diverted water from his mill. After the Suppression in 1541, the monastery buildings and lands passed to Sir Thomas Eustace, a Catholic loyalist. In 1604 it passed to the Harringtons, in 1617 to Sir Charles Wilmot and in 1624 to Sir Thomas Raper. The church consisted of a nave with aisles, chancel and two transepts, and building was probably complete by 1170. The south arcade of choir and nave which remains is slightly later in date, and has alternating round and square pillars supporting capitals with peculiarly Irish motifs. The three west windows are 12th century, but the three east windows and the tower (now housing carved fragments and some medieval tiles from the Abbey) are 19th century. Joining the south aisle to the cloister is a 12th century doorway, while excavations in 1931 brought to light a north door in the aisle, parts of the original cloister (now rebuilt) and an early tower which blocked the eastern two-thirds of the transept arches. The decorative stonework at Baltinglass shows an interesting fusion of Cistercian and Irish Romanesque architecture.

JCKAS 5, 1908, 379; Arch. Journal 88, 1931, 380; Leask, Churches II, 26

BALTINGLASS HILL (328) Burial Mound and Hill-fort

MAP 8 P 14
OS½" 16S.88.89

Access : Up through fields, over ditches and across boggy hillside to top of hill. Not signposted

On top of the hill there is a double ring of stones which once retained a mound of stones. At the most northerly point of the ring there is a Passage-Grave with short passage, and a stone basin bearing faint decoration. Towards the south-south-west of the ring there is another Passage-Grave, this time with five recesses off a central chamber, and two stones decorated with spirals. The third and earliest grave is in the north-western portion of the ring, overlain by the stones of the inner ring. There are also other minor structures. The Passage-Graves were built in the Late Stone Age, but in the Early Iron Age (500 B.C.–A.D. 500 ?) the ring of stones was surrounded on the outside by a large defensive stone wall, while further down the hill-slope are two further concentric stone walls which probably also belong to the Iron Age fortificatory system.

PRIA 46 C 1941, 221

CASTLERUDDERY (441-442) Stone Circle and Motte

MAP 8 P 14
OS½″ 16S.91.94

Stone Circle
Access : Through field-gate into field. Signposted
A stone circle, 100 feet in diameter, with an interior and exterior facing
of stones with a bank in between. Some very large boulders are used in
this circle, and some are lying down.
JRSAI 75, 1945, 266

Motte
Access : Across bank with barbed wire fence into field. Not signposted
A motte surrounded by a ditch which is rounded at the southern side
but squared at the north. Further to the south is a raised area, which may
also have been used like a bailey for defensive purposes.

CASTLETIMON (304) Ogham Stone

MAP 8 R 14
OS½″ 16T.30.86

Access : Directly beside road. Not signposted
An Ogham stone, placed in a niche beside the road, bearing the inscription
NETA-CARI NETA CAGI.
JRSAI 3, 1854-5, 187 and 40, 1910, 61; Macalister, Corpus I (1945) 51

CROSSOONA (418) Ring-fort

MAP 8 P 14
OS½″ 16S.93.89

*Access : One-third of a mile up a laneway, then through gate, up another
laneway for about 300 yards and fort is on right. Not signposted*
A ring-fort with bank and ditch, and the interior covered in trees. Not
worth a visit.

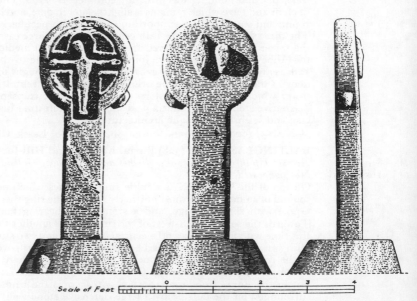

Scale of Feet

Fig. 82. St Valery's Cross, Fassaroe, Co Wicklow.
Probably 12th century.

Fig. 18. The Dwyer-MacAllister Cottage, Derry-namuck, Co. Wicklow.

MAP 8 R 13
OS½″ 16 O.26.10

DOWNSMILL (135) Church

Access: Through gate into field. Not signposted
A small medieval church, possibly late 16th century in date. The east gable has a small 16th century window, and there is a belfry on the west gable. The interior is covered in brambles.

MAP 8 P 14
OS½″ 16S.96.91

DWYER-MACALLISTER COTTAGE (449) Derrynamuck *Fig. 18*

Access: Up path for about 300 yards, through farmyard. Signposted
The famous rebel, Michael Dwyer, was trapped in this cottage by the English in 1799, together with a small group of men. One of these men, Samuel MacAllister, drew the fire upon himself and was killed, but in this way enabled Dwyer to escape. The cottage is two-roomed, with rope chairs, a settle bed, a table with wooden vessels and a churn, a roasting spit, cooking utensils and pikes of the period displayed inside.

MAP 8 R 13
OS½″ 16 O.24.18

FASSAROE (337) St Valery's Cross *Fig. 82*

Access: Directly beside road. Signposted
A small granite cross, allegedly brought here from elsewhere. It has an unpierced ring at the top, with a representation of the Crucifixion on one side and two worn human heads on the other. Its date is uncertain, but it is probably 12th century.
JRSAI 88, 1958, 101

MAP 8 Q 14
OS½″ 16T.
10/13.96

GLENDALOUGH (134) Churches, Round Tower etc. *Figs. 83 and 84*
Signposted

The monastery in the 'Glen of the Two Lakes' founded by St Kevin in the 6th century was one of the most famous religious centres in Early Christian Ireland. The old Irish annals often refer to it, telling of the deaths of its abbots and illustrious monks or of the raids the Vikings made on it. After St Kevin himself, the most illustrious name associated with Glendalough is that of St Laurence O'Toole—the only canonised Irish saint—who was raised from Abbot of Glendalough to be Archbishop of Dublin in 1163. Also in 1163 one of the many fires which occasionally raged at Glendalough struck and did great damage to the churches. On arriving in Ireland, the Normans appropriated the monastery, and then united it with the See of Dublin in 1214. After this Glendalough declined and fell into decay, until restored in the years 1875-80 and again in 1911-12. The monastery which St Kevin founded was probably centred around the Upper Lake, but when the community became so large some centuries after the foundation, the monastery was moved further down the valley to the area around the present Cathedral. The monuments are scattered over a mile and a half in the valley, and they are described here going from the top of the valley towards the bottom.

1. Temple-na-Skellig
Access : Only approachable by boat
A small rectangular church with twin-light east window, and which originally had a flat-headed doorway. The church has been partly reconstructed. West of the church is a platform where wattle and daub houses may once have been placed.

2. St Kevin's Bed
Access : Only by boat, and up or down cliff-face by ladder
A small man-made cave in a cliff-face about 25 feet above the level of the Upper Lake. Although it is said to be St Kevin's living quarters, it may be a Bronze Age burial place much older than St Kevin.
JRSAI 67, 1937, 290; Antiquity 11, 1937, 350

3. St Kevin's Cell
Access : Up path
The foundations of a small bee-hive hut, traditionally said to be St Kevin's house.

4. Reefert Church
Access : Up path
A nave-and-chancel church (11th century?) with flat-headed west doorway and a number of round-headed windows. Note the projecting corbel-stones at the exterior corners which held the wooden rafters. Outside are some cross-inscribed grave slabs.

5. Site of Church
Access : Along path
A platform beside a stream. The foundations of a church can be seen on the platform.

6-8. Crosses and Stone Fort
Access : Along path into field
A stone fort and two stone crosses standing near each other.

9. Stone Cross
Access : In field very near car-park
A simple cross with the arms partly damaged.

10. Cross
Access : Over wall and down into field
A small cross with incised grooves forming another cross on the face.

11. St Mary's Church
Access : Across stile, through field and across another stile
A church where the chancel was added later to the original nave (10th–11th century ?) The west doorway has a cross inscribed on the under side of the lintel. The east window has Romanesque moulding on the exterior.

The following are situated in or close to the main cemetery beside the main road:

Gateway
The Gateway—the only surviving example in Ireland—was presumably the main entrance to the monastic enclosure. The steps up to it are modern. It consists of a square building with round arches in the north and south walls, and originally there was another storey above it. A large cross is engraved on a large stone on the right, inside the second arch.

12. Round Tower
A very good example of a Round Tower with a height of about 100 feet and with the door about 10 feet above the ground. The conical roof was re-built in the last century, but with the original stones.

Fig. 83. Map of the monastic ruins at Glendalough, Co Wicklow.

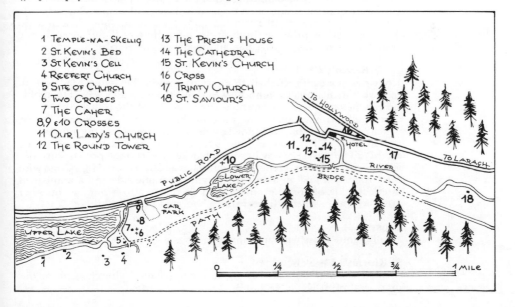

*Fig. 84. Three figures sculpted over the doorway
of the Priest's House, Glendalough, Co Wicklow.
The top part is now missing. 12th century.*

13. The Priest's House *Fig. 84*
A tiny rectangular building of unknown use with the remains of a Romanesque arch on the exterior of the east wall and with a carving over the
south door (a part is now missing) showing a robed figure in the centre
and a figure kneeling on either side of him. Built probably in the 12th
century.

14. The Cathedral
The largest church in Glendalough, it has a nave and chancel as well as
a sacristy. The lower portion of the nave wall with large square blocks, is
the oldest part (11th century?), and the antae and a flat-headed west doorway also belong to the oldest period of the church. The upper parts of the
nave were built later, and at an even later stage (12th century) the chancel
was built, necessitating the construction of a Romanesque chancel arch.
The sacristy was probably built at the same time as the chancel. In the
church are some Early Christian and medieval grave-slabs.

15. St Kevin's Church
Known as St Kevin's Kitchen, this is a nave-and-chancel church (11th–12th
century?) with a small Round Tower above the west doorway. The roof is
entirely of stone, and is prevented from sagging in the centre by the wall
of a small chamber above the nave of the church. The Round Tower,
which acted as a belfry, was added to the church later. Only the foundations
now remain of the chancel, and beside it still stands the stone-roofed
sacristy. The west doorway has been blocked up, and the present entrance
is through the chancel arch. In the church is a 12th century High Cross with
the Crucifixion and an abbot (St Kevin ?) on one side and a number of
interlacing motifs on the others, and there are also a number of other
architectural fragments from various churches preserved there.

Cross
A tall granite cross with an unpierced ring.

St Kieran's Church
A small and not very interesting nave-and-chancel church lying to the
south-east of St Kevin's Church.

16. Cross-slab

Access : Just east of the Royal Hotel, at junction of road to the Wicklow Gap
An upright slab carved with one large and one small Latin cross in relief.

17. Trinity Church

Access : Over stile, down steps into field beside road
A nave-and-chancel church (11th–12th century?) with both west and south doorways. The south doorway is round-headed. The west doorway is flat-headed and leads to a small rectangular area which was added later. Above this rectangular area once rose a Round Tower, but this was blown down in 1818. The chancel arch is simple, the windows round-headed and pointed. Note the corbel-stones on the exterior corners for holding the wooden rafters.

18. St Saviour's Priory

Access : Along path on the far side of the stream from St Kevin's Kitchen for about half a mile, then down into field on left where church is situated in a grove of trees
A nave and chancel church containing the best Romanesque decoration to be seen in Glendalough. The church is said to have been founded by St Lawrence O'Toole in 1162, but it may have been built a little before that date. The chancel arch and the east window both bear a fine selection of Romanesque geometric, animal and human face motifs, but unfortunately some of the stones were wrongly replaced when the church was heavily reconstructed around 1875. Much of the nave was reconstructed when a new building was added to the north of it during the later medieval period. In this addition, a stairs rises to a second floor above the chancel.
Official Guide; Price, in Essays and Studies presented to Eoin MacNeill, ed. Ryan (1940) 244; Leask, Churches I, 34, 71, 74, 76, 96 and 159

KILCOOLE (267) Church

MAP 8 R 13
OS½″ 16 0.30.08

Access : Down a laneway. Key obtainable from Thomas Delaney, Seaview, Kilcoole
A nave-and-chancel church probably built in the 12th century. The chancel probably once had a steep-pitched stone roof with a small attic room over the chancel. The nave has a small round-headed window in the south wall. The western portion of the church was added later as a two-storey living quarters. There is a good collection of eighteenth century tombstones in the graveyard.

KILCRONEY (417) Church

MAP 8 R 13
OS½″ 16 0.24.17

Access : Through St Joseph's Home of the Brothers of St John of God at Kilcroney. By following the signpost for 'Farm' you will come past the church. Not signposted
The church was dedicated to St Cróine, about whom nothing is known. It stands on a plinth which may have belonged to an older church, and the present flat-headed south-doorway may have stood in the west wall of the older church before it was put in its present position when the whole church was heavily rebuilt at some unknown date. In 1530 the church was occupied by monks from St Mary's Abbey in Dublin.
JRSAI 59, 1929, 179

Going mountain-climbing?—Don't go alone

KILLINCARRIG Fortified House

MAP 8 R 13
OS½″ 16 0.29.11

Access: Through stile and field, then over fence into another field. Not signposted
One of the few surviving houses of the early 17th century in Ireland, this is an L-shaped house which was the first to be taken by Cromwell on his march from Dublin to Wexford in 1649. On the ground floor it has a main hall with a fire-place, a kitchen at right angles and a stairs in a tower projecting from one side of the hall. The house has 23 single or double mullioned windows, and two chimneys.
Leask, in Studies in Building History ed. Jope (1961) 246

KINDLESTOWN (323) Castle

MAP 8 R 13
OS½″ 16 0.28.12

Access: Through gate into field. Not signposted
One of the few examples of a type of halled castle used in the 13th and 14th centuries, this castle was probably built by the Archbolds in the 13th century. Although rather ruined, sufficient remains to show that the ground floor was roofed by a continuous barrel vault, and imprints of the original plank shuttering can still be seen. The upper storey was divided into a number of rooms with large or small windows.

LEMONSTOWN (419) 'Mote'

MAP 8 P 13
OS½″ 16N.90.05

Access: Over a number of fields. Not signposted
This round mound situated on a hill-top surrounded by a circle of trees may have originally been a Bronze Age burial mound (possibly with a Passage-Grave underneath?). But probably in Early Christian times it appears to have been fortified by a bank and ditch outside it. A Bronze-Age Food-Vessel was found in the mound in 1818.
JRSAI 63, 1933, 48

MOYLISHA (368) 'Labbanasighe' Wedge-shaped Gallery Grave

MAP 8 P 15
OS½″ 19S.93.68

Access: Up a laneway for 300 yards, then turn left at top, and two fields further on there are trees on the right and beside them, in an enclosure, is the tomb. Not signposted
A wedge-shaped Gallery-Grave in a mound of stones which was 4 feet high and 42 feet long. The tomb itself consists of a short entrance chamber, and a longer burial chamber behind it. Around the tomb itself there is a setting of stones placed in the form of a U. A mould for a bronze spearhead was found in the tomb, suggesting a date of about 1,000 B.C., but it may be even earlier than that.
JRSAI 76, 1946, 119

PIPER'S STONES Athgreany (416) Stone Circle

MAP 8 P 13
OS½″ 16N.93.03

Access: Across fence into field. Signposted
A stone circle still consisting of 13 granite boulders, some standing, some lying. The date of the circle is unknown. It got its name because 'bag-pipe' music is said to be played on the spot by the fairies.
JRSAI 61, 1931, 128

RAHEEN-AN-CHLUIG (262) Church

MAP 8 R 13
OS½″ 16 0.28.17

Access: Through Raheen Park housing estate, up lane and into field. Not signposted
A small rectangular church, built probably in the 12th or 13th century, with the remains of a door in the south wall and round-headed windows in the east and west gable.

RATHGALL (422) Hill-Fort

MAP 8 P 15
OS½″ 19S.90.73

Access: Along path for 100 yards. Signposted
A fine stone fort built on a small hillock. There are three concentric stone walls with ditches outside them placed at various distances apart. Recent excavations have shown that the innermost wall was a kind of citadel, and was built later than the other walls; it dates to the medieval period or later. The fort was probably built in the early centuries of the Christian era. It has been tentatively identified as a seat of the kings of South Leinster.
JRSAI 41, 1911, 138; Antiquity 44, 1970, 51

ST MARK'S CROSS (280) Blessington

MAP 8 P 13
OS½″ 16N.98.13

Access: Direct to cemetery in which cross stands. Signposted
A granite cross set in a square base. The cross is tall and thin, and the arms are proportionately wide in relation to the small unpierced ring. Tradition says that it had another pair of arms! Although called St Mark's Cross, it was known as St Baoithin's Cross in the 19th century. It originally stood some distance away at Burgage, but was moved to its present site when it was in danger of being submerged while the Liffey valley nearby was being flooded for a hydro-electric scheme.
JCKAS 12, 1935-45, 137

SEEFIN (317) Passage-Grave

MAP 8 Q 13
OS½″ 16 0.07.16

Access: Up about 700 feet through heather to top of mountain. The best approach is from near Kilbride military camp. Not signposted
A Passage-Grave under a mound of stones. The chamber is approached with two stones bearing concentric diamond-like motifs resembling the human face. The burial chamber has two side-chambers on each side and one at the back. One roof stone of the chamber near the entrance bears a decoration consisting of five lines. The corbelled roof of the chamber is incomplete, and entrance is most commonly effected through a hole in the top of it. The grave has probably been open for a long time, as an Early Christian equal-armed cross can be seen on one of the roofing stones. Being situated on top of a mountain, a climb up to it is worth it for the view alone.
JRSAI 62, 1932, 153; 63, 1933, 46; 67, 1937, 313 and 93, 1963, 85

THREECASTLES (491) Castle

MAP 8 Q 13
OS½" 16 0.01.16

Access : Through gate into field. Not signposted

A rectangular castle with a barrel vault at the top of the third storey. There is a well-preserved fire-place in the second storey, and a turret stair leading to the roof. The castle is alleged to have been built in the early 14th century, but it could well be later. The English and Brian O'Toole defeated the Fitzgeralds here in a battle in 1547. Two other castles are said to have existed in the neighbourhood, but nothing remains of these.

MAP 8 R 14
OS½" 16T.31.94

WICKLOW

Founded by the Vikings in the 9th century, the town was granted to the Fitz Geralds in Norman times, though the Byrnes held sway there for a considerable time up to 1542, and burned the town in 1580.

Romanesque Doorway

In the 18th century Church of Ireland church of St Thomas, a fine Romanesque doorway of mid-12th century date has been inserted in the porch, though some of its stones have been wrongly re-set. It comes from a medieval church which was dedicated to St Thomas, a 12th century Bishop of Glendalough, and some of its features resemble those at St Saviour's Priory in Glendalough, built about the same time.

Leask, Churches I, 160

Franciscan Friary

Access : Through Parish Priest's garden. Not signposted

The O'Tooles and the O'Byrnes founded a monastery here for the Conventual Franciscans in 1279 in gratitude for a victory won over the Fitzgeralds. The monastery was granted to Henry Harrington in 1564. All that remains are a portion of the nave, the south transept with a 13th century window, and the arch of a 15th century tower.

JRSAI 58, 1928, 143

Aisle	A side division, usually of the nave of a church
Anta, plural Antae	Projections of the north and south walls of a church beyond the east and west gables
Arcade	A series of arches on pillars or columns
Arch	A concave construction of stones supporting each other and spanning a space
Architrave	A moulding above or on either side of a doorway
Bailey	An enclosure beside a castle or at the foot of a motte
Bank	A ridge of earth
Barbican	A building defending the gate or entrance of a castle
Barrel Vault	A vault with semi-cylindrical roof
Bartizan	An overhanging defensive turret
Bastion	A tower projecting from the wall of a fortification
Bawn	A fortified enclosure attached to a castle
Bee-hive hut	A small stone hut, shaped like a bee-hive, with stones in a circle piled on each other in corbel technique until they reach a point at the top
Bell-cot	An ornamental structure at the top of a gable to contain bells
Boss	A raised knob
Burgundian Arch	An arch with a flattened top
Cairn	A mound of stones
Capital	The head of a column, usually supporting an arch
Capstone	A stone covering a megalithic tomb
Causeway	A stone pathway
Cenotaph	A monument to someone buried elsewhere
Chancel	The east end of a church where the altar stands; sometimes reserved for priests
Chapter Room	A room in a monastery where the monks assembled for meetings, readings etc
Chevaux-de-Frise	Stones placed in the ground with their points upwards; designed to hinder access

Choir	Same as Chancel
Choir-stalls	Seats placed in a row in the choir of a church
Cloister	A covered passage, forming a square, giving access to various parts of a monastery
Cloister-garth	An open square enclosure surrounded by the cloister
Colonnade	A range of columns placed at intervals
Columbarium	A round building in which doves were housed
Column	A round stone or stones used for support
Corbel	A projecting stone
Corbel Technique	A method of roofing whereby stones are placed in a circle, with each row oversailing each other until they meet at the top
Court Cairn	A type of Megalithic Tomb—see Figs. 1-2
Courtyard	An open space inside a castle
Crenellation	The stepped pattern in battlements
Crossing	That part of a church where nave, choir and transepts meet
Cruciform	Shaped like a cross
Crypt	An underground cell or chapel, often forming part of foundations
Cupola	A dome
Curtain Wall	A high wall surrounding a castle, often having towers at intervals
Ditch	A trench
Dolmen	A type of Megalithic Tomb—see Figs. 1, 19 and 79
Domestic Buildings	Those buildings in a monastery where the monks lived, worked, ate and slept
Donjon	A tall tower which acted as a final retreat
Dove-cot	A round building used to house doves
Drawbridge	A wooden bridge giving access to a castle across a moat, and which can be pulled up to prevent people entering the castle
Earthwork	Anything made by the throwing up of earth
Foliate	With leaves
Forecourt	An open semi-circular court placed in front of something such as a megalithic tomb
Fresco	A wall-painting incorporated into the plaster while it is still wet
Gable	The pointed end-wall of a building
Gate-house	A building through which access is gained
Gazebo	An ornamental round house, usually part of a garden
Gothic	A style of architecture using the pointed arch and common from the late 12th century
High Cross	A tall cross of stone—see Figs. 8, 38 and 62-3
Hood-moulding	A narrow band of stone projecting out over a door or window
Interlacing	Bands laced together
Keep	A tower
Kerb-stones	Stones at the edge of a mound to keep it in place
Lancet	A tall narrow window
Lavabo	A building containing water for washing
Lintel	A flat stone covering a doorway
Machicolation	An opening in the floor of a parapet or turret through which defenders could drop things on intruders
Manor	Land kept by a nobleman for his own use
Martello Tower	A round tower erected on the coast for protection against sea invasion
Medallion	A round ornament

Megalithic Tomb	A tomb built with large stones—see Figs. 1-3
Misericord	Wooden Choir-stall
Moat	A ditch filled with water
Mortar	A cement of lime, sand and water used to bind stones together
Motte	A round mound, flattened on top, used by the Normans as a fortification
Moulding	An ornamental shaping
Mullion	An upright stone dividing a window into parts
'Murder-hole'	A hole in the ceiling of the entrance passage to a castle through which things could be dropped on intruders
Nave	The main western portion of a church
Niche	A recess in a wall
Ogee-headed window	A window topped by a curve which is partly convex and partly concave
Ogham	A type of script making use of notches and used for Old Irish inscriptions—see Fig. 6
Order	Receding lines of stones in a doorway
Oriel window	A projecting window
Palisade	A fence of pointed wooden stakes
Pantry	A food store
Parapet	A breast-high wall on a platform at the top of a building
Passage-Grave	A type of Megalithic Tomb—see Figs. 1 and 56
'Pattern'	A pilgrimage made to a holy place and the religious exercises involved in it
Pietà	A representation of the Virgin Mary holding the dead Christ across her lap
Pilaster	A column projecting from a wall
Piscina	A basin for washing sacred vessels and provided with a drain for water; it is usually placed in a niche in the wall
Plinth	Projecting part of a wall base immediately above the ground
Portal Dolmen	A type of Megalithic Tomb—see Figs. 1, 19 and 79
Portcullis	A sliding door in the form of a grid with points on the bottom and standing above a gate; it could be lowered in time of danger
Quatrefoil	Composing four segments of circles
Quernstone	A stone used for grinding corn
Radio Carbon	A modern scientific method of dating the age of an object by measuring its carbon content
Rampart	A mound or wall surrounding a fortified place
Recess	A niche or receding part in a wall
Refectory	A building in which people eat
Rock-cut	Cut into the rock
Romanesque	A style of architecture using rounded arches and common in the 12th century
Rood	A crucifix
Rood-screen	An ornamental partition dividing nave and choir in a church
Round Tower	A tall slender tower used as a bell-tower and as a refuge in time of danger—see Fig. 10
Runic	The alphabet or script used by Scandinavian Vikings
Sacristy	A building beside a church where vestments, sacred vessels etc were kept
Screen	A partition, usually dividing nave and chancel in a church
Scriptorium	A place or building used for writing
Sedilia	Wall-seats used for those celebrating the Mass

Sheela-na-Gig	Grotesque and often lewd small sculpture
Shingle	Thin wooden roof-slate
Souterrain	Underground passage built of stone
Stalagmite	A column-like mass of carbonate of lime formed on cave floors by water dripping from the cave roof
Star-shaped Fort	A fortification whose wall-projections give the ground-plan of the fort the shape of a star
Stucco	Ornamental plaster work
Transitional	A style of architecture containing elements of the Romanesque and Gothic architecture, and intermediate in time between the two styles
Transept	The side-arms of a church, running north and south
Trefoil	Composing three segments of circles
Triple-light	A term used to describe windows divided into three divisions
Tudor	A style of architecture used in the period 1485-1603 and later
Turret	A small tower
Twin-light	A term used to describe windows divided into two divisions
Tympanum	The semi-circular stonework panel enclosed within an arch over a doorway
Wall-walk	A wide space on top of a wall to allow people to pass
Weather-slated	A term used to describe the application of slates to a wall to make it rain-proof
Wedge-shaped Gallery Grave	A type of Megalithic Tomb—see Figs. 1 and 3
Wicker-work shuttering	Plaited twigs (or their imprint) placed against the mortar of a ceiling
Vault	An arch or series of arches forming a roof or ceiling
Vill	An assemblage of houses

Abbreviations/Journals

Arch Journal	The Archaeological Journal
CLAJ	The County Louth Archaeological Journal
JCHAS	Journal of the Cork Historical and Archaeological Society
JCKAS	Journal of the County Kildare Archaeological Society
JCLAS	Journal of the County Louth Archaeological Society
JGAHS	Journal of the Galway Archaeological and Historical Society
JNMAS	Journal of the North Munster Antiquarian Society
*JRSAI	Journal of the Royal Society of Antiquaries of Ireland
Kerry Arch Mag	The Kerry Archaeological Magazine
NMAJ	North Munster Antiquarian Journal
PRIA	Proceedings of the Royal Irish Academy
TRIA	Transactions of the Royal Irish Academy
UJA	Ulster Journal of Archaeology

*For the sake of convenience, the early volumes of this Journal with the titles 'Journal of the Kilkenny Archaeological Society', 'Journal of the Kilkenny and South East of Ireland Archaeological Society' and 'Journal of the Royal Historical and Archaeological Association of Ireland' are all quoted as JRSAI.

Abbreviations/Monographs

Dunraven, Irish Architecture   Dunraven, The Earl of, Notes on Irish Architecture (ed M
Stokes) Vol I (1875); Vol II (1877)

Leask, Castles   Leask, H G, Irish Castles and Castellated Houses (1964)

Leask, Churches I–III   Leask, H G, Irish Churches and Monastic Buildings Vol I—
The First Phases and the Romanesque (1955); Vol II—
Gothic Architecture to A.D. 1400 (1966); Vol III—Medieval
Gothic and Last Phases (1960)

Macalister, Corpus   Macalister, R A S, Corpus Inscriptionum Insularum
Celticarum Vol I (1945)

Megalithic Survey, Vol I   De Valéra, Ruaidhrí and Ó Nualláin, Seán, Survey of the
  Co Clare   Megalithic Tombs of Ireland, Vol I—Co Clare (1961)

Megalithic Survey, Vol II   De Valéra Ruaidhrí and Ó Nualláin, Seán, Survey of the
  Co Mayo   Megalithic Tombs of Ireland, Vol II—Co Mayo (1964)

Petrie, Round Towers   Petrie, G, The Ecclesiastical Architecture of Ireland anterior
to the Norman Invasion (1845)

Short Select Bibliography

General

Killanin, The Lord and Duignan, M V, The Shell Guide to Ireland 2nd edition revised 1969.
Evans, E E, Prehistoric and Early Christian Ireland—A Guide 1966
Illustrated Ireland Guide (Bord Fáilte) 1969
Raftery, Joseph, Prehistoric Ireland 1951
Ó Ríordáin, S P, Antiquities of the Irish Countryside (1968)
De Paor, Máire and Liam, Early Christian Ireland (1958)
Norman, E R and St Joseph, JKS, The Early Development of Irish Society (1969)
Gwynn, A and Hadcock, R N, Medieval Religious Houses—Ireland (1970)

Prehistoric

De Valéra, Ruaidhrí and Ó Nualláin, Seán, Survey of the Megalithic Tombs of Ireland,
Vol I—Co Clare (1961); Vol II—Co Mayo (1964)
De Valera, Ruaidhrí, The Court Cairns of Ireland, in PRIA 60 C 1960, 9
Ó Ríordáin, S P and Daniel, Glyn, Newgrange (1964)

Early Christian and Medieval:

Champneys, Ecclesiastical Architecture of Ireland 1910
Dunraven, The Earl of, Notes on Irish Architecture, 2 Vols 1875-77
Henry, F, Irish Art, 3 Vols 1965-70
Henry F, Irish High Crosses
Leask, H G, Irish Castles and Castellated Houses 1964
Leask, H G, Irish Churches and Monastic Buildings, 3 Vols 1955-66
Lionard, P, Early Irish Grave Slabs, PRIA 61 C 1961, 95
Macalister, R A S, Corpus Inscriptionum Insularum Celticarum 2 Vols 1945-49
Map of Monastic Ireland 2nd edition 1964
Petrie, The Ecclesiastical Architecture of Ireland anterior to the Norman Invasion 1845
Westropp, The Ancient Forts of Ireland, TRIA 31, 1896-1901, 579

History

The Course of Irish History ed Moody 1967
Curtis, E, History of Ireland (1968)

List of Selected Museums and Folk Parks

Museums

Ashford, Co Wicklow	Mount Usher Motor Car and Carriage Museum
Cork	Municipal Museum, Fitzgerald Park
Dublin	Chester Beatty Library, Shrewsbury Road
	Joyce Tower Museum, Sandycove
	Kilmainham Jail Museum, Kilmainham
	Municipal Museum, William Street
	National Museum of Ireland, Kildare Street and Merrion Street
	Trinity College Library
Edgeworthstown	Edgeworth Museum
Enniscorthy, Co Wexford	Castle Museum
Kilkenny	Rothe House Museum, Parliament Street
Kinsale, Co Cork	Civic Museum, Old Court House
Limerick	City Museum and Art Gallery, Pery Square
Loughrea, Co Galway	Ecclesiastical Museum beside Cathedral (key at Curate's House on other side of Cathedral)
Maynooth, Co Kildare	Ecclesiology and Physics Museum, St Patrick's College
Newgrange, Co Meath	Display Centre beside Car Park
Rossnowlagh, Co Donegal	Co Donegal Museum, Franciscan Friary
Sligo	Yeats Museum
Stradbally, Co Laois	Steam Engine Museum
Waterford	Reginald's Tower Museum
Wexford	Maritime Museum on old Lightship at Quayside
Youghal	Clock Tower Museum

Folk Parks

Bunratty, Co Clare
Glencolumbkille, Co Donegal

*Figures on the 12th century
St Manchan's Shrine
(National Museum of
Ireland, Dublin)*

The numbers refer to the pages

MAP SECTIONS

Legend

──────────	Trunk Roads
──────────	Link Roads
──────────	Other Roads
─ ─ ─ ─ ─ ─	County Boundary
▲ 497	National Monuments

Symbols

⊓	Megalithic Tomb
⬭	Stone Circle
⊥	Standing Stone
⚏	Ogham Stone
●	Stone or Earthen Fortification
†	Early Christian Church or Monastery including Romanesque
▲	Medieval Abbey or Friary
⛊	Early Christian and Medieval Remains
⊕	Medieval Church or Cathedral
⛫	Round Tower only
⊕	High Cross or Medieval Cross only
⛉	Castle
⬟	Motte
■	Miscellaneous

1

SCALE 10 20 MILES 30

10 20 30 40 Kilometres 50

Key to Sections and Counties

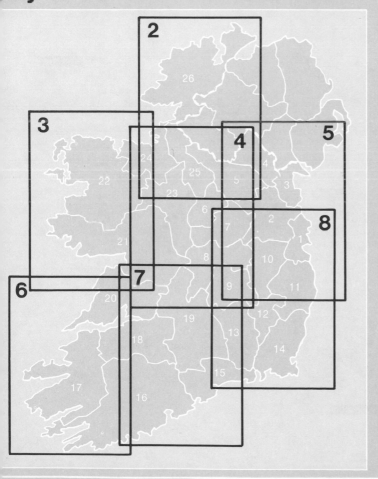

COUNTIES

1	DUBLIN
2	MEATH
3	LOUTH
4	MONAGHAN
5	CAVAN
6	LONGFORD
7	WESTMEATH
8	OFFALY
9	LAOIS
10	KILDARE
11	WICKLOW
12	CARLOW
13	KILKENNY
14	WEXFORD
15	WATERFORD
16	CORK
17	KERRY
18	LIMERICK
19	TIPPERARY
20	CLARE
21	GALWAY
22	MAYO
23	ROSCOMMON
24	SLIGO
25	LEITRIM
26	DONEGAL

G   H   J   K   L   M

1

✠ 24 Tory Island

25
Clonca Church
and Cross ▲
271   ✕ Crosses
Carndonagh Cross   ✕ Carrowmore
● Cooley
Cross

23
● 319
Doe Castle   Buncrana
⌂ 435
✠ Rathmullan
Priory ▲   ⊕ Fahan Cross-slab

Gortahork
Creeslough

Bunbeg

Aran Island

140
⊕ Grianan of Aileach ●
Burt Castle ⌂   ⊞ Derry

DONEGAL

Dunglow

Letterkenny
Conwal ✠
┬ 453

✠ Raphoe

463 ⊙
Beltany Stone Circle   ◉ Strabane

TYRONE

Glenties
Ballybofey

4

✠ Glencolumbkille
𝝅 139

● Omagh

Killybegs

Donegal

⌂ Donegal Castle
174 175

FERMANAGH

5

Creevykeel
Megalithic Tomb
𝝅   𝝅 477
338

◉ **Ballyshannon**

◉ Enniskillen

murray ✠ 117

6

Drumcliffe High Cross   Corracloona Megalithic Tomb
✠ 119   405
LEITRIM   ■ 508
Maheraghanrush   Sean Mac Diarmada's House
Sligo   Megalithic Tomb
Abbey 𝝅   377
433 ▲ 189   ⌂ 390 Park's Castle

Clones
Round Tower 111 ⼎
High Cross 112 ✠   𝝅 367
Clones

Knocknarea Cairn
153A ▲   **Monaghan**
𝝅   ┬ 118
𝝅 Sligo   ▲ 69 Creevelea Friary

lithic Cemetery 153B
GO   ● 277
Ballysadare   𝝅
Churches   277A

7

152 Heapstown Cairn
Ballymote Castle ⌂   373 ▲   𝝅 465
▲ Ballindoon Friary   Drumlane Church
arrowkeel Megalithic Cemetery 518   ♠ 4   and Round Tower

8

342 Ballinafad Castle   Cavan
167 ▲   68   ✠ Kilmore   **CAVAN**
Boyle Abbey   Fenagh Churches

● 159   ● Carrick-
𝝅 488   on-Shannon
■ Jamestown Gate

ROSCOMMON

9

Cloonmorris Church
and Ogham Stone ≛⊕

Rathcroghan ● 294
𝝅 473   Granard Motte 263 ■

Loughcrew
Megalithic
Cemetery

Inishmurray ✝ 117

Donegal

Drum

6

Belderg

⛰ 386

Ballycastle

Killala Bay

Esky

Sligo Bay

Sligo
Abbe

433

189

Knocknarea Cairn

353A

Sli

Breastagh Ogham Stone 415 ⛩ 389

⛩ 269 Rathfran Friary

Dromore

Carrowmore Megalithic Cemetery 153B

elmulre

ishglora ✝ 99A

Killala Round Tower 105

Enniscrone

Bangor

103 Moyne Abbey

Rosserk Friary 104

SLIGO

Ballysadare
Churches

7

Inishkea North
✝ 379

✝ 99B Fallmore
St. Dairbhile's Church

Ardnaree Friary ▲

Ballymote Castle

Ballina

Ballina Dolmen 145

MAYO

308

Errew Abbey 307

Lough
Conn

402

⛩
293
✝

479

Carrowkeel Megalithic Cemet

8

Dooagh

23

Foxford

Swinford

Gorteen

Ballaghaderreen

Frenchp

9

ickkildavnet Castle 458

Rockfleet Castle

454

235

Burrishoole Friary

Mallaranny

Newport

Ballylahan
Castle
325

Turlough
Round Tower
100

172
Strade Friary

48 Meelick Round Tower

159

Clew Bay

Castlebar

Bellavary

Clare Island
97

198

196

Murrisk Abbey

Westport

483

Balla

403 Balla Round Tower

Ballyhaunis

Cas

Louisburgh

96 Aghagower
Round Tower
297

Ballintubber Abbey

501

222A

222B

Emlagh Cross 397

Cloonfad

Ballymoe

10

Lough
Mask

Ballinrobe

Claremorris

248 Dunmore
Castle
and Friary
273

Dunmore

439
Glin
Cas

Inishmaine
Abbey 102

246

359

Fearlagar Castle
428

Castl

Delogan

Aghalard Castle 243

146

244

Kelly's Cave 413

251

95B

48 ▲ Kilbennan Round Tower

Tuam ⛪
Cathedral

505

Tuam High Cross

Mou

11

Cong Abbey 432

245

412 ✝
Inchagoill
Churches

231

95A

50 ▲ Ross Errilly
Friary

Killursa Church

166 ▲ 278
Knockmoy Abbey

369

Maam

Recess

Lough
Corrib

470

Aughnanure
Castle

49
Annaghdown
Churches

Oughterard

Claregalway Friary ▲ 165

GALWAY

12

Roundstone

242

431
Pearse's Cottage

Screeb

Moycullen

Athenry Castle and Abbey

406

164

Carna

Inveran

St. Nicholas' Church

Lynch's Castle

46

Galway

Turoe Stone
327

Athenry

Loughrea

13

Spiddal

Galway Bay

Drumacoo Church
254

Kiltiernan Church
✝ 446

Loughrea Fr
498

499

Black Head

ARAN ISLANDS

Córcomroe
Abbey
11

272
Isertkelly Castle

Ardrahan

365
Drumharsna
Castle

Thoor Ballylee

Gleninagh Castle
509

Ballyvaughan

✝ 12

Newtown Castle

Ballinalacken

259

Kilmacduagh
Churches
Round
Tower 51

See Map Page 82

Cahermacnaghten

Poulnabrone
Dolmen
354

13

Temple Cronan Church

206

252 Ardamullivan Castle

Carran Ch

Lisdoonvarna

Kilfenora
Church
Crosses

8

270B 270A

448

Killinabov Ch

Cliffs of Moher

14

G   H   I   J   K   L   M

FERMANAGH

Enniskillen

LEITRIM

Drumcliffe High Cross
† 119

Corracloona Megalithic Tomb
405
508

Miltowmn

Maguires Bridge

Lisnaskea

Sligo
Abbey 189
433

Maheraghanrush
Megalithic Tomb
377

Manorhamilton

Sean Mac Diarmada's House

Upper
Lough Erne

Clones
Round Tower 111
High Cross 112

Clones

Knocknarea Cairn
53A

† 118

390 Park's Castle

Sligo

Dromahair

Swanlinbar

Cootel

arrowmore Megalithic Cemetery 153B

Ballysadare
Churches

277

69
Creevelea Friary

7

SLIGO

277A

Drumshanbo

Drumlane Church
and Round Tower

4

Cavan

CAVAN

Ballymote Castle

152 Heapstown Cairn
373   465
Ballindoon Friary

Carrowkeel Megalithic Cemetery 518

342 Ballinalad Castle

Meadow

68
Fenagh Churches

Kilmore

8

167
Boyle Abbey

Carrick-
on-Shannon

Ballyjamesduff

159

488

Jamestown Gate

ROSCOMMON

Mohill

Cloonmorris Church
and Ogham Stone

Drumlish

Granard

Loughe
Megali
Cemete
1512

Frenchpark

Elphin

Ballinalea

Granard Motte 263

9

Rathcroghan 294
473

Strokestown

Longford

Abbeylaragh

Castlepollard

215

220 Fe

Emlagh Cross 397

Ballintober Castle

Ballymoe

Lanesborough

LONGFORD

St. Mel's Church †

Castlepollard

Multyfarnham Friary

10

248 Dunmore
Castle
and Friary
273

439
Glinsk
Castle

Roscommon Castle
181

Roscommon

362 Abbey

Inchcleraun
91

Abbeyshrule Abbey

Taghmon Church
265

Kilbennan Round Tower

Tuam
505
Tuam High Cross

Castlestrange Stone 320

Athleague

Rinndown Castle

213 Inchbofin

WESTMEATH

Mullingar

11

166   278
Knockmoy Abbey

Mount Bellew Brid

487

Lough
Ree

Glasson

Ballymore

155
Hill of Ushnagh

GALWAY

467

Athlone
520
Athlone

223 Bealin Cross

galway Friary

Kilconnell Friary
47

250
Clonmacnoise 81   336

Moate

Ciara

Kilbeggan

313 Durrow High Cross

Eden

12

Athenry Castle and Abbey
406   164

371

512
Clontuskert
Priory

Tihilly Church and Cross

Tullamore

daingean

327
Turoe Stone

Clonfert
Cathedral

Gallen Priory
504

Rahan Churches
82

Kiltiernan Church
446

Loughrea

Loughrea Friary

498   499

Clonony Castle

OFFALY

Portarlington

13

65
harsna
stle

272
Isertkelly Castle

Meelick
Friary

Derryhivenny Castle
283

Lorrha Churches
357

510
Castletown and Glinsk Cross

Lea Cast

Thoor Ballylee

462
Pallas Castle

361

Birr

Mountmellick

259

Portumna Castle
Abbey 515

361   378
451   Lackeen Castle

Kinnitty

497

Port Laoise

Dunama

252 Ardamullivan Castle

363

348

Mountrath

LAOIS

Timahoe Round Tower
114 B   1

14

Killodiernan
Church

Roscrea Church
Cross Castle 211   126

125 Mohaincha Church

Abbeyleix

Tuamgraney
Church

Inishcaltra
5

513   Rathurles

Aghaboe
Church   Motte
353

Rathdowney

Newtow
Killeshi

224
St. Finghin's Ch
15 Quin Abbey

Nenagh Castle

113

Templemore

Nenagh

Killaloe Cath
and Churches
16
278

TIPPERARY

M N P Q R S

6
7
8
9
10
11
12
13
14

ARMAGH

DOWN

Downpatrick

Newcastle

St. John's

Monaghan

MONAGHAN

Armagh

Newry

Warrenpoint

111
Cross 112
Clones

367

Cootehill

Castleblayney

Kilkeel

326
249
424 Carlingford Castles
476 Proleek Dolmen
Carlingford Lough

Castleblayney

460

Cohaw
Megalithic Tomb

382
208
Inishkeen
Round Tower

388 Dun Dealgan

474

Dundalk

CAVAN

Carrickmacross

Shercock

St. Mochta's House 312

92
480
Dromiskin High Cross and Round Tower

Baileborough

LOUTH

Ardee Castle
298
Roodstown Castle
144

Virginia

264

94
Termonfeckin Castle and Cross
170

Loughcrew
Megalithic
Cemetery
151 290

Robertstown Castle 256

Killary Cross

Monasterboice

Magdalene Tower
511

107
Castlekeeran Crosses
108 158
Teltown
Kells

Mellifont Abbey 93
Slane Friary 188
Newgrange

Millmount Fort

Drogheda

Kells Crosses
Round Tower

149

106
Donaghmore Round Tower

409 410
147

215
220 Fore Abbey

Rathmore Church 289
Athlumney
Castle 287

482 496

495

199 179
Duleek Priory and Cross
440

Hill of Ward
150

Cannistown
Church 239

356

309

322 Athcarne Cross

265
481
Delvin Castle

Bective Abbey 187

109 Skreen Church

472 Fourknocks
Megalithic Tomb

non Church

Trim Castles/Churches 468
514 186

469
261

148 Tara

110

MEATH

310 Baldongan Church

Skerries

Mullingar

489 257
400

DUBLIN

157
Lusk Round Tower

Rush

Lambay Island

Killucan
Crosses

232
Donore Castle

Dunshaughlin

Swords Castle 340

St. Doulagh's Church

Edenderry

Cross

Cross

Dunsoghly Castle 230

Finglas Cross

Swords

36 St. Mary's Church
Howth

Maynooth Castle
485

Taghadoe Round Tower 70

404

Clondalkin
Round Tower
32

St. Michan's Church

Cross

285

Newcastle Church

DUBLIN

302 Marino Casino

401
34
Christchurch Cathedral
St. Patrick's Cathedral
St. Werburgh's Church

Dublin Bay

494 Monkstown Castle
444 Archbold's Castle Dalkey

KILDARE

Ardrass Ch

190

207
226 291
493

Tallaght

216

35 Killiney Church
225 Tully Church/Crosses

Allenwood

464
343

33

Jigginstown
House

394

275 Kilteel Church
Cas

162

Newbridge

Kildare Cathedral
Round Tower

305

Threecastles

491

Ballyedmonduff 437

Fassaroe 337
Cross

417

262

Punchestown

280
St. Mark's
Cross

135 323
Killincarrig House
267 Kilcoole Church

Lea Castle

Monasterevin

Dun Aillinne

71
Old Kilcullen Cross
Round Tower

419

416 Piper's Stones

Dunamase Castle

Ardscull
Motte

Castleruddery
Stone Circle
441

134
Glendalough

Wicklow
Church
Friary

Round Tower
114 B 114 A

Moone
High Cross

442

328

449
Dwyer-MacAllister
Cottage

503

Castledermot Churches
and Crosses 200

471

203
418

Baltinglass Abbey

WICKLOW

Wicklow

304
Castletimon Ogham Stone

116

452

Rathvilly

Aughrim

Avoca

	A	B	C	D	E	F

Cliffs of Moher

✝ 13
Carran Ch   Temple Cron
⊕ π
270B 270A
Kilfenora ▲ 8
Church   448
Crosses   Leamaneh ⊕ Killinaboy
Ennistymon   Castle   Coloh
⊕ 17
Dysert O'Dea
Church Cross ▲ 16
Round Tower
▲ 204
Ennis Friary 170   ▲ 19
Claracas
▲ 176   Mog

Kilkee

195 ▲

Kilrush
▲ 185
Carrigaholt   ⚓ 10   Yh   201
Castle 427   Scattery Island   Askeato
Loop Head   Mainistir na   C
River Shannon   349   Galliaghduff ▲
Carrigafoyle Castle ▲
Kerry Head   258   Shanid Castle
Lislaughtin
Friary   ● 459
Ballybunion
Newcastle West
LIM
Rattoo Round Tower ⌂ 55   260
Listowel
⊕ 303
268
Abbeyfeale   Glenquin Castle
Dromcollher
✝ 67   86 ⊕
Ardfert ▲▲ 358   Tullylease Chur
Churches 54   2
Tralee ▲ 295
56 ⊕   57   Newmarket
Tralee Bay   Ratass Church   Castleisland
Camp   430   Farranfore   Kanturk Castle 517
Killagha Abbey ▲   Cloonbannin
238 ●
DINGLE PENINSULA   Ballymalis
See Map Page 107   Kilcoolaght 364 Castle   236 ✝ Aghadoe Church 296
Ogham Stones 329 Beaufort 53 and Castle
519 Reask   Dunloe 385 ▲   Millstreet
Blasket   Ogham Stones 183 ▲ Ross Castle   420
Islands   Dingle Bay   311   Ballyvourney
Muckross
KERRY   Muckross Friary   Glenflesk
Glencar   Macre
Leacanabuaile Fort   Carrigaphooca Castle 255
414 ● ● 227
500 ✝
59   Kenmare
Cahirciveen
Valentia Island   ● ✝ 228   Sneem   Kinneary
380 ● 492 ✝ 60   Inchigeela
168   Glengarriff   374 ⌂   ● 233
Ballinskelligs   ✝ 143   Kinr
Abbey   346 ✝ Staigue Fort   450 ⌂   Dunmanway   Rou
✝ 61 Skelligs Derrynane   425
Ogham Stone   Ballynacarriga Castle
426 ✝   Laragh
Ardgroom   Glengarriff   Clon
436   Timole
Kilnaruane ⊕
Pillarstone   Bantry
Bantry Bay

Dursey Island

Drombeg ⌂ Coppinger's
Stone Circle 381 ⌂ Court
Skibbereen
Knockdrum Fort 284 ●

▲ 169

⊕ 22

L M N O P Q R

farnham Friary
265 Taghmon Church
Rathmore Church 289
Hill of Ward 150
482 496
Athlumney Castle 287
Cannistown Church 239
Bective Abbey 187
Trim Castles/Churches 468
514 110
186
489 257
400
199 Duleek Priory and Cross
440
356
322 Athcarne Cross
309
472 Fourknocks Megalithic Tomb
109 Skreen Church
148 Tara
261
MEATH
310 Baldongan Church
157
DUBLIN
Lusk Round Tower
WESTMEATH Mullingar
155 l of Ushnagh
Killucan Crosses
232 Donore Castle
481 Delvin Castle
Swords Castle 340
Dunsoghly Castle 230
Finglas Cross
St. Michan's Church
Maynooth Castle 485
St. Patrick's Cathedral
302 Marino Casino
401
Christchurch Cathedral
St. Werburgh's Church
36 St. Mary's Church
313 Durrow High Cross
Tihilly Church and Cross
Churches
Taghadoe Round Tower 70
Cloudalkin Round Tower
404
32 285
KILDARE
Ardrass Ch
Newcastle Church
190
207 494 Monkstown Castle
226 291
444 Archbold's Castle Da
33
493
464 343
35 Killiney Church
216
225 Tully Church/Crosses
276
162
337
417
262
135 323
Killincarrig House
267 Kilcoole Church
275 Kilteel Church
Ballyedmonduff 437
Fassaroe Cross
Kildare Cathedral Round Tower
Jigginstown House
Newbridge
394
Threecastles
491
305
Punchestown
280 St. Mark's Cross
Lea Castle
Dun Aillinne
l Glinsk Cross
Dunamase Castle
419
416 Piper's Stones
Castleruddery Stone Circle 441
134 Glendalough
449 Dwyer-MacAllister Cottage
Wicklow Church Friary
Old Kilcullen Cross Round Tower 71
Ardscull Motte
LAOIS
Timahoe Round Tower
114 B 114 A
Moone High Cross
503
Castledermot Churches and Crosses 200 471
328
203 418
442
Baltinglass Abbey
WICKLOW
304 Castletimon Ogham Ste
116
452
Haroldstown Dolmen
Clonmore Castle
Killeshin Church 115
Browneshill Dolmen 306
422 Rathgall Stone Fort
352 Nurney Cross
CARLOW
438
486 Ballymoon Castle
137 Aghowle Church
368 Moylisha Megalithic Tomb
Grangefertagh Round Tower
Freshford Church
399 Dunmore Cave
282 Ballylarkin Ch
376
331
344
Clara Castle 274
351 Ballyloughan Castle
350
Kilkenny Churches 72
Rothe House
St. Canice's Cathedral
Black Friars
Kilkenny Castle
393
Gowran Church
521 Ferns Castle/Churches
133
218
coly bey
Burnchurch Castle 321
Tullaherin Round Tower 161
78 Ullard Church
372 475
180 Kells Priory
191 Kilfane Church
Graiguenamanagh Church
WEXFORD
455
Killamery High Cross
Kilree 76 Ch Cr RT
80 Jerpoint Abbey
77 Clonamery Church
3 St. Mullins Churches/Crosses
Enniscorthy Castle
375
392 Vinegar Hill
75
334
73A 73B
KILKENNY
Ahenny High Crosses
124
79
Kilkeeran High Crosses
443 St. Mary's Church
123
147 Tibberaghny Pillar
445
Carrick on Suir Castle
132
Granagh Castle 253
229 Rathumney Castle
492
516 506
434 Rathmacnee Castle
Reginald's Tower
205
Ballyhack Castle
Dunbrody Abbey
Clonmines Medieval Town
457 Tacumshane Windmill
Gaulstown Megalithic Tomb 398 421
Knockeen Dolmen
154
384 237 Matthewstown Megalithic Tomb
429 Slade Castle